CARTESIAN STUDIES

Albert G. A. Balz

UNIVERSITY OF VIRGINIA

NEW YORK

Columbia University Press

MCMLI

194.1
D445X
B 198

76014

FOREWORD

THE ESSAYS included in this book were published at intervals throughout more than a score of years. I am indebted to the editors of the *Philosophical Review,* the *Journal of Philosophy,* the *Review of Religion,* and of *Studies in the History of Ideas* for their courtesy in granting permission to republish them. They are republished with few changes, and most of these are trivial.

The essays have, I hope, a certain unity of theme. They are concerned in the main with the doctrines of Descartes concerning the nature of man. Most of them, however, are devoted, not primarily to an exposition of these doctrines as expressed in the writing of Descartes, but to the interpretations and developments of them by his successors, both followers and opponents. They have in view also the diffusion of Cartesianism in the history of thought, both philosophic and scientific.

The doctrine concerning the nature of man, as expressed in the Sixth of the "Meditations," is customarily described as "dualistic." In Descartes' own terms, man turns out to be, not a unity of nature, but a unity of composition. He is a substantial immaterial soul intimately related to a body, and this body is a changing aggregate of "modes" referable to matter substance. It may be urged that a dualistic conception of man was no new thing in the history of thought. Descartes may be regarded as having reformulated—or perhaps rediscovered—a conception coming down from remote antiquity. The rediscovery, in any event, was expressed in a new context of ideas and in an age of many changes in the meanings of traditional terms; the formulation of the doctrine definitely associated it with the institution of modern science and the metaphysical perspective in which science was to view existence.

The influence of this view of man as a unity of composition pervaded all subsequent reflection. Philosophy, broadly speaking, tended more and more to make the theory of knowledge a precondition of all other efforts of philosophical speculation. Epistemological analysis, however, had recourse to notions concerning the nature of man and his experience that we today would call "psychological." These psychological investigations were largely determined by Descartes' dualistic view of man. In this manner his doctrine, with its consequences and attendant difficulties, was transmitted to epistemology and thus to other areas of philosophy. In effect, then, philosophical thought tended to move in a circular fashion, expressing in its terminal speculations the consequences of Cartesian influences upon psychology and epistemology. Moreover, the movement was stimulated by the development of the physical sciences. In some such way as this, Cartesian doctrine pervaded all efforts of the modern mind. Even opposing philosophies, seeking to overcome the difficulties entailed by the "dualism," or repudiating it in order to assert a completely materialistic philosophy, were governed by the position they sought to transcend or to deny. Moreover, fine art and literature were pervaded by similar influences. The studies that follow are efforts to disclose something of this diffusion.

This volume could not have appeared without the assistance of the Department of Philosophy of Columbia University, of the Research Council of the Richmond Area University Center, and of the Research Committee of the University of Virginia. I am deeply grateful to them for making possible the realization of a plan that had been entertained for many years.

To Miss Jill Hanckel King are due many thanks for her assistance. I wish also to record my gratitude to Mr. John Hunton Moss for his expert help in preparing these studies for republication and to him and Mr. James Reese McKeldin for assuming the responsibilities of proofreading.

ALBERT G. A. BALZ

Charlottesville, Virginia
April 2, 1951

CONTENTS

CARTESIAN STUDIES

GERAUD DE CORDEMOY
1600–1684

IN ORDER to distinguish the soul and the body, states Bouillier,[1] Cordemoy maintains *en bon cartésien* that the existence of the soul is more assured than that of the body. Moreover, as Bouillier adds, the existence of the body can become assured only through faith. But these points, with which the historian of Cartesianism concludes his account of Cordemoy, would more properly be used in an introduction. The distinction of soul and body is recognized by Cordemoy as the very first step in metaphysics and epistemology. It is this, however, because through it alone can we arrive at physics. Cordemoy's *Le Discernement du corps et de l'âme* carries a most significant subtitle, *Pour servir à l'éclaircissement de la physique*. There could scarcely be found a more emphatic contemporary statement concerning the vital bearings upon physical science of the dualism of body and soul effected by Descartes. The directly perceptual world of Aristotle and medieval tradition—after all it is only the common-sense world—is certainly the world that science must explain. The beginnings of modern science come with the recognition that mind had not been very successful in explaining this perceptual world in the terms which it directly suggests. The task of the first modern scientists was twofold: it was necessary to define the subject-matter of inquiry in terms of the concepts and methods to be employed, and simultaneously to determine the concepts and methods through a definition of the subject matter. The subject matter was nature or the physical world, of course, but the problem was to decide upon just what is to be meant by the term "nature." This must be defined by determining the objectives of science; the objectives could be defined only in terms of concepts and methods —and this in turn fixed a content for the term "nature." The objective was a quantitative knowledge of a qualitative world, or

[1] *Histoire de la philosophie Cartésienne,* 3d ed., Paris, 1868, I, 516.

at least of a nature whose mask is qualitative. The problem of
the common-sense and perceptual world must be attacked circui-
tously, by a flanking maneuvre. The problem once solved, physics
will be a science of nature by means of which we may understand
how the perceiver comes to have the world that he perceives, in
relation with a world he does not perceive. Before this can be
accomplished, however, the perceiver must be recognized for what
he is, in order that the province of physics may be defined. This
province, once defined, must necessarily include the human body.
The human being, like everything else, is a portion of the commonsense and perceptual world and is also a fact within the province of physics. Since the human being, again, is the perceiver,
the distinguishing of the directly perceptual world from the world
that will be studied in physics may well begin with him. Thus,
the discerning of mind from body is a preliminary step that serves
for the clarification of physics. As the satirical and peripatetic
Jesuit Daniel remarks, the world of Descartes is well ordered, and
freed from an "infinité d'accidens, de qualitez, d'especes intentionelles." [2]

The successors of Descartes were concerned with the problem
of mind and body for more than one reason. On the one hand,
they were interested because of moral and theological reasons;
and then the problem is metaphysical in its own right, so to speak.
On the other hand, they were sometimes interested in the mind-
body problem because of an even deeper interest in physical science; in this case a satisfactory conception of mind and body
was a preparation for physics. To begin with, the dualism was to
free physical science of many encumbrances. To return to it from
the excursion into physics was, of course, to re-encounter a difficulty. But since we can be more assured of the existence of the
soul than of the body, theology may provide a solution of the
problem.

Geraud de Cordemoy, whatever fund of tradition he may have
brought to the study of Descartes, did not fail to perceive the
impact of the Cartesian dualism upon traditional ideas. If the

[2] *Voyage du monde de Descartes*, nouvelle édition, Paris, chez Nicolas Pepie, 1702,
p. 4.

discerning of soul and body leads to an *éclaircissement* for physics, he thinks it leads also to a just appraisal of older conceptions.
He is not misled by the doctrine of animal spirits or by the definition of spirit as subtle matter. Nor will the notion of "form" bridge
the gap between soul and body. He uses the conception of the
animal spirits, for example, but it is a purely physical and physiological principle; fluidity and subtlety are not signs of an approximation to spirit. If the principle that moves animals, he
affirms, is to be called *âme* or *forme*, this principle is by no means
identical with *esprit*, which is separable from the body.[3] Cordemoy's task, indeed, is precisely to assign to soul that which belongs to it and to body that which belongs to body. This task is
defined by taking seriously the Cartesian dualism of spiritual
and extended substance. If body be extension, then the human
body is extension, and all that is not extension must be attributed
to the soul. Thus the realm of physical inquiry is defined, for
we must note that this discerning of body and soul is not undertaken in the interests of psychology or of metaphysics or of theology, but of physics—*pour servir à l'éclaircissement de la physique*, as the title informs us. The Cartesian ideal of an universal
physics, and the Cartesian conviction that the human mind is capable of it, are shared by Cordemoy. To realize the ideal and
justify the conviction, we must first know what the soul encom-
passes.

And so Cordemoy states the following principles:

If I think in any fashion whatever, it is because I have a soul.

Si ie conçoy diversement les differens objets; si dès l'abord i'en
apperçoy quelque chose; si pour les mieux connoistre ie les considère
plus long-temps; si après avoir discontinue ie récommence: En un mot,
si i'ay des *idées*, des *perceptions* de *l'attention*, & de la mémoire; c'est
que i'ay une Âme.

If I consider my own thoughts or those of others [he continues], if I
consider truth, and many other things that have nothing to do with extension ("que ne tiennent rien de l'étendue, de la figure, ny du mouve-

[3] *Traité de métaphysique*, p. 107, in *Les œuvres du feu M. de Cordemoy*, Paris,
Remy, 1704. This volume is hereinafter referred to as *O*. All references to *Le Discernement du corps et de l'âme en six discours, pour servir à l'éclaircissement de la
physique*, are to the edition of 1666, chez Florentin Lambert, hereinafter indicated
as *D*.

ment") : if I am capable of conceiving purely intelligible things, it is because I have a soul.

If I consider the things that depend upon extension, figure, and motion, in a word, if I am capable of imagining, it is because I have a soul.

If I judge, whether the object be corporeal or spiritual, it is because I have a soul.

If I doubt, it is because I have a soul, and a soul which lacks something.

If I am free in my judgments, if I have a will capable of good or bad, if I have liberty in my volitions, it is because I have a soul.

If I love, hate, experience sadness, if I have desires, it is because I have a soul.[4]

Thus the province of physics is made clear.

Everything that we admire in the works of Art, or of Nature, is a pure effect of movement and of arrangement. But in order that we may be able to know this by means of examples, I think I can choose examples that will best convince us, a watch and the body of man. Everyone is sufficiently persuaded that the arrangement of the parts of a watch is the cause of all its effects . . . we need not seek *form, faculties, occult virtues,* or *qualities* in it.[5]

We are, indeed, assured that the watch is not animated (*animée*) *for the very reason that an explanation in terms of motion and arrangement is possible.* This clarification of the field of physics, we note, has two sides. On the one hand, thought may dispense with the terminology of the School and its implications; on the other hand, by the attribution to the soul of everything that is not extension, figure, and motion, nature as the field of physical inquiry is simplified and its universal features revealed.

This confident determination of the subject matter is but the other side of an assurance of human capacity for knowledge. Heine somewhere tells how Voltaire, in a letter to Mme du Deffand professes that he is enraptured by her remark to the effect that such things, if there be any, which men can *not* come to know are certainly of such a kind that knowledge of them would be of no importance to man. There is in this a boundless confidence in human capacity, even with that qualification of utility. For Cordemoy, in an earlier day, there is little doubt in the competence of reason. The fact that thought could so easily determine the field

[4] *D*, pp. 146–51.   [5] *Ibid.*, pp. 59–60.

of physics is evidence of its capacity to constitute the science. Perhaps, he says, our power of knowing, at least in this world, may not be so great. But it is certain that we have enough for knowledge and that we shall not lack it if we use well our light and our power of not judging until we really know. God has given us "toutes les lumières dont nous avons besoin." We have "les idées très-distinctes" for knowing the things of nature, in so far as it is useful to know them. What then is this utility? Cordemoy explains that our knowledge of things, or the knowledge we may obtain if we will, is such that we can recognize them as useful or harmful, even if we cannot know what they are. To know what things are, he explains in a note, means to know what are figure, situation, or the movements of the insensible parts of things.[6] The adequacy of our knowledge is assured by the "notions parfaites" that God has given the soul, whether for the purpose of knowing itself, or of knowing its body, or of knowing that marvellous relation which constitutes their union. Indeed, for such knowledge all that is needed is the reflection of the soul on that which it is, on itself; and by the same means it may know, so far as is useful to it, everything which composes the universe. This possibility of knowledge extends not only to nature and to man, but even to God. And so Cordemoy thinks of a philosophy capable of making a "juste discernement" of everything, and of reasoning on foundations other than our prejudices. No one can commence better than by beginning with that which he possesses in himself and by the examination of all the ideas he has of the soul and of the body.[7]

What, then, for Cordemoy, is this field of physics for which he has provided an "éclaircissement"? And the soul, discerned as distinct from the body, what is it? What, as a branch of universal physics, is the physics of the body? And what is this marvellous connection that obtains between body and soul? What is the secret of their union, of which he speaks in the Dedication to the King?

Let us first turn to the field of physics. The problem of knowledge as the task of organizing a universal science of nature re-

[6] *O, Un Discours physique de la parole*, pp. 74–75.
[7] *D*, Préface.

quires first of all the discovery of the least common denominators of things. In a sense (as we have learned from Cordemoy already) we cannot know the nature of these common denominators. What figure is—that we cannot know. There are, then, certain ultimate facts in terms of which we may know things, but which, in themselves, remain brute given facts. What are these?

It is difficult to resist the inference that Cordemoy's physics is as much a reaction against Cartesian doctrine as an adoption of it. Descartes, defining matter as a substance the essence of which is extension, furnished a conceptual common denominator of the stuff of things. In this definition the manyness of things tends to be obliterated. In terms of tradition, a thing and a substance are somehow one and the same. The number of substances is the number of things. But Descartes had reduced them to one, so far as the system of nature is concerned. In the *tourbillon* theory he was doubtless endeavoring, among other aims, to provide a scientific means of thinking of the manyness of things, of the particular, in connection with the oneness of all things with respect to substance. Cordemoy seems to have felt that physics was in danger of eliminating the differentiations of things. He does not directly refer to Descartes, but directs his objections against what seemed to him to be a widespread opinion among the physicists.

It is therefore bodies in the plural, rather than extended substance, that is fundamental for Cordemoy. Every body is an extended substance. And matter is an assemblage of bodies. "On sçait qu'il y a des Corps & que le nombre en est presque infiny: On sçait aussi qu'il ye a de la matière; mais il me semble que l'on n'en a pas des notions assez distinctes, & que c'est de la que viennent presque toutes les érreurs de la Physique ordinaire." [8] But the term "body" does not stand for the thing of common sense. Its meaning for Cordemoy, indeed, would be better indicated by the term "atom." Matter is a composite of bodies, and everything of common experience is a *portion* of matter. There is a great difference between a *part* of matter and a *portion*. Every body, he says, considered as entering within the assemblage of material things is a *part* of matter.[9] Bodies then are extended sub-

[8] *Ibid.*, p. 1.   [9] *Ibid.*, pp. 2–3.

stances, and they are the units of composition. The composites are things, and these are portions of matter. "Matter," it seems, is a collective term for all physical things, rather than that of which they are composed. The units of composition, defined as extended substances, are *indivisible because each is a single substance*. Each excludes all others, and so they are characterized by impenetrability. Each body, since it is extended, must have that extension *terminated*—otherwise there would not be many bodies, but one. This termination of a body is its figure. Relations of situation obtaining between bodies define their place, and alterations of these relations mean that they move. From these definitions it follows that Cordemoy repudiates infinite divisibility. This fallacy, he thinks, has arisen because people have confused the notion of matter in general and the thought of particular things, and have concluded from divisibility into imperceptible portions the infinite divisibility of matter.[10] No unit-body by itself can affect our sense-organs. Hence it follows that what we perceive is matter, not bodies, *i.e.* assemblages of unit-bodies rather than the units themselves. Even great men have committed the fallacy of confusing matter and body, and so have attributed to matter that which properly belongs to body, that is, have said that it is a substance and that it is extended.[11] Cordemoy recounts several "inconveniences" that follow from this fallacy. It is obvious, however, that the fundamental difficulty he finds in a physics resting on this error is its inability to explain movement and rest. In the continuity of matter, when defined as one substance the essence of which is extension, there is no room for the differentiation of one thing from another, and so no separation of things. And without this separation neither motion nor rest is intelligible. To Cordemoy, it would seem, the Cartesian maxim, to the effect that the infinity of figures would suffice to explain the diversity of things, was unintelligible on a basis of the Cartesian reduction of nature to one extended substance. He does not, so far as I have noticed, literally state that extension constitutes the essence of substances. Extension belongs to or pertains to body; every body is an extended substance. But the plurality of bodies

10 *Ibid.*, pp. 4–5.   11 *Ibid.*, p. 8; cf. p. 15.

makes difficult the assertion that extension defines their essence.
His thought seems to be that a particular extension, whose "termination" makes a particular "figure," is that which defines the
essence of a body. The figures of bodies are diverse, and so their
combination to make portions of matter, or things, leads to the
different figures of things. Since some of the bodies have similar
figures, there are portions (things) that are similar in figure.[12]
Finally, if we use the terms "quality" and "form" they can mean
only the different arrangements of the parts of matter, and nothing else.

Another Cartesian, with almost an official position as the ex-
pounder of Cartesian doctrine, expresses a recognition of the
same difficulties. Régis seeks to provide a place for the particular
by distinguishing between primary matter and the particular as
differentiated within universal extension. By the term "Matière
première" we must understand

le sujet de toutes les formes . . . de tout ce qui se trouve dans les corps
particuliers par quoy ils diffèrent les uns des autres. . . . Or la matiere
premiere ne diffère de la quantité qu'en ce que la quantité est une substance étendue considérée comme telle ou telle selon la grandeur; au
lieu que la matiere premiere est cette même substance étendue considérée
comme capable de recevoir des modifications qui font qu'elle est un
corps de telle ou de telle nature. Ainsi, par example, dans un morceau
de cire, l'étendue considérée en elle-même est ce qu'on appelle *Corps,*
l'étendue considérée come telle ou telle selon la grandeur est ce qu'on
nomme *Quantité,* & cette même étendue considérée comme le sujet des
modes qui constituent la forme de la cire, est ce qu'on appelle *Matiere
premiere.* D'ou il s'ensuite que le mot de Corps est un terme absolu, &
que les mots de quantité & de matiere premiere ne sont que des termes
respectifs.

If we make this distinction we shall avoid the error of taking
quantity and primary matter as absolute things existing really
outside of the understanding. Régis thinks that his definition of
primary matter is Aristotle's, with the addition (which Aristotle
forgot to make) that primary matter is "extension itself considered as the immediate subject of the modes in which the primary
forms of purely material beings consist." With Aristotle we may

[12] *Ibid.,* p. 23.

say that primary matter is not a determinate thing. Every body
consists at bottom of primary matter and is resolvable into it.
Thus, for Régis, Descartes has supplied a content for the Aristotelian term. But this leaves Cartesian doctrine with the problem
of supplying an equivalent for the Aristotelian form "par quoy
plusieurs choses different les unes les autres." Against the scholastics, however, Régis asserts that we must deny that the material
forms are substances or substantial. Now, he thinks, upon the
basis of Cartesian doctrine, material forms are either "geometrical" or "physical." God, we must posit, having created extended
substance or primary matter, has divided it into an infinity of
parts of one or another figure, and, secondly, has done so in such
a way that there exist voids between the parts; finally, the "division" that He has placed between the parts consists in the diversity
of movements with which they were endowed upon the instant of
their creation. With this set of conceptions and distinctions, Régis
is prepared to introduce the theory of the *tourbillons.* Both for
him and for Cordemoy the fundamental difficulty for physics upon
the Cartesian basis was to make provision for the specific differences of particular things in connection with their reduction to
one substance, the essence of which is extension. And this question becomes acute precisely because the perceptual qualities of
things must be included within the realm of spiritual substance
and can no longer serve as the means of differentiating one thing
from another. The *éclaircissement* of physics by the discrimination of soul from body is not accomplished without raising new
problems, or at least without necessitating a reformulation of the
old.[13]

The second Discourse is devoted to the thesis that all changes
whatever in matter can be explained by local movement, even
changes of quantity (*accroissement ou décroissement*), of quality
(alterations), and of form (generation and corruption). What
changes of quantity, quality, and so forth, really mark are not
differences in the nature of movements, but diversity in the degree of motion and so in its sensible effects. Motions do not differ

[13] *Système de philosophie* . . . Paris, 1690, T. I, Livre premier de la physique,
Partie I, pp. 283–85; Livre second, Partie II, chs. i–iv.

qualitatively—and here Cordemoy is rejecting qualitative physics—but in amount. He is cognizant of the mechanical schema of
interpretation and of its significance. The rules of mechanics obtain not only in the parts of matter that we can see but also in those
that we cannot.

Cordemoy's common denominators for the physical world are
therefore extended substances, or bodies, figure, and local motion. Given these and the intervals (or pores) existing between the
bodies forming material things, all that is needed for a universal
science of nature is given. In this way he envisages that science
which Descartes had taught him to perceive. It remains for him
to remove from a special branch of physics, the study of the human body, the inconsistencies and ambiguities that had marked
Descartes' treatment of the matter.

Only spirits can be sensitive (*sensibles*), as only bodies can be
moved, says Cordemoy. Beasts are bodies and nothing more. The
body of the beast and that of man fall within the province of physics. Cordemoy adapts the conception of animal spirits to the needs
of the case. The nerves are "des suites & des alongements du
cerveau mesme." [14] They are conceived to be like tubes, and are
sometimes full and sometimes empty of spirits. He follows Descartes in asserting that the most subtle and warmest parts of the
blood mount from the heart to the brain. Into additional details
concerning his account of the body we need not go. We may be
content with noting that he extends the conception of subtle matter
as operative principle beyond the body. Subtle matter is the cause
of all movements, whether of masses or of "sensible liquors." In
its pure unmixed form it is the cause of light. The cause of the
motions of artificial and natural machines is one and the same—
it is subtle matter.

The mechanical conception of bodily activity, as well as the
form taken by the body-mind problem for Cordemoy, are interestingly illustrated by his theory concerning words. On the part of
man, he asserts, the means of knowing other men is the word.
Souls, indeed, could communicate much more readily were they

[14] *Traité de Métaphysique*, in *O*, p. 106.

not united to the body. This union is what necessitates the employment of signs. The failure of minds to understand other minds, it follows, is due to difficulties, not in conceiving the thought which others express in signs, but in the signs themselves.[15]

Beasts, since they are bodies and not bodies plus souls, cannot possess language in the sense in which men have it. Throughout the discussion Cordemoy holds in mind the thought that words, or language, involve the existence of both body and soul. We must not attribute to other bodies the possession of souls unless we find acts of those bodies that cannot be explained by the body alone as cause. The extreme unlikeness of character that distinguishes symbols and thoughts shows the difference between body and soul, and at the same time indicates the secret of their union. Two elements must be distinguished in the word: that which comes from the body and that which comes from the soul. Now in so far as expressive acts can be explained mechanically (at bottom, by means of the animal spirits), we need not suppose a soul involved in the use of signs. Cordemoy concludes that the cries and vocalizations of beasts can be explained mechanically, without an appeal to a soul. Now he recognizes that, if these cries and other expressive acts of beasts be not words at all, in the sense in which they convey meaning and imply a soul, then we must face the fact that these activities nevertheless serve as a means of communication. How is this to be explained?

The basis of explanation is his general conception that God has established a certain proportion, that is, a harmony, between our human bodies and the other bodies of the universe. The same would apply to beasts. Thus, the cries of animals attract those of the same species and repel those of others. The explanation of this lies in the varying structure of animals. The responses of beasts to sounds and the vocalization of beasts are to be explained by wise adjustments of the bodily mechanisms of the various species; and these adjustments are the provision of the Creator. Thus the "word" in the animal is purely a case of mechanics. But in man it reflects the endowment of a soul. The word in man signifies not merely mechanical adjustment and action but also that there

[15] *Un Discours physique sur la parole*, in *O*, Preface, and pp. 1–2, 36–37, 60–61.

is perception and the experience of willing for or against the movement excited in the human body by the sound-stimulus. A perception is a thought, and so belongs to the soul.[16]

Cordemoy, be it noted, has no intention of compromising his position that there is nothing common to body and soul save the fact that both exist. The Cartesian appeal to the pineal gland has no attractions for him. Man, for him as for Descartes, is somehow one being. But he perceives clearly enough that Descartes had made him incurably dual. Moreover, if we remain faithful to Cartesian principles, no common denominator can be found for the spiritual and the mechanical facts. How seriously Cordemoy takes this is neatly illustrated by his answer to the question how one may possess a better understanding than another. Does this difference pertain to the soul? Cordemoy perceives that if we study men as bodily machines we cannot escape the conviction that one of these machines may be better constructed than another. One human body may possess better vision, for example, than another. How can we resist the logical temptation to reduce the differences of intellectual power to differences in the construction of the bodily machines? But if this be done, shall we not in effect dispense with the need of souls? If the differences can be explained in terms of machine construction, why cannot mind as a whole be explained in terms of the body? In short, if mechanism explains anything, why will it not explain everything? Now Cordemoy asserts that souls are in principle universally the same. Here is the Cartesian dictum concerning the universality of common sense taken seriously—and without the irony! Yet he also asserts that differences in power of conception, of clarity of thought, and so forth, are due to differences in brain construction. If men of "slow understanding," he says, were disembarrassed of an inadequate brain equipment, their slowness of comprehension would cease.[17]

His escape from this difficulty is by means of a first step towards Occasionalism. Finding neither in nature as mechanism nor in man as spirit an explanation of the union of the two in the human being, appeal is made to God. God effects a union of antithetical

[16] *Ibid.,* pp. 50–51.   [17] *Ibid.,* pp. 60–61.

things. The Author of Nature joins movements and thoughts as man artificially joins thoughts and signs.[18] The soul's rapidity or slowness of comprehension depends upon the brain with which it is in union, for brain activity and thought must correspond one to the other. The Cartesian dictum that good sense is universal in mankind is by no means an innocuous statement. Taken together with the definition of mind or soul as in essence thought, the essential and thoroughgoing rationality of every mind is in principle implied. As this makes the problem of error grave, just so it raises the problem of the differences of intellectual ability between individual men. The essential rationality of mankind, the fact that thought defines the very essence of each individual soul substance, does not facilitate a hypothesis concerning the capacity for clear and distinct ideas varying in degree from man to man. When all things lose their qualitative differences of rank, and are reduced to mere quantitative differences in extension, then in an analogous way selves and minds, which are equally spiritual substances, the essence of which is the capacity for rational thought, tend to assume equality. This is the germinal situation from which came the faith of the enlightenment that when the obstacles to the free exercise of mental powers shall have been removed, men will quickly attain, as individuals and as forming societies, the rational and the good life. In so far as the immediate followers of Descartes were reluctant to deny the essential equality of human souls, the inequality of bodily machines served as a way of escape. This is a natural suggestion because it is relatively easy to ascribe differences in the powers of imagination, perception, and memory, to the body. But since these faculties are really in the soul, along with the principle of clear and distinct ideas itself, the thought presents itself that either the body explains all differences of capacity from man to man, or else it explains none. Thus, slowness of understanding, for Cordemoy, is the fault of the body, not of the soul in itself.

In this statement of the situation I have perhaps made the alternatives and issues clearer than they were in the mind of Cordemoy. With respect to this one comment may be ventured. The

[18] *Ibid.*, pp. 15–16.

choice of the one alternative, that is, that responsibility for the apparent inequality of minds rests upon the inequalities of their adjoined bodies, is not without its dangers in view of the general framework of ideas. The point of view is apt to raise a question concerning God's providential designs. For, it may be asked, Why should the Creator have inflicted upon one soul the handicap of a relatively imperfect bodily machine and given another a much more perfect one? [19]

Whether Cordemoy's doctrine is a complete Occasionalism— whether it deserves the name or not—is not a question that need detain us. The interesting matter is not what his doctrine shall be called, but how it came about that this sort of answer was advanced at all. There is an appearance of artificiality in all Occasionalism. Taking the antithesis of body and soul seriously, and combining with this all the evidence that indicates that man is one being, mind reaches an *impasse*. There is no way out save by invoking the Deity as the efficient cause of the union of body and soul (or of their apparent union).

However, when we seek to comprehend the genesis of this doctrine, we are driven far beyond such a simple statement. We shall be compelled, indeed, to see in doctrines of this type a revision of the traditional conception of design. The impact of the new scientific ideas, revealing nature as one system, with all things as instances of extension, and motion as the principle of explanation of every happening within the system, would seem to have brought about a sharp opposition between a world of design and a world of mechanical action. To whatever extent this opposition may have been perceived, and so generated an enmity towards the new science of nature, the antagonism and enmity did not prevent the development of quite a contrary point of view. For mechanical explanation could be subordinated to explanation by design on the condition that design was restricted to the world as a whole, while mechanical explanation was left as the (human) view of its details. Mechanical action, in short, could be envisaged as the divinely ordained means for carrying out the plan of Deity for the universe as a whole.

[19] Cf. note 20 below and the text on pp. 21–27.

For Cordemoy the unification of body and soul in man, despite their antithesis, is possible precisely because mechanical principles of explanation give a specific content to the notion of divine design. Mechanism provides a clear insight into the very process by which the Deity accomplishes His purposes. Certainly mechanical operation is easier to comprehend than miracle. The mechanical arrangement of the universe, that is, the mechanical design of the whole of nature, implies the harmonious articulation of its various parts. The proportion that God has established between our bodies and the remainder of the universe is only a special instance of a general proportion obtaining throughout the universe of created beings. The notion of a Deity who more or less arbitrarily and unexpectedly intervenes in the course of events, or affords a special manifestation of His power in famine or pestilence, in miracle, in signs and portents, was certainly familiar enough to the world. That God should intervene was no new thought. To systematize that intervention, to make it orderly (and thus to conjoin even this thought with the spirit of the scientific movement), and to purify both this notion of intervention and the concept of design from the grossness of tradition—to do all this was both incidental to the development of Occasionalism and that which suggested the doctrine.[20]

One other point must be considered. Cordemoy's physical doctrine is essentially an atomism. Body—*corps*—is the indivisible unit of composition of matter. Between bodies are pores or intervals, whatever these are. Bodies are extended substances, each

[20] There is interesting corroboration of the spirit of this position in the *Lettre écrite au R. P. Cossart, de la compagnie de Jésus, pour montrer que tout ce que M. Descartes a écrit du systême du monde, & de l'âme des bêtes, semble être tiré du premier chapitre de la Genèse* (5 *Novembre* 1667), in *O.* Descartes, says Cordemoy, goes into details. But obviously his teaching is only a more extended explication of what Moses says in Genesis. Descartes' principles are simply a philosophical and exact way of explaining the same marvels that Moses describes historically. We might add the statement that originally, before the Fall, man's body and soul were in complete harmony with the whole of the universe. The Fall brought a disturbance of the whole proportion (*Traité de Métaphysique, O.* The letter is referred to by Daniel, *Voyage du monde de Descartes,* p. 5.) In *De la nécessité de l'histoire . . . (O),* Cordemoy suggests the use of history for the education of young princes. History should commence with Genesis, and a wise instructor can use philosophy and theology, without being burdened by syllogisms, to explain Creation and the Order of the Universe and to give a high idea of the power and wisdom of God.

terminated in its extension, that is, each possessing specific figure. The separation of soul from bodily machine is really but one instance of a division prevailing throughout nature. There is as much need of an explanation for the conjoint behavior of the units of physical nature as for that of body and soul. The explanation of the latter through the activity of the Deity both illustrates and suggests the activity of the Deity throughout the universe. In this direction lies the completion of the doctrine in Occasionalism.

We may turn to the question of the first cause of motion. That this should be the title of the Fourth Discourse is in itself significant—its very place suggests that it is the more general question which must precede the more limited body-soul problem. Adopting in this discussion the geometric method, Cordemoy lays down two axioms:

1. On n'a pas de soy, ce qu'on peut perdre, sans cesser d'estre ce qu'on est.
2. On ne peut conçevoir que deux sortes de substances, sçavoir *l'esprit* (ou, ce qui pense) & le corps: C'est pourquoy on les doit considérer comme les causes de tout ce qui arrive; & ce qui ne peut venir de l'une, se doit nécessairement attribuer à l'autre.

From this it follows that the first mover of body is not body; it can be only a spirit, and, moreover, only the spirit that commences motion can continue to move bodies.[21] The point is that the unitary body substance, Cordemoy's atom, cannot cause a motion. For, if it did, it would lose something of itself and so in that measure cease to be. But the atomic bodies are fixed in their being. Their motions cannot come from anything extended, or from anything material. Matter is a composite of bodies. The phenomena of motion, accordingly, demand a nonmaterial cause, not merely for their beginnings but also for their continuation. In these statements Cordemoy is asserting the insufficiency of the mechanical conceptions of science. All relations in the physical

[21] *D*, pp. 94–97. See also the *Traité de Métaphysique*, in *O*, pp. 111–12, to the effect that God is the cause of corporeal and spiritual substances and that the one is capable of being extended and the other of thought and will; but God is not extended and is not body.

world are cases of motion. But none of them is intelligible in terms of the entities of which that world is composed.

From this it follows that God's intervention is continual. We say that an object *B* causes *C* to move, and *C* causes *D* to move, and so forth. But since no body can transmit anything to another body, God's activity is present in every case of change. The encounter of two bodies is "une occasion à l'esprit, qui a meu les premiers, de mouvoir les seconds." [22] To think that one body moves another is to confuse occasions and causes.

The motions of our body are then similar to any other motions whatever. Our will is not the cause of them. Cordemoy refers to reflex action to demonstrate that our bodies move before we will them to move.[23] The soul can be said to move the body only in the sense that one body moves another—a statement which reveals how for him the relation between body and soul is but one instance of the general problem of relations.

As the laws expressing the orderly relations between things (or between the constituent bodies) are laws established by the Deity, so the relations of the body and soul are instituted by God. The power of the First Spirit "a aussi posé entre nos ames & nos corps des loix qu'elle [that is, this spirit] ne voile jamais; & tandis que ces corps sont constituez d'une certaine façon, elle en dirige toûjours certains mouvemens selon nos desirs, ce qu'elle fait avec tant de promptitude, & se conformement a nos volontez" [24] that we believe that we ourselves are the cause.

As the unity of the world, consequently, is an order imposed upon its discrete elements, so the unity of body and soul resides in the regularization of the activities of the other. The union of body and soul cannot be similar to the union, in the ordinary sense, of two bodies. Nor can it be analogous to the union of two souls.[25] The relation of body and soul is a special case of organization precisely because the things to be related have nothing

---

[22] *D*, p. 104.
[23] Reference is made also to the fact that vital movements cease despite the will; moreover, we cannot control the speed of the movements of the subtle kind which cause bodily motion. *Ibid.*, pp. 105–6.
[24] *Ibid.*, pp. 117–18.
[25] Cordemoy's conception of union is covered by the following definitions and axiomatic propositions:

in common. The whole meaning of the union of body and soul must be given in a *harmony,* an *appropriateness,* a *correspondence,* between a state of the soul, an idea or volition, and a state of the body, whether a perception or an action. If the spirit wills a movement of a certain sort, and the body does move conformably, then this *is* (one might say "phenomenally") the union of body and soul. This doctrine furnishes a certain meaning to the statement that God is everywhere, without being dependent upon matter, and that the soul is wherever there are motions directed by it. In this sense the whole of the soul is in the whole of the body.[26]

In all of this, it will be evident, the Cartesian antithesis of body and soul is accepted. The members of this dualism, however, will bear with unequal weight upon psychological, epistemological, and theological problems. God, it is clear, is as different from matter as is the soul. God and the human soul are together opposed to matter as the spiritual to the material. Moreover, the knower and the thing that perceives, feels, and imagines, reside in the soul. The Cartesian dualism sets over against the material universe, not man, but man's soul. And while it makes the human soul and God of essentially the same substance, matter remains

---

Definition I: "Deux corps sont unis autant qu'ils le peuvent estre, quand leurs étendues se touchent mutuellement & avec un tel rapport, que l'un suive nécessairement les déterminations de l''autre." *Definition II:* "De mesme, on diroit que deux esprits séroient unis, si leurs pensées se manifestoient mutuellement & avec un tel rapport que l'un suivist nécessairement les déterminations de l'autre." *Axiom:* "D'ou il résulte que l'union des choses ne se fait que par ce qu'elles ont rapportant: Et conséquemment si un Corps & un Esprit sont unis, ce n'est pas par la rapport de deux étendues, car l'Esprit n'en a point. Ny par le rapport de deux pensées, car le Corps n'en a point" (*D*, pp. 120–22). This may be completed by the definitions and axiom of the second part of the Fifth Discourse. "*Def. I:* On dit qu'un corps agit sur un autre, quand à son occasion cét (sic) autre corps commence d'estre arangé ou meu autrement qu'il ne l'estoit auparavant. *Def. II:* De mesme on dit qu'un esprit agit sur un autre esprit, quand à son occasion cét esprit conçoit, imagine, veut, ou pense, en quelque façon que ce soit, autrement qu'il ne faisoit auparavant. *Axiom:* D'ou il résulte qu'une chose n'agit l'autre qu'autant qu'elle y peut apporter de changement suivant sa nature . . ." Hence a body cannot cause movement in a soul, or a soul cause thought in a body (*D*, pp. 128–29). We are led to the conclusion: "Mais si ce corps, ou son mouvement, ou sa figure, ou autre chose dépendante de sa nature peut estre apperçeu de quelque esprit, en sorte qu'à son occasion cet esprit ait des pensées qu'il n'avoit pas auparavant, on pourra dire que ce corps a agy sur cet esprit, puisqu'il luy a causé tout le changement dont il estoit capable souivant sa nature" (*D*, pp. 129–30).
[26] *D*, pp. 124–25.

the antithesis of that substance. The older distinction between the Creator and the created is supplanted by, or, better, cut across by, the distinction between the spiritual and the material. Aforetime, perhaps, the existence of the world was considerably more assured than that of the soul. But for Cordemoy it is necessary to believe, if not to demonstrate, that the existence of the soul is more certain than that of the body, or of body in general. Appropriately enough, this assertion is a portion of the title of the Sixth Discourse.

There are some, says Cordemoy, who assert that were it not for the teaching of religion there would be grave doubts of the existence of the soul. However, he adds, while the confirmation that faith affords is welcome, yet it is not necessary for the conviction that the soul exists. Indeed, it is astonishing that people should doubt on the subject. Nothing is clearer to the spirit than the spirit itself. One may doubt the existence of the body, but not of the doubt itself. Doubt is a thought and who can believe that a thought is the same thing as that I call a body? Is it asserted that I feel the body? But persons whose fingers have been cut off may feel pain at the ends of the fingers—but they do not imagine they have extended parts that really are lacking. There is no ground for believing in extension if the sole reason for the belief is that I feel it. I may think I have a body without really having it. But I cannot think without really having a thought. In this way Cordemoy removes the Cartesian argument from a logical, methodological, and epistemological context to what is essentially a psychological context. The soul or mind (*âme* or *esprit*) is "that which thinks of something." But we have seen that all psychological processes, ideation, perception, attention, memory, imagination, judgment, and will, are unequivocally assigned by Cordemoy to the soul. All are *pensées*.[27] Without the soul, all is extended substances and motion. Within the soul is my immediate experience, that which I am. That I am aware of extension by feeling—that I sense it—is not certain evidence that such a thing

---

[27] The thing I think about is called an object. "Ce que l'on conçoit de l'objet s'appele *idée*; on la nomme *perception* à l'abord, *attention* à la continue; & *mémoire*."

exists. The existence of the soul is *more* assured than that of the body.

What then belongs to me *à cause du corps?* What belongs to me because of the union of body and soul? To both questions Cordemoy must reply that in one sense nothing pertains to me because of the body or because of the union of soul and body. But in another sense body and soul can be understood only in terms of one another. Let us remember that there is a certain proportion between them. This proportion is a part of the Deity's universal adjustment of things to one another, an adjustment presumably perfect before the Fall, so far as man is concerned. The order that God imposes, so to speak, upon the relations and motions of the elements of matter is the expression of this adjustment, of this universal harmony. My soul, that is, the realm of spiritual events, is proportioned to my body, the realm of physical events with which my soul is intimately related. What has already been observed of the appanages of the body, says Cordemoy, leads me to know that "si ie remarque de la figure, du mouvement, & des organes différens en moy, c'est parce que i'ay un Corps." [28] The same thing may be remarked concerning nutrition, the transportation of the body, waking, sleeping, and so forth.

Something must result from the union of soul and body. Anything that cannot be explained as due either to body or to soul must be due to their union. Cordemoy then employs the conception of animal spirits as the neurological basis for the explanation of the mechanism of sensation and perception. I therefore can possess the senses without being more than a body. All such processes are reducible to brain motions. The same may be said of such matters as hunger and thirst. However, to assert that one may possess such processes, and still be body and nothing more, is a statement limited to physiological processes. In other words, Cordemoy here distinguishes between neurological sense-processes and the sensation or perception itself, the end-results of the causal chain, which are psychological facts. "Mais il n'est pas possible . . . que je les sente [that is, the bodily processes]

[28] *Ibid.*, p. 152.

& que je m'en apperçoive, des qu'elles arrivent, sans avoir une Âme, & sans que cette Âme soit unie au corps que je nomme le mien." [29] The terms "sensation," or "perception," may thus signify two entirely unlike universes of discourse, that of bodily mechanism and that of spiritual process. Sensing is something utterly different from, although allied with, a stimulus-reaction circuit. Cordemoy illustrates his distinction by giving an account of nerve-process that may be called quite fairly sensori-motor, and then adds: "Mais cela n'est pas sentir." [30] On the other hand, were I a soul without attachment to a body, I should not perceive a process resulting from (let us say) an injury to my finger, and should have no interest in it—and "cela n'est pas sentir la douleur." But

il est certain que si par la puissance qui a fait ce corps & Âme, ils sont en telle disposition, qu'il y ait un rapport nécessaire entre les pensées de l'une & les mouvemens de l'autre, en sorte que cette Âme ait interest que les mouvemens de ce corps soient toujours iustes, & les organes qui y servent, bien ordonnez, elle ne pourra s'appercevoir de l'état violente & contraire à l'oeconomie de ce Corps qu'avec douleur.[31]

Similarly, the soul, taking an interest in everything making for the conservation of the body, perceives the need of alimentation, and so feels hunger.

As the above quotations indicate, and as is further shown by Cordemoy's discussion of pleasure and pain, he continues the standpoint broached, but not developed, by Descartes. The latter's rather incidental statements to the effect that sensations are to be viewed as agencies making for bodily welfare, for the control of the body and its adjustment to the environment, and as signs of the relation of the organism to things are carried somewhat further by Cordemoy. Pleasure and pain are to be explained— or rather to be understood—in terms of what is useful and what is harmful to the body. They are the soul's feeling of the equilibrium or inequilibrium of the bodily economy. He adopts the thought of Descartes that sensation and the passions are due to the fact that man consists of soul and body. With Descartes the idea was connected with the possibilities of interaction through the pineal

[29] *Ibid.*, p. 176.   [30] *Ibid.*, p. 177.   [31] *Ibid.*, p. 178.

gland and at the same time was related to the problem of why man, the rational being, is so largely irrational. With Cordemoy, of course, the conception that sensation and the passions are fruits of man's composite nature is altered in the direction demanded by his rejection of every possibility of interaction. In so far as useful, sensation reflects the orderly proportioning of things in the world by God. In so far as sensation and passion indicate inequilibrium, a disordered condition, they represent a failure of that proportion. To account for it, presumably, Cordemoy would appeal to theology, the divine plan, and the Fall.

The sphere of the psychological and the neurological are thus sharply distinguished. The correspondence between them, however, is so exact that the effects of habit obtain in both spheres. Cordemoy seems to think that a process in the body, when the soul is added, involves the additional fact of a feeling in the soul. Then this feeling (for example, of pain or hate) leads to a change of disposition in the soul, that is, to an activity of will. This volition is then the occasion of an alteration in the bodily process. Whether this character of sequence involved in the preceding statement is merely incidental to Cordemoy's mode of expression, or represents his real meaning, is difficult to determine. It is clear enough what results. For if once a *pensée* has been joined to a movement of the brain, he says, "jamais l'âme n'a cette pensée, par quelque occasion que ce soit, que ce mouvement ne soit excité de nouveau." [32] Again, desire is the thought that the soul has of following that which can serve the body, and fear (*crainte*) the thought of avoiding that which may injure the body. Thanks to the principle of habit, the correlations of desire and fear with bodily processes become fixed, and when the one recurs, so will the other.

In all these ways Cordemoy recognizes that the fate of the soul is in some sense bound up with the career of the body. The soul is a name, not for a substantialized knowing principle, but for a self with its own life and inner way of being. Yet this soul reflects at every moment its specific attachments to the body. It adds to the bodily process a new datum. The motions of the brain are diverse in correlation with the diversity of objects. And in cor-

[32] *Ibid.*, p. 194.

respondence with the diversity of brain perturbations the states
of the soul vary. Strictly speaking, the states of the soul are conjoined with the perturbations of the brain. The doctrine that the
perturbations of the nerves form the "occasions" for the formation by the soul of the idea of the object, that is, the perception,
was evidently regarded as peculiar to the "Cartesians." Daniel,
representing the Jesuit opposition, takes it as characteristic of
them. He points out that as a consequence our ideas and perceptions of objects do not depend necessarily upon the objects, "mais
uniquement de l'organe interieure." [33] But, explains Cordemoy,
the soul does not conjoin the sensation with that "qui la cause im-
médiatement" ("cause," of course, to be taken in the sense of
immediate occasion). Rather, it relates the sensation with the
places from which the *"ebranlemens"* (that is, the stimuli) customarily proceed. It connects the sensations of pleasure and pain,
Cordemoy states in the *Traité*, with its own body, and other sensations with their various objects or causes. That is, the soul "ap-
pliquant toujours sa sensation à la chose, pour la perception de
laquelle elle luy est donnée, il luy arrive ordinairement de la
confondre avec cette chose." [34] It is useful, says Cordemoy, that
the brain should be stimulated from a distance by means of subtle
bodies, and it is useful that the soul should *rapporter* the sensation
occasioned by the motions of the brain to the objects which start
the train of motion.[35]

This transference of the sensation to the "object" is a most
interesting illustration of the effects of taking the Cartesian dualism seriously. If the soul and body are utterly unlike, their union
is definable only as a correlation or correspondence of a state
of the one with a state of the other. Outside the soul are motion,
extension, figure, but nothing more whatever. Whatever commerce the soul can possibly have with the extra-organic world
is indirect, and that in two senses. It is indirect in that it is limited
to a somewhat inexplicable correspondence of events utterly unlike. It is indirect in a second sense, in that this correspondence is
really limited to the correlation of a state of the soul with a state
of the brain, not with an extra-organic thing or event. The move-

---

[33] *Voyage du monde de Descartes*, p. 58.   [34] *O*, p. 117.   [35] *D*, pp. 212–13.

ments of the nervous system are connected by a chain of causes (that is, occasions) with that which lies outside the human body. But the occasions of states of the soul are, so to speak, the termini of these chains of causes, the motions in the brain. We should therefore expect to find the soul transferring its states, its sensations, to the correlated motions of the brain rather than to the objects from which these motions proceed, as Cordemoy expresses it. At least there is precisely as much reason for the transference of the sensation to the brain-motion, to the terminal portion of the chain, as to any other portion. The soul has no sensation save when certain movements of the brain constitute the occasion. But Cordemoy acknowledges that we never perceive these brain-perturbations.[36] Moreover, it is a question as to the sense in which, according to his principles, the soul can perceive any motions at all. But laying that aside, it is clear that he felt the difficulty concerning the very existence of the extra-organic world brought about by his strict adherence to the antithetical character of soul and body. He does not seem to entertain the problem specifically, but he recognizes that the soul does, in fact, conjoin, or *rapporter,* its sensations to extra-organic rather than to intra-organic occasions, and he recognizes in addition that this is something to be explained. His explanation, so far as it goes, is simply that it is useful for the soul to do this. It is useful, however, only because the soul is wedded to the body, and this transference of the sensation is primarily useful to the body and only indirectly to the soul. We are creatures composed of soul and body. As creations of the Creator we fall within that general proportioning for which the Deity is responsible. Because of the orderliness of the world, it is useful for the soul to attach its sensations to the early rather than the later links of the chain of causes, and in this sense guide the body. It can hardly be doubted that Cordemoy feels assured of a certain efficacy of the soul. If it learns, the body profits thereby, because God will parallel this improved condition of the soul with its appropriate correlate in the organism. In this very indirect sense there is an interaction of soul and body. Cordemoy seems to imply that the soul gradually comes to make the trans-

[36] *D*, pp. 228–29.

ference of the sensation to the extra-organic object. The hint is not developed, nor is the efficacy of thought by means of God worked out. The background of the matter is the general conception of God's proportioning of things. In asserting that God's instrumentality provides that the soul shall have the state appropriate to the body and the body a condition appropriate to the condition of the soul, Cordemoy defines none too clearly a mode of interaction giving efficacy and concrete meaning to the union of soul and body. He is carried over whatever obstacles such ideas may have presented to him by the notion of God's providence.

For Cordemoy himself, the problems of the nature and efficacy of the soul, of the nature of the body and its "marvellous union" with the soul, are satisfactorily solved. The world of things, the subject matter of physics, has been stripped of every quality that by an inveterate habit we incorrectly attribute to it. Because we have reached a knowledge of the self, we have attained a clear idea of things. In obtaining a clear idea of the union of the soul with the body we secure a clue to the relations of one thing with another. With all this the soul achieves a vision of its true worth.

Elle renferme en soy tout ce qui la peut satisfaire; & estre dans une joye sans pareille, elle n'a qu'à faire reflexion sur ce qu'elle est; elle n'a qu'à bien examiner les notions parfaites que Dieu luy a données, soit pour se connoistre elle-mesme, soit pour connoistre le Corps qu'elle anime, soit pour connoistre quel est ce merveilleux rapport qui fait toute leur union.

And beyond this lies even more.

Elle peut par le mesme moyen connoistre (du moins autant qu'il luy est utile) toutes les autres pieces qui composent cét universe; enfin elle peut par ces lumieres connoistre Dieu mesme, & le connoistre assez pour l'aymer plus que toutes choses.[37]

[37] *D*, Preface.

CLERSELIER, 1614–1684

AND ROHAULT, 1620–1675

CLERSELIER, says Condorcet, had for Descartes "un enthou-
siasme ou ploutot un culte." This enthusiasm, indeed, has consequences somewhat unusual in the history of philosophy. Clerselier saw in Rohault, Condorcet continues,

l'homme le plus propre à repandre les vérités que Descartes avait
enseignées, et qui n'existaient encore que pour un petit nombre de sages,
et, malgré les disproportions de la naissance et da la fortune, il choisit
Rohaut [*sic*] pour son gendre, au milieu des cris d'une famille indignée,
qui ne concevait pas qu'on aimat mieux trouver dans son gendre des
talents et des vertus, que des aieux et de l'or et qui appelait cela sacrifier
sa fille; comme si un philosophe honnête et respecte du public n'était
pas plus propre à faire le bonheur et la gloire de sa femme, qu'on homme
mediocre, riche et titre.[1]

Rohault's career seems to have been launched under favorable
skies. Condorcet adds, however, that Rohault made not a single
discovery that could be cited. He neither added to nor corrected
the philosophy of Descartes, the eulogist continues, but he taught
this philosophy with clarity and with method. His books carried
this doctrine to the public, and were "biens faits et bien écrits
pour le temps."

That Condorcet should have eulogized Rohault serves to coun-
terbalance somewhat the statement that he made not a single dis-

---

[1] *Œuvres*, O'Connor and Arago, Paris, 1847, Vol. II, *Éloge de Rohaut*, p. 95. In his
Preface to his second volume of Letters of Descartes (given in the *Œuvres de Descartes*, Adam & Tannery, 1901, V, 628–36), Clerselier states that Paris is filled with
a number of persons who, either from a desire "d'insulter à cette nouuelle façon
de Philosophe" or from a curiosity to know what it is all about, go to the Assembly
held every Wednesday "chez Monsieur Rohault, tres-scauant Mathematicien, & fort
experimenté dans les Méchaniques, & celuy de ma connoissance qui est le plus
versé dans cette Philosophie . . ." (p. 630). "Monsieur Rohault si connu non seulement a Paris, par les conferences qu'il y a faites longtemps en public & en particulier
sur la philosophie de Monsieur des Cartes; mais encore dans toute la France par
le traité de physique & par les entretiens qu'il a donnez au public . . ." *Sentimens
de M. des Cartes touchant l'essence & les proprietez du corps, opposez a la doctrine
de l'église, et conformes aux erreurs de Calvin, sur le sujet de l'Eucharistie*, par
Louis de la Ville, Paris, chez Estienne Machallet, 1680, pp. 69–70.

covery. For Condorcet, Rohault's carrer is worthy of eulogy because of the latter's fervent discipleship and educational function. The student of the history of philosophy, however, will probably find in Rohault's work an interest that seems to have escaped Condorcet. It is true that if we follow the conventional treatment of Descartes neither Rohault nor Clerselier have much interest for the student of today. They testify to the significance of Cartesianism for the generations immediately following Descartes rather than to the import of that philosophy for the mind of today.

The tradition established in the histories of philosophy interprets the *Cogito, ergo sum,* both in itself and as the terminus of the methodological doubt, as really meaning a Cartesian discovery that the immediacy of self-consciousness is the one ineluctable fact upon which philosophy may be built. Descartes, in short, begins with a psychological and a psychical fact. It is difficult, however, to credit Descartes himself with this doctrine. He certainly did not express it in so many words. He tells us that the *cogito* proves that I am a mind, the whole essence of which is to think; he does not state that my immediate consciousness of my inner states constitutes the essence of mind. It must be admitted that he was led more and more in this direction, in all probability because of an increasing recognition of the epistemological difficulty arising when the dualism of substances, giving sensations the status of spiritual facts, made the relation of these data to things problematic. Certainly it is true that this difficulty was of the first importance in leading his followers to define the Cartesian point of departure as the immediate awareness of our states of consciousness.

At the time of Clerselier and Rohault, however, this "psychological" interpretation of Descartes had not become fixed. It is more accurate to say that they represent a stage in the development of this point of view. Whatever interest the work of these two men has for the history of philosophy thus depends upon their conception of the Cartesian philosophy. Rohault, as we would say, was a physicist, not a philosopher. Condorcet however, thinks of Rohault as a disciple of Descartes the philosopher. That Rohault made not a single discovery to add to Cartesian doctrines means, for Condorcet, that he made no contribution to physics. Even for Condorcet the time had not come when physics is something that does not concern philosophers, when selective interest views Descartes primarily as epistemologist, metaphysician, and psychologist. In the circumstances, it is of the highest interest to ask what Cartesian doctrine meant to Clerselier and to Rohault. What was the doctrine that Clerselier acclaimed with enthusiasm? What were the verities that Rohault was to convey to a wider public?

It is important to note that Clerselier was in religion a devout and sincere man. Bouillier quotes Bayle to the effect that it was doubtful if any one in Paris went to mass more often than "le bon M. Clerselier." [2] He is, at the same time, imbued with a passion for the advancement of knowledge. Such a passion, for a religious man who was also possessed of an enthusiasm for the Cartesian philosophy, would bring about an acute consciousness of the Cartesian break with traditional science and philosophy and an uneasiness concerning the accord or disaccord of the new system of thought with theology. Descartes, as Clerselier understands him, has proclaimed the authoritative competence of reason for the acquisition of knowledge; he has made the recognition of human rationality the point of departure for the intellectual life. There is dynamite in this, and Clerselier knows that the Cartesian proclamation of the authority of reason lays upon the expounders of the new doctrine the burden of demonstrating its harmony with theology.

Clerselier understands that Descartes, in asserting rationality to be the essence of the human soul, had asserted the necessity for the free exercise of reason for the acquisition of certainty. This was not, of course, an unrestricted defiance of authority. The tradition of a separation of the realms of reason and of faith was firmly established. But he evidently feels that this insistence upon the competence of reason and the universality of good sense is, in principle, a denial of this separation of the fields of reason and of faith. For this reason the vigor with which he demands

[2] *Histoire de la philosophie cartésienne*, 3d ed., I, 505.

independence of mind in matters of philosophic inquiry is no greater than the vigor with which he protects the new philosophy from the charge of impiety.

In referring to the public lectures by Rohault, Clerselier admits that the audience may be surprised by the novelty of the doctrines, but insists that the auditors are convinced by the agreement of the experiments with Rohault's reasonings. The great number of persons of condition who applaud Rohault should lead all those who possess a desire to know and to rid themselves of deception to honor his assembly by their presence. For then they will render themselves the judges and arbiters of his explications. Why, inquires Clerselier, should one depend on the judgment of others when one can enlighten himself and ask of his own reason that which one should believe? Submission to the judgment of others may be proper to infancy of mind, but it becomes a mark of laziness and baseness to remain in this submission. The very men, says Clerselier, to whom the world appeals as to authority, are those who showed greatest independence of mind. Aristotle, above all men in antiquity, deferred least to the opinions of those who preceded him. For this very reason we are not doing an injustice to Aristotle if, after his reign of two thousand years, we treat him in the very fashion in which he treated his predecessors.[3] Descartes, for Clerselier, is an innovator, yet one who restores an ancient tradition of inquiry. He has rightly directed the mind in the search for truth. The learning of the Schools, we read in another place, is vain. Words alone make the difference between this pretended knowledge and the knowledge of the peasant. In despair some wish to introduce the reasoning *des chymists,* and others the dogmas of Epicurus—but these efforts fail, and most of the advocates return to the *philosophie commune.* The philosophy of Descartes, however, suffers a different fate. It agrees with Aristotle, with the real Aristotle, of course, not the Aristotle of the commentaries. Neither Descartes nor his followers abandon the true Aristotle save where new inventions, such as the telescope, lead to new discoveries. The Car-

[3] *Œuvres de Descartes,* V, 630–31; cf. note 1, above.

tesians pass from the metaphysical method of Aristotle to a more physical and more particular method.[4]

Descartes, then, has pointed to *la lumière naturelle* as the foundation of knowledge. Man possesses all that is necessary for knowledge if he will but cultivate and exercise his rational endowment.[5] This is the meaning of the *Cogito:* man finds within his natural capacity for knowledge the competent instrument, the method of its employment, and the criterion of valid use. Descartes the physicist, the natural scientist, represented to Clerselier the installation of science. This was his innovation as against the vain learning of the Schools that had remained in the same state for centuries, without the least advance or the least discovery.[6] But now this vigorous championship must be protected from the charge of impiety. There can be no modification of the claim that man is competent to know. Medieval philosophy, in effect, had acknowledged the impossibility of the task to which it had devoted so much effort. The separation of the provinces of reason and of faith was, in principle, a confession that rational demonstration of dogma could not be achieved. The Cartesians, and certainly 'le bon M. Clerselier,' were not prepared to challenge dogma. But the competence of reason and the universality of good sense cannot be proclaimed from the house-tops without suggesting that authority must have a subordinate place. Obeisance to authority and acknowledgment of the verities of the faith seem to be graceful and prudential gestures rather than an expression of sincere conviction. The Jesuits perceived the danger and saw in skepticism concerning the competence of reason a better safeguard of the faith than any alleged harmony of Cartesianism and theology could provide. Bayle states that the Jesuits feared the attractiveness to youth of the new philosophy more than they

[4] Rohault, *Entretiens sur la philosophie*, Paris, 1671, Preface. This work appeared during Rohault's life, but the tone of the Preface suggests that it was written by some one else. Clerselier published the *Œuvres posthumes de Rohault* after the latter's death and contributed a Preface to them (Paris, 1684). The *Entretiens* are not included in the *Œuvres posthumes*. It is possible that the Preface to the former is by Clerselier.

[5] Cf. Clerselier's celebration of the natural light in his Preface to the *Œuvres posthumes* of Rohault.

[6] Cf. Rohault, *Entretiens sur la philosophie*, Preface.

feared the possibility of discord between this new philosophy and religion.[7] Clerselier perceived that the enemies of Cartesianism sought to discredit the doctrine primarily on moral and theological grounds. It is probable that Clerselier himself had felt some anxiety on the score of the possible conflict of the master's tenets and the faith. He evidently addressed questions to Descartes on the subject of the Eucharist, and Descartes replies to the question.[8] To whatever extent he may have been troubled by a conflict in his own mind between Cartesianism and religion, he must have resolved such conflicts to his own satisfaction, for he retains his piety and champions the cause of the new philosophy. Descartes the metaphysician, Descartes the discoverer of the real difference between body and soul, becomes for Clerselier the supporter of the essential truths of religion. If Descartes be an innovator in this sense, it is not because he has overthrown the truths of religion, but rather because he has finally placed them upon a secure foundation.

This may be examined in greater detail. Clerselier avers that he cannot suffer without anger that detractors should with impunity accuse Descartes' doctrine of favoring in some way "les libertins & les athées." "Sans mentir, c'est traitter cruellement un Philosoph qui a sappé les deux principaux fondémens du libertinité & de l'athéisme, en prouuant inuinciblement l'existence de Dieu & l'immatérialite de nos Ames." Let the detractors be permitted to say what they will concerning the principles of his physics, but not his morals; let them rail at his opinions, but spare his person; let them, if they will, treat of the extravagance of 'ses petits globes & sa matière subtile'; they may, if they will, consider as a play of marionettes the movements of the heart, the circulation of the blood, the diverse agitations of the gland, the course and distribution of the animal spirits—but let them not question Descartes' fidelity to the truths of religion.[9] In the Preface to the *Œuvres posthumes de Rohault* Clerselier affirms the necessity of distinguishing between theology, the faith, and the

[7] *Receuil de quelques pièces curieuses concernant la philosophie de Monsieur Descartes*, Amsterdam, 1684, "Avis au lecteur."
[8] Letter of March, 1646, *Œuvres de Descartes*, Adam and Tannery, IV, 371–73.
[9] Clerselier's Preface to the third volume of Letters; in *Œuvres de Descartes*, V, 641.

thoughts and opinions of men. The support that Cartesian doctrines will bring to theology is not recognized by common sense.
For

l'imagination de la pluspart des hommes ne s'accomode pas des nouvelles
découvertes. La nouveauté des sentimens, mesme les plus avantageux à
la Religion, les affraye; et ils se familiarisent facilement avec les principes
les plus faux, & les plus obscurs, pourvue que quelque ancien les ait
avancez. Et lorsqu'ils se sont ainsi familiarisez avec ses principes,
quelqu'-obscurs qu'ils soient, ils les trouvent évidens, & les regardent
comme très-utiles quoy qu'ils soient très dangereux. Ils s'accoutument
mesme si bien, à dire & à écouter ce qu'ils ne concoivent point, & à se
défaire d'une difficulté réele une distinction imaginaire, qu'ils démeurent
toujours très-satisfaits de leurs fausses idées, & ne souffrir qu'on leur
parle un langage qui soit clair & distinct: semblables en celà à ces
personnes qui sortant d'un lieu obscur apprehendent la lumière & ne
peuvent la supporter, s'imaginant qu'on les aveugle, lors mesme que
l'un tache de dissiper les tenebres qui les environnent.

Two elements in the Cartesian doctrine, Clerselier thinks, are
fundamental for the establishment of faith upon rational bases.
Descartes has demonstrated the existence of God and he has discovered the real distinction between body and soul. Clerselier
perceives, moreover, that this demonstration and this discovery
are not simply so many portions of the Cartesian philosophy,
metaphysical items to be placed side by side with his physics and
not essentially related. Rather they are indissoluble, and at bottom are one. The demonstration of the existence of God and the
discovery of the nature of the soul, together with that of body,
provide the very foundation for a universal science of physics.[10]
In this respect Clerselier understands Descartes better than do
many later commentators. He knows that both with respect to
interests and to results Descartes is breaking with the past. But
he knows equally well that Descartes is not as radical in con-

[10] "Iamais homme a-t'il mieux revé, que lors que, dans ses Méditations Métaphysiques, il nous a clairement fait connoistre la distinction réelle qui est entre l'ame &
le Corps; & lors que, poussant plus loin ses pensées pour éstendre de plus en plus
ses connoissances, il a déduit & démonstré l'existence de Dieu par un argument si
conuaincant & si naturel, que nous nous seruons tous les jours sans y penser d'un
semblable, & mesme nous n'en auons point d'autre, pour nous assurer de l'existence
de tous les Estres qui sont dans le monde." Third Preface, *Œuvres de Descartes,*
V, 638.

scious intention as he seems to be. Perhaps it would be better to state that neither master nor follower perceived the full consequences of the Cartesian principle that reason carries within itself its own luminosity and is the sole source from which we may derive the criteria giving meaning to truth and falsity. In a sense, the Cartesian philosophy was several revolutions rather than one —and perhaps neither Descartes nor Clerselier perceived all of them.

To one of these revolutions, the new conception of the distinction between science and metaphysics, we must now turn. To Descartes, says Clerselier, is due a great advance, because he wrote of metaphysical things—*des choses Métaphysiques*. There is a great difference between *les vérités Métaphysiques* and *les choses Métaphysiques*. The former are just certain clear and evident propositions which every one knows and which are rules for judging the truth of things. But they do not lead us to a knowledge of any existence and are not conceived as the properties of a substance. They are simply truths residing in the understanding and do not subsist outside it. By "metaphysical things," however, is understood

des Choses ou des Substances intelligentes, ou bien des Propriétéz qui appartiennent à ces Substances, lesquelles sont détachées de la Matière, & ont une propre subsistance indépendante d'elle; qui sont connues sans elle, & premièrement connues qu'elle.[11]

Thus Clerselier makes the distinction between metaphysics and science (physics) virtually depend upon the type of existents with which they deal. Metaphysics, by and large, is concerned with spiritual beings; science or physics with corporeal entities. Thus the Cartesian dualism effects a radical distinction between metaphysics and science upon a new basis. It becomes a step in the modern opposition of philosophy and science. Before Descartes, indeed, some great men have spoken worthily of intellectual things. But, says Clerselier,

s'il m'est permis de dire icy ce que i'en pense, vous n'en trouuerez aucun, qui ait conçu bien distinctement en quoy consiste précisément l'Essence d'une chose Spirituelle, & qui l'ait si nettement distinguée de celle des

---

[11] Second Preface, *ibid.*, pp. 632–33.

choses Matérielles, qu'il n'ait point confondu les fonctions des autres. Monsieur Descartes est le seul à qui nous avons l'obligation de nous en avoir donné les véritables notions, & de nous avoir en mesme temps decouuert le moyen dont il s'est seruy pour parvenir à une connoissance si distincte & si exacte. Car quiconque voudra méditer auec luy, ne pourra douter, non plus que luy, de l'existence de son Âme, c'est à dire de sa propre existence, en tant qu'il est vne chose qui pense; qui est la véritable notion que l'on doit avoir de la Substance Spirituelle, & par quoy l'on reconnoist manifestement qu'elle est distinguée de la Substance Corporelle, comme ayant en soy des Propriétéz ou des Attributs totalement differens de ceux que nous conceuons pouuoir apparténir à la Substance Corporelle, ou Éstendue.[12]

The dualism of body and soul has the most important consequences for morality. It provides the means of checking *les libertins*. But it is not the concept of the immateriality of the soul that is sufficient. Clerselier feels that it is idle to assure *les libertins* that the soul is a thinking substance without providing an equally fundamental concept of the substance of matter. Evidently men are so accustomed to thinking of the soul as the form of the body that its definition as a thinking substance is not sufficient to convince them that the soul is neither material nor mortal. The point is that *les libertins* will assume that the soul as thinking substance is nothing more than the form of the body and so will participate in its mortality. It is necessary to show that the essence of body is of such a character that the term "soul" could in no sense be applied to what is material. Our perception of the true nature of the soul, of spiritual substance, prepares us to perceive the true nature of the body. But to complete this it is necessary to bring about the perception that corporeal substance by its own nature excludes all thought, desire, and feeling. We can fully discern the distinction between body and soul only when we have perceived that extension is the essence of corporeality. Unless the essence of body be such that everything spiritual is by that essence excluded from the body, *les libertins* will maintain that the essence of the body is capable of thought.[13] Thus, the Cartesian dualism is made to possess implications for morality no less striking than for physics.

[12] Preface to *Œuvres posthumes.*   [13] *Ibid.*

The critical importance, in the opinion of Clerselier, of the Cartesian dualism is emphatically expressed when he adds that the body-soul distinction "est de toutes les véritéz celle qui est la plus féconde & la plus nécessaire, soit pour la Philosophie, soit pour la Théologie, soit aussi pour la morale Chretienne." To the support of this Clerselier would bring the conception of animals as automata. So far from this conception leading to a doubt as to the human soul, for Clerselier at least, it is rather a reinforcement. He points out with approval that Rohault indicated the danger of believing animals to have souls nobler than the animal body. Doubtless it was dangerous because if animals could be given a soul nobler than the body, but without attributing to them a spiritual soul, then men might be regarded after the analogy of animals. The human soul might then be thought of as something nobler than the body, perhaps nobler than the souls of animals, but yet not a wholly different substance. He recognizes that there are many who think the Cartesian doctrine concerning animals strange and dangerous because it may lead to the denial of a soul to man. But for Clerselier himself the opposite doctrine would be the more dangerous.[14]

This new doctrine of the soul, he thinks, must supplant the traditional notions. The traditional view furnished a series of images to mediate between the object and the soul. But Descartes has shown us that this explanation is a tissue of unintelligible conceptions. The contrast between the Cartesian doctrines and those of his opponents is illustrated, says Clerselier, by the case of perception. If we ask how vision is produced, the answer is as follows: the object emits its image; this image is received in the eye; from there it is transported to the common sense; thence it passes to imagination, and from imagination to *la fantaisies*; finally, the understanding, which does not know this corporeal image, forms a spiritual image similar to the corporeal; and this spiritual image is that which the understanding perceives, and by means of it the object. But those who assert this do not know what such an image is or how the object forms it or sends it on. They do not know how it is received or how transported to the

14 Third Preface, *ibid.*, p. 644.

common sense, and so forth, not to mention that they cannot tell what imagination and the common sense are. They think they triumph over Descartes because when he has explained the process he reaches the point where he must confess his inability to explain further. This point, of course, is reached when the transition from brain to soul is to be made. Descartes confesses, says Clerselier, that he can give no explanation why a movement in the brain should excite a thought in the soul, if not that "the soul has been made of such a nature that certain movements of the body have been joined to certain thoughts of the soul, and reciprocally certain thoughts of the soul to certain movements of the body, by the order and disposition of the Creator who has made and united together these two natures and who has joined them harmoniously the one with the other." [15] Clerselier reproaches the adversaries with not recognizing that after Descartes has demonstrated that these two natures are so different and without common attributes it is impossible to render an account of their union, or of such facts as the action of the soul on the body, other than by referring this union to the will of the Creator. To ask for more than this, says Clerselier, is to prove that one does not know the nature of the soul and of the body. In short, the dualism is demonstrated. Nothing can be said as to how body and soul form a unity save to acknowledge that they do and to recognize in the fact two things, the power of the Creator and the limits of our knowledge.

In this Clerselier indicates the fact that the opponents of Cartesianism had not been slow to perceive the consequences of the dualism of mind and body. To him, however, this dualism had the merit of bringing the problem of perception within the field of physics and of sweeping away a swarm of imaginary entities. At the same time, the dualism, defining the true nature of the soul, provides an unshakable foundation for faith, for the immortality of the soul, and for morals. The correlating of the physical and spiritual by the Creator, to which Clerselier appeals, and which was to be worked out in detail in Occasionalism, is obvi-

[15] *Entretiens*, I, especially pp. 38–39.

ously the pivot upon which turns the employment of Cartesianism in the interests of theology.

Considering the relations between Clerselier and Rohault, it is likely that the latter represents quite accurately the point of view of the former in his reaction to Cartesianism. If the work of Descartes represented to Clerselier a clarification of questions concerning the fields of physics and of metaphysics, it meant something similar to Rohault. The latter, however, is a physicist in interest. His purpose is the establishment of a science of nature. Cartesian conceptions, especially the dualism of soul and body, provide the necessary determination of the subject matter of this science, and at the same time make possible its harmonization with theology. Aristotelian science had been intimately associated with theology: to replace Aristotelian science by Cartesian and at the same time to maintain the intimate association of science and theology was Rohault's conception of the task of thought.

The first step is to get the soul out of physical nature. The Aristotelians, he says, have been led by the notion of the *Âme raisonnable* as the form of man which can exist by itself to the notion of forms in general as entities that can exist by themselves apart from matter. But while the rational soul is the form of man, it is, Rohault continues, a veritable substance that may exist independently of the body that it informs. With respect to other things, the case is different.[16] What Aristotle meant by matter Rohault is not sure. But matter is really just extension in three dimensions. Carrying over the dualism to the question of beasts, he interprets the traditional terminology on the new basis. By soul is meant a substance which thinks, doubts, judges, feels, loves, and hates. But philosophers have also used the term to mean the principle of sensitivity and the principle of nutrition and growth. Beasts may be said to possess sensitive and vegetative souls, but in the new context the expressions have a new meaning. The *âme sensitive* of beasts consists of the figure and disposition of all the parts of the body, but more especially of the blood and spirits (*esprits,*

16 *Ibid.*, II, 167–68, 170–71, 189 ff.

that is, animal spirits). A similar interpretation must apply to the vegetative soul. Rohault, it must be noted, refuses to admit that beasts may possess only material "souls" and nevertheless may reason, even if the admission be qualified by the statement that they do not know that they reason. His standpoint seems to be that the very essence of the (spiritual) soul is the power of reasoning, and a material soul that reasons, although it may not possess rational consciousness, is an unintelligible notion. It is the capacity for reasoning that is primary in the notion of the soul as spiritual substance, not self-consciousness.[17]

In an analogous manner he carries over the implications of the dualism to the interpretation of qualities. Thus, since animals are merely machines, we cannot infer from their "expressions" of joy and rage that they possess these feelings. Sensible qualities, he avers, were taken by the School as belonging to things. But, he continues, in the new philosophy sensible qualities are placed in the senses; or, as he explains, it would be better to say that the qualities are *in the soul which feels them.* Joy and rage are not things or properties of things at all. They exist where they are felt, and that is in the soul. "The sense-qualities of things" is an admissible expression if the phrase be safeguarded. The dualism of matter and mind substances effects both a separation of accidents and the things said to possess the accidents and also defines a new connection. In this respect, that the accidents are in the soul that senses, they are removed from things. But in a different meaning of the phrase, the sensible accidents are in systematic unity with things. The new philosophy substitutes for the relation of substance and accidents (in the ancient meaning of the terms) a new connection. "Substance and accident" in the context of modern philosophy stands for a systematic causal relation between the things and the impressions of sense, that is, between the states of matter and the states of the percipient soul.[18]

Thus, the causal connection between the specific differences in extension and sensations in the soul is the central factor in substituting for Aristotelian science the newer science, while preserving the theology with which that Aristotelian science had been

[17] *Ibid.*, I, 50–53.   [18] *Ibid.*, pp. 74–75, 85.

associated. For Clerselier and Rohault, as for many others, the conception of the soul advanced in the new philosophy was a positive gain for religion, theology, and morality. The idea of the soul was freed in this doctrine from just those elements of meaning that related it all too firmly to finite and perishable things. Its immortality, in the older context, was not easy to demonstrate, if, indeed, it did not remain a mystery to be accepted by faith. The Cartesian conception of the soul seemed to possess all the advantages for faith and none of the disadvantages that the older concept had possessed. Clerselier and others quite evidently felt that belief in the immortality of the soul had been shaken. Perhaps they were convinced that responsibility for this lay with the inadequacy of the doctrines of the School. Or perhaps they perceived the strategic advantages for the advancement of the new philosophy as a whole that might be gained by insisting upon the immortality of the soul as something completely assured by the Cartesian position. One cannot resist the inference, in any case, that incredulity concerning immortality was associated in the minds of such men as Clerselier with the moral conditions of the day. Accordingly, the new conception of the soul, with its assurance of immortality, seemed to have profound advantages for the welfare of society. With all this went the advantages for science itself, for the whole of nature was freed for investigation that could employ a new economy of conception. Nothing after all was lost. What the world of matter had lost had been gained by the soul. The approach to metaphysics and theology is primarily by way of the soul, not by way of a world of things. The causal connection between extension and sensation in the soul defines the central problem for metaphysics. In the subsequent history of the effort to organize Cartesian doctrine and traditional belief, this causal connection comes to define the exact point at which faith must supplement reason.

LOUIS DE LA CHAMBRE
1594–1669

THE Sieur Louis de la Chambre, *Conseiller du Roy en ses Conseils, & son Médecin Ordinaire* (as he styles himself) is scarcely one of those who have contributed to the larger movements in philosophy. Bouillier [1] refers to Guy Patin's admiration for La Chambre. He was, said Patin, "un des premiers et des plus éminents de l'Académie française, en raison de sa doctrine, qui n'était pas commune." This estimate of La Chambre reflects, one suspects, Patin's hatred of the Cartesian philosophy and his devotion to Gassendi rather than the real achievements of La Chambre. We have here an example of the passions surrounding the controversies of that day. To be a Cartesian or to be an opponent of Cartesianism involved loyalties and enmities embittered by a dozen conflicts of tradition and advanced ideas, and these conflicts were not lessened by the fact that the parties to them did not fully comprehend the genuine issues at stake. Could we recapture the intellectual environment within which La Chambre wrote, perhaps his doctrine would become more impressive in losing some of its fantastic elements and his controversies be revealed as unexpectedly vital. For the issues that he took with such seriousness had then their day in court. For the historian, however, his work is of interest as symptomatic of intellectual changes in large measure lying beyond his conscious recognition of their real import. A study of La Chambre, accordingly, taken as a means of historical diagnosis and illustration, may prove to be not without its profits.

The historian of Cartesianism includes La Chambre among the Gassendist opponents of Descartes. As a Gassendist, La Chambre would be equally an opponent of the School. It was not easy, however, to oppose Descartes without succumbing to his influence. Bouillier says of these Gassendist anti-Cartesians that they made war upon the spiritualism of Descartes and, while not daring

[1] *Histoire de la philosophie cartésienne*, 3d ed., I, 557–59.

openly to profess materialism, insinuated it clearly enough. This may have been true of some of them. But Bouillier is scarcely justified in his generalization. With respect to some of them, as for example Samuel Sorbière, and probably also La Chambre, he misinterprets the situation. The implication of Gassendist teaching was, of course, materialism, however Gassendi might have refrained from it, either with sincerity or with insincerity. But such opponents of Descartes as La Chambre and Sorbière were at bottom opposed to his physical doctrines and to certain ideas concerning method. With respect to Cartesian conceptions concerning the soul as spiritual, immortality, and the existence of God, they were not essentially opposed. On the contrary, they found in Cartesian spiritualism a means of maintaining or reinstating elements of faith and theology, while substituting for the science of the School the newer view concerning the constitution of nature.

If La Chambre opposed the Cartesian spiritualism, he at any rate also succumbed to it. Descartes seems to have taught him that even if there were nothing in the understanding that had not come from and through the senses something radical took place when the materials of sense reached the understanding. Descartes' spiritualism, of course, was but a part of the body of his doctrine. The establishment of a universal physics, with mathematics as the instrument and mechanism as the principle of interpretation, was equally a Cartesian influence. Descartes therefore also taught La Chambre that in de-anthropomorphizing nature, in revealing it as a mechanical system, we make the problem of the nature of man acute. The problems of human knowledge, of psychology, and of morals must undergo a decided revision and restatement.

La Chambre, it appears, never got out of his head the notion that spirituality meant "subtle matter," that is, the sort of conception that in antiquity led men to identify the soul with flame and the atoms of fire, rather than with the sensibly grosser elements of earth or water. He does not identify the soul with the animal spirits. This, however, is not due to the fear of openly acknowledging materialism. Rather it is due to the fact that

Cartesian teaching drove him in the direction of Cartesian spiritualism, while tradition, the School, and the Gassendist materialism drove him towards a rematerialization of Descartes' soul-substance. The result can scarcely be dubbed a compromise; it is rather a case of intellectual indigestion. It is also a testimony to the timeliness of Descartes' definition of spiritual substance, a testimony to the fact that Descartes had brought into clarity of statement ideas that were latent and diffused in the whole intellectual situation.

La Chambre's writings,[2] of course, express the interests of a physician. These interests included, however, a rather generous infiltration of concern with the occult arts, with chiromancy and astrology particularly. As a physician, that is, as one who had a tincture of natural science in the fields of anatomy and physiology and neurology, such elements of intellectual currency as the notion of "animal spirits" were parts of La Chambre's equipment. Given his Gassendist background, his study of Descartes, and his interests as physician and physicist, we should expect him to be interested in the mechanism of the body as used in the explanation of "psychological" processes. He must have been impressed especially by Cartesian ideas concerning man, the mechanism of bodily activity, the automatism of animals, and the like. His interest would naturally center about the neurologi-

---

[2] Bouillier lists the following bibliography for La C.: *Art de connaître l'âme*, 1653; *Système de l'âme*, 1664; *Discours sur la haine et de l'amitié qui se trouvent entre les animaux*, Paris, 1667, in 8; *Traité de la connaissance des animaux*, Paris, 1664, in 4. The present writer has had access to only the first and fourth of the books just listed. References in what follows are to *L'Art de connoistre les hommes*, Amsterdam, *chez* Iacques le Jeune, 1669, in 12; and *Traité de la connoissance des animaux, où Tout ce qui a esté dit pour, & contre la raisonnement des bestes, est examiné*, Paris, *chez* Iacques d'Allin, 1664, in 12.

La Chambre uses the name Louis de la Chambre in the works which the present writer has used. In Larousse, however, his name is given as Marin Cureau de la Chambre; it is so given in the Adam and Tannery edition of the *Œuvres* of Descartes, and by Condorcet in his Eulogy. La Chambre wrote also a book entitled, rather formidably, *Nouvelles pensées sur les causes de la lumière, du débordement du nil et de l'amour de l'inclination* (1634). Larousse attributes to him a work called *Nouvelles conjectures sur l'iris, a receuil des épitres, lettres et préfaces de M. de la Chambre* (1664), and *Caractères des passions* (1640–62). In the *Traité* the latter work is referred to and the statement made that he expects to present to the public a third volume of the *Caractères*. La Chambre's relations to Descartes can be gathered by reference to the Adam and Tannery edition of the *Œuvres* of Descartes (Index des Noms Propres, in Vol. V).

cal interpretation of imagination, perception, memory, and thought, rather than about epistemological and metaphysical problems. With such a background, we should expect his adherence to the doctrine of the automatism of animal life, including the human body. But from the School he has gathered such notions as that of sensible species, that of the hierarchical ordering of nature and the things comprised within it, and that of the interpretation of things in terms of design. He pays, of course, due deference to the traditional religious doctrines. It seems clear, however, that his piety of expression is not just an instance of the current fashion in writing, but is representative of conviction. Condorcet, referring to his "strange assertions," states that far from being persecuted, he rather had the reputation of being a religious philosopher. "On pardonna donc à la Chambre ses opinions en faveur de sa piété," Condorcet conjectures, "ou peut-être dut-il au peu de succès de son ouvrage le bonheur d'échapper à l'envie. Elle avait pour lors de plus grands objets, Pascal et la memoire recente de Descartes." [3] In some sense La Chambre managed to combine the materialistic implications of his Gassendist standpoint with a proper deference to the Church, and with these he unites a strain of thought that we may call Cartesian. Perhaps this was a rather extraordinary alliance, but La Chambre was no profound thinker to whom such combinations would present difficulty. At any rate, the influence of the School, of the hierarchical conception of nature, of the traditional notions of animal spirits and a vital soul or animating principle, counteracted the Gassendist drift towards materialism and the Cartesian doctrine of automatism. Descartes, indeed, in his doctrine of spiritual substance and of man as a whole somehow composed of a bodily machine and a spiritual essence, had raised an obstacle to materialism and to a mechanistic interpretation of vital activities. His reservations concerning the pineal gland and the violence of his separation of man from the animals were ideas that could work in two ways. If animals are machines, why not man? But, if the human body be a machine, and yet the spiritual

[3] *Œuvres*, O'Connor and Arago, Paris, 1847, Vol. II, the *Éloge* of La Chambre, pp. 3–4.

soul can affect it by way of the pineal gland, then the body is not a machine after all, and one may grant at least a sensitive and vegetative soul to the animals. Cartesian influences thus served as both a reinforcement and a deterrent with respect to materialism and automatism. Descartes' position had made man the most exceptional creature in the universe; in fact, man is the exception, for he is a part of extension and nature on the one hand, and akin to deity and angelic beings on the other. This position in one sense fitted theological tradition and religious convictions.[4] It is not easy to determine the exact influence of Descartes upon La Chambre. He speaks in several of his letters of awaiting the arrival of La Chambre's *Caractères*. The two must have had mutual acquaintances in the world of letters. But how direct this influence was, or how extensive, it is difficult to say. If conjecture is permissible, the considerations just pointed out would suggest that it was twofold. On the one hand, reacting against automatism, La Chambre endows animals with the power of knowing; he retains the essentially triplicate view of man as body, animating or vitalizing soul, and spiritual power. With this goes an infusion of occult ideas. On the other hand, Descartes, either directly or indirectly, must have impressed him with the meaning of spirituality, of spiritual substance and the nature of thought, as that meaning is defined in Cartesianism by the dualism of substances.

With all this there is a point of fundamental importance, especially in view of what I have called the symptomatic value of La Chambre's work. He is, or thinks that he is, a man of intensely practical purposes. The art of knowing men is for him no merely theoretical interest. It is, or should be, a science of supreme practical value. Chiromancy and the reading of character from physiognomy are not superstitious. They are, to him, applied arts hitherto unhappily lacking the necessary scientific foundations. He wishes to employ the more recent advances in anatomy, physiology, and neurology to secure this foundation. In this sense his interest is naturalistic and practical. The spirit of his work, as illustrated especially in the Preface to the *Art de connoistre les hommes,* may be expressed approximately in the statement that

[4] On this point see the essay on Clerselier and Rohault.

happiness depends on knowledge of our fellows, on moral insight into the nature of man. A practical knowledge of human nature, in self and in others, is its basis. The study of man is the beginning, and morality as the art of living is the completion. The first book of the *Art de connoistre les hommes*, has as title the words: *"L'idée de la perfection naturelle de l'homme."* In Descartes, in Montaigne, and in Pascal there is found everywhere the feeling that the problem of human happiness is the primary ground even for the advancement of science. Natural, scientific knowledge must provide the foundations for happiness. Even for a skeptic this is a persistent motive. The skeptic, just as much as those who were not skeptics, believed that the cultivation of human faculties must supplant traditional theological conceptions as the ground of *La Sagesse*. The criticism of received opinion, the reaction against Scholasticism, and resolute skepticism were all complementary aspects of the Cartesian insistence upon the principle of the essential rationality of the human spirit. Descartes, just as much as did Locke, insists that "men must think and know for themselves." The Lockean analysis of experience in order to discover how men come by their ideas and the Cartesian proposition that good sense is of all things the most universally distributed are expressions of a common impulse. For Locke affirms that only "so much as we ourselves consider and comprehend of truth and reason, so much we possess of truth and reason" (for the "floating of other men's opinions in our brains makes us not one jot the more knowing, though they happen to be true").[5] And Descartes affirms that every mind possesses within itself the very source of certainty and uncertainty in knowledge and that the human mind is universally the same. The ancients cultivated wisdom, but that wisdom was not *La Sagesse*. Perhaps they perceived that knowledge is power, but not in the Baconian sense. It is somewhat ridiculous to range the name of La Chambre along with these exalted ones. In many ways, however, he was the child of his age more truly than were Descartes and Locke. Prophets represent a future as well as a past; but La Chambre represented his own day.

[5] *Essay*, Bk. I, ch. iv, sec. 23.

It is quite possible that he escaped Cartesian influence in many ways because of his eminently practical interest. From the standpoint of the physician, the soul-substance of Descartes, in principle isolated from the body despite the patent artifice of the pineal gland, must have seemed an obstacle to the founding of an art of knowing men. We cannot credit La Chambre, of course, with the recognition of his own implicit mechanism and the difficulties that a later age has found with it. Descartes himself had given a magnificent example of the mechanistic method of interpreting the human body. Moreover, he had suggested the view of sensations as signs of needed bodily adjustment and as signs of bodily conditions. The passions were due, according to him, to the fact that men are composites of body and soul. But this statement, expressing the difficulties of Descartes' own dualism, was really irrelevant to physiology and neurology. La Chambre is unable to carry through his design, which is in principle the establishment of a complete knowledge of human nature on what we should call physiological and neurological foundations. On the one hand, Descartes' doctrine placed reason and will, and, in the final analysis, everything we should call psychical, beyond the scope of this plan. On the other hand, the conception of animal spirits, which La Chambre should have turned into a purely scientific conception, rendering unnecessary such principles as the vegetative and sensitive souls, is associated in his mind, not with the clarifying influence of Descartes, but with the Aristotelian science of the School. The result of all this is that animal spirits, the vegetative and sensitive souls, understanding, reason, and will are left without definitely assigned relationships. Had La Chambre consistently followed Descartes in his definition of nature as extension, the human body and animals would have been brought within the one universe of discourse. But he must have felt, quite obscurely, that this would have left the human mind outside the field and so rendered his art of knowing men unachievable. Accordingly his conception is that, if men can be known, if their powers, passions, dispositions, and all the sources of the motivation of conduct can be explored, then the field of investigation is the body. The body must be so defined as to include the possibility of such knowledge. Thus, the body is not merely a machine, nor are animals merely automata. Accordingly the likeness between men and the animals is saved as against the dualism of Descartes. It is in this sense that even La Chambre's insistence upon the power of animals to reason is an expression of an essentially practical interest.

The *Traité des animaux* is a controversial treatise. In the *Avant-propos* the author makes clear that he had written an earlier treatise on the *Connaissance des bêtes*.[6] This book had been attacked by one Chanet,[7] in a work that La Chambre describes as *De l'instinct & de la connoissance des animaux,* and to this attack the *Traité* is a reply. The content of the earlier work of La Chambre's, which he describes as dealing with the *Connoissance des bestes,* is fully indicated in the *Traité,* since the author introduces each of the four parts of the latter by an extended *abbrégé* (*sic*) of the earlier treatise. The *Traité,* then, is intended not so much to introduce new ideas as to defend and to provide details in supplementation of the doctrine of the first work.

In the *Avant-propos* he gives a general defense of his doctrine that animals think. Other writers have sought to explain their behavior by instinct. But if one appeal to such a faculty, he appeals either to a mystery or to what will turn out to be reasoning power itself. The new fashion of denying reason to animals is unreasonable. Moreover, it is impious—although it may be that La Chambre has his tongue in his cheek when he says this. Equally new-fangled, it seems, is this idea of finding in reason that which distinguishes man from the animals. Some other basis for the exceptional dignity of man must be found. This difference is not the presence of reason in man and the absence of it in the animals. Rather, it is a difference in the kind of reasoning possible to men and that possible to animals.[8] "Que les bestes raisonnent, & que leur Raisonnement ne se forme que de notions

[6] Apparently he does not furnish the exact title under which the work he refers to was published. Perhaps the reference is to the *Caractères des passions.* At any rate, he implies in this *Traité* that the *Traité* is a supplement to the *Caractères.*
[7] *De la connaissance et l'instinct des animaux,* La Rochelle, 1646.
[8] Cf. p. 288 of the *Traité.*

& de propositions particulières, en quoy il est différent de celuy des hommes qui ont la faculté de raisonner universellement, & que cette faculté est la vraye différence de l'homme qui marque la spiritualité & immortalité de son ame" is La Chambre's contention. That which would provide the really distinctive mark of man, he affirms,[9] would be a knowledge of man's proper substance. But such is our ignorance of the ultimate differences of things that we must use those properties and powers nearest to the essence, rather than the essence, to indicate the nature of things. This is why philosophers employ reason as the distinctive mark of man. To do even this adequately, however, we must understand by reason a faculty, universal in animals, but distinguished in man by spirituality. The latter, for La Chambre, is virtually equivalent to ability to think in universals and abstractions. It is a special faculty of mind, not mind as a whole, that is of "spiritual" nature. The term "substance" reflects, not a Cartesian, but a scholastic meaning. In other connections the Cartesian meaning appears to determine the implications of reason and will.

What, then, is the function that defines the "mental" similarity of men and the animals? This is imagination. This faculty is central in La Chambre's whole view of the constitution of man and of the animals. On the one hand, imagination is related to the scholastic vegetative and sensitive souls; on the other hand, it must bring together corporeal functions (vegetative and sensitive powers) and those functions which are spiritual and immortal (that is, the faculty of reasoning in terms of universals and the faculty of will).

The outline of the *Traité* supplied in the *Avant-propos* indicates this role of imagination. He proposes, he says, to demonstrate: in the first part, "que l'imagination pour connoistre les choses en doit former les images"; in the second part, "que l'imagination peut unir les Images qu'elle a formées & par conséquent faire des propositions"; in the third, "qu'elle peut unir plusieurs propositions & les lier ensemble par des termes communs en quoy consiste la Raisonnement." The fourth part,

9 *Traité*, pp. 269–70.

he explains, is to contain the replies to the objections ordinarily advanced against the reasoning of beasts.

Imagination, our author explains, means in this book, not a faculty distinct from common sense or from *"la phantaisie,"* etc., but a general faculty which comprises all the powers of the sensitive soul that serve for knowledge, in the same way as *entendement* comprises all the faculties of the intellectual soul, such as the apprehensive, discursive, cogitative powers, the active and passive intellect, and so forth.

When we turn to the body of the work, we learn that images are of three kinds. There are exterior images, which are sensible images representing only the accidents of things. They are, so to speak, images of sense. Secondly, there are the images of imagination. Finally, there are the images of the understanding (*entendement*), concerning which there will be much to say later.[10]

La Chambre's scheme, as far as it can be made out, is approximately as follows. Things shed images (he calls them portraits), and these are the sensible species of traditional terminology. These portraits, however, make known to imagination only the sensible accidents, that is, the sense-qualities. The portrait is not, so far, a thing or the image of a thing. Imagination, because the sense-organs are affected by the portraits, takes these quality-images, adds to them the image of body, and so forms the image of a thing, of a thing and its properties.[11] Thus, imagination produces a composite which is akin to its own composite nature and conformable to its function of knowing things, as La Chambre expresses it.

The reasoning of animals is a matter of joining and separating the images by imagination, which gives affirmative and negative propositions. This faculty, however, cannot form universals or abstractions; [12] neither can it reflect upon itself, this capacity being reserved for *entendement* alone.[13] La Chambre is aware of the

[10] *Ibid.*, pp. 4 ff.
[11] The reader may be interested in Clerselier's reaction to this account of perception, a reaction based on his passionate Cartesianism. See the essay on Clerselier and Rohault.
[12] *Ibid.*, p. 9.   [13] *Ibid.*, pp. 156–57.

danger that he will be suspected of making imagination equal
to *entendement,* and this, he observes, is far from his intention.[14]
Here we find a characteristic element of what may be called his
psychology. The animal's powers (and man's) are to be understood primarily in relation to the needs of life. They are auxil-
iaries to the body's career and welfare. In our own phraseology,
the activities of animals and men are of two sorts; those aimed at
securing enjoyment and satisfaction and those of avoidance, re-
treat, escape, and withdrawal. In this measure La Chambre's psychology is naturalistic and so far free from traditional bias. The
position is quite in harmony with Descartes' "psychological"
view of sensation, not with his uncertain treatment of sensation
in epistemological and metaphysical contexts. But these remarks
apply only to the faculties that fall below *entendement* in the
comprehensive sense. In conformity with this psychological point
of view, La Chambre asserts that the knowledge of imagination
is limited to corporeal things that are necessary for life and,
moreover, is limited to those things appropriate to the nature of
each species. The knowledge of *entendement,* in contrast, extends
to all things whatsoever.

The details of his defense could have for us only an antiquar-
ian interest. Those of them that concern the language of animals
are most deserving a moment's attention. Animal's possess language and communicate their thoughts. Their language differs
from man's in one important respect. The languages of both are
matters of institution, that of the animals having been instituted
by God, those of men (at least since Adam) having been devised
by humanity itself. Animal cries are the elements of language.
Now these cries, affirms La Chambre, do not of themselves signify
the passions they represent.[15] Their connection with the passions
is due to the institution of Nature, or better, he adds, of God, who
has given to the various cries and expressions the significance that
it pleased Him to assign to them. The animal's employment of
such signs is, however, deliberate and with recognition of their
function in communication.

Let us now turn to man. In the *Traité* we learn that knowledge

14 *Ibid.,* p. 267.   15 *Ibid.,* p. 399.

is an action, which cannot be conceived otherwise than as a "representation of objects that is made in the soul." [16] Imagination knows by forming portraits of things, and the knowledge of animals is limited to the manipulations of these corporeal images. But what, then, of man?

Before proceeding with the question of human knowledge, let us consider the plan of *L'Art de connoistre les hommes*. The book falls into two parts. In the first, the anatomical, physiological, and psychological foundations for the art are set forth. In the second, supposedly upon the basis so provided, the means employed in the art are expounded. This leads to an exposition of physiognomy and chiromancy, with some attention to astrology. Let us not be too hasty in judging La Chambre. Let us recall that he was a physician, a scientist, a Gassendist, a member of the Academy, and admired by some eminent contemporaries. He is as modern (in the eulogistic sense) as he is medieval (in the derogatory sense). Were he living today, his interests, one may imagine, would lie in applied psychology, vocational guidance, psychoanalysis, and medical psychology. So much may be remarked with respect to the plan of supplying a scientific basis for occult arts.

La Chambre's mechanism, if the paradox be pardoned, is a vitalism. His drift towards mechanical explanation is both helped and hindered by the influence of Descartes. Still more is his tendency towards mechanistic explanation thwarted by the "vitalistic" implications of the traditional *anima, âme*—the vegetative and sensitive principle. Of course, more than one of his contemporaries uses the term, but many of them carefully explain that the vegetative or sensitive soul can be only a name for certain kinds of mechanical operations. But La Chambre does not reveal such an unambiguous position. The conception of the animal spirits, again, suffers from a similar ambiguity. It has been associated with the notion of vegetative and sensitive principles. The new physiological mechanists—Descartes, Harvey, and Boyle, for example—certainly intended to strip the term of what, for them, was a traditional, scholastic, and unscientific con-

[16] *Ibid.*, p. 3.

notation. But the phrase the "animal spirits" remained ambiguous for many men, all the more because Descartes' distinction between the spiritual and the material was not fully understood. This distinction was associated with that between the animal spirits and the body. Hobbes asserted the incomprehensibility of the Cartesian notion of spiritual substances. It is not easy to determine whether he really did not understand or perversely refused to understand. At any rate he falls back upon the tradition that associated spirituality with "subtle matter," and these with the notion of the animal spirits. It would have made for clarity had Descartes and others discarded the phrase "animal spirits," since it was difficult to disinfect the words of connotations wholly at variance with the assumptions of their physiology. There can be little doubt that the confusion of spirituality in the Cartesian sense with meanings derived from the older physiology and carried by the words "animal spirits" was widespread. For Bayle in his Dictionary, in the article dealing with Gomez Pereira, saw fit to urge that what the "chymistes" call "spirits" is essentially body and matter. Now La Chambre was a student of Hobbes; he is quite prepared, on the whole, to define the faculty of thinking by means of abstract ideas in terms of Cartesian spirituality. But he is helped over various difficulties because the elusive connotation of "animal spirits" blinds him to their existence. In the *Traité* which we examined first, although presumably the later writing, a sharp distinction between imagination and *entendement* was noted. We were there informed, for example, that the latter is a spiritual faculty. It is absent in animals. It is the power that makes possible reasoning in terms of universals and abstractions. It "subtilise sur toutes les choses les plus sensibles." [17] When we turn to the *Art de connoistre les hommes*, we encounter something of the language of a Cartesian-like dualism, something of its implications, criss-crossed by old ideas concerning the *anima* and by scientific and pseudo-scientific ideas concerning the animal spirits. Again it is imagination that defines the point where body and mind are divorced and where they form a junction, if not a union.

[17] *Ibid.*, p. 201.

Man, we are told, consists of body and soul, *corps* and *âme,* both of which are by nature perfect and in possession of all that is necessary for the performance of their functions.[18] The term *âme* is used in a more, and in a less, restricted sense. It comprises occasionally what in other contexts is described as the spiritual power or spiritual faculties, *entendement* and *volonté.* In the more restricted usage, it conveys the meaning of the vital principle, the principle of the vegetative and sensitive functions. This unclear usage is illustrated by the difficulty of determining its relation to the animal spirits. La Chambre, as physician and scientist and even as Gassendist, would tend to employ the latter term in a revised sense and so to substitute for the *anima* a description of bodily activities in terms of nerve processes. This tendency is checked, however, by the use of the term *âme* in such a way that it is clearly not identical with the animal spirits. Whether this means that it is not identical with them so far as it includes the spiritual faculties, or that it is not identical even in the restricted sense, it seems impossible to decide. In some passages there is the suggestion that the corporeal soul uses the animal spirits as its agency. So a triplicate arrangement is implied, the animal spirits, the vital soul, and the spiritual faculties. When it is asked how the soul moves the body, the question is answered —or rather not answered—by asserting that the animal spirits follow the movements of the soul itself. There is a sort of sympathetic coharmony of soul and animal spirits.[19]

In brief, two views conflict at every step. The dual view would discriminate between body, which would include vegetative and sensitive processes as just bodily activities describable in terms of motions (of animal spirits), and soul, or spirit, consisting of two faculties, reason and will. When La Chambre expresses this point of view, imagination vibrates uncertainly between body and

18 Bk. I, p. 13.
19 This notion of a harmony or conformity of body and soul seems to have been a characteristic expression of the age. Evidently it is an expression of a pervasive teleology. With Clerselier it is apparent as minimizing the difficulties presented by the dualism of body and soul and their inability to affect one another. Similarly, it plays a great role with Cordemoy. Occasionalism may be regarded as an extended expression of this vague notion. The interested reader may be referred to the essays on Clerselier and Cordemoy.

soul, being definitely attributed to neither.[20] The other and competing view may be described as hierarchical. According to this
âme would be a comprehensive term standing for a whole set of
functions, varying from the (vitally) more fundamental and
"grosser" functions, such as nutrition, through the sensitive and
imaginative powers, to the spiritual (that is, most subtle and
rational) processes of reason and will.[21] In the *âme intellectuelle*
"l'Entendement connoist & la volonté se meut." "Dans la sensitive [soul] l'imagination fait la connoissance, & l'appétit sensitive forme ses mouvemens. Et dans la naturelle [the vegetative
soul?] il y a aussi quelque vertu qui connoist à la mode ce
qui luy est bon & mauvais, & un appétit qui cause tous les
mouvemens que nous y remarquons."[22] The *âme naturelle* is
more or less what we should call instinct and its correlated impulses. La Chambre writes also of a *faculté estimative*, which
seems to be related in one context to the natural soul and in others
to higher powers.

La Chambre's uncertainties concerning the imagination are
characteristic of the situation that arose when the ideas of Descartes concerning the soul came into contact with notions derived
from the School. Imagination seems to be placed midway between sense and the capacity for thinking in terms of abstract
ideas. It is claimed both by body and by mind. Descartes, indeed,
had distinguished unmistakably two opposed meanings of the
terms "imagination" and "memory." The one meaning is corporeal, referring to traces in the brain. The other is spiritual, and
memory and imagination as functions of soul-substance are
faculties of the mind and wholly incorporeal.[23] Strictly speaking,
the brain-process can be called imagination only by a transfer of
the term that may be practically useful but is really not legitimate
at all. La Chambre, dealing with imagination, beautifully illustrates the conflict of Cartesian conceptions with those of the
School. He does not follow Descartes in using the term in two

[20] Cf. *L'Art de connoistre les hommes*, Bk. I, ch. i, esp. p. 21.
[21] Cf. *ibid.*, p. 28, where reference is made to the rational, sensitive, and vegetative
functions.
[22] *Ibid.*, p. 93.
[23] *Œuvres*, Letters CC, CCXXXVII, ed. by Adam and Tannery.

senses, with the difference in meaning clearly defined. He doubles the images. In the *Traité* we are informed that both imagination and *entendement* possess images, each having such as are fitted to the nature of the function possessing them. The caption at the beginning of the section in which this is set forth reads as follows: "Les Images que forme l'Imagination, sont différentes de celles qui partent des objets comme celles de l'entendement." Later he says:

L'Entendement pour connoistre, forme des Images conformes à la nature: donc l'Imagination pour connoistre, doit aussi former des Images conformes à sa nature. Car puisque ces deux Facultez ont cela de commun qu'elles Connoissent, il fault aussi qu'elles avent quelque action qui leur soit commune pour former la Connoissance. Or il est certain que l'Entendement forme ses Images parce qu'elles sont spirituelles & qu'il n'y a que l'Entendement qui les puisse produire: Il faut donc que l'Imagination produise aussi les siennes, puis qu'il n'y a point d'Action qui puisse estre commune à ces deux facultez que la production des Images.[24]

The passage of the sensible species from sense to its sublimation as an idea in the intellect is cut across by the separation of the understanding, as the faculty of abstract ideas in its spirituality, from the imagination, with its limitation to the generic image. The purpose of this view is easy to discern. La Chambre's *Traité* is written in order to refute Chanet's criticism and to demonstrate that animals can think. If animals be granted only the sensitive and nutritive principles, it is clear that they cannot think. But if they be granted in addition the capacity of thought, without further qualification, the distinction between man and the animals is lost. La Chambre escapes the dilemma by limiting that reason which man alone possesses to the faculty of abstract ideas; and then, while denying this to animals, he urges that imagination can join images to form propositions, from which he concludes that animals can think, since they possess imagination.

There is another side to the matter. Human conduct is a matter of motion, and the art of knowing men will concern the motivation of conduct. Unqualified acceptance of dualism would have made both unintelligible to La Chambre. The *âme naturelle*, the facul-

[24] *Traité*, pp. 32–33.

ties of desire and passion, if they are bodily, would be merely
motions of animal spirits, unaffected by man's reason and will.
But all faculties have their *mediocrité*, our author asserts, and
by this he means their adequate functioning, their moderation.
The very source of this moderation is a natural *indifférence* (that
is, a judicial aloofness) of the *âme raisonable*.[25] La Chambre,
in a word, is aiming at rational control of appetite and passion.
Therefore reason, through will, must be intimately related to
body, that is, to the vegetative and sensitive and appetitive
faculties.

The foundation of the art of knowing men is a psychology of
feeling and passion. To these are attributed two dimensions, at-
traction and repulsion, to which correspond good and bad. The
doctrine is based on the general principle that there exists a conformity between particular parts of the body and the inclinations
and dispositions, the whole falling under the natural perfection
of man. It is a harmony of structure and function interpreted in
terms of design. The body is the instrument of the soul, and

qu'autant que celle-cy a de facultez & de puissances différentes, il faut
qu'il ait autant de diverses Parties pour en estre les organes: Parce que
l'instrument doit estre proportionné, & à la cause qui l'employe, & à
l'action qu'elle doit faire par son moyen. Et comme chaque puissance a
une action qui luy est propre, il faut qu'elle ait aussi un Instrument qui
luy soit particulier, c'est à dire qui ait la consistence & la figure qui sont
propre à cette action-là.[26]

An inclination is a constant disposition to movement. Some inclinations, we learn, are purely spiritual. All dispositions to
movement are in the soul, and the seat of the inclinations is the
appetite, which in this context is said to be the only part of the
soul that can move. But appetites are blind, so that the *entendement practic et estimative* must command. Inclinations are permanent dispositions. They are either natural or acquired. The
former consist of images that nature impresses on the animal at
birth, and these are what are termed instincts.[27] The final definition of inclination is: *"Une disposition permanente, & une
facilité contractée de longue-main, que l' Appétit a de se mouvoir
vers certains objets qui luy sont agréables."* [28]

[25] *Ibid.,* p. 19.   [26] *Ibid.,* p. 56.   [27] *Ibid.,* p. 72.   [28] *Ibid.,* p. 75.

One cannot resist the temptation to pause at this point for the sake of calling attention to such an account of instinct. Nature impressing these images at birth is La Chambre's version of an attitude or conception which found a generally similar expression in the cruder forms—not the Cartesian—of the doctrine of innate ideas. Mr. Gibson remarks that "there existed a widespread tendency, among writers upon philosophical subjects in the seventeenth century, to rest the validity of what they regarded as the fundamental principles of knowledge and conduct upon a vague and often unexplained appeal to Nature. . . . Thus, the objective and universal validity of the principles of knowledge and morality was identified with their naturalness. . . . From this identification of objective and universal validity with naturalness a further step was commonly taken, by which our recognition of the truth of propositions possessing these characteristics was referred in some way to the operation of Nature, or of God acting through Nature, upon our minds. Thus came to be widely accepted, in various forms, a theory of natural and innate principles." [29] This statement suggests a question: was not the "further step," as Mr. Gibson expresses it, equally an earlier step? Is Nature, or God's operation through Nature, the explanation of the presence of the innate principles, or did men look for and believe in innate principles because they were convinced of Nature's operation or of God's through Nature? Perhaps the two thoughts are at bottom one. Science was about to substitute the conception of natural structure and the functions expressing that structure for the view of things given by interpreting them in terms of design. On a wide scale, the discovery that the mechanistic view of nature could be used in the interests of design illustrates the point. The argument that the bodily machine proves a divine Designer is given by La Chambre. [30] Generalizing it, we may say that nature as a machine implies a Designer of the natural machine as a whole. Thus, the conception of design, which no longer explains the nature of any *particular* as such, does explain why nature is just the system that it is. Man, as a

[29] *Locke's Theory of Knowledge and Its Historical Relations*, Cambridge, 1917, p. 29.
[30] Preface, p. 6.

part of nature, falls within a general structural plan. The part is in conformity with the remainder of the system. That nature should so affect animals, at birth, or before, or even the mind, as to furnish it with the principles of our knowledge of nature and of our conduct (for good conduct must somehow be natural) could well be taken as a corollary when nature is viewed as a machine designed by God. The traditional notion of a hierarchical system, in which every substance or thing had its assigned place and role, is thus queerly translated into naturalistic terms —with, of course, not too much recognition of what radical consequences might be drawn from the new version of things. To conceive the operation of nature as the operation of God through Nature is, then, quite in harmony with the conception of the natural system as one vast instance of design. The wholesale conception thus supplants the occasional and particular applications of the notion. The real difference is that the momentary intervention of the Deity, as in miracle, is precluded. But those stanch upholders of tradition who were suspicious of new ways of demonstrating the works and glory of God were deeply justified in their suspicion. The harmonious ordering of the system of nature, with its especially significant illustration in the organization of the body and the harmony of body and mental capacity, seems quite compatible with the notion of God's architectonic and providential functions. At first sight the newer conceptions seemed to give a richer content to certain inherited ideas. Nevertheless, suspicion was justified. There lurks in the situation the danger that instead of giving new contexts to old ideas there will be effected a simple substitution of new ideas for old; and this would be a very different matter. The struggle for existence and the survival of the fit may provide a substitute explanation for the "proportioning" of body and soul which plays such a part in contemporary discussions of the souls of animals. Mechanism in nature, instead of explaining design, may be taken as an alternative method of explanation. The adherent of the School might well doubt the assurance that new ideas formed a rational justification and completion of tradition. La Chambre's vacillating eclecticism is in spirit symptomatic of this situation.

This account of La Chambre's thought may be concluded with brief references to two questions: What is the effect upon his theory of knowledge of the competing view concerning body and mind? What is the effect upon his practical interests of these competing ideas?

With respect to knowledge, the chief problem is to explain how the rational soul's activities are related to those of imagination. The images of the understanding, we have learned, differ radically from the images of imagination itself, for the images of each faculty are in conformity with the nature of the faculty to which they pertain. Hence the images of the rational soul, or of the "spiritual" portion of the soul, are spiritual; they are consequently wholly dissimilar from those of imagination. It is obvious that two possibilities, corresponding to the two competing views of the nature of body and mind, define the situation. On the one hand, if understanding be spiritual (in the Cartesian sense, of course) and imagination a bodily function, then the images of the one are spiritual and those of the other are corporeal. Knowledge turns upon the relation of the one image to the other. The spiritual image must be conceived as a correlate of the corporeal, as something arising in the rational portion of the soul as the appropriate reaction of that faculty to a certain activity in the corporeal function. From the other point of view, the image of the understanding would arise from the image of the imagination; it would be a later stage in the history of the sensible species. Continuity between functions rather than correlation of entities of different nature would obtain.

La Chambre, as may be expected, adopts neither position to the exclusion of the other. *Entendement,* we are told, forms its images, which are spiritual, after the model of the images of sense and imagination. But we are also informed that *entendement* can spiritualize the images of imagination.[31] On the one hand, it seems that the images of the imagination, which are corporeal in nature and are images of the corporeal, are duplicated in the spiritual portion. On the other hand, he explains that the image that comes into being because the understanding has

[31] Page 108.

spiritualized the image of the imagination is spread or diffused throughout the (rational) soul.[32] It is in this way that the body communicates with the soul, and the whole of the soul is put in possession of the communication from the body. La Chambre, of course, tells us nothing of this process of spiritualization. It overcomes for him the difficulty that the rational power cannot directly apply itself to matter, that is, to the corporeal image. It is obvious that the ambiguity in the term "spirit" helps him over the difficulty. The spiritual image in many contexts means nothing more than ethereality. This is supported by considerations he adduces in order to make intelligible the alleged "diffusion" of the spiritual image. He states that the sensible image can multiply itself and spread itself through the air and through other bodies; but if the sensible image can do this, he argues, then all the more can the spiritual image accomplish the feat. Again, he is led to the notion of this diffusion in order to explain how the image which is in the intellect can pass from this faculty into the faculty of will. This is sufficient to illustrate how he artificially combines the sensible species and image of tradition with the separation of the corporeal from the spiritual as demanded by the two-substance position.[33]

Let us turn now to the second question concerning the effect of these competing views upon La Chambre's program of establishing a practical science, an applied psychology. The spiritualization of the image explains how body communicates with soul. But how does the soul communicate with the body? This is the critical problem if the art of knowing men is to be a practical art. The answer is found in the fact that will, *volonté*, although spiritual (and along with the *âme raisonnante* asserted to be independent of body),[34] communicates with the body through motion. But just as La Chambre felt compelled to devise two sorts of image in order to relate understanding and imagination, so now he is obliged to duplicate motions. Will can affect body, because motion is common to things corporeal and spiritual. The will cannot communicate with body by *connoissance*, says La Chambre, any more than the *pensées* of *entendement* can be carried over into

[32] Page 109.   [33] Cf. pp. 130–31; 133 ff.   [34] Page 102.

imagination. "Les choses spirituelles ne peuvent jamais devenir corporelles." [35] Elsewhere he remarks that spiritual images or ideas cannot be transformed into phantasms of imagination.[36] The infinite capacity of the understanding, which can form an idea of everything created, means that it far surpasses imagination. But a similar contrast must exist in the case of motion. As the former hypothesis was symptomatic of his inability sharply to distinguish between the old and the new meanings of "spirit," so in the case of the effect of will upon the corporeal we find a similar symptom. Motion in and of spirit cannot be identical in meaning with corporeal motion, but spiritual motion cannot be a mere figure of speech. In reply to arguments, La Chambre appeals to the fact that angels, although spiritual beings, do flit hither and thither. This proves that motion can be common to spiritual and corporeal beings. But his real argument, which although merely verbal to us was evidently not so to him, is based upon a distinction. The motion of spiritual beings is of a kind appropriate to the nature of such entities, just as the motion of corporeal things is of a kind appropriate to the character of things.

In this way he relates body to soul and soul to body. In this way he recoils from the consequences of the antithesis of spirit and matter, which would have defined knowledge and action as a correlation of a spiritual entity with an antithetical corporeal entity. And finally, in this way, by means of distinctions that are verbal, he escapes the necessity of choosing between Darcartes and the School.

It may be hoped that in the diagnostic sense this study of La Chambre possesses some value. His writings can scarcely deserve any other use. He indicates the genuine novelty of Cartesian ideas. He illustrates the way in which the problem of the relation of body and mind becomes central for epistemology, physical science, psychology, and even morals. The impact of Cartesianism, manysided as it was, affected traditional ideas concerning the nature of man and the ethical problem not less than older notions concerning the sphere of science. Giving man over as

[35] Pages 134–35.   [36] Pages 130–31.

subject matter within the compass of a universal science of physics, and so finding a common denominator for the animate and the inanimate, for the simple and the highly organized, Descartes at the same time excluded man from universal physics, and therefore alters radically the perspective within which man and his knowing and volitional processes must be viewed. Moreover, this alteration applied equally to man as subject matter for psychology and as a moral agent. Descartes could scarcely have upset the world of Scholasticism and left the place of man and his salvation unaffected. That a member of the Academy, a protégé of Richelieu, and a physician should have experienced an infiltration of Cartesian ideas that mastered him, while leaving him without mastery of the ideas, is not a matter of surprise but an illustration of the conflicts with which modern inquiry begins. La Chambre's metoposcopy and astrology are precisely as unintelligible as the foundations upon which he proposed to base the art of knowing men. He is unable either to reconcile two dissimilar contexts for inquiry or to choose between them. The history of psychology down to the present, not to mention the story of epistemology, demonstrates that this conflict has not yet been wholly resolved.

SAMUEL SORBIÈRE
1615–1670

NOW there is in your mind something or other, I do not know what, opposed to Descartes, that indicates a virulent and bitter poison, so that you can scarcely refrain from depreciating him and his work as far as in you lies. However I well know him to be a philosopher more learned than you, myself, and almost numberless others, so that I dare to affirm this with any and every solemn assurance. Has he perchance despised you? What then! You think his Method to be sheer folly; but perhaps there is more wisdom in it than you comprehend. (*sed et forte magis accedit ad sapientiam, nec ea plura animo complecteris.*) Did then this great man wish to hold himself up to the whole world for derision? Who can think so? Did he err so disgracefully in Physics, a man who was such a Lyncæus in mathematics, which is the most certain, if not the most noble, branch of Philosophy? Look forward to the coming age, in which he is destined to triumph, which will bring this purpose of yours to naught. But, you will say, this philosophy is absurd to me and to others. Show these absurdities, demonstrate one of them, and I shall believe you. What glory for you if you should take your pen against him! To be sure the reply will bring out the truth. Nothing is lacking to you whose mind and pen are most ready; if you discover something evidently false, you will place everybody under obligations, and at least you will compel the author to put forth his doctrine more fully and clearly. Gassendi, who has recently entered into a sacred friendship with Descartes, you wish to excite against him. Do you yourself, who are free from this friendship, urge the several difficulties in your own mind, and show us, or better show to him, by a single experiment or argument anything absurd in the Physics of René, or henceforward desist from this passion for denunciation. If you dare not attack him under your own name, how many will you find who will gladly affix theirs? [1]

In these words Mersenne, in a letter to Sorbière, characterizes the latter's attitude towards Descartes. Mersenne probably regarded him as a truculent and insincere spirit—a judgment concerning him that seems to have been somewhat widespread in the

[1] From the manuscript letter given in Latin in the *Œuvres de Descartes*, Adam & Tannery, IV, 515. Sorbière's *Avis à un jeune médecin*, a rare small book printed in 1672, after Sorbière's death, has been translated by Frank Lester Pleadwell and published in the *Bulletin of the History of Medicine*, XXIV (May–June, 1950), 255–87. The translation is accompanied by an account of Sorbière's life and work.

learned world of his day. Bouillier, referring to the fact that Sorbière had passed from Protestantism to Catholicism, notes that the sincerity of his conversion was doubted because he seemed over-eager to exploit it.[2] He has, to be sure, recorded his admiration of Descartes, but he was passionately loyal to Gassendi, who was to him "the best of men." He urges Gassendi to refute Descartes and accuses the latter of excessive ambition and of being animated by the desire of founding a sect. Thus his admiration for him is seriously qualified, and it is not easy to discern to what extent it is sincere.

Sorbière may have been both truculent and insincere. He attempted to *envenimer les rapports de Descartes et de Gassendi*, as Bouillier states. His attitudes towards Descartes and Gassendi, however, expressed not merely his personality but also his relation to the intellectual situation. He was a man capable of recognizing the intellectual cross-currents, but incapable of mastering them. As a follower of Gassendi, as physician, man of letters, and man of the world, he stood in a complicated situation. Whether from lack of courage or from lack of ability, he could neither repudiate Descartes nor follow him. He illustrates the inability of the age either to assimilate the spirit of Cartesian teaching or to escape its influence. Hostility and reluctant admiration, worldly prudence and unreasoned attachment to tradition, a recognition, in part intellectual and in part emotional, that between Descartes and tradition there could be no compromise— out of these were born misunderstanding that fostered compromise and a compromising attitude that engendered misinterpretation. Sorbière possessed a genuine passion for what we may call physical science. In this he was evidently sincere, whatever may be true for the rest. Science, a universal science of nature, is the very ideal of intellectual effort. The future lies with the physics of Gassendi, however, rather than with that of Descartes; this is evidently his firm conviction. But he is a compromising and none too courageous spirit. The deferences and prudential gestures of Gassendi are not sufficient for him. This, it seems, is the reason for his interest in Cartesian ideas: they furnish a defini-

[2] *Histoire de la Philosophie Cartésienne*, 3d ed., 1868, I, 561 ff.

tion, as he adapts them to his purpose, of a field for metaphysics (and so for religion and theology) within which the truths of faith and theology can be ensconced, safe from imprudent extensions of Gassendist-Epicurean, or more simply, of "scientific" ideas. In what follows this external addition of Cartesian ideas to current scientific ideas will be set forth.

Not the least remarkable achievement of modern thought is the sterilizing separation of science and philosophy. Metaphysics appears to be a corrective rather than a completion of physics. Theology is an enterprise to be maintained in spite of science. Historically, psychology has provided the more or less slender connection between philosophy and science. It is difficult for the student of the history of philosophy to avoid the fallacy of viewing such philosophers as Descartes in the light of this opposition of philosophy and science. He forgets that Descartes himself knew of no such separation. He fails to appreciate that for him theology and metaphysics were most intimately related to the study of nature. The student of history is unwittingly led to think of Descartes' doctrines in the field of physics, physiology, and astronomy as mere appendages to his "philosophy"—to the method of doubt, the arguments for the existence of God, the criterion of clear and distinct ideas, and the dualism of substances. But for Descartes himself these "appendages" were the very culmination of his efforts. Such a halving of his achievements would have been to him a violent misrepresentation of his teaching and purpose. His aim was defined in his own mind by the vision of a comprehensive structure of knowledge. The *Cogito* meant the establishment of Reason in the seat that authority had occupied. The demonstration of the existence of God, whatever personal satisfaction it may have given Descartes, was no mere gesture of deference to theological and ecclesiastical tradition. That could have been accomplished in another way. He could simply have accepted the existence of God as a certainty of faith. In terms of his own conception of the nature and function of reason and of the problem of inquiry, the acceptance of God's existence on the basis of faith was impossible for the prosecution of his task. The *Cogito* and the criterion of clearness and distinctness

of idea were in effect a proclamation of the independence and
competence of reason. To secure a rational structure of knowledge we cannot begin upon a basis of faith. Reason, in short, is
not competent to master the subject-matter of inquiry unless it is
capable of demonstrating the existence of God. This demonstration, then, was not bravado or a *tour de force:* it was quite simply
the laying of foundations necessary for the science that was to
represent the compass of enquiry. The distinction between theology and metaphysics on the one hand and physical knowledge on
the other was a distinction between substructure and superstructure. The physics of inanimate nature, of animate nature, and
even of the human body—these were not for Descartes adjoined
to theology and metaphysics, but were built upon them.

The contemporaries of Descartes and the men of the immediately succeeding generations dissected Cartesian teaching in
various ways. Only by dissection could the joinings of compromise be effected. From one point of view the difficulty was to
follow Descartes' lead in the intellectual mastery of the physical
world without admitting the competence of reason in matters of
theology. From another point of view the puzzling question was
how to utilize the Cartesian demonstration of God's existence in
the interests of faith and of authority without suggesting that
faith and authority could be dispensed with. Descartes' doctrines
concerning the soul, to indicate another point of view, not only
assisted in saving its immortality from the Maw of universal
mechanism but also suggested the capacity of the individual to
secure his salvation without intermediaries. The mystical tradition could scarcely view the criterion of clearness and distinctness
without suspicion, and Thomists might well suspect that the Cartesian *Cogito* rendered a distinction between the sphere of faith
and the sphere of reason quite unintelligible.

Sorbière affords an interesting illustration of the conflict between Cartesianism and tradition. A follower of Gassendi, he is
necessarily opposed to Descartes as regards the main principles
of physical science, while of course participating in the reaction
against Scholasticism. His admiration for Gassendi was unmeas-
ured, and Bouillier quotes his statement to the effect that some

day men will wonder why ten years after the publication of the *Syntagma Philosophicum* there should have been adherents of any other doctrine than that of Gassendi. Sorbière, however, did not remain unaffected by Descartes, as will appear later. Moreover, he was not wholly satisfied with Gassendi's mere gesture of assent to such doctrines as the spirituality and immortality of the soul. He thus becomes in fact a Gassendist who seeks to demonstrate the existence of God and the existence and immortality of a spiritual soul and would employ Cartesian ideas to accomplish this.

The prevailing interest in Epicurus, for which Gassendi was largely responsible, was an expression of enthusiasm for the application in science of the atomic conception. Sorbière's letters bear testimony to the extraordinary vogue of Epicurus, but equally give evidence that this vogue was accompanied by a repudiation of the Epicurean atheism and the Epicurean failure to admit spiritual substance and an immortal soul. In a sense this was largely prudential. On the other hand, it also represented an accommodation of mind. If the field of science could be freed by making obeisance to authority with respect to God and immortality, so much the better. Thus Sorbière opposes Epicurus' view that the universe is infinite, with its implication of the possibility of a plurality of worlds; he opposes also the attribution of immovability and eternity to this infinite universe, and insists upon the architectural character of the world as against its origin in a blind concourse of atoms.[3] Of course, in writing to Mazarin anything else would have been imprudent. But the other side of the matter is illustrated in the letter to the Comte Christophe, Delphique Burgrave of Dona, in which he urges the latter to consider Epicurus' method of physical inquiry, while protesting that he does not wish to wean his correspondent from that of Descartes.[4] In letters to the Bishop of Laon, Sorbière denies the eternity of the atoms, asserts that reason and faith are not opposed, and vindicates the Providence of God and the immortality of the soul.

[3] Letters XXXV, XXXVII, XXXIX, in *Lettres et discours de M. de Sorbière, sur diverses matières curieuses*, Paris, 1660. All references to Sorbière, unless otherwise noted, are to this volume.
[4] Letter XVI.

He even asserts that the search for final causes is necessary. God has for man a special care, as is indicated by the admirable structure of our body and the conjoining of the soul with it. Epicurus thinks that man's industry is a result of his possessing hands: but Sorbière retorts that hands were given man in order that he might be an industrious animal.[5]

Sorbière, in short, is an early example of the scientist who feels the necessity of reconciling science and theology. Throughout his Letters and Discourses there is present the spirit of compromise. The restriction of science to physical nature is prudential. Gassendist doctrine, however, left the interests of faith outside the sphere not only of science but also of all inquiry. The Cartesian standpoint integrates theology, metaphysics, and science. From the Gassendist point of view we establish physical science and prudently proclaim, in effect, its irrelevance to theology and metaphysics. It is Gassendi, and not Descartes, who would foster the deliberate avoidance of theological and metaphysical questions by science. Sorbière, because of Gassendist teachings, because of a faltering spirit, or because of inability to comprehend, must ignore the Cartesian position as to the necessary linkage of theology, metaphysics, and knowledge of nature. On the other hand, the Gassendist gesture towards faith is felt to be insufficient. Therefore Sorbière proclaims that there is no real conflict between science and theology,[6] views nature after the fashion of Gassendi, admires Montaigne and Charron, and devises arguments to demonstrate the existence of God and the immortality of the soul.

With this goes another interesting fact. Sorbière expresses the growing tendency not merely to distinguish science and meta-

---

[5] Letter XXXIX.

[6] Sorbière asserts that the Scriptures, with respect to matters of physics, leaves us with complete liberty of belief (Letter LXVI). With this should be considered his praise of Hobbes' efforts to secure tolerance and to avoid all religious dissensions by taking the position that the doctrine of Jesus as the Christ is alone fundamental for salvation (*discours sur sa version de la politique de M. Hobbes*). Sorbière's enthusiasm for the newer modes of thought, for "science," is displayed by his interest in the *innovateurs modernes*, among whom he reckons Descartes and Hobbes, as well as Telesius, Cardan, Campanella, Bacon, and Helmondt. Hobbes, with respect to politics, he says, is like the men of science who invent new systems, who seek to reconstitute medicine and to apply mathematics to all problems.

physics but even sharply to oppose them. In the intellectual history of the period this growing opposition is a matter of the first importance. To oppose inquiry into nature to metaphysics was a means of winning freedom for physical inquiry while making possible an external harmonization of science and theology. By eschewing metaphysics, science, in effect, avoided an order of problems that would necessarily have brought rational inquiry and authority into conflict.[7] In two discourses ("Que le peu de cognoissance que nous avons des choses naturelles, ne nous doit pas destourner de leur estude," and "De la vérité de nos connoissances naturelles"), both delivered before an assemblage of physicists *chez* M. de Montmort (June 14, 1658, and August 19, 1659), Sorbière indicates that this separation of science and metaphysics is *already a matter of agreement within scientific circles.* Thus, he states that in this assemblage it is understood that metaphysical thoughts are to be avoided. He promises that in his discourse he will treat *physiquement de cette vérité que nous recherchons dans la connoissance des choses naturelles.* He defends the search for natural causes and urges that even if we have little knowledge of first principles or even of the details of physics this should not deter us from the study of this science in which we meet with much pleasure and find *quelque utilité.* He therefore is aware that in fact physical science and metaphysics have been separated from the standpoint of the interests and procedure of science. The separation amounts to virtual antagonism. The avoidance of metaphysics is a condition of progress in the science of nature. Moreover the inference can scarcely be avoided that for him the subject matter of metaphysics differs radically from the subject matter of scientific inquiry. This is suggested by the fact that he is conscious of the consequences for morals of the separation of science and metaphysics. All appearances in nature turn upon movements; were morality to fall within the field of scientific inquiry, the causes of virtue would be reduced to movements. Herein lies a chief reason for his addition of Cartesian ideas to Gassendist-Epicurean atomism as providing the instru-

[7] Yet in the Discourse on Hobbes, Sorbière even inveighs against men like Voetius, who attack Descartes because the latter seeks to demonstrate the existence of God by natural reasons.

ments of inquiry into nature. The soul, as the seat of morality, falls without the subject matter of science.

Physical science, safeguarded by the opposition of science and metaphysics, surrounded by a circumference of skepticism, with this skepticism counterbalanced by arguments for the existence of God, the spirituality and immortality of the soul—these factors define the compromise of Sorbière.

Arguments for the incorporeality of the soul, he asserts, can be drawn from the nature of the will as well as from the nature of the understanding (*entendement*). The will often repudiates what is agreeable and what is due to sense, and, consequently, what is due to the corporeal. But as will is planted, so to speak, in the understanding, the principal part of the soul (which is the *âme raisonnable,* or immortal principle), it is sufficient to attend to the nature of understanding.

The first proof turns upon the position that understanding is wholly different from imagination (*intellection, entendement* as contrasted with imagination or *la phantasie*). Sorbière notes the error of those who do not recognize that intellection and imagination are distinct faculties, and who, not observing this distinction, look upon imagination as common to beast and men, with the sole proviso that in men imagination is *plus exquise* and receives the name *entendement.*[8] However, there is in man a form of intellection enabling him to comprehend things that cannot be imagined. We conceive things for which there is no image in the brain and for which we can fashion no image. Sorbière's illustration is that we cannot imagine the sun as many times larger than the earth, although we know it to be so. Since intellection has no image, it follows that it is immaterial, just as the imagination is proved corporeal by its need of material images. *Entendement* does make use of the images of sense and imagination, "comme de degrès par ou il monte à l'action qui luy est propre, qui est de dépouiller ses idées de toute matière, & en cela mesme il fait rémarquer son immatérialité."

[8] Sorbière, incidentally, is skeptical about Descartes' theory of the pineal gland— or we know so little about the hidden springs of nature, he urges, that there may be a million organs in the body that must be understood before we can conjecture how things happen within it (Letter LXIII).

The second line of demonstration is drawn from the fact of reflection by understanding upon itself. When the *entendement* considers its own functions, when it conceives or understands, it makes a reflection upon itself. For Sorbière this is a case of a thing acting upon itself. It therefore forms an exception to the axiom "nothing acts upon itself." But this axiom is a law of the corporeal. The eye does not note that it sees, or the imagination that it imagines. These faculties and their actions are corporeal. *Reflexion* is the work of a superior faculty, cut free from matter and incorporeal in nature.

The third line of argument depends upon this, that men not merely form universal notions, but even conceive the reason for universality. Beasts in a sense can form universals, as when dogs recognize that a thing is a man and not a horse. But they do not understand universality as such. They cannot know the abstract, as color, but only the colored. Sorbière adds that additional proofs can be drawn from the objects of the understanding, which include the incorporeal as well as the corporeal. He quotes Aristotle to the effect that the understanding must be of a very simple nature, free from all admixture, because it is capable of understanding all sorts of things. The soul cannot be organic, since it knows the organ which is intermediate between the faculty itself and the object. If it were corporeal, it would never suspect the existence of the incorporeal. But the reverse does not obtain. The soul can and does know the corporeal, although not itself corporeal, because what is higher in excellence comprehends within itself eminently all the inferior qualities.

Here, it is obvious, there is an ill-digested combination of Gassendist and Cartesian teachings, further confused by scholastic connotations of terms. Gassendi, admitting a spiritual soul, the subject of rational insight and superior to the material or corporeal soul, proceeds as if the corporeal soul alone existed. The spiritual soul, in effect, lies beyond the province of inquiry, and in the serious business of philosophy and natural philosophy may be omitted from the reckoning. This gesture having been made, Gassendi can attack Descartes' protestation that his objections relate to the method and the arguments of Descartes rather than to the conclusions, by arguing that this protestation is so completely inoperative that it is meaningless. Sorbière, however, is evidently driven by Descartes to give a serious account of what Gassendi had vaguely admitted in an ineffective gesture. On the other hand, it must be noted that Sorbière uses the term "spirituality" quite sparingly, and his term "incorporeality" reflects a Scholastic distinction affected by Epicurean atomism. The latter gives a content to the "matter" of the traditional distinction, while the "form" breaks into portions, represented in part by the material soul and in part by the incorporeal rational principle. It is worth noting that Sorbière employs Cartesian doctrine for his purposes. In a letter addressed to the Bishop of Laon, with the title "Qu'il y a des Natures incorporelles, contre l'opinion d'Épicure," he advances the argument that the method of doubt leads to the notion of a substance that thinks, and, as there is in it no idea of extension, it must be without dimensions. He does not acknowledge the source of the argument, but does admit that it is not of his own invention.[9]

The immortality of the soul, he asserts, is most impressively shown by establishing the incorporeality of its essence, coupled with the fact that we cannot conceive of death as anything other than the separation of parts. Moreover, the spirituality of the soul satisfactorily disposes of the ancient question regarding its seat. In addition to the argument drawn from the nature of the soul, its immortality may be demonstrated by three proofs of a different character. The first is that of universal consent; the second, the universal desire for immortality; and the third is the demon-

[9] The chief sources for Sorbière's arguments concerning the soul are Letter XVII, to Mazarin, and Letter XXXIX, to César d'Estrée, Bishop of Laon. In this connection it is worth while to point to Sorbière's discussion of God. The existence of God, he thinks, is really a first principle intelligible in itself. But he adds that there are two basic arguments for the existence of God: one of these, based upon what he calls *Anticipation universelle*, is a version of Descartes' use of the idea of God as innate. This idea, he states, is universal in man, and this universality cannot be due to legislation, tyranny, or fear, for "elle naist avecque nous," "elle se forme au mesme temps que nostre âme, & démeure cachée iusques à la première qu'elle a de se produire." He then attempts to explain, not the cause of the idea of God (which is God himself), but the causes that occasion the idea's passage from its hidden and implicit condition to its explicit presence in the mind. In brief, it is the comparison of impressions made by the senses that evokes the idea. (Letter XIX.)

stration drawn from God's moral government of the world. The latter argument, of course, depends upon the necessity of another life in order that the balance of merit and reward may be secured. Finally, in refuting an argument of Epicurus againt the immortality of the soul, Sorbière employs Gassendist teaching. Drunkenness and similar facts do not demonstrate the corporeality of the soul, but only this, that the brain is not in a condition to receive the influence of the soul. The brain, in short, is an instrument of the soul, at least of that soul which is a rational incorporeal principle, and drunkenness, like death itself, is rather a sign that the instrument is unavailable than a proof that the soul suffers from the condition of the body or is perishable.[10]

Sorbière's *mélange* of ideas is further illustrated in his discussion of truth. Here again the utility for science of Cartesian dualism appears. He employs this dualism to give content to the otherwise empty gesture of Gassendi with regard to the question of the spirituality and immortality of the soul. The Cartesian dualism swept the field of physical inquiry free of the cobwebs of forms. Whatever there may be in things animate and inanimate or in experience that suggests forms and formal principles may somehow be relegated to the soul-substance. For Sorbière, the field is thus cleared for a discussion that is to be conducted *physiquement*. Metaphysics is disavowed, and this disavowal is in effect the exclusion of problems concerning the soul, immortality, and God from the province of physics. This being premised, scientific knowledge itself must be treated *physiquement*. Thus, in his discourse "De la vérité de nos connoissances naturelles," beginning with a disavowal of metaphysics, Sorbière proceeds to leave the spiritual soul out of the reckoning. The result is that even thought is included in the subject-matter of physics. Truth is commonly said to be the conformity of thought with the thing it represents. But thoughts are brain-movements, just as sensations are movements prolonged from without. Interior movements, or thoughts, may harmonize with one another or may be found to be more or less in conformity with sensation movements. Thought, being movement, can be compared only to move-

10 Letter XL.

ment. The contrast of thoughts in the soul and motions in things becomes for physical science (metaphysics having been laid aside)
the contrast between motions that lie within our bodies and those
that lie without. Movements that are without the body, however,
are beyond our reach, and therefore we must speak "soberly"
of them, for they can be only conjectural. The "way of ideas"—
if we may represent Sorbière in this fashion—is the way of internal motions. Truth results from comparison of movements of
thought, that is, internal movements, one with another, or of these
with movements prolonged from without, that is, sensation movements. Even mathematical verities are movements chained to one
another, like toothed wheels, of which the first makes all the others
move. The proof of the value of mathematical speculations, born
wholly within the brain, is in applications to sensible movements.
Nothing in physics is more certain than what our experience demonstrates and our senses confirm.[11] And here enters the influence
of Hobbes. To reduce this discussion of truth to a more common
currency, says Sorbière, and speaking more logically, we must
regard philosophical truth as consisting in the use of words and
in their signification, not in the things these words represent. Truth
is a property, not of things, but of propositions. Since Sorbière
translated the *De cive*, it is scarcely questionable that in the above
position we have a manifestation of the influence of Hobbes. This
tends to be confirmed when we turn to a letter to Mazarin in which
Sorbière maintains that *La Politique* is as capable of demonstration as geometry. Science, properly speaking, he says, has to do
with the truth of theorems or general propositions and the consequences that can be drawn from them. Truth of fact should not be
called science, but simply knowledge.

La science par laquelle nous sommes asseurés qu'un Théorème que l'on
propose est vray, est une connoissance par les causes, qui commence par

---

[11] "De sorte que la verité dont il est icy question ne sera autre chose, que la conso-
nance des mouvements, soit de nos pensées toutes seules tandis que nos sens ex-
ternes se reposent; soit de nos sensations, lors que nos sens continuent à faire leurs
fonctions ordinaires; qui sont de faire en nous des mouvemens assez forts, dont
le contrecoup dure quelque temps, avant qu'ils s'affoiblisse, qu'il se perde entière-
ment, ou qu'il devienne, peut-estre, le mouvement de la pensée: ce qui luy arrive
lorsqu'il est si foible que nous ne sçavons plus ce qu'il est devenu." Discourse: "De
la vérité de nos connoissances naturelles."

la generation du sujet, & qui en dérive par un bon raisonnement. Mais que la science par laquelle nous sçavons tant seulement, qu'il est possible qu'un Théorème vray, est une connoissance qui n'a pas son origine dans les causes; & qui commence par l'expérience des effets, d'ou elle rémonte vers les causes, par une légitime ratiocination. Que par l'une et l'autre de ces méthodes on tend à Démonstration; & soit que l'on déscende, ou que l'on monte, on marche toujours dans le mesme chemin. Que néantmoins la Démonstration que se forme en la descente de la cause vers les effets a bien plus de force, que la démonstration qu'il faut pousser en haut, & en laquelle l'effet a précedé la connoissance de la cause. Pour ce qu'il est bien plus avantageux d'avoir les causes toutes présentes, & de n'avoir à penser qu'à la manière de laquelle nous nous en pourrons bien servir; que d'avoir à rappeller le passé, & à connoistre quel il peut avoir esté: Ce qu'il nous faut faire, lorsque ne connoissons que les effets, nous devons en rechercher les causes qui ne sont plus, ou qui nous sont cachées. Que cela estant, nous n'avons point de science par démonstration, à priori, avec une préalable connoissance des causes, qu'en celles, don't l'invention & la naissance, les principes & les progrès dependent de nostre franc arbitre.

Thus, with respect to geometry there are theorems concerning quantity that one can demonstrate; the causes of the properties of each figure are contained in the lines we trace, while the constitution of the lines depends on our free will. Since we alone are the authors of the figures, it follows that geometry has demonstrations of the first order. But as natural things and their causes are not in our power, but are dependent upon the will of the Creator, we cannot deduce the properties of things from their causes, since we do not see the causes. All that we can do is to remount the ladder as far as we can and show that it is not impossible for such and such to have been the causes. This sort of demonstration is a *posteriori*, and the science of it is physics. In the case of politics and ethics, a genuine science of justice is possible. They are capable of demonstration *a priori*, because we know the principles involved, and men have made laws and pacts that are the causes of justice. Justice is a matter of human institution, and before the establishment of laws and pacts neither the public good nor justice existed.[12]

Whatever may be the case then, with respect to incorporeal

[12] Letter LXXXXI.

beings and so with respect to metaphysics and theology, the subject matter of science is motion. From the physical standpoint,
thought and passion, sensation, and even morals are questions
of physics, for in themselves they are motions. But even here we
must be more precise, thinks Sorbière. For if the subject matter
of scientific knowledge be motion, only the motions that occur
within the organism (commonly called thoughts or sensations)
would be in the strict sense, the subject matter. The universe, as
it exists beyond the body, is a sea of motions continuous with the
motions of the body. Knowledge of this sea of motion is obtained
by inference from effects, the internal motions, to causes, the
external motions. Knowledge in the eulogistic sense, or science,
however, is deductive, from principles or causes to effects or consequences. Mathematics is a genuine science, as is politics, because both are born wholly in the brain and are deductive. Knowledge of fact is not science, because it is knowledge from effects
—ultimately effects in the organism—of causes which reside without. The determination of the sphere of a universal physics is
not the result of a metaphysical deduction; rather, to metaphysics
and theology must be turned over everything that is excluded
when the subject matter is defined *physiquement*, in terms of motion. We are said to know things by way of ideas. But, as things
are motions, they are accessible to us only in the sense in which
external motions are prolonged in bodily ones. And from the
standpoint of physical science, ideas, too, are motions. The consequence is that the whole subject-matter of inquiry, in the immediate sense, consists of motions of and within the body. Thought
and sensation, in so far as they are anything more than motion,
fall within the province of metaphysics. The field of scientific inquiry, in so far as it lies beyond the limits of the body, is a field
of conjecture rather than of science in the emphatic sense. Epistemological representationism, from the standpoint of physics,
must be translated into the harmony of motions in the brain. The
subject matter of a universal science is extension and motion. The
human body is of course, included within this subject matter.
The immortal, rational and incorporeal principle, and thought
and will in so far as these are functions of the incorporeal princi-

ple, are by definition excluded from the field of scientific inquiry. Incorporeal things—God and the soul—are excluded from physics; and exclusion from physics is just what defines the field of metaphysics.

The field of incorporeal things, Sorbière asserts, is indeed accessible both to faith and to reason. It is subject to authority, both human and divine.[13] From incorporeal things, however, we cannot pass to corporeal. Reason may seek to demonstrate the spirituality and immortality of the soul and the existence of God, but these efforts remain, in the end, metaphysics, and merely metaphysics. Physics is "la seule science humaine qu'il y a dans le Monde."

[13] Letter XIX.

LOUIS DE LA FORGE AND
THE CRITIQUE OF
SUBSTANTIAL FORMS

THE PURPOSE of this essay is not to study the philosophy of
Descartes, but rather to discover, if possible, what a Cartesian
disciple conceived that philosophy to be. We are concerned, therefore, with a contemporary's interpretation of the philosopher.
Louis de la Forge writes with the intention of setting forth the
meaning of the new doctrine. He certainly believes himself to be
wholly faithful to Cartesian principles. He has but a slight interest in independent philosophical construction. He is aware of
ambiguities in the master's teachings, and it is part of his purpose
to clarify them; but he never doubts that what Cartesian principles meant to him they meant to Descartes himself. In employing La Forge as the chief thematic material, we shall find occasion
for corroboration and illustration by reference to Dom Robert
Desgabets.

Descartes recoiled from some of the consequences of his metaphysical foundations for science. Gilson indicates that he was
loath to accept the dualistic view of body and soul. This view
imperiled, as he well knew, the unity of the human being, and his
protests that the two substances can be united in the one being
express his sensitivity concerning the issue. The pineal-gland
theory cannot be dismissed as a mere gesture. The earnestness of
his desire to reconcile his doctrine of substance with the requirements of the Eucharist is matched by the seriousness with which
he entertains the theory of the functions of the pineal gland. Moreover, there persisted a conflict between his biological account of
the nature of sensation—sensation as bodily phenomenon providing guidance to the organism—and the status of sensation in terms
of the dualism of soul and body.

The followers of Descartes had to begin, in a sense, where Descartes had arrived. While Louis de la Forge and many others

were faithful enough to the philosopher's teachings, they were forced to a shift of emphasis. Taking fuller cognizance of the consequences of the body-soul dualism, their approach to metaphysics and epistemology is altered. It was scarcely possible to recapitulate the original process and so to pass from the doubt to the dualism, even in the degree in which we may say that Descartes had done so. Knowledge of the terminus affected the interpretation of the procedure leading to it. If the dualism was for Descartes a conclusion he had reached, but nevertheless found difficult to accept, it was for the follower a principle in the light of which every Cartesian statement must be interpreted. The method of doubt and the *cogito* are thought in terms of the dualism; the latter is even viewed as responsible for the former. The dualism, for a follower like La Forge, is not only a metaphysical conclusion; it is rather a statement of "psychological" and physical fact determining the first steps in epistemology and metaphysics. All inquiry is concerned with subject matters defined by the dualism of substances; the latter, then, defines and controls the issues involved in the inquiry.

To the Cartesians, however, the new philosophy was not just another philosophy, but in many ways final and also, for the first time in history, science in the eulogistic sense. What mystifies a man like La Forge is the strength of opposition the new doctrine encountered. His practical problem is to state the Cartesian philosophy in such a way as to facilitate conviction. He was faced by the fact that the doctrine had the reputation of being revolutionary. He recognized ambiguities of statement, if not of meaning, in the Cartesian writings. To eliminate the ambiguities and to overcome the prejudices against novelty was the expositor's task. In addition to this, of course, it was necessary to overcome by extension certain of the residual difficulties in the doctrine itself.

La Forge believed that the novelty of Cartesian philosophy and the secret of the prejudiced opposition it encounters lie in the dualism of substances. He is keenly conscious of the great intellectual economy provided by the new definitions of matter and of spirit. But novelty and economy are sharply defined by contrast with a background, and this background is scholasticism. The dualism has taught La Forge that the principles of the School are useless and obscure. When we have learned that there are only two kinds of being, bodies and spirits, all existence is simplified. Such a view contrasts radically with the complexities and unintelligibilities of "formes substantielles des Corps, qualitez réelles, impresses, intentionelles," and similar conceptions. But La Forge is aware that novelty of contrast with established doctrine can be most effectively ameliorated by a demonstration of the doctrine's essential respectability. This is to be accomplished by demonstrating that Cartesianism represents tradition. In brief, Descartes must be revealed as an Augustinian even if he cannot be pictured as an Aristotelian and a Thomist. Accordingly, La Forge devotes the Preface of his book [1] to a proof that the Cartesian view of the soul is identical with that of St. Augustine. Moreover, he seeks to prove that St. Augustine's views are opposed to those proclaimed by the School. To this end he insists that the saint did not confuse spirit and corporeal or animal spirits, or confuse processes in the brain with events in the mind. Augustine, like Descartes, assures us that we may conceive of a substance which is not the subject of sense and imagination.

With these strategical advantages gained, La Forge proceeds to the details of exposition. That which is to be expounded, clarified, and given systematic statement, is the dualism of body and soul with its immediate consequences. Ambiguities of statement in Descartes' writings must be removed, together with waverings and uncertainties in his teaching. The meaning of the dualism for the study of man and nature is to be set forth. The problem

---

[1] *Traité de l'esprit de l'homme, de ses facultez et fonctions, et de son union avec le corps, suivant les principes de René Descartes*, Paris, Girard, 1666. All references are to this work. Accents are very sparingly used in this edition, and no attempt has been made to put in the omitted accents in the quotations or to modernize the spelling. The references to Desgabets (born in the first years of the seventeenth century, died March 13, 1678) are to the documents forming the Appendix (pp. 299–422) in Paul Lemaire, *Dom Robert Desgabets, son système, son influence et son école, d'après plusieurs manuscrits et des documents rares ou inédits;* thèse pour le Doctorat présentée à la faculté des lettres de Grenoble, Paris, Alcan, 1901. Of Desgabets' many writings, a very little was printed during his life or shortly afterward. Many unpublished manuscripts remain. A valuable collection was published for the first time in the appendix to Lemaire's volume.

fixed by the dualism itself, the relation of mind and body, may
then be solved. When all this has been accomplished, the metaphysical foundations for the new knowledge of nature will have
been established, and the fears of the theologian may be abated.
La Forge may have limited his task to man because of a lack of
competence in physical science. As a physician his chief interest
is in man. But it is more reasonable to believe that the limitation
is a direct expression of his comprehension of the cardinal principle of Cartesianism, and therefore of the practical needs of defense, of propaganda, and of popularization.

The first step in the removal of the ambiguities of the Cartesian
doctrine and in assuring its comprehension is to inquire why
there should be any ambiguities or difficulties of comprehension
at all. Descartes' language is misleading at times, and his readers
have been misled.[2] But the difficulty is vastly deeper than a question of mere terminological consistency. The real problem is why
the fundamental Cartesian ideas are not apparent to everyone.
The idea of the soul as a substance the essence of which is thought
and of matter as in essence extension—these ideas are clear and
distinct. They are, moreover, innate.[3] Nevertheless, men must be
persuaded of these ideas. All men are rational, for good sense is
the most universally distributed of things, and human relation-
ality is the very fountainhead of these clear ideas. Notwithstanding all this, the Cartesian dualism appears to the generality as a
novel and revolutionary conception.

La Forge understands that there is something paradoxical here.
Ideas that are universal, innate, and so clear and distinct that they
are indubitable appear for the first time (with some reservations

[2] La Forge admits that he may scandalize some very scrupulous Cartesians by his
use of the term "idea." Descartes used it not only for the forms, that is, the thoughts,
of the spiritual substance, but also for the forms of the animal spirits. La Forge
proposes to restrict the term to the former usage, and is at great pains to indicate
that he is really faithful to Descartes' meaning when imposing this restriction (Preface; also pp. 98–99).

[3] Innate ideas are three in number—of the substance that thinks, of extended
substance, and of the union of the two. The real meaning of "innate idea" is the
possession of a faculty for producing them; they are innate in possibility, not in
act, like figures in wax, but not as so many states of soul disposed like pictures in
a gallery (p. 142; ch. xx).

concerning Augustine) in the teaching of Descartes. Why is it
so difficult to bring them from potency into act? It is necessary
even to prove the proposition that everything that thinks is immaterial. For there are some who go so far as to admit that the
universe is composed of spiritual and corporeal substances, but
nevertheless do not consider that thought belongs peculiarly to the
first, since they believe it may be communicated to the second.
In addition, there are opponents who think that body alone exists,
and urge that the sole difference between one body and another
depends upon the relative grossness of subtlety of matter. The
primary Cartesian ideas are necessarily accepted by the mind
that understands them. Since they are generated by the intrinsic
nature of good sense or reason itself, there can be no obscurity
in them. Yet the fact is that the Cartesian ideas seem obscure.
How does it come about that they are so? And how was Descartes
enabled to rid them of the obscurity which somehow attached to
these ideas? [4]

The answer to this seeming paradox, La Forge believes, lies
precisely in this fact, that neither idea is clear and distinct without
the other. Unless we conceive matter as a substance the essence
of which is extension, we cannot properly conceive spirit as a
substance the essence of which is thought. Conversely, the idea
of spirit brings into clarity what matter really is. Augustine, in
effect (although La Forge does not say this), is ambiguous in
expression concerning spirit because he had an inadequate conception of matter. Descartes succeeds because his ideas of spirit
and matter are equally clear and distinct. La Forge and Desgabets are in complete agreement about this. In philosophical
thought as well as in popular opinion, confused ideas of spirit
and body have prevailed. The source of confusion lies in this,
that immateriality has been taken to mean *subtle matter*. Men
possess the bad habit of conceiving all things after the manner
of bodies, a habit rooted in the prejudices arising in infancy.
Even the term "spirit" confuses men because of its original signification—La Forge says that in every language its primitive
meaning was "breath." This confusion of spirit and subtle matter

[4] Page 24; cf. pp. 186–87.

has been conserved in and fostered by the scholastic distinction between matter and form.[5] Some men have thought of the soul as a body or as a harmony of the body. Others, instructed by faith, have declared it to be immaterial. But since the latter did not know what immateriality really means, they thought of the immaterial soul after the analogy of the forms of nature. Thus they were led, on the one hand, to endow the soul with all the functions found within the human organism—and so the Cartesian definition of the essence of the soul as thought is incomprehensible to them. On the other hand, they were led to construe the soul in corporeal terms as subtle matter. The total result was an idea partly spiritual, partly material, and altogether monstrous.

Philosophical language has preserved in more or less disguised fashion these very confusions. Forms, it is true, have been declared immaterial. But what immateriality really meant in this context, that is, for La Forge, the context of scholastic teaching? Immateriality of form has not been defined in terms of matter defined as that the essence of which is extension; it has been contrasted with the unity of matter and form. If form has been regarded as immaterial, nevertheless its immateriality does not conflict with the unification of form and matter in a thing. Forms are immaterial in the sense that form in its purity may be somehow attained by dematerializing the thing as a unity of matter and form. Immateriality is thought of, in effect, as a matter of degree, and if forms are said to be immaterial, they are not immaterial *substances*. These very uncertainties in the notion of the immateriality of form, La Forge thinks, have made possible the identification of form with subtle matter, if, indeed, this identification has not defined the meaning of form. Even at best the School, when given credit for the proposition that forms are immaterial, does not represent or anticipate the Cartesian truths. For example, the School asserts that the soul is a spirit because

[5] Page 25. Desgabets, in the essay "De l'union de l'âme et du corps" (Lemaire, pp. 326–47) ridicules the idea of identifying the soul with subtle matter. His appreciation of Descartes' contribution to clarity in the ideas of spirit and matter is emphatically expressed. He, too, asserts that the whole subject of the union of soul and body has been in a state of confusion because men did not know what an immaterial substance really is.

it is not extended. But this, says La Forge, is not the Cartesian doctrine. Descartes insists that the soul is not extended because it thinks. It is not an immaterial form, but thinking substance in the sense of a substance the very essence of which is thought. The Cartesian meaning therefore signifies that thinking cannot be a function of matter or a property of a thing defined as the unity of matter and form. Matter, whether gross or subtle, is incapable of thought.[6]

These confusions with which Scholasticism is beset, as La Forge thinks, have been carried over into epistemology. The School thought that the gap between thought and things—a gap that the Cartesian truths make undeniable—could be bridged. The notion of the intentional species was taken as the solution of the problem concerning the relation of thought and things. But when we start, as we must, with the dualism of substances as defining thought and things, a new account of perception and of knowledge is demanded.

At this point it is imperative to recognize that Scholasticism and Cartesian doctrine are two radically different contexts within which terms must be defined. It is impossible to carry over into the Cartesian context the meanings given to matter, form, and intentional species by scholasticism. Of this La Forge is, on the whole, quite well aware. From the Cartesian standpoint, the intentional species, if produced by body, must be extended; the species is corporeal, material, in the sense in which matter is the very antithesis of spirit or thought. But for the School the fact that the species is produced by a thing or comes from a unity of matter and form does not necessarily imply that it is corporeal or extended or material in the Cartesian sense of the term. It is produced by the form, and form is in principle unextended. It is a likeness of the thing and is generated by the form of the thing. It represents the nature of a given particular thing because it is produced by the form of that thing. At the same time, however, it contains the universal nature of the species to which the par-

---

[6] Pages 187–88. La Forge rejects the doctrine of the School to the effect that the soul is virtually, although not really, extended. Virtual extension, if it means anything, means parts outside of one another, and hence implies extension.

ticular body belongs. A form is identical in nature throughout
the whole of the species to which particular examples belong,
although it is numerically different in the various individuals.
The scholastic species is an image of the thing, but the thing is
both matter and form. It is then impossible to preserve the meanings of the term in the Cartesian context. The species in this context is like the thing in the sense in which every thing is extension and motion. It is figured motion leading from the thing to
the organs of sense. The scholastic species is simply supplanted
by the Cartesian mechanism of perception.

The question of knowledge has been obscured, La Forge tells
us, for two reasons. Most thinkers have regarded bodies as well
as spirits as capable of thought. Again, men confound the ideas
or notions that the spirit immediately apprehends with the corporeal species serving sense and imagination.[7] On the principles of
Cartesianism, La Forge insists, the meaning of corporeal species
must be strictly confined to the field of extension and motion.
If knowledge be regarded as the reception of corporeal species in
the *puissance cognoscitive,* even mirrors must be said to know.
The reception of species, however, if it means anything in the
Cartesian context, means local motion and nothing more. Imagination and memory are just other cases of local motion.[8] Scholasticism has led men to study the nature of knowledge by looking
at corporeal things instead of regarding the nature of spirit as
such.[9] If corporeal species are only accidents or modes of body,
their whole nature is to be extension and motion, and accordingly
they can be received by an extended subject alone. They cannot
be received into spirit at all.[10]

Thus, a double adjustment must be effected. The species, since
it must be extended and material in the Cartesian sense, must be
conceived in just those terms into which every material phenomenon is resoluable. It is defined as "l'impression que fait l'objet
interieur ou exterieur sur nos sens interieurs ou exterieurs." The

[7] Page 98.   [8] Pages 92–93.   [9] Page 95.
[10] Page 110. Desgabets regards the corporeal species as traces formed in the substance of the brain by the course of the animal spirits and contrasts these with the
"idées spirituelles de l'âme"; there is, he says, a *liaison fort étroite* between the two
(Lemaire, p. 335).

corporeal species, says La Forge, must be considered in four stages: in the object, in the external sense, in the pineal gland, and in that part of the brain which serves as the organ of memory. Extra-organically and intra-organically the species is reducible to extension and motion. In the brain it is a motion or, with respect to memory, a trace.

Si vous considerez dans leur origine, ou dans leur cause, ces especes ne sont rien que les diversitez qui se trouvent dans les Corps . . . soit dans la figure & l'arrangement de leurs parties, soit dans leur mouvement ou leur repos, à raison desquelles ils peuvent faire quelque impression sur les fibres des nerfs qui se rencontrent dans l'organe de quelqu'un de nos senses exterieurs; si vous les considerez maintenant dans cét organe, ces especes sont toutes les manieres differentes dont ces Corps agitent ces nerfs, & ouvrent par leur moyen certains pores des ventricules . . . sur la glande ces especes ne sont autre chose que la diversité que l'ouverture de ces pores aporte dans le cours des Esprits, & dans la situation de la glande; enfin dans la siege de la memoire, ces especes sont la disposition que laisse le cours des Esprits en passant par ces pores qui ont esté ouverts par l'action des objets de dehors.[11]

In short, the perceptual process from the source to the brain is the transmission of motion, and whatever meaning the corporeal species may have in terms of the process depends upon this.

The second adjustment necessary for the theory of corporeal species in dualistic terms follows from the distinction between the immediate object of spirit and the physiological correlate. The terminus of the chain of motions is a motion. The reception of the "species" is not even the production of an idea. Since all knowledge is within spirit and the acts of knowing do not extend beyond the soul, it is impossible that the corporeal species could be the forms by the immediate perception of which we are said to have thoughts. The impressions within the soul and the corporeal species (as the train of motion at any point in the process of perception) bear no resemblance to one another.[12] The corporeal species is not, then, the immediate object of the mind. Since thought is the essence of spiritual substance, and since mind in knowing never goes beyond itself, the act of perception or knowing—for all knowing is perceiving—and the immediate object

[11] Page 113.   [12] Pages 103–4, 110–13.

are both within the soul substance. All operations of the spirit are reducible to two: "apercevoir ou connoistre" and will. Sense, imagination, reminiscence, and understanding (*entendement*) are modes of the first, while judgment, inclination, and appetition pertain to the second. There is, indeed, a sense in which understanding is unique; it is not dependent upon the body for its specific acts. But the specific contents of sense-perception, reminiscence, and imagination, although like the ideas of pure understanding they are spiritual entities, are occasioned by equally specific bodily processes.[13] The immediate object of the mind is then a state of itself; it is a thought or idea, a spiritual content. "Pensée" is defined as "cette perception, conscience, ou connoissance intérieure que chacun de nous ressent immediatement par soy mesme quand il s'apercoit de ce qu'il fait ou de ce qui se passe en luy." [14] "Connoistre" is "simplement apercevoir ce qui est interieurement representé à nostre Esprit." [15] "Les Idees ou Notions Spirituelles, cette forme de chacun de nos Pensees par la perception immediate de laquelle nous avons connoissance de ces mesmes Pensees," [16] are the objects of perception.

The corporeal species is not an image or picture. The pictorial image is a state of the soul itself.[17] Sensation is not less a perception or thought because it has body as its object. The physiological sense-process, of course, is neither a feeling nor a thought. All of this leads necessarily to the central fact—a fact upon which depends the solution of the problem of mind and body and also of the problems of epistemology—that there is a systematic correlation between the spiritual entity which is the immediate object of the spiritual activity of perceiving and the "corporeal species" defined as motion in the brain.

The fallacy of construing spirit as immateriality and imma-

[13] Pages 75–76. Reminiscence must be distinguished from memory; the latter is a corporeal faculty which retains by means of vestiges the species of the corporeal objects, while reminiscence is the activity proper to spirit in the process of recall (pp. 84–85).   [14] Page 14.   [15] Page 96.   [16] Page 99.
[17] La Forge states that, before speaking of the spiritual ideas to which the corporeal species are attached, it is necessary to meet the charge that he is not faithful to Descartes (pp. 114–15, 143). He has evidently met the belief that Descartes in the *De l'homme* wrote as if the corporeal species were exactly like a painting of the object.

teriality as subtlety of matter resulted in the belief that the species
was qualitatively similar to the object itself. From this further
consequences flowed. In the first place, the object in the external
world was taken to be the qualitied thing of perception. That is,
in effect the things that uninstructed common sense regards as
existing independently were taken as being in themselves what
they seem to be for perception. But La Forge insists that the thing
is really extension and motion and nothing else. Again, the School
taught men to think that similarity in real being was necessary
for "intentional" or "representational" similarity. The species
could represent the thing for knowledge, because it really resem-
bled the thing. Thus, knowledge was regarded as dependent upon
a real similarity between the beginning of the perceptual process
in the thing and its "mental" terminus. Moreover, thinks La Forge,
the principle that there is nothing in the understanding that was
not first in sense reinforced this view of perception. In turn, the
intentional-species theory of perception reinforced the principle.

La Forge insists that Cartesian principles oblige us to reject all
this. Sensitive knowledge, indeed, cannot be wholly different from
knowledge of and by the understanding. The reason for the resemblance between knowledge of sense and knowledge of understanding, however, is not found in the notion of the corporeal
species or in some process of dematerializing the species, but in
the fact that sensation and understanding are faculties of one and
the same spiritual substance, and the ideas of one and the other
are entities within the soul and partake of its nature.[18] There is
a difference between the two kinds of knowledge. The distinction
is that between the confused character of the sense-idea and the
clearness and distinctiveness pertaining to the idea of the understanding. The confused nature of sensation is, indeed, a proof
that there is nothing in things similar to the qualitative properties
of the sense-idea. Cartesian principles, for La Forge, assure us

[18] Page 29. Ideas as modes of thought are identical. They differ in four ways: (1)
according to whether they represent clearly and distinctly, or confusedly; (2) according to the things represented; (3) according to the powers they serve, whether
sense, imagination, reminiscence, or pure understanding; and (4) finally, according
to the causes which contribute to their production (ch. x, pp. 138–42). Desgabets
states that all the ideas that come to us by way of the body are equally spiritual, and
do not bear the slightest mark of matter (Lemaire, p. 339).

of the through-and-through perspicuity of the material world. Mathematics applied to extension and motion is exact science. The fact that an idea is clear and distinct is the very sign that there are in things properties similar to those implied in the idea.[19] La Forge states definitely that the Cartesian doctrine cuts directly across the principle that there is nothing in understanding that was not first in sense. Two meanings could be given the principle, and neither is true. It is not true that images of understanding resemble the things in nature according to real resemblance. Nor is it true that all knowledge is derived from the sense-impressions arising within the spiritual soul.[20]

The representative function of ideas can be comprehended, says La Forge, only when spirit is placed "en parallele" with the body.[21] Spirit and body are alike in that both are substances, possessing essential attributes. For this reason each has specific traits—figure, mobility, and divisibility for the one, volition, understanding, and reasoning for the other. Just as the body at every moment possesses a specific figure, is in a specific condition, so the soul at every moment has a specific idea. Extension as such is indivisible, and so body is in general inseparable from its parts; in the same manner, the soul is inseparable from its functions. The diverse figures of body are only so many unlike ways in which the superficies is diversified and limited. Ideas are the different forms in which the acts of the soul are "revestus," limited, and determined.[22] But these likenesses of body and soul are due to the fact that each is a substance. They do not indicate a resemblance of substantial nature. A state of the one remains a mode of existence wholly unlike a mode of the other. From this it follows that knowledge does not depend upon similarity in "real being." But now, characteristically, new difficulties arise. It is difficult, La Forge uneasily confesses, to understand perceptual knowledge. He is evidently somewhat nonplussed because the new truth—or rather this recent attainment of truth—makes knowledge as the relation of idea and thing more difficult instead of less difficult to understand. However, ideas do in fact represent things. There must obtain a dependable relation between idea in the

[19] Page 103.   [20] Page 122.   [21] Pages 127–28.   [22] Pages 128–29.

soul and the thing. We must redefine "resemblance" for epistemological purposes. Thus, a thing may be said to resemble another according to its intentional or representative being when
it has the power to make us think of that other, even if the former
has no real, positive, or sensible relation to the latter. Desgabets
sums up the possibilities for scientific knowledge of things by
pointing to three alternatives. First, we may assert that there exists in the perceiving subject a quality similar to the quality characteristic of the perceived thing itself; but this is fallacious, for
it confuses preception itself with things. The second possibility
is this: we may say that knowledge is a relation between the perceptual quality on the one hand and local dispositions plus a
sensible quality (unlike the perceptual quality) in the things perceived; but this view is really meaningless. We seek to retain
the thing as qualitative without being able to give any intelligible
meaning to the notion of a quality that is not a quality of the perception in the soul. Thus, there remains only the third, the Cartesian, view: perceptions in the soul, on the one hand, and "local
dispositions" and nothing else in the thing, on the other hand,
without resemblance between the two orders of fact. Thus for La
Forge and Desgabets ideas undeniably represent things which
they in no sense resemble, and upon this knowledge depends.
Since ideas do represent things, it must be possible for them to
to exercise this representative function. La Forge, however, remains uneasy concerning the issue. He must have suspected that
"intentional resemblance" was not an explanation so much as the
thing to be explained. Since "esprit" is a thing that thinks, it must
of necessity be a thing that can represent by means of a thought
that which is not a thought at all. The power to do this must be
regarded as a consequence of the essence of the soul.[23] In this
sense there can be no question why and how the soul not merely
knows, but knows physical things.

In certain respects, however, this answer is too easy. The rational principle, as the power of knowing and of distinguishing
the true from the false, cannot doubt that its clear and distinct
ideas constitute knowledge. In short, matter, as the field of ex

[23] *Ibid.*, pp. 102–3, 130–31. *Desgabets*, Lemaire, pp. 376–77.

tension everywhere penetrable by mathematics, and the clear and distinct ideas of understanding are related by the very nature of thought itself as a principle. There is really no question—God having been demonstrated not to be a deceiver—whether and how spirit can know matter. Clearness and distinctness of idea define knowledge. But difficulty arises, because the ideas of sense, which are not clear and distinct, but confused, claim to know things by representation. Such ideas are not pure products of the understanding, but are somehow conditioned by bodily operations. Even in terms of the new theory of the perceptual process, ideas are remote from things. As Desgabets states, all of them are equally spiritual even if some do come by way of the body. Moreover, the new doctrine of the mechanism of perception is of no help. All that it provides is a more accurate and specific statement of the difficulty. The theory of the mechanism of perception explains the causal relationship between the terminal point in a chain of motions, that is, the movement of the pineal gland or its trace, and the extra-organic thing. It shows us that the relation of idea and thing is really the relation of idea in the soul and movement or trace in and of the gland or brain. But idea and brain process are each within opponent substances. If the sense-impression be conditioned by anything physical, it is conditioned by the brain movement. But what this conditioning means remains as obscure as before.

Since knowledge of things by way of innate ideas and the pure ideas of understanding presents no difficulty; and since La Forge also believes that there is no difficulty in the case of ideas which we have because we determine ourselves to think; there, then, remain only the ideas of sense whose role in knowledge is obscure.[24] The problem is twofold. What relation is there between the sense-ideas of particular things and the universal ideas of the pure understanding? And again, how can a sense-idea in its specific qualitative being represent, not a thing in general, but a spe-

[24] Pages 131–34. The soul is partially independent of the body for its ideas. The *entendement pur* is able to perceive all sorts of objects of thought without the aid of the corporeal species. Thus, some of the soul's ideas are independent of its correlation with the body. Moreover, the will may contribute ideas that, with respect to some aspects at least, are independent of bodily occasions (pp. 84–85).

cific and particular material thing? In the first case the inner de-
materialization of the species must be replaced in the new context
by a new mode of conceiving the relation between sense-impressions and pure ideas. The problem is whether, and how, the clear
ideas of understanding can be applied to, or can employ, the confused ideas of sense in a systematic organization of knowledge.
The answer will define the role of observation and experiment in
science. The second problem depends upon a demonstration that
there is some systematic and exact relation between the sense-
percept, with its specific qualities, and a given particular nuclea-
tion in extension, which is the "thing" said to be represented by
the former. Matter, as Desgabets says, is differentiated by "local
dispositions"; what assurance have we that there is a constant
relation between the local dispositions defining a thing in the field
of extension and the percept we are said to have "of" that thing?
This is the point that La Forge recognizes to be critical for epistemology on a Cartesian basis; and he recognizes, moreover, that
the solution depends upon the solution of the mind-body problem.
Or, to state the matter more accurately, the relation of soul and
body must be so construed as to justify the substitution of "intentional" resemblance for real resemblance between idea and
thing.

The union of soul and body, La Forge declares, is the most
remarkable thing in all creation. We must not becloud the question with vague notions of corporeal species. Nor can we depart
from the strict terms of the dualism of substances. Some of the
followers of Descartes appear to believe that the soul and the body
are united by a special mode of being. If they mean, as they apparently mean, that this something is neither spirit nor body, they
are wholly unfaithful to Cartesian doctrine. They are like those
who conceive matter and form to be united by a middle term differing from the one and the other. If we wish to avoid such ambiguities, let us simply ask, are such alleged uniting principles
or qualities extended or nonextended? [25]

There are two approaches to knowledge of the properties of the

[25] Pages 189–90.

spirit. We may inquire, why has the soul at a given moment such
and such thoughts rather than other possible thoughts? We are
directed towards the properties possessed by the soul in virtue of
its union with the body. This approach, however, never furnishes
the clue to the essence, the real attributes, of the soul. This essence is apprehended by a "sentiment interieure" alone; thought
always implies this immediate awareness. La Forge here virtually equates thought, consciousness, and spirituality. The nature of thought consists "dans cette conscience, ce tesmoignage, &
ce sentiment interieur par lequel l'Esprit est adverty de tout ce
qu'il fait ou qu'il souffre, & generalement de tout ce qui passe immediatement en luy, dans le temps mesme qu'il agit, ou qu'il
souffre." [26] The essence of spiritual substance is not thought as
rational reflection, for the latter is only a special mode of thought.
The *sentiment intérieur* is present in every *pensée*. Hence, the
substance that thinks is a being the essential nature of which is
to perceive everything happening within itself, whether it is active
or is acted upon. What the spirit does not perceive, that is, is not
conscious of, is foreign to spirit. Spirit is essentially something
that perceives itself and perceives what happens within itself,
and whose being is in this perceiving. It follows that the soul
thinks always.[27] Since sense experience and reflection are equally
modes of thought, La Forge is beginning where Descartes arrived. It is not the rational principle of the *Discourse*, the Good
Sense or Reason, which is the power of judging and distinguishing
the true from the false, that is the opposite of extension, but consciousness or the states of consciousness. The opposition is the
antithesis of self-consciousness and matter. The corporeal species
in the brain is just that of which we are not conscious at all; it is
therefore not an idea. We are conscious of a qualitied state of the
self, and therefore this of which we are conscious cannot be a state
of the brain or a thing. The union of body and soul is thus the
union of consciousness and a nervous system.

The mystery of this most mysterious thing in creation is the
attachment of conscious spirit, not to body in general, but to a
particular organized body. The soul cannot be in a place. One

[26] Page 54.   [27] Pages 54–55.

bit of extension is as irrelevant to its nature as another. Why is it connected with a particular body? The place of the soul can mean only the fact of its connection with a certain body.[28] The body is somehow involved in the specific contents of consciousness. Why is the soul aware of just what it is aware of? Obviously, it is due to the union of the soul with its body. Desgabets states that the dependence of the soul upon the body is proved by various facts: bodily sleep affects the soul; the soul depends upon the growth of the body; if the body lack a sense organ, it is deprived of certain states; the understanding is passive, in part at least, and must get its ideas in some way through corporeal action; and there are many other facts of similar point. But union can mean only a certain dependence; the closest union that the nature of spirit and extension permits is only this, that states of the first depend upon movements of the latter, and the reverse. The union consists "dans une mutuelle & réciproque dépendance des pensées de l'un & des mouvemens de l'autre, & dans le commerce mutuel de leurs actions & passions, soit que ce soit la volonté de l'Esprit qui est uny qu'il ait obligé à cette dépendance, soit qu'un autre l'y astraint." [29] The metaphors customary in the writings of his day, such as that which compares the relation of the soul and the body to that of a pilot to a ship, are quite inadequate.

In these conditions the problem really becomes theological. The cause of the union of soul and body can be God alone. The union cannot be due to bodies. God may have employed an angel to effect it, La Forge admits, but there is no reason to think so. God's will, however, is only the general cause of the union. More specifically, the causes which unite a given consciousness and its states with a given body and its states are two: the constitution of the individual body and the powers of volition pertaining to the individual soul.[30] Through the will of God, a given body and a given soul are united, and the individual constitution of each explains peculiarities in the processes of the other.

[28] Pages 179–83.
[29] Page 196. The statement is elaborated on pp. 205–13. For Desgabets' views of dependence of soul on body, see in Lemaire, "De l'union de l'âme et du corps," pp. 344–45, p. 331.
[30] Pages 227–29.

Thus, through the will of God, body and soul are united. And more specifically, through the will of God *this* body and *this* soul are united. However, the same power is effective in an additional sense. Body and soul, of course, do not affect one another. Efficient causality does not relate corporeal species in the gland and conscious state. The former is the occasional cause of the latter; and acts of will are occasioning causes of new forms of the motions in the animal spirits. Within the limits fixed by the constitutions of the particular soul and particular body there is a further limitation—*the constancy of the correlation between a given conscious state and a given movement of the animal spirits.* God, in short, after joining *this* body and *this* soul, could conceivably have left the career of each without systematic relation to the other. We must admire His wisdom in this respect. He could have joined to each *espèce matérielle,* to every form that the course of the animal spirits takes, whatever thought He pleased. This He has not done. He has rather taken into account the train of causes from the extra-organic object to the gland. Accordingly He has willed that the thought joined to a given movement of the animal spirits should be just that particular thought which *ordinarily* represents the (extra-organic) cause that makes the spirit take this form. This means that the correlation of conscious state and the movement of the animal spirits is systematic and fixed, without exception. There would never be an error in taking a given sense-impression as representing a certain movement in the animal spirits. The given movement in the animal spirits, however, may arise through constellation of internal conditions in the absence of the specific extra-organic cause which usually determines the animal spirits to this movement. There is no invariable connection between a given brain process and a certain cause affecting the sense organs. Illusion and hallucination are possible, but relatively rare. If I am conscious of a certain shade of red, then it is certain that my animal spirits are moving in one special way. In this there is no possible failure of correlation. But my animal spirits may take on this motion even when I am not affected by that condition in the physical world which usually obtains when I am conscious of this shade. God's principle, that a given conscious state shall have one, and but one, correspondent in the series of brain events never fails.[31]

This is by no means a statement of psychophysical parallelism, or even of systematic Occasionalism. The correlation of thought and brain state is limited to sense.

Par les pensées, qui sont naturellement unies à certaines formes du cours de l'Esprits, que la volonté de l'Ame ne sçauroit séparer, i'entens seulement ces sentiments confus qui sont causez par l'action des objets sur nos sens, lesquels il est manifeste que l'Ame ne peut ny oster ny changer.[32]

The connection with respect to other ideas is arbitrary. The visual or spoken word as a sense process has a natural correlation with a particular sense perception. But we can "attach" to the word an idea which is not at all a perception of this sense process. The understanding as active, La Forge seems to mean, is an independent source of ideas. There are ideas which we possess because we will to think them. There are, however, some ideas and some movements which depend upon one another absolutely in the same sense that one cannot be without the other. These ideas are ascribed directly or indirectly to sense. This is the maximum closeness of union between soul and body.[33]

It may, however, be objected that the distinction between natural correlation and the voluntary correlations of will may nevertheless fall within the scheme of occasional causes established by God. The understanding and the will may generate an idea independently of sense. But if for every such idea there is a correlated brain-process, and this same brain process occurs whenever this particular idea is present, the system of correspondence remains universal. Nevertheless it is clear that La Forge really means to limit the systematic correlation of idea and bodily process to the interrelation of body and soul in and through sense. For he states quite unmistakably that there is an infinity of things of which we may think, but which we cannot imagine. And we may recall in memory these very thoughts. Such pure conceptions, because they are pure and not images do not leave vestiges in the brain. This proves that since we can recall these conceptions there exists a

[31] Page 217.   [32] Page 225.   [33] Page 195.

purely intellectual memory—a point in which Desgabets seems to differ from La Forge. We must then conclude that for La Forge some ideas may arise and may be recalled without the existence of any correlated brain process. In general, the situation is that in so far as the soul generates ideas from its own intrinsic nature, not even the coöperation of the body, in the sense of occasioning cause, is necessary. But in so far as an idea cannot be accounted for save by the fact that the soul somehow dwells in an animal body, that idea implies the presence in the body of a process with which the idea is specifically correlated. La Forge's doctrine, accordingly, is neither a psycho-neural parallelism nor a complete statement of Occasionalism.[34]

The function of sense-impressions in knowledge of things is thus made conceivable by a divinely guaranteed correlation of sense idea and brain process with respect to sense ideas, despite the antithesis in nature of soul and body. This partial psycho-neural correlation is the very union of body and soul. In the place of a correspondence of a form apprehended by the mind with the formal component in the thing we have a constant connection between an entity in the soul and the movement of the animal spirits in the brain, and less certainly and directly, a connection of the former entity with extra-organic "local dispositions." The ideas occasioned in the soul by its compresence with the body constitute a natural but divinely decreed symbolism for specific events in the material world. The possibility of representation is based upon the fixity of the natural symbolism.

But this is only half of the total problem. The correlation of sense impression and motion does not alter the fact that the sensation is confused. How, then, can there be knowledge, which is a matter of clear and distinct ideas, drawn from, secured by, or con-

---

[34] Pages 344–45. The essential difference between imagination and understanding explains why understanding has no need of organs, and is a faculty independent of body. La Forge seems to have regarded the correlation of word and thought, and of pure conception with the brain process which is the physical meaning of the word, as equally arbitrary. The only necessary connection is that between the word as movement in the gland and the sense-perceived word. Desgabets seems to differ from La Forge in his assertion that with every mental process there is always some liaison with movements of the animal spirits (pp. 343 ff.).

nected with the confused ideas of sense? That a given sensation stands always for one and the same motions in the organism, and (with due allowance for the role of the organism) in the world— all this is not a knowledge of the motions themselves. How does sense knowledge become clear and distinct? Or how do the clear and distinct ideas of understanding, independent of sense with respect to origin and significance, lend clearness to the ideas of sense? Or, finally, is it possible that sense ideas become of themselves clear and distinct? If they remain to the end confused, how can they be employed in the interests of knowledge?

The problem, of course, is that of knowledge of particular things. For the School, a thing, a substance composed of matter and form, is a unique and richly qualitied entity by means of which its specific character is defined. But La Forge has placed the bundle of specific qualities and their specific combination within the soul; nothing save extension and motion remains without. The anti-Cartesian continually maintains that without forms and real qualities matter as extension is perilously near being nothing at all. Even if things be local dispositions, understanding must deal with sense impressions. Only by means of subjective sense impressions can the ideas of understanding be directed upon things. The ideas from sense, confused as they are, are the only guides to understanding in its proposed enterprise of coming to know a world of particular things and events. The infinitude of figures, said Descartes, suffices to express the diversity of things. But *what* figures express *what* things? The difference between sugar and salt is expressible in a mathematical way; but the difference to be expressed is not the difference between a salty and a sweet taste, but some other difference, a difference of extension and motion which the tastes suggest, which the tastes symbolize, but which is not revealed in and by the sensation.

The perceptions of sense are both clear and confused. They are clear in the sense that the sensation forces us to perceive that something acts upon our body and that one impression is different from another. They are psychologically clear. With respect to their representational function they are confused for two reasons. First, they lead us to attribute to things qualities that are subjective. In addition, sensation does not picture the action of the object (that is, the motions to the pineal gland), but affords us feelings only, such as heat, which have no resemblance to the real properties of things. The sensation of heat does not represent clearly and it gives no direct inspection of that which is in the object itself as the property of producing the sensation of heat.[35] From sense we derive the ideas of memory and imagination (at least of the memory and imagination that have corporeal correlates), and accordingly the latter suffer from the confused character of their origin in sense.

The notion of substantial forms, of real qualities, and the like ideas resulted from an uncritical acceptance of the world as it appears. A natural inclination leads us to project our subjective states into extra-organic things. Now we cannot prevent this projection of sense qualities into things; but, enlightened by the Cartesian determination of what spirit and matter really are, we can recognize the true status of sense qualities. This done, we are left with the world of objects reduced to extension and motion, while all the specific differences between things are represented in sense and imagination by the qualitative variety of the perceptual and imaginal states of the soul. The two great common denominators of things, that is, extension and motion, are given by the clear and distinct ideas of understanding. Sense will convince us of a difference between a thing that naïve experience declares to be hot and a thing that naïve experience declares to be cold. The clear and distinct ideas of understanding assure us that this difference is somehow a matter of differences in extension and motion. So far, all this is divinely certified and guaranteed, for the competence of reason in the field of clear and distinct ideas is assured by the fact that God is not a deceiver, and the symbolism of sense is assured by God's ordinances concerning the union of mind and body. Something remains to be discovered: we must know what motions and extensions heat sensation points to and what motions and extensions the sensation of cold symbolizes.

[35] Pages 268–71, 272–73, 276–77. A disembodied soul—the human soul after death—will have no confused ideas of sense. It will know body, but will have no impressions of color, heat, etc. Pages 405–12.

In the end, La Forge is unable to resolve the question and to overcome the contrast between the clear and distinct ideas of motion and extension on the one hand and the confused representations of sense on the other. This epistemological situation is a reason why he makes a further approach towards Occasionalism. Extension and motion, as ideas of the understanding, are not co-implicative, but independent notions. Extension and motion are radically external one to the other. The essence of matter is extension, and a thing is a bit of extension. Motion is not a real property of things, and the interaction of things is not conceivable in terms of things as so defined. Incidentally, of course, to urge that the interaction of things is inconceivable furnishes a support for the inconceivability of interaction between body and soul. La Forge is clearly uneasy because the very notion of "thing" is about to evaporate into nothingness. He must deny agency in things—a heavy body does not fall because it inherently possesses a specific power of falling or a specific quality of motion. Once more, qualitative differences are states of the spirit, and for them in the thing must be found quantitative differences. Now force and motion must be distinguished from extension as such; but then either the former must be a mode of extension, which is absurd, or else motion and agency must be properties of incorporeal substance alone. It follows that the motions of things are due to God. Nothing in the extended thing, in its nature as extension, explains its motions. The motion of a thing is not an expression of its intrinsic character.[36] God is then the sole, the universal, and the total cause of movement. If we assert the subjectivity of sense, we deny qualitative variety of motion. Ultimately, the perceived interactions of things, the variety of motions, the falling of the heavy body, and the rising of the light body are all cases of the confused ideas of sense.

The confused character of the sense idea is not dispelled by the application of a clear and distinct idea. The impression called heat remains what it is whether or not heat in the thing be a mode of motion. The clear ideas are not adequately represented in the confused ideas of sense.[37] The sense ideas, indeed, can be noth-

[36] Pages 242–43, 246–53.   [37] Page 272.

ing more than occasions for the application of the clear ideas of size, figure, extension, and movement. La Forge, who is unable to explain the technique which understanding is to follow in utilizing these occasions, feels that even the confused character of sense ideas must be justified in terms of God's providence. The reason for this confused character of sense ideas is the soul's inability to perceive the minuteness and delicacy of the nerve fibers, and the size, movement, and figure of the motions that go on within them. That is to say, a constellation of minute effects in the brain is necessary to provide an "occasion" sufficing to lead the soul to perceive that the body has been effected. It might be thought that it would be better were the soul able to intuit directly the motions in the nervous system, not in sum, but in detail and separately. But the lack of this capacity is proof of the providential arrangement of things. If the motions in the nerves were directly apprehended, so that the thought of such motions would be present in the soul upon the occasion of the motions rather than a sense feeling, then the soul would relate its experiences with the brain or the gland and with this alone, rather than with the body as a whole. Did this occur, the soul could not take cognizance of the welfare of the body as a whole; the world, for the soul, would in effect shrink to the pineal gland, for the soul would be joined to the gland and to nothing more. The confusion of the sense impression is therefore the reason why the soul is attentive to the career of the body amid a world of things.[38]

Knowledge—scientific knowledge—of nature in its details involves three factors: the clear and distinct ideas whose source is the pure understanding; the confused ideas of sense as occasions for the employment of the former; and things as nuclei in the universal field of extension. In two ways knowledge depends upon God. In the first place, the systematic correlation between the terminal brain motions and the sense experience itself, which insures the connection of body and soul, makes possible the soul's concern with the welfare of the body, and serves also to point beyond the body to the world of things. The systematic correlation guarantees that sensations are symbols for fixed values. The ob-

[38] Pages 274–76.

jective applicability of the ideas of understanding and of mathematics, not to extension as such, but to the events and things in a world order, depends upon this constancy in the symbols. Again, since motion and extension are independent variables, and since perceived motions are part of the qualitatively varied confused impressions of sense, the relevance of the clear idea of motion to the apparent motions of things depends upon God. Motion as a universal idea, with the possibility of quantitative statement, is applicable in nature only because God, as cause of motion, guarantees in the (apparent) interaction of things a set of occasions which is reliably systematic.

Thus, the Cartesian dualism renders substantial forms and intentional species meaningless. The facts that suggest these ideas are discovered to be, not at all items in an objective world, but subjective impressions within the things that think. Substantial forms, from the point of view of the Cartesian La Forge, do not constitute a subject matter, but a system of symbols for a subject matter. And the latter is known only when it is apprehended as quantity and given exact statement through the pure ideas of understanding. That which is clearly and distinctly understood is true. Through divine providence we have innately the ideas of the nature of matter, of spirit, and of the relation between these two. In all of this there is nothing hypothetical. If there be a place for hypothesis, we must assume, that place is defined by the task of discovering exact values in terms of extension and motion for the natural symbolism of the confused ideas of sense. All agency, all qualitative variety, is removed from the physical world by the Cartesian determination of what matter is and what spirit is, and science is possible.

The dualism of matter and spirit, if it makes possible a science of nature, defines at the same time a subject matter for the science of mind. Substantial forms, intentional species, and real qualities are, indeed, not the subject matter of physical science. The apprehension of those who, like Desgabets' correspondent, think that matter without forms and real qualities is equivalent to nothing and physical knowledge has no subject matter is unnecessary. For the subject matter which they had naïvely believed to be the subject matter of physics has not vanished in disappearing from physics; it has become the subject matter of psychology.

These are the truths that all men may perceive if they will but dispel the prejudices that have obscured the natural light and if they will free themselves from their enslavement by the authority of Plato, of Aristotle, of Epicurus, or of any other philosopher. For it is shameful to submit to the authority of a philosopher when that philosopher is not sustained by reason; but it is honorable and advantageous to a man of good sense to submit to the dominion of reason, even if it be not sustained by any authority whatever.[39]

[39] Page 452.

CARTESIAN DOCTRINE AND THE ANIMAL SOUL

An Incident in the Formation of the Modern Philosophical Tradition[1]

THE Cartesian philosophy made the distinction between man and the animals a philosophical problem. By this statement is meant no more than that the question was one with which philosophers were concerned and with which they felt it necessary to deal. Moreover, agreement with the doctrine of the automatism of ani-

---

[1] The primary sources used for this study are the following:

(1) *Essai philosophique sur l'âme des bêtes, où l'on traite de son existence & de sa nature et où l'on méle par occasion diverses réflexions sur la nature de la liberté, sur celle de nos sensations, sur l'union de l'âme & du corps, sur l'immortalité de l'âme, &c. et où l'on réfute diverses objections de Mr. Bayle,* a Amsterdam, chez françois Chanouion, 1728. The author's name is not given, but this seems without doubt to be the work attributed to a certain Boullier. The historian of Cartesianism, Francisque Bouillier (*Histoire de la philosophie cartésienne,* 3d ed., Paris, 1868, p. 162, n. 1) refers to *Essai philosophique sur l'âme des bêtes,* by Boullier, 2d ed., Amsterdam, 1737, 2 vols. in 12. In this paper I shall assume that the work before me is that referred to in this *History of Cartesianism.* The book contains an "Avertissement," a "Discours préliminaire," and two parts. The first bears the general title: "Où l'on preuve qu'il doit y avoir dans les bêtes un principe immateriel." The second part bears the title: "Où l'on recherche quelle est la nature de l'âme des bêtes." The author evidently knew many of the writings of the period on the subject. He mentions Dilly, Cudworth, Bayle, Henry More, Locke, Cordemoy, Pardies, Daniel, Régis, La Forge, Fontenelle, Willis, Digby, Shaftesbury, and Leibnitz.

(2) Dilly (Dillyiel) *Traité de l'âme et de la connoissance des bêtes* . . . Amsterdam, 1691. Bouillier (cited above) refers to a book of the same title by Dilly as printed at Lyon, 1678.

(3) Sigismond Gerdil, *Réceuil de dissertations sur quelques principes de philosophie et de religion,* Paris, 1760. The third dissertation bears the title: "Essai sur les caractères distinctifs de l'homme & des animaux brutes, où l'on prouve la spiritualité de l'âme humaine par la nature de son intelligence."

(4) The *Dictionnaire* of Bayle. References are to the translation by Bernard, Birch, Lockman, and others, London, 1739. The articles on Pereira, Rorarius, and Sennert, especially, have been utilized.

(5) Daniel, *Voyage du monde de Descartes,* nouvelle édition, revue & augmentée d'une cinquième partie, ajoutée aux quatre precedents, par le P. G. Daniel, de la Compagnie de Jesus, Paris, chez Nicolas Pepie, 1702. Also, Daniel, *Nouvelle difficultez proposées à l'auteur du voyage du monde de Descartes,* Paris, 1790 (The Privilège du Roy is dated 1693).

mals was taken as a decisive test of philosophical affiliation. The Cartesian arguments for the existence of God can be taken as a criterion for determining whether an alleged champion of the new philosophy really understood Descartes. In a similar way, adherence to automatism formed a test of fidelity. If one were a genuine Cartesian, one proclaimed that animals are machines. But if one asserted his discipleship, but denied that animals are machines, that discipleship was a mockery.[2]

---

(6) *Amusement philosophique sur le language des bestes,* attributed to one Bougeant; Paris, 1739.

(7) De la Chambre, *Traité de la connoissance des animaux, où tout ce qui a esté dit pour, & contre le raisonnement des bestes, est examiné,* Paris, 1664.

(8) *Histoire critique de l'âme des bêtes, contenant les sentimens des philosophes anciens, & ceux des modernes sur cette matiére,* par M. Guer, avocat, Amsterdam, chez F. Changuion, 1749, 2 vols. in one.

(9) J. B. Du Hamel, *De corpore animato, libri quatuor, seu promotae per experimenta philosophiae, specimen alterum,* Paris, 1673. Also Ioan. Bapt. du Hamel, *De consensu veteris et novae philosophiae, Libri duo,* Paris, 1663.

Other relevant documents of the period will be referred to as needed. For an interesting compilation of the old and the new meanings of terms, the following is of great value : Chauvin, *Lexicon, rationale sive thesaurus philosophicus ordine alphabetico digestus, in quo vocabula omnia philosophica, variasque illorum acceptiones, juxta cum veterum, tum recentiorum placita, explicare; & universe quae lumine naturali sciri possunt, non tam concludere quam recludere conatur,* Rotterdam, 1692.

In the footnotes the works above listed will be referred to by the author's name only, except in cases where more than one work of the same author is used. I have not attempted to bring the quotations into conformity with modern usage by modernizing the spelling or by altering and supplying accents. It should be added that in order to avoid burdening the text with corroborative materials I have preferred to add to the number and length of the footnotes.

[2] Daniel, p. 430. Dilly also forms an excellent witness to this. Descartes alone, he states, has taught us to know the nature of the soul and has defined the "caractere veritable" that distinguishes us from the beasts. Moreover, "La connoissance de cette question [*i.e.,* of brutes] est absolument necessaire pour la parfaite intelligence de la Philosophie: car soit qu'on se range du costé des Philosophes qu'on appelle nouveaux, ou qu'avec le grand nombre & la foule ou se tienne attache à la philosophie des Anciens & principalement à celle d'Aristote, on est obligé de s'en instruire à fond" (Preface). The question is especially important for the new philosophers because of "la liaison estroite, que ce point particulier a avec les principaux fondemens de leur Metaphysique & de leur Physique" (*ibid.*). Daniel (*Nouvelle difficultez* . . . pp. 4–5) makes the objector state that the very "pierre de touche" of Cartesianism, the very test of the fidelity of the disciple, is furnished by adherence to "la doctrine des Automates." It is worth noting in addition that Descartes was not acquainted with the *Antoniana-Margarita* of Gomez Pereira, a work published in 1554 in which animals were taken to be machines. Descartes, in a letter to Mersenne, states that he has not seen this work and does not think he needs to see it (Letter CCXLIV, Adam and Tannery ed.). Bayle doubts if Descartes had heard of the work, which Bayle says is scarce (*Dictionnaire,* article, "Pereira").

The question as to whether animals are or are not machines led to an extended controversy. The problem had a many-sided meaning for the intellectual situation of the age. Whatever its merits in itself, for the historian of ideas it is a privileged illustration of the conflicts within seventeenth- and eighteenth-century thought. The Cartesian dualism, with a knife-like stroke, had divided existence into two portions. If one thought with Descartes, animals either belonged to both spheres of existence, or they belonged to one of these two. Or, if the thinker defined existence as a single sphere, both animals and men fell within it, but he could not accept Cartesian metaphysical principles. If to some inquirers the conception of animals as merely automata was an important discovery, to many it was a stone of stumbling. In either case the doctrine did not have primarily a "scientific" interest. The position was welcomed less because it supplied a metaphysical foundation for the scientific study of the animate order than because it furnished a new support for ancient convictions. Religion and theology—in their traditional forms—might be weakened on one side by the newer ways of thinking, but on another side might find compensatory strength through the doctrine of the animal machine. On the other hand, to maintain unimpaired the older metaphysical supports for religious and theological tradition implied a denial not merely of the new attacks upon this tradition but also a rejection of the alleged new reinforcements. In short, to admit the value of new demonstrations of the existence of God or of novel assurances of human immortality was to many minds suspiciously like acknowledging that the older foundations of belief were inadequate. In reply to a comment of Mersenne to the effect that in the *Meditations* he has said not a word concerning the immortality of the soul, Descartes replied that Mersenne should not be astonished,

car ie sçaurois pas demonstrer que Dieu ne la puisse annihiler, mais seulement qu'elle est d'une nature entierement distincte de celle du cors, & par consequent qu'elle n'est point naturellment sujette à mourir avec luy, qui est tout ce qui est requis pour establir la Religion.[3]

[3] Letter CCXXIII, Adam and Tannery ed., III, 266.

But many Cartesians found a much more positive support for religion in the doctrine, especially when the distinction of substances was reinforced by the automatism of animals. On the other hand, the conception of animals as machines was a difficulty to many, both Cartesians and anti-Cartesians, precisely because it could not be reconciled with certain historical ideas and constituted a veiled threat against theology.

The Cartesian position that animals are automata was a by-product of the dualism of finite substances. The grounds that determined the dualism of the human body and soul, however, did not in themselves dictate the doctrine of the automatism of animals. What it implied was this, that in so far as animals possess powers resembling powers in man, what was done with these powers in man must receive a similar treatment in the animals. If in man such faculties are resident in the soul substance, then, if they are possessed by animals, there must exist an animal soul. If animals think, and if thinking in man implies a soul, then the animals too are endowed with a soul. As a consequence of this, the situation bristled with dangers. Many Cartesians discovered in the dualism a new method of assuring such desiderata as the immortality of the soul and also a new means for asserting man's essential superiority to the order of nature. It was all the more imperative that man should escape inclusion in nature after nature had come to be defined as a vast network of relations in space. But with this gain went commensurate dangers. In the traditional scale of creation from matter to God, man's position above the animals and lower than the angels was quite secure. The Cartesian dualism in one sense destroyed the hierarchy, but safely placed man's soul above physical nature. However, when the animal is envisaged in terms of the dualism there is danger that too much will be proved. Man might lose his uniqueness in creation. In so far as it could be shown that man possesses powers and activities not granted the animals, then at least this much was fixed, namely, that the animal soul, if there were one, must be of an order different from and inferior to the human. On the other hand, the more successfully physiology and neurology could be worked out on the dualistic, that is, on the mechanistic basis, the more facts that could reasonably be explained as due to the machine, the less need for an animal soul. But success in dispensing with an animal soul brought precisely the danger that the argument would be extended to man, to the undermining of his privileged position. If the animal can satisfactorily be described as a machine, then the more varied and the greater the powers of the animal, the greater the probability of the inference that man too is an automaton.

These considerations will be illustrated in detail later. Enough has been said to indicate that the problem was inescapable. There are two general observations, however, that should be made by way of introduction. In the first place attention should be called to the stereotyped and patterned character of treatments of the problem. The arguments for automatism are constantly repeated: they follow a fixed pattern, with varied details. But this is equally true of the arguments against automatism. In the same way, there is a stereotyped character about the attacks of the automatists upon the defenders of animal souls—the defenders being in the main Scholastics. And finally, even those who wish to compromise and to maintain an animal soul, while adopting the Cartesian definition of spiritual substance, are forced again and again to the same pattern of thought. This constant reiteration, with variation only of details and no genuine advance in thought, deserves comment. It indicates that the intellectual situation was marked by the conflict of incompatible metaphysical ideas, not by interests in specific scientific inquiries. A vast number of books were devoted to the controversy. If occasionally the problem was treated with levity and as an opportunity for wits, nevertheless it was in most cases treated with extraordinary seriousness. Yet it remained a metaphysical problem. Guer, who amuses himself at the expense of all parties—the automatists, the advocates of spiritual souls for animals, and the advocates of substantial forms—finally says, in effect, that there is not much to choose among them so far as a real advance in knowledge is concerned. Between the substantial forms, which the Cartesians say are mere words, and the Cartesians' constant reference to "a certain motion of the animal spirits," Guer thinks there is really little to choose. And it is evident that this author suspects that, religion aside, there is little merit to the controversy.[4]

This leads directly to the second observation. There were many common factors in the attitudes of the Cartesian automatists and the anti-Cartesians. For both of these groups the vital interest of the problem lay primarily in its real or imagined connections with traditional religious, theological and ethical ideas. The problem for the Cartesian was the adjustment of animal automatism to the task of supporting tradition by means of the Cartesian metaphysics as a whole. Bayle notes the many theological advantages of this automatist position. He indicates that, since automatism deprives the brutes of even sensibility, it follows that the brutes do not suffer. In this way the Cartesian may avoid contradicting the principle that only sinful creatures suffer. Moreover, automatism, which deprives the animal of suffering, leaves unimpaired the proof of original sin by an argument from the suffering of infants.[5] Bouillier, moreover, thinks that Descartes, who was the first to bring to light "la grande verite de la distinction de l'ame et du corps," was led to the automatist position by religious reasons. He would never have subscribed to it, Bouillier thinks, had he not felt that the notion of the soul of brutes was dangerous to the interests of religion. For the anti-automatists, on the other hand, the refutation of the doctrine of automatism provided an opportunity for casting discredit upon Cartesianism as a whole.[6] Moreover, there was more than one effort to overcome the difficulties of automatism by employing Cartesian ideas to justify a new application of scholastic principles. Finally, skepticism found in the doctrine an opportunity to display the essential insolubility of the problem by giving a vast array of pros and cons. Boullier observes that while many books on the question treat it as a philosophical problem, there frequently occurs an effort to manipulate the controversy for the purposes of skepticism and therefore to make it an indirect attack

[4] Guer, pp. 276 ff.
[5] *Dictionnaire*, article "Rorarius," n. C; Vol. VIII.
[6] B, Part II, p. 184.

upon religion and morality.[7] He notes the diabolical cleverness
of the maneuver: the hypothesis of automatism is made ridiculous
by the skeptic and so rejected; then, insisting upon the essential
similarity of animals and man, the skeptic concludes that the
difference between animals and men is one of degree only. This
similarity is made all the more striking because the hypothesis
of automatism is applied by Cartesians to the human body as
strictly as to the animals. In any case without bodies not even
Cartesians will admit passions and pleasure and pain for men.
Given the similarity between animals and men, with the body as
the source of the passions, the skeptic reaches a naturalistic and
hedonistic system of ethics. Thus, even the skeptic turned to the
doctrine of automatism with an intellectual ax to grind. It is no
wonder that Boullier and others thought the dangers real and
compromise necessary.

It must be recognized that the problem of the animal soul was
bound up with the much-discussed question as to whether animals
reason, or possess intelligence. In the intellectual conditions that
prevailed, however, this matter could scarcely be investigated or
the problem formulated, without taking a stand with respect to
the metaphysical problem of the soul. With the Cartesians, the
issue is clear. With their opponents, the issue is not so clear; by
distinctions in the sources of knowledge and in kinds of ideas,
they seek to retain for the animals some measure of knowledge
and intelligence and to find a way of escaping a choice between
automatism on the one hand and endowing the brute with a soul
too similar to the human on the other hand.

Boullier adopts the artifice of representing a Cartesian as setting forth the doctrine of automatism. The doctrine that Boullier
thus puts into the mouth of "the Cartesian" is, of course, his
own version rather than an exact account of some contemporary
treatment of the subject. It departs from the teaching of Descartes
himself. Moreover, Boullier's statement of automatism is shaped
beforehand so as to facilitate refutation. Our author provides us
with a pattern that reflects not only the theory of animals as ma-

[7] B, "Avertissement." It is evident that the writer has Bayle in mind.

chines but also the attitude and motives of those who found the doctrine unacceptable. In setting forth Boullier's pattern we shall have opportunity to observe certain interesting variants.

The Cartesian, as Boullier represents him, begins with the statement of his presuppositions.

Je présupose connue la distinction réelle, et la différence essentielle des deux substances, avec celle des proprietez et des opérations qui sont propres à chacun. *Descartes* l'a montré, S. *Augustin* l'avoit prouvé longtems avant lui, et, à la honte du Genre-humain, il ne falloit qu'un peu de bonsens pour s'en convaincre; tout sentiment est une perception et une pensée; il ne peut se trouver que dans un sujet qui se connoît soi-même, c'est-à-dire dans un esprit, et par consequent le sentiment ne peut se trouver dans la matière. Il y a une contradiction, il y a impossibilité métaphysique, que la matière sente, et soit capable de sentiment, comme il y a contradiction qu'elle pense. . . . On ne sauroit contester non plus, que le Corps humain ne soit une machine.[8] . . .

These are the presuppositions of the Cartesian—but it is important to note that they are the presuppositions of Boullier also. It is not merely the exposition of the Cartesian position of automatism, but also its refutation, that assumes the dualism of substances. Boullier is not the sole instance of this. We must, in short, recognize several types of refutation. There is the type which is based upon an acceptance of the dualism of substances, but despite this common ground seeks to disprove the thesis that animals are only machines. Admitting that matter cannot feel or think, it is urged that beasts must have souls that in some degree are quite similar to human souls and wholly distinct from matter. It is worth noting that Père Roche devotes a chapter to an attack upon those who attribute to beasts souls that are immaterial, and so far spiritual, although urging that these animal souls are

[8] B, Part I, ch. i, p. 11. On the next page a machine is defined as "un tout formé de l'assemblage regulier de diverses parties tellement disposées, enchaînées, & proportionées l'une à l'autre, qu'il en résulte un mouvement uniforme & regulier, par rapport à ce tout." ". . . A Beast is a meer Automaton or Engin: that is, an Animal destitute of all Knowledge, and consequently may be thus defined: A Beast is an Artificial Engin or Machin of GOD, furnished with a various and wonderful structure of Organs, containing in itself a material principle of Life, Motion and Sense" (*An Entire Body of Philosophy, according to the Principles of the Famous Renate des Cartes* . . . Written Originally in Latin by the Learned Anthony Le Grand, Now Carefully Translated from the Last Corrections, Alterations, and Large Additions of the Author, Never Yet Published. . . . London, 1694, Part VII, p. 254).

destructible despite their immateriality.[9] Again Louis de la Forge
urges that if it were demonstrated that animals possess cognition
it would necessarily follow that they possess spiritual souls. But
he refuses to admit that this conclusion would imply the essential
substantial sameness of the brute and the human soul, for, he
says, it is not necessary to believe that "tout ce qui est Spirituel
soit de mesme espece." [10] In various other ways the dualism of
substances is accepted—the identification of spirituality, thought,
and feeling granted—and nevertheless the doctrine that animals
are merely machines is rejected and some opponent theory advanced. Again, there are refutations of automatism which do not
rest upon any essential agreement with Cartesian metaphysics.
The proponent of Scholasticism argues against the machine
theory, but on the basis of a radically different system of thought.
Refutations of this type, then, imply a virtual rejection of Cartesianism as a whole, so that the argument against automatism
becomes in principle an attack upon the Cartesian system. And
finally, we should, perhaps, note those eclecticisms which present
a confused mixture of Cartesian and scholastic principles serving
as a basis of compromise between the opposed views.

There is one other observation to be made concerning the attitude of Boullier, since it is typical of many of the refutations
based upon agreement with the doctrine of two substances.
Boullier accepts the doctrine that the human body is a machine.
In fact, Boullier and many others, whatever they propose about
the brute soul, sense the difficulties inherent in the pineal-gland
theory and the notion of the soul as capable of redirecting the
flow of the animal spirits. These ideas were, indeed, largely given
up. Huet records the fact that Cartesians had formerly greatly
admired the pineal-gland theory: it is significant, however, that

[9] *Traité de la nature de l'âme et de l'origine de ses connoissances, contre le systeme
de M. Locke & de ses partisans,* 2 vols., Amsterdam, 1759, ch. x.
[10] *Traité de l'esprit de l'homme, de ses facultez et fonctions et de son union avec
le corps, suivant les principes de Rene Descartes,* Paris, Girard, 1666, p. 31.
Guer asserts that four points of view have dominated the modern controversy: first,
the view of those who insist that beasts have spiritual souls; second, those who
admit only instinct; third, those who assert the existence of a "substance mitoyenne"
between matter and spirit, called substantial forms; and finally, the view that
defines beasts as pure machines, II, 15.

Huet thinks that this admiration is a thing of the past, no longer regarded as an essential element in Cartesian philosophy.[11] The result of this indifference to the pineal-gland theory is a clarification of the issue. The objective of a refutation based on dualism is not primarily to disprove the thesis that the animal body is a machine, for even the human body is that, but rather to prove the existence of a soul adjoined to the animal body. As with man, so with the animals: the machine alone is insufficient to account for the facts of behavior. The definition of the organized body as a machine may raise the difficult question of the efficiency of the soul. But this question is not rendered more difficult by the existence of an animal soul, for it arises in its most acute form in connection with man conceived as a dual being.

To return now to Boullier's Cartesian. He begins with neurology and a statement of the "marvelous union" of body and soul. The "union" is described as a "certain reciprocal dependence between the two substances," or it is said to consist of a "mutual correspondence of thoughts and movements," with the result that the soul is at every moment acting on the body and producing movements, while in similar fashion the body acts upon the soul.[12] In some manner the soul may contribute to the movements of the body, and the bodily processes may contribute to the events in the soul. But this is not to be taken as equivalent to a denial that the body is a machine. Boullier's Cartesian proceeds to distinguish between those processes which proceed from the pure mechanism of the body and those that depend upon the union of body and soul. Thus, there are "absolute involuntary" movements, independent of the soul. The "principle" of the life of the body is not within the spiritual substance. The Cartesian is impressed with the appropriateness, the utility, of the involuntary response to a stimulus. This utility of response, of course, might well occur if the process, arising in the sense organs, led to and

---

[11] *Censura philosophiae cartesianae*, Lutetiæ Parisiorum, 1689, p. 97.
[12] Part I, pp. 15 ff. Boullier represents the Cartesian as stating that God has given the soul a confused, but strong and constant, sensation or perception of the sensorium (the pineal gland?), with the result that the soul perceives the movements of the pineal gland in the form of sensations, and in virtue of the correlation of sensorium and body, is thus able to perceive the movements of the latter.

through the soul and thence back to the body and its muscles. But, thinks the Cartesian, it is simpler to explain the facts by means of the bodily mechanism only. The correlation of stimulus and reaction is due to the structure of the machine.

This implies a fundamental merit of the machine hypothesis, that is, its economy. But this economy refers not so much to scientific methodology as to theology. The Cartesian is driven to a denial of souls to animals. Animals are automata. This conclusion is demanded by metaphysics. As an incidental by-product it provides economy in explanation and brings neurology and physiology within the realm of natural science. But, as we shall see later, a chief objection to the animal soul (that is, to a spiritual substance adjoined to the animal body) is theological and religious. At the same time, however, refutations of automatism may rest upon the same basis. This defines an intellectual crisis. The hypothesis of automatism must be subordinated to teleology.

The Cartesian thus urges that the sufficiency of the automaton indicates the perfect workmanship of the Creator.[13] To prove automatism, the Cartesian is made to appeal to the facts of habit, reflex action, natural antipathies, and the passions. We must recognize that Boullier does not make his account of the Cartesian position internally self-consistent. This may be due to his desire to make his refutation easier. It is equally probable, however, that the inconsistencies attributed to the Cartesian by Boullier fairly represent the confusions characteristic of many Cartesian writers of the day. Boullier represents the Cartesian as stating that the power of the bodily mechanism is "extrêmement" limited by the laws of the union of soul and body. These laws permit the mechanism to operate without interference only so long as its operations accord with the purpose of this union. The limitations upon mechanism are expressive of divine purpose. Now the purpose of the bodily mechanism is *not* the conservation of the body, either directly or indirectly. Rather, since the soul is the nobler thing, the body is its instrument—it is a means of obtaining "certaines connoissances," "certaines sensations"; finally, the body provides the soul with the matter and with the occasion for

13 Part I, ii, p. 23.

the exercise of a great number of virtues.[14] Since the soul must preside over the conservation of the body, perception is interposed between impression in the brain and bodily movement. Thus, the existence of the bodily machine, and its control by the soul in whatever sense and measure that control obtains, are intelligible in terms of the role God has designed for man and in these terms alone.

It is not easy to discern precisely what Boullier attributes to the Cartesian. In his account there may be the afterconsequences of the pineal-gland theory. Or of the occasionalistic position: that is, in some cases the occasioning cause for the spiritual event lies within the body, while in other instances the occasioning cause is within the soul and is thus logically prior to the bodily correlate. Boullier's Cartesian, at all events, seems to mean that the body-machine may operate on occasion in complete independence of the soul and, perhaps, without the soul's awareness of the activity; in other respects the soul becomes aware of the bodily situation and somehow directs the machine. An idea, arising within the soul from its own intrinsic energies, occasions the bodily reaction and to that extent has a certain control over it. The operation within the body remains mechanical, however, since only the direction of the animal spirits can be altered by the soul substance, if, indeed, that is possible.

The sufficiency of the bodily machine and the soul's control over the mechanism, in whatever sense this control occurs, are equally expressive of the excellency of craftsmanship displayed by the Creator. But laying aside the case of man and turning to the animal, the teleological character of the arguments is clear. The striking fact about animal behavior is its adaptation to the conditions of action for the fulfillment of bodily needs. This, in the Cartesian's terms, is the harmony between the automaton and the world of things, a harmony the natural end of which is the conservation of the machine. If the things and events of nature can be explained in terms of mechanical principles, it is all the more probable that a creature without moral significance, that is, the animal, can be understood in terms of similar principles.

[14] *Ibid.*, pp. 26–27.

However, the animal cannot be satisfactorily described *as* a machine unless we can demonstrate that it *is* a machine. The success of our description of the animal as a machine may well suggest the automaton hypothesis. This is insufficient. Mechanism as a methodological procedure needs a sanction. This seems to be what Boullier's Cartesian has in mind. The animal machine, if it be a machine, is this precisely because mechanism is the plan according to which divine purposes are carried out.

You cannot deny, urges the Cartesian, that God *could* make a machine similar to the body of a horse or a dog—a machine capable of self-maintenance. Moreover, God could well establish such a harmony between the automaton and the bodies that environ it that the impressions made by things, combined with the internal conditions of the automaton, would result in movements "convenables aux objets, proportionez au bien de la machine." [15] There is

une organization particulière dans les bêtes, que le Créateur y aura produite, & qu'il aura differemment reglée dans les diverses espéces d'animaux, mais toujours proportionnément aux objets, toûjours par rapport au grand but de la conservation de l'individu & de l'espèce. . . . L'idée d'une telle harmonie paroît grande & digne de Dieu.[16]

The same point of view is expressed by Dilly. We are enjoined to consider the animal with this in mind, that the animal is made so as to exist without recourse to any inner conscious principle of control. Moreover, we must consider the environing bodies with the recognition that they, as well as the brute, were made by one and the same Author. It follows that the animal is designed to pursue the useful and to avoid the injurious. In general, the Creator made animals and things with a view to their interadjustment. A horse will refuse to go forward when it sees a precipice because God has disposed his organs to such an effect that the objects cause the animal spirits to flow to the muscles of arrest.[17]

The end of animal life is nothing more than its own conservation. With man, however, the lower must be subservient to the nobler. Now since man indubitably has a soul—and this is ad-

[15] Part I, iii, pp. 35–36.   [16] *Ibid.*, p. 40.
[17] Dilly, ch. xvii, p. 213.

mitted by all parties to the controversy [18]—it follows that the human bodily machine is neither an end in itself nor able to define the end of man as the composite of soul and body. From this it follows that when something more and other than bodily conservation is the end, mechanism is necessarily limited; it is somehow limited by the laws of the union of body and soul. In some sense, then, the control of the mechanism by the spiritual substance is demanded by the very nature of the end of man. In the case of the animals, the end of life is continuation of life, and nothing more; translated into other terms, this means that mechanism and self-maintenance imply each other. In so far as the maintenance of bodily life can justly be defined as a purpose of man's existence, to this extent we shall expect to find man a machine. Where the whole end of a living thing is merely maintenance and conservation, we can expect to find nothing save a machine. Mechanism is a principle of economy, even for God. For the maintenance of life a machine is quite appropriate. Anything more would be wasteful. The Creator's wisdom would be in question were animals more than machines. In the circum-

[18] It is important to note that the controversy concerning the animal soul, at least in the stage with which we are now interested, is prior to a universal materialism. None of the sources upon which this study is based indicate that the doctrine that man is wholly a machine is seriously entertained. That is, none of the parties to the controversy deny the existence of the human soul, as something distinct from matter, whether or no the Cartesian soul substance be accepted. Some writers recognize the danger implied in proclaiming the sufficiency of mechanism for the animal: that is, they perceive that the argument may be extended to man. Dilly refutes this very argument by pointing out that man is immediately aware of his thinking (pensee) and insists that thought cannot be a derivative of extension (Dilly, ch. xi). Bougeant points out that I am immediately aware of my own existence as a thinking being, but acknowledges that other men may be, so far as I can know, mere soulless machines (pp. 9–10). Similarly, Guer reports the same argument. The inference to the possession of souls by other men is precisely on a par with the inference to the souls of beasts (pp. 120 ff.). To make a machine having all the activities and appearances of a human being is within the competence of God, as Bougeant points out (pp. 9–10). But none of this implies a real skepticism concerning the existence of the human soul. These arguments are recognized to be just factors in polemic, mainly useful in counteracting the theological arguments against the animal soul. The skeptic may use similar arguments, but not so much in order to entertain the possibility that man is soulless as to advance the skeptical position in general and to throw discredit upon pretensions to knowledge. Certainly the function of Bayle's criticisms is not to demonstrate that man is an automaton. Gerdil, it is significant to add, writing at a later time and in reaction to De la Mettrie, takes of course a very different attitude (cf. pp. 154–157).

stances—and this is evidently the background of the Cartesian's argument—the hypothesis of automatism is the simpler, in this special sense of the word.

The argument of the Cartesian continues in the same strain. Man is capable of making machines of surprising capacity; all the more may we expect inventive mechanical capacity on the part of God. The phenomena of animal instinct afford an especially clear demonstration of the animal's automatism. For animal instinct does, indeed, imply reason—but an "exterior reason," a creative reason that produces rational effects by mechanical means.[19] It is the misinterpretation of this that has produced the notion of a world soul. The Cartesian, in short, substitutes for the world soul the universal mechanical process that is the manifestation of the perfect divine creativeness. The spirit of the argument is throughout teleological. The instance of man's exceptionableness provides no difficulty. For, whether the creature be animal or man, whether or not there be adjoined to the mechanical system a soul, in every case we are confronted with the extraordinary complexity of the machine. That is, from the Cartesian's standpoint, since the soul merely redirects the courses of the animal spirits, but is not their source, the complexity and variety of stimulations and reactions imply proportionate intricacy in the nervous system of man. The presence of a soul in man does not imply less complexity in his bodily machine. Accordingly, the opponent of automatism cannot draw support from the unimaginable complexity that must characterize the animal body if animal behavior is due solely to the body. Since bodily events are one thing and mental events another, the addition of an animal soul does not simplify the operations of the animal body.[20] Back of this argument lies, of course, a general presupposition, namely, that where "natural" ends alone are involved, the Creator is content with mechanism. But where the ends are moral, that is, essentially supernatural, mechanism is insufficient. We

[19] Bayle tells us that this doctrine of an "exterior reason" was advanced in *Essais nouveaux de morale*, Paris, 1686, but does not give the name of the author. The doctrine seems to be an illustration of the fact that, in the controversy before us, design and mechanism are virtually co-implicative.
[20] Part I, pp. 46 ff.

may say either that the existence of the human soul proves that man is more than nature, or we may say that because God has designed for man more than the life of bodily conservation, with respect to both individual and species, he has endowed man with a soul. And this, indeed, is the real meaning of "the empire" that the soul has over the body.

The Cartesians, states our author,

disent de belles et bonnes choses quand ils nous parlent de la fécondité des loix du mouvement, des miraculeux effets de la Méchanique, de l'étendue incompréhensible de l'Entendement divin. . . . Je regarde cette idée féconde et presqu'infinie des possibilitez méchaniques, des combinaisons de la figure & du mouvement, jointe à celle de la sagesse & de la puissance du Créateur, comme le forte inexpugnable du Cartésianisme.[21]

But withal, the question is factual. Let us agree that God does not deceive. If, however, the facts seem to demand an animal soul in order that we may understand them, then, if animals really are machines, it follows that God does deceive us. Boullier states that this retort to the automatist was made by both Pardies and Daniel. Boullier, however, recognizes that the retort is insufficient. The dangerous argument is as follows: if the Cartesian arguments succeed in demonstrating that animals are automata; if it be proved that all the activities of animals can be explained upon this hypothesis; then, by similar reasoning, we cannot be assured that any man, with the exception of oneself, possesses a soul.[22] The Cartesian argument is in danger of being too impressive, to the unholy glee of the Pyrrhonians to whom Boullier refers.

The argument occurs in a special form. Thus, according to Dilly, Pardies argues that it is unworthy of God to give animals organs such as eyes and ears which must be merely for show and must be without function; for, if matter cannot think, and if sensation and perception are special modes of thought, the sense organs of the animals provide no sense impressions and therefore are without any utility whatever. Dilly insists that Pardies

[21] Part I, p. 58. [22] *Ibid.*, pp. 61–62. Cf. note 18, above.

misrepresents the situation. The sense organs in the animal machine do possess a real office (although they cannot, of course,
provide even occasions for sensations in the soul when no soul
exists), for the sense organs permit things to influence the automaton and so make for its preservation.[23] Dilly is probably
quite unfair to Pardies. We must bear in mind that behind this
controversy lies an agreement concerning this, that God does
things in a reasonable and proportionate manner. If man be
unique in possessing a spiritual substance added to his bodily
machine, it is extraordinary that this bodily machine should so
greatly resemble these other machines, called animals, which do
not possess any souls whatsoever. One would expect the human
body to be so unlike the animal body that the uniqueness of man
would be as strongly suggested by the peculiarity of his body as
by his possession of a soul. If the human eye be similar to the
eye of the dog, why should we not expect visual sensation in the
latter as well as in the former? The difficulty is by no means confined to Pardies. Du Hamel, in his eclecticism, illustrates the
point clearly. It is difficult to deny sensation and feeling to animals, since they are endowed with eyes, ears, and other organs
adapted to sense perception. It is equally difficult to admit that
extended substance can feel or think. If corporeal substance be
capable of perception, how can we distinguish soul and body at
all? Brutes distinguish one thing from another—shall we deny
them perception and attention? If we do, how shall we explain
why the images or forms in the brain do not blur one another?
In short, it is not easy to see how we can show the utility of sense
organs at all unless we posit a soul with powers of perception and
discrimination to take advantage of their functioning.[24] Dilly argues from the "marvellous activities" that man performs without
the employment of the soul. Actions, such as reflex adjustments
of which we are not aware and which we do not control, prove how
far mechanical explanation will extend. If such as these and the
process of prenatal growth can be explained mechanically, how
can we limit the possibilities of mechanical explanation with re-

[23] Dilly, ch. xxiii.
[24] Du Hamel, *De corpore animato*, p. 304.

gard to the brutes? [25] But others, and among them Du Hamel, feel
that the marvels of animal behavior—for example, the wonders
of instinctive behavior—are just what constitute the chief obstacle to the automatist theory.

We may leave these details and return to Boullier. It must be
admitted, states Boullier, that if God can make a machine which
"par la seule disposition de ses ressorts exécute toutes les actions
surprenantes que l'on admire dans un chien . . . il peut former
d'autres machines qui imiteront toutes les actions des hommes." [26]
In God's mind are comprehended all the possibilities of movements and of their combinations. If between the machines made
by men and the creatures of God, such as animals and men, there
is but a difference of degree, that is, of the complexity of mechanical construction, and if the machine imply a machine-maker
whose power and intelligence are commensurate with each other,
then most dangerous conclusions will follow. For just as human
power and intelligence suffice to explain the possibilities of man-
made machines, just so we need not infer from animal and human
machines a being of infinite power and intelligence, but the
presence in the world of intelligences other than "Dieu & son
propre Esprit." The fabricator of man may be more than human,
but less than Omnipotence. God would prove to be a hypothesis
out of all reasonable proportion to the facts.[27] Guer states that
the Peripatetics have several retorts to make when God's competence as a maker of machines is urged. In the first place, they may
reply that if God be capable of making a machine of such complexity as man, He may be equally capable of inventing a midway substance, something between matter and spiritual substance, so that animals may be more than machines and less than
man. In any case, the Peripatetic continues, the argument is in
effect invalid. For the doctrine that animals are machines depends upon the possession of so much knowledge concerning the
details of machines and especially of the alleged animal machines that we may decide whether mechanical explanation is
possible. And finally, the Peripatetic retorts that in countering the

[25] Dilly, ch. xvi.   [26] Part I, p. 63. Cf. Daniel, *Nouvelle difficultez*, pp. 70 ff., 100 ff.
[27] Part I, p. 64.

question: can you prove that God cannot make a machine exactly like an animal? we may ask: how can you prove that God can do so? [28] The argument from God's competence is irrelevant.

The entire situation can be inverted, urges Boullier. If we once admit, what the facts really suggest, that man and the animals differ in degree rather than in kind, we may argue with equal force to the conclusion that animals and men are alike machines or that souls are present in both cases. If men are machines with souls adjoined, which the Cartesian admits, then we may insist that animals with respect to the possession of souls connected with the body differ from man only in degree. The fact is that animals and men resemble one another too much to make a radical difference between them wholly intelligible. This conviction is present throughout the writers who criticize the doctrine of automatism. Even some Cartesians feel the need of explaining why their position carries so little conviction. The intelligent activities of man are due to a rational soul. But animals act in ways that suggest intelligence. This, for the Cartesian, is an indication of divine skill in design. But why is it so difficult to obtain assent to automatism if God's competence is granted? The reason is that man insists upon humanizing the animals. We believe ourselves to be the cause of our acts; we think that our souls are the conservators of our bodies; we are convinced of the soul's power to affect and guide the body; and so, not believing that our bodies are independent of the soul, we find it difficult to think of the animal as a machine.[29]

Because of considerations such as the above, Boullier thinks, the issue cannot be settled. Nor can it be settled by the usual arguments from language.[30] It is idle to base argument upon what

[28] Guer, II, 291–97.
[29] Cf. Abbe Lanion (Guillaume Wander), *Méditations sur la métaphysique*, Cologne, 1684; given in Bayle's *Réceuil de quelques pièces curieuses concernant la philosophie de M. Descartes*, Amsterdam, 1684.
[30] Organized discourse in man can be interpreted mechanistically. It may be argued that corresponding to the diversity of verbal signs (as stimuli) there exists an equivalent diversity of responses following mechanically from the stimuli. On the other hand, if language in man necessarily implies a soul, then in some degree animal communication will imply a similar foundation (Boullier, pp. 64–66). De la Forge, as Boullier indicates, deduces "une notable différence entre les Hommes & les autres animaux" from the fact that language is a matter of "institution." De la

is possible for God. Concretely, the facts imply in man the presence of a soul. The real question is therefore whether we can discover in the behavior of animals facts that point to something analogous to what we know to exist in man, that is, a soul. Since in fact God did not make man a machine, although we may admit God's competence for the task, when we turn to the animals the safer course to pursue is to expect God to have followed an analogous plan. This is better than an appeal to mere abstract possibilities.[31]

An animal soul, in short, is something that one can understand. The limits and possibilities of mechanism are unknown. This attitude of Boullier's, then, represents an interesting contrast to a later standpoint. It is not souls, but machines, that are speculative conceptions. The concept of the soul is for Boullier traditional and quite in harmony with the theological tradition. The new metaphysics, it is true, has given a new and better meaning to the soul, defining it as a spiritual substance; and in doing so it advances a new conception concerning the corporeal in general and the human body in particular. The soul, so to speak, is not a speculative conception, but universal mechanism is. Every man, if he attends, must reach at least his own soul as indubitable fact, and he has a clear and distinct idea of it. But mechanism, like the Lockean "way of ideas," is a new thing. And this leads at

---

Forge argues that the natural, involuntary and unlearned bodily expression of the passions are universally the same in all animals of the same species, including man. But since languages differ from one human society to another, and even the deaf have not one but a diversity of sign systems, language in man is clearly owing to "institution." But language in this sense, as caused by "institution," is characteristic of man alone. Hence it follows that language is inexplicable upon the basis of bodily mechanism alone, for then animals would also have languages due to "institution." Language in this sense implies a principle other than mechanism (De la Forge, pp. 350–54). But Boullier states that Daniel has refuted this argument. De la Chambre urges that "la voix des Bestes se fait avec dessein & intention d'exprimer leurs pensées" (p. 400). De la Chambre denies to animals the power of abstract thought, but imagination, which animals possess, is capable of a certain sort of judgment and of the formation of propositions. Thought in this sense is possessed by animals; their language is commensurate with this capacity of imagination.

[31] Part I, pp. 66 ff. For Dilly the hypothesis that beasts are machines implies more artifice than the hypothesis that a soul is attached to the animal body. God, in the case of the animal, dispensed with the assistance of a soul principle and accordingly showed greater creative competence. Hence the doctrine of the automatism of animals makes for the greater glory of God.

once to the essential element in Boullier's refutation of the Cartesian. The animals show many indications in their behavior of consecutive activities directed towards an end, representing the ideas, desires, interests, and designs of a particular being. Even admitting that many of the stories told concerning animals are mythical, nevertheless enough remains to indicate that animal behavior approximates that of man. The scientific way of looking at these facts is to interpret them by analogy with what we know, and this means to adopt the hypothesis of an animal soul. The theory of animal machines is speculative and metaphysical.

To this a teleological point of view may safely be annexed.

Comme le but général de la Sagesse divine paroît être de raporter & subordonner le Monde corporel aux Intelligences qui se raportent elles-mêmes à Dieu, le but particulier de l'organization d'une certaines [sic] portion de matière doit être de servir à quelque principe immatériel, certainement plus excellent qu'elle: ce que notre ame éprouve dans l'état d'union, nous decouvre le but de l'organization de ce corps qui lui est uni; & de là nous tirons légitimement cette conséquence, que tout corps organisé, toute machine qui se conserve elle-même, est faite pour loger une ame, c'est-à-dire, un principe immateriel, auquel cette machine soit subordonnée comme instrument de sensation & d'action.[32]

Now it must be emphasized that the writer has just urged the essential irrationality of the notion that machines are made for the sole end of conserving themselves as machines. ". . . à quoi bon dans l'Univers des machines qui se conservent elles mêmes?" [33] For our author, mechanism implies a final cause. This, he insists, is obvious with respect to detail. The ear and the eye as mechanisms are unintelligible even as mechanisms unless we observe that they are made for audition and vision. What is true of the part is true of the whole—what is the end for which the machine exists? Its self-perpetuation? This is incredible, not because such an answer is teleological, but because it is inadequately mechanistic. The man-made machine is designed for a purpose, and that purpose is in every case specific. But self-conservation is not a helpful element in the effort to comprehend a machine—it tells us nothing specifically concerning its nature as a machine. The body, human or animal, becomes mechanistically intelligible precisely

[32] Part I, pp. 79–80.   [33] *Ibid.*, p. 77.

when we can see that it is organized for the accomplishment of a purpose. In the end, so Boullier really thinks, the body is a machine devised to serve the soul. It is the vehicle of sensory information and of muscular adjustments that assure the conservation of the creature of God in its adventurous career amid things. Of course, it might be said with respect to this frame of ideas, that were the soul not attached to the body it would be independent of things and immune to their harms and dangers. The soul needs the body only because it has one. Concerning this Boullier has nothing to say. The matter is cared for, of course, by the general mystery of man's existence—that is, the plan of salvation.

We may conclude, then, bearing in mind the wisdom and the veracity of God, that there is

une ame dans les bêtes, c'est-à-dire, il y a dans les bêtes, un principe immateriel uni à leur machine, fait pour elle, comme elle est faite pour lui, qui reçoit à son occasion differentes sensations & qui leur fait faire tant d'actions qui nous surprennent, par les diverses directions qu'elle imprime à la force mouvante renfermée dans la machine.[34]

As our author points out at the very beginning of the second part of his work, new embarrassments await those who champion animal souls. The proponents are in danger of proving both too much and too little. The Peripateticians lay themselves open to the attacks of a Pyrrhonian like Bayle and also to those of the Cartesians. For they urge the existence of a sensitive soul in animals, while denying a rational soul. This provides an opportunity for the raillery of Bayle. The Peripateticians think they can explore the souls of animals as the anatomist explores their entrails. They assert a sensitive soul, whereupon the Cartesians triumphantly show that they have proved too much. The latter insist that the inference from animal behavior to a sensitive soul is no more valid than an inference from the same facts to a rational soul. But even the Peripateticians are unprepared to grant a rational soul to animals. If Père Daniel can challenge the Cartesians to show why, on their principles, men are not machines, one may justly demand of Père Daniel that he prove why the sensitive soul he assigns to brutes will not suffice for man.

[34] *Ibid.*, pp. 84–85.

Boullier insists that the Peripateticians can never refute automatism by recourse to a distinction in the order of kinds of souls. That is, Boullier is himself a Cartesian at this point. The term "soul" means spiritual substance, the antithesis of material substance, or it means nothing at all. Boullier agrees with the Peripatetics that animals are not machines. And of course animals are not upon the same order of being as men. But the concept of a "substance mitoyenne entre le corps & l'esprit" (as Guer describes it) will not assist in refuting automatism. In Guer we learn that not even God could create a substance that is neither matter nor spirit. It is of the essence of every being that feels and knows to be spirit, and of every being deprived of knowledge and feeling to be matter. The notion of a substance midway between spirit and matter, endowed with possibility of sensitive knowledge (but not spiritual knowledge), is wholly untenable. To say knowledge or feeling is to say spiritual substance. It is possible to urge that between the knowledge of the beasts and that of man is a difference of degree, and perhaps of great degree. But nevertheless it will not serve to make this distinction. Unless beasts are to be granted spiritual souls, knowledge must be denied them.[35] This is the predicament in which, according to Bayle, the Peripatetics find themselves.

Equally unavailing, as Bayle points out when quoting Pardies, is the doctrine of some writers to the effect that animals possess a soul, but that this soul is *material*. If a material soul will explain the activities of brutes, by analogy those of men will be explicable in similar terms.[36] Bayle regards as likewise futile the theory he attributes to Willis, according to which there exist two souls, one corporeal but subtle, and the other spiritual. If the corporeal soul suffices for the animal, it may for man, and all the more since we can imagine that the human soul is even more subtle than the soul of the brute.[37] Bayle is well aware that the notions of animal

---

[35] Guer, pp. 198–201, 209 ff., 228 ff. Daniel, under the guise of a debate between Aristotle and Descartes, insists that no one has demonstrated that a being midway between spirit and matter is impossible, which all the more makes the plan of the Cartesians to explain animals as machines a chimerical program (*Voyage*, p. 201).
[36] *Dictionnaire*, article "Rorarius," note E.
[37] *Ibid.*, note K.

spirits and of subtle matter have much to do with the position of those who seek an escape from automatism without becoming Cartesians. He insists that what the "chymists" call "spirits" is as essentially body or matter as are dirt and flesh.[38]

Notions such as those of a corporeal soul, of a "substance mitoyenne," of an additional something adjoined to the animal body are all, for the convinced Cartesian, mere verbalisms. Peripatetic views of souls are reconcilable neither with Descartes nor with Epicurean views of matter. Dilly represents the Peripatetic as defending his notion of the soul by insisting that it contains no difficulty unless one accept "Epicurean" views of matter. Atomism renders unintelligible the relation of form and matter. But if matter be properly understood as Aristotle defines it, that is, as primary matter, pure possibility (*puissance*), that is, as a being empty, without quality, quantity, quiddity, or existence, but capable of receiving all of these, then the Peripatetic view of the soul is intelligible, and the animal soul is not a difficult conception. But Dilly thinks that in escaping the atomists the Peripatetic becomes an easy victim of the Cartesian. For all of this definition of matter is merely an affair of words. Soul and matter are antithetical substances—and with this there is an end of Peripatetic views and of all intermediary substances.[39]

The Peripatetic view everywhere turned upon a distinction between rational and sensitive knowledge. The Cartesians were

[38] *Ibid.*, article "Pereira," note E. Henry More's repeated insistence that the soul or spirit cannot be identified with the animal spirits, and that subtle matter is matter, not spirit, is another indication that the confusion was widespread. (*The Philosophical Writings of Henry More*, ed. by Mackinnon, New York, 1925, pp. 123, 135, 137).

[39] Dilly, chs. xiii, xxiv. Bougeant insists that we know of only two substances, and a substantial form which is neither matter nor spirit is an "opinion monstrueuse." An intermediary substance, incapable of reasoning, but capable of feeling and knowing, is a "pure supposition without proof and without foundation," a thing of which we can form no idea whatever (pp. 14–17). Bougeant's own suggestion of a solution to the problem of animal souls is worth noting as the *reductio ad absurdum* of the whole controversy. He suggests that the souls of brutes are indeed spirits; but this can be sustained without conflict with the dogmas of religion, and at the same time the identification of soul and immortal principle can be retained. This is done by the hypothesis that the souls of brutes are demons, fallen angels, whose inclosure within the animal bodies is an indignity constituting a foretaste of the eternal torments of hell to which they are ultimately condemned.

quick to perceive that the old distinction must be radically rein-
terpreted on the new basis. Descartes himself found the primary
meaning of spiritual substance in the power of reflection and
in the power of intuiting clear and distinct ideas. But he had, of
course, recognized that the definition of matter as extension compelled the inclusion of sensation, perception, and imagination,
within the soul substance as modes of thinking. Boullier, a convinced Cartesian to this extent, recognizes that the similarity in
human and animal equipment with respect to the organs of sense
is a crucial point. There is a certain reasonableness about the
position of Daniel, let us say. Daniel admits that the movements
of the blood, heart, and reflexes are mechanical. In general the
body is a machine and its peculiar organization contributes to the
determination of its motions. But there is also an animal soul,
midway between matter and spirit, conferring the capacity for
sensation and perception, yet not for reasoning and thought. The
soul of the beast is "une substance qui a des sensations, ou des
connoissances sensitives sans penser & sans raisonner." [40] Now
Boullier, as convinced a dualist as any Cartesian, cannot agree
with this manner of assigning to animals a soul. The Perpateti-
cian, insisting upon a sensitive soul and an intermediary substance, at least confesses that sensation is not a bodily or a wholly
material and mechanical function. But a faculty belongs either
to the soul, and therefore is spiritual, or else to the body, and
in this case the term "soul" is completely inapplicable. Either
reason and sensation are lodged within the same substance and
are existentially of the same order, or else sensation is a purely
corporeal fact, and in no sense can the term "knowledge" be
applied to it. If sense organs imply sensation and sensitive knowledge, and if sensitive knowledge implies a soul, then we must
conclude that where there is sense there is a spiritual substance.
A substance of this kind, being the seat of sensation, which is a
mode of thought, may just as well comprise a rational faculty also.
If reason itself be no more incompatible with matter than sensa-

---

[40] Daniel, *Voyage*, Cinquième partie, pp. 437, 504 ff., 509–10. This part contains
the "Lettre d'un Peripateticien, a l'auteur du Voyage du monde de Descartes" but
it is evidently a representation of Daniel's own position.

tion, as Boullier urges, then the soul that contains the power of sensation in all probability contains the power of rational reflection also.[41] Boullier is thus led to assert that the brute soul is one that thinks. In his generous eclecticism the influence of Locke seems here to unite with the influence of Descartes. Boullier reinforces the preceding argument by a somewhat hesitant statement that all the faculties of the soul seem to be "enveloped" within sensation. The soul begins with sensation in infancy, and our author implies that the higher faculties develop from sensation. Referring his readers to Locke, he points out that every sensation comprises a confused idea of an object. Grant the animals the faculty of sensation—a sensitive soul—and you must grant them thought as well. Moreover, you must grant the animals self-consciousness, "le sentiment de leur propre être." Thus, our defender of animal souls assigns to animals precisely what constitutes for the automatist a fundamental objection. Dilly, for example, would agree that all physical states are modes of thought. To think is to have activities of whose existence we are immediately certain. We are immediately certain of these acts in and through these very acts themselves and in the very moment in which we have them. Dilly is attacking Pardies' distinction between material "connoissance" and spiritual "connoissance." Pardies insists that spiritual knowledge is a reflection upon itself, while material knowledge is merely perception: this enables Pardies to allow knowledge to animals. But Dilly insists that the reflective moment in thought is identical with the spiritual experience itself. A percept and the reflective awareness of it fall within one state of consciousness, and so both must be spiritual. Every psychological state, as we should say, involves awareness as an integral element; and awareness, for Dilly, implies the spiritual soul. If we deny self-consciousness to animals—and for Dilly this is obviously necessary—then we must deny them thought in every sense of the term. Otherwise they would be in the peculiar condition of having thought without knowing that they have it.[42]

For Boullier, then, the animal soul is a thing that thinks and it is possessed of "le sentiment de son propre être." This leads

---

[41] Part II, p. 90. [42] Dilly, chs. ii, iii, xi, xiii.

us to what Boullier himself recognizes as the crucial difficulty for the defender of a spiritual animal soul. The problem is to discover a specific difference between the brute and the human soul. Bayle, as Boullier states, has insisted upon this problem. The skeptics' program is to minimize the difference between the brute and the animal soul, with the result that we shall be driven into a dilemma with equally repellent horns. Bayle urges that ascribing a sensitive soul to brutes fails to provide a specific difference between animals and man. Sensation and perception imply self-consciousness. Then animals possess souls identical in essence with the human. Either man and the brute are both machines, or else they possess souls of identical character. Boullier cannot accept even Bayle's suggestion that freedom may define the difference between man and the animals. The meaning of soul as spiritual substance forces Boullier to insist that whatever is a fundamental trait or faculty of the human soul must be present in some measure in the animal. The brutes then possess freedom.[43]

Boullier then confronts the argument that Bayle bases upon observed differences between one man and another, and between animals and men. If the child and the adult, the stupid man and the philosopher, the monkey, the Negro and "un bel esprit Européen" (to use his examples), are alike with respect to soul, then we must look elsewhere for an explanation of the diversities and inequalities manifest in their activities. But where can we look save to their bodies? Some bodies, we must admit, facilitate the activities of the soul more than others. The fact is that, if we could transpose the souls of the dullard and the philosopher, the latter's soul in the dullard's body would never reveal the philoso-

[43] Bayle, Boullier states, urges that the liberty of spontaneity cannot be denied animals even if we deny them liberty of indifference. His purpose, he adds in a note, is to disclose the chimerical character of the latter notion of liberty by furnishing a Pyrrhonian balance of pros and cons. If liberty of indifference is unnecessary for animals, it can be dispensed with for man, since the souls of man and of animals are of identical substance. In this way the dilemma rearises: either there is a substantial difference between the brute and human souls, or the brute soul is a meaningless conception (Part II, pp. 101 ff.). If the higher faculty of thought can develop from sensation, then will is an equally possible development from a lower source. "Le seul principe sensitif paroit renfermer un fonds d'activite auquel il ne manque que des idees distinctes, pour devenir un principe libre" (Part II, p. 105).

pher, and the dullard's soul in the philosopher's body would appear to be not the soul of a dullard but of a philosopher. Or, to leave such fancies, Bayle may urge that between the stupid and the intelligent is a difference greater than that between the animal and the stupid man. If the human soul is everywhere the same, we must explain the difference between stupidity and genius by unlikeness of the bodies to which souls are adjoined. Granting this, the difference between animal and man can be accounted for by dissimilarity and inequality of body. This is all the more convincing if the distance between stupidity and genius in man is greater than that between man and the animals—and many of the contributors to the animal-soul controversy would make this admission. We may even go further and allege that a human soul, placed within an animal body, would appear to have all the deficiencies of the alleged animal soul. Thus, the Peripatetic's inference from animal behavior to a soul limited to sensitivity may be mistaken; the real fact may be that the animal possesses a quite complete soul, but, cramped by the animal body, is so limited in expression that we mistakenly infer the presence of a more limited soul.[44]

Boullier's reply to this argument is to assert that Bayle has drawn a false analogy between extension and spirit. All differences between bodies are mere accidents of one and the same essence, extension. Bodies are composites. But souls are individual unities, simple, indecomposable, and accordingly specifically dif-

[44] Bayle, *Dictionnaire*, article "Rorarius," notes D, E, and p. 763. Similar arguments are advanced by Guer. Comparisons between animal and brute souls are dangerous. Le Gendre, says Guer, argues that you cannot admit a soul of brutes and insist that it is inferior to the human. This inferiority may obtain in some respects, but in other respects the brute soul may be finer than the human—a thing suggested by animal behavior. That is, an argument based upon the analogy between human and animal activities is double-edged (Guer, pp. 138 ff.). The difficulty may be presented in another way. Either the soul has some efficiency and real function, or it has not. If the former, bodily activities depend upon it. Now the acts of brutes are similar to those of man. If human activity expresses a soul, so does the activity of the animal. But, if animal acts go on without a soul, then we should conclude that the human soul is there in man, but without efficiency. The correlation of body and soul in man can then be explained neither in terms of the character of the body nor of the character of the soul. The automatists are thus driven to God for an explanation of the union of body and soul, which is extremely dangerous, since God thus becomes responsible for our actions (Guer, pp. 258 ff.).

ferent every one from another. There is no spiritual substance
in general, with thought as its essence. There is a plurality of
spiritual substances, and each is an individual. Thought is a generic perfection that each possesses. But souls may possess different degrees of perfection. The essence of each soul is defined, not
so much by the generic essence (that is, thought in general), as
by a certain concrete fund of thought and activity that defines the
individual substance.

Ainsi dès que l'ame de la Bête a quelque pensée, elle convient avec celle
de l'homme, dans l'attribute general de pensée . . . mais elle en différe
par des proprietez specifiques, & parce que le fonds de pensée & d'activité
qu'elle renferme est beaucoup plus petit que celui de l'ame humaine.[45]

Here, then, we have the reintroduction of the medieval hierarchy, the scale of beings from matter to God, within the system
of Cartesian soul substances. Above the vast monotony of extension, wherein all differences are mere accidents, there stands a
system of souls that participate in the attribute of thought in an
infinite number of ways; and according to differences of participation each of these souls possesses capacities for perception and
thought unlike those of any other. We have here an order of intelligences, from the lowest brute to the most gifted man—and beyond man are the angels. Each individual soul, fixed within the
limitations defined by his specific difference, may exploit more
and more fully his capacity, but always within the restrictions of
these limits.[46]

[45] Part II, p. 115. The arguments of Boullier against Bayle are quoted with approval
by De Crousaz, in *Examen du Pyrrhonisme ancien & moderne*, par M. de Crousaz,
de l'Academie Roiale des Sciences, Gouverneur de Son Altesse Serenissime Le
Prince Frederic de Hesse Cassel . . . a la Haye, chez Pierre de Hondt, 1723,
Part III, sec. 10, pp. 480 ff. De Crousaz maintains a position similar to that of Boullier.
[46] In Part II, ch. iv, Boullier uses this point to refute Bayle's (conjectural) extension
of an argument of Addison's to the effect that each soul may by proper exercise become in time a higher soul, taking a place on a higher rung of the ladder. But for
Boullier the perfecting of the soul can occur only within the limits set by the
specific constitution of the individual soul. Otherwise, he insists, if we admit that
a soul capable of thought is capable of such development as to comprise all thought,
we shall be obliged to admit the potential equality of a human and the divine mind
(cf. p. 128). In short, our author attributes to Cartesian souls the fixity of the
species and also a certain singularity definitive of the individual soul, while this
places limits upon its perfectibility.

The animal mind reveals its limitations in that it cannot possess "idées spirituelles & abstraites" and is not "susceptible" to the idea of a God, of a religion, of the morally right and wrong; nor does the animal soul possess the ideas and principles upon which the arts and sciences are founded.[47] These deficiencies are proved by experience. Again the objection arises—and the figure of the Pyrrhonian Bayle is in the background—are these deficiencies due to the restrictions placed upon the animal soul by its body? And once more emerges the real basis of Boullier's doctrine: this suggestion, if admitted, will imply a blunder on the part of God. The craftsmanship of God implies that He does that which is fitting, and therefore He assuredly furnishes for every type of soul a set of bodily conditions appropriate to and suitable for the effective exercise of that soul. In this sense, indeed, although our author does not state the point specifically, the study of the particular animal body will indicate the character and limitations of its soul.

We remain without a definition of the nature of the animal soul. We know that the animal soul is (1) spiritual substance; (2) a thing that thinks; (3) incapable of "spiritual" and abstract ideas; (4) duly proportioned to the body and the body to it, that is, each is suited to the other; and finally (5) that the animal soul possesses in some degree each of the faculties of the human soul. But how is it that the thing that thinks cannot form abstract ideas? In what sense does the animal soul possess the faculties of the human soul, and still be in principle incapable of a range of ideas and volitions characteristic of the human soul?

At this point Boullier beautifully illustrates the process of syncretism that is typical of the age. On the one hand the Cartesian dualism has defined the situation so that a psychological function is either lodged in the spiritual substance or else it is not psychological at all, but corporeal and mechanistic. There is no

---

[47] Part II, pp. 134–35. "Il est possible qu'un Etre ait des sentimens, ait des perceptions, & s'appercoive qu'il les ait, sans avoir reçu la Capacité de réfléchir sur ces Perceptions, pour avoir soin de les mettre dans sa Mémoire, pour s'informer de leurs Causes, pour remorter à leurs sources, ou pour en prévoir les suites, & prendre làdessus des mesures." De Crousaz, *Examen du Pyrrhonisme ancien & moderne,* pp. 481–82.

middle term. On the other hand, since the soul is spiritual substance and one thing, and since its essence is thought, everything within the soul is either thought or potentially thought. Again, the physiological conditions of sensation in animals seem analogous to those in man. In addition to all this, Boullier has studied Locke and thinks that Locke provides us with a natural history of ideas in the soul corresponding to things outside. Finally, the unity of the soul substance, the essence of which is thought, has forced Descartes to look upon sensations and perceptions as thought, but with the reservation that they are *confused* thoughts. These factors Boullier uses—we need not inquire with what consistency—to define a situation in which he can reintroduce the conception of the sensitive soul and thus define the animal soul by preserving the intermediary character of the older conception, while adjusting it to the conditions defined by the Cartesian dualism. We therefore discover that the animal soul is a sensitive principle, an immaterial thing, a thinking substance—

en un mot, un esprit qui n'a que des perceptions confuses & dont l'activité est modifiée & reglée sur ces perceptions, c'est-a-dire, qu'il a divers desirs confus qui correspondent à la varieté de ces sensations & dont elles sont en quelque sorte l'objet.[48]

Moreover, because the animal soul is a sensitive principle, its relation to the body is so necessary for its activity that it cannot exist without the body. Significantly enough, Boullier then declares that in order to appreciate his hypothesis, the reader must follow him through a long "digression" concerning the nature of sensation. If the animal soul be the sensitive soul, then in sensation must be found that which at one and the same time provides the likeness of human and brute souls and provides the difference between them.[49]

What then is the character of the brute soul? The soul of man possesses the faculties of clear and distinct ideas and also of confused ideas, of sensation. The faculty of will, acting upon the faculty of forming clear and distinct ideas, leads to the activities of reflection, judgment, reasoning, and free choice. The animal

[48] Part II, p. 140.
[49] The digression occupies pp. 141–74 of Part II. It is considered on pp. 149–154.

soul, possessing the faculty of sensation only, is incapable of clear and distinct ideas.

Vous voyez donc qu'une ame qui ne seroit capable que de sensations ne ressemblera à l'ame humaine que par les attributs inséparables de toute intelligence, & qui doivent nécessairement entrer dans l'idée générale d'une substance qui pense.[50]

Strictly speaking, the animal soul does not possess the power of choice or volition. Nevertheless, "Dans toute substance qui pense il y a toujours quelque chose d'analogue à l'entendement & à la volonté." [51] The animals, Boullier seems to imply, possess confused desires and impulses that are the analogue of the human acts of will. The animal soul perceives things by means of sensation. But with man the faculty of clear and distinct ideas adds to (or transforms?) the sensations from things, and this is beyond the capacity of the animal soul. Distinctness of percept, that is, the percept of the thing as an organized whole, is due to the higher faculty in man. What Boullier seems really to mean, is that man alone can perceive, while animals possess sensations without the capacity of organizing them into perceptions of objects.[52] The animal, being incapable of reflection, is incapable of virtue or of vice, of memory or of anticipation.

Throughout the discussion Boullier is obviously troubled by the fact that the animal's behavior seems to imply precisely these powers of reflection, foresight, and will. Boullier meets the difficulty in two ways. On the one hand, wherever animal behavior suggests reflection and knowledge in the eulogistic sense, we may be certain that the mechanism of the body is responsible for such behavior. The Divine Designer, so to speak, may secure certain types of activity in either of two ways: in the case of man, by means of a soul capable of the higher levels of thinking; in the case of the animals, by means of mechanism. On the other hand, for Boullier sensation is thought. To that extent the principle that whatever is in the human soul must have its analogue in the animal is satisfied. Sensation, however, is confused thought, and therefore is not reflective knowledge—thought in the emphatic

[50] Part II, p. 176.   [51] *Ibid.*
[52] *Ibid.,* p. 180.

sense. In this way the animal may be denied reason, but nevertheless we may say that the soul of the animal is a substance whose essence is thought.[53]

The real difficulty in this situation is teleological and theological. The opponents of automatism were not slow in grasping the opportunity. The argument is developed as follows: animals suggest by their activities that they are endowed with the capacity to remember, to learn by experience, to exercise foresight, and to plan for the realization of ends. In short, they display intelligence, a power for thinking that is something more than susceptibility to sensation. But if animals do not possess souls, while their behavior certainly suggests that they do, then God is a deceiver. We persistently believe that animals are not machines at all. The argument appears again and again. Dilly answers Pardies' use of the argument by insisting that the error is man's and that God is not responsible for it—employing the Cartesian account of error.[54] But the argument can be inverted, and Boullier does this. It is equally valid to argue that, since God does not deceive and animal behavior forces us to the conclusion that animals possess souls whose essence is thought, it is legitimate to believe the conclusion. The trouble with the whole question, as Boullier's treatment reveals, is in restricting the scope of the argument so as to exclude the inference to reflection and clear and distinct ideas as powers of the animal. The manipulation of ideas is so characteristic of the whole controversy concerning the brute soul that it is worth while to add a comparable situation which Daniel puts into the mouth of his Peripatetician:

. . . les bestes agissent, comme si elles connoissoient, comme si elles sentoient, comme si elles raisonnoient: Cela prouve rien selon vous. Les hommes parlent comme s'ils connoissoient, comme s'ils sentoient, comme s'ils raisonnoient: cela ne prouvera aussi rien selon moy, parce que cela doit ne rien prouver selon vous.[55]

The facts concerning animal behavior that give rise to the difficulties we have been considering are the activities of advance adaptation and the guidance of action towards remote ends. The

[53] *Ibid.*, p. 181.   [54] Dilly, ch. x; Guer, p. 302.
[55] Daniel, *Nouvelles difficultez*, p. 84.

facts must be allowed for without an encroachment upon human prerogatives. The question is complicated by the necessity of providing for some measure of efficiency in spiritual substance with respect to the control of the body. Boullier insists that the hypothesis of a sensitive (spiritual) soul, joined to a machine, suffices to explain the facts of animal behavior. Rational powers need not be attributed to the soul of the brute. But the facts do demand something more than a machine. The machine, of course, embodies the wisdom of the Creator. Within the design of the Creator, however, and indeed as a part of that design, the sensitive soul in the brute is necessary for the initiation and redirection of movements. Just as the similarity and the difference of the brute and the human souls are defined by the difference between the confused and the clear percept falling within sameness of substance, so the distinction between the two orders of spirits is defined by the difference between confused and clear volition.[56] As sensations are confusions of minute perceptions, so the confused desires of animals are "une multitude ou suite de petits efforts," and these are exactly analogous to the various "suites" of minute ideas. By the wise provision of the Creator some of the animal's perceptions are associated with pleasure and some with pain. Given all this,

Il ne faut plus autre chose, si ce n'est que le Créateur ait tellement ajusté les ressorts de cette machine faite pour l'âme de la bête, que les désirs confus qui correspondent aux sensations douloureuses ou agréables, produisent dans le cerveau diverses impressions lesquelles, en vertu de la structure générale, feront mouvoir la machine d'une manière propre à éviter la cause de la douleur, & à s'unir à celle du plaisir.[57]

God would not provide for the action of the body upon the soul without providing for the action of the soul upon the body. A machine by itself could have no "interest," and nothing could with propriety be regarded as useful or injurious to a machine.[58] Given the sensitive soul, however, the brute is by nature something that will take account of the useful and the injurious. Pleasure and pain, as passions, would not exist at all in a mere machine. Their appearance in the sensitive soul attached to the machine

[56] Cf. pp. 149–154.   [57] Part II, p. 188.   [58] *Ibid.*, p. 190.

would be unintelligible unless those feelings were effective in guiding the machine. The sensitive soul will then direct the activities of the animal machine in conformity with the associations between pleasure and pain and the sensations. This process of association occurs in accordance with the reciprocal harmony, the inner adjustments, which define the artifice of the Creator in uniting with the animal body a sensitive soul.[59]

Since the arts and sciences depend upon distinct ideas and universal principles, the animals are incapable of them. In the strict sense of the term, then, animals do not reason.[60] But if animals do not reason, how is it possible to explain or explain away the appearance of reasoning found in animal behavior? Boullier states that there are three classes of activities which are commonly cited as evidence of reasoning power: the activities of instinct, the "docility" of animals, and certain activities of adjustment to specific conditions which do not seem explicable in terms of either instinct or habit.[61]

The phenomenon described by the term "instinct" caused a great deal of discussion in the brute-soul controversy. Remarkably enough, instinct is often conceived of in the same way by those who oppose and those who advocate automatism. The automatists and the anti-automatists, in many cases, agree that instinct must be regarded as a case of mechanical adjustment. Dilly states that instinct is a set of actions that every member of a species does naturally; instincts invariably make for the conservation of the animal; the instinct consists only "dans la disposition particulière" of the animal's brain at birth.[62] The animal automatists, then, dispose of the case of instinct as of any other animal power: instincts are factors in the mechanical design of the Creator. Their place in the economy of the machine is defined by their serviceability in the struggle for existence. Now many of the anti-automatists, agreeing in essentials with the automatists' description of an instinct, are equally positive that it is a portion of the bodily machine. Their reasons for this, however, differ somewhat. The perfection of adjustment involved in what is called

[59] *Ibid.*, pp. 186–87.
[61] *Ibid.*, p. 196; chs. x, xi.
[60] *Ibid.*, ch. x.
[62] Dilly, p. 177.

"instinctive behavior" cannot be attributed to the soul without grave danger. For, if instinctive behavior is due to mind, then the remarkable achievements of animals would imply a power of reasoning quite superior to that possessed by man. The advocate of animal souls must then agree with the automatists that instinct belongs essentially to the body. There is abundant evidence to show that this objection to assigning instinct to spirit was a commonplace of discussion in the controversy, a commonplace of serious weight. An eclectic such as Du Hamel is driven in both directions. Instincts are related to the goals that the Creator has fixed for animal life: procreation, care of the young, self-maintenance. Instinct cannot be due solely to atomical arrangement or mere stimulation: the inner organization of the animal must be involved. But on the other hand, the instinctive process involves knowledge, for it is augmented by sense-experience—and how can there be sense-experience in the absence of a soul? In the end Du Hamel leaves us perplexed. He can only conclude by warning us not to put the animals on a plane with man, or to make them only a shade inferior to man, or to concede them liberty and free will.[63] If instinct be due to reason, freedom of will would be implied. And since instinctive activity is the very perfection of art, infallibility would have to be granted to the beasts. Boullier, although upholding a spiritual substance in the brute, cannot of course admit such consequences. If animals are endowed with such perfection of thought as instinct would imply, the integrity of the Creator would be open to suspicion. A certain moral obliquity would be chargeable to God. For if animals have this endowment, then in brutes the gift of reason is subordinated to ends that are purely "animal," that is, to nutrition and propagation. But this is unworthy of the Creator, for a rational soul cannot be intended to subserve the gratification of merely bodily desires and the mere conservation of life. Hence instinct must be a bodily power, and adaptation to the conditions of bodily life its function, that is, its purpose according to the divine plan.[64]

[63] Du Hamel, *De corpore animato*, pp. 320–31.
[64] Part II, pp. 197–99.

On the other hand, it is quite worthy of the Creator's goodness to attach to the animal body a *sensitive* soul. It is true that the animal body is made for the service of the sensitive soul; but the animal as a whole is made for the good of the universe. The brute soul, although in a sense blind, is nevertheless an immaterial agent arranging the diverse parts of matter and forming of them an organized whole. The soul of the animal, it is clear, is necessary as a principle of organization: it remains, at bottom, the organizing form of the Peripatetic.[65] Pleasure and pain are the guiding factors in the sensitive soul and are therefore the very conditions that enable the soul to organize the life of the animal.

In a similar fashion, Boullier concludes that the docility of animals even less demands the attribution of reasoning power to them. Learning implies something more than the body machine, for mechanism may explain habit, but not its formation. As with intelligence in man, so in the brute a duly proportioned principle of correction is needed. The effects of new objects upon the body, and thence upon the sensitive soul, together with the effects of the latter upon the body, produce new traces in the nervous system. Learning builds up new mechanisms upon the mechanisms of instinct. With this view of instinct and learning, neither too much nor too little is granted to the brute.[66]

In the twelfth and thirteenth chapters of the second part, Boullier seeks to refute a class of objections to the doctrine that animals possess sensitive and spiritual souls. This class of objection consists of those which govern the whole controversy: they depend upon certain theological ideas. Their refutation, like the objections themselves, reflect not so much the advance of science as the reconciliation of new metaphysical and scientific ideas with tradition.

Descartes had taught men to understand by "soul" a spiritual

---

[65] *Ibid.*, pp. 207–9.
[66] Part II, ch. x. As for the third class of acts, alleged to be inexplicable either by habit or instinct, Boullier dismisses them on the grounds of inaccurate observation and our failure to appreciate the possibilities of mechanism, particularly when we fail to remember that mechanism means divine design. Boullier extends mechanical explanation wherever it suits his purposes. Cf. Part II, ch. xi.

substance. Wherever the Cartesian influence reigned, there the term "soul" meant spiritual substance, the essence of which is thought (as reflection, as conscious experience, as immediate experience), or else the term meant nothing at all. Moreover, spirituality meant immateriality, and since immateriality meant indestructibility, immortality was implied. The immortality of the animal soul seemed to follow from its nature as spiritual substance—and Cartesian anti-automatists, such as Boullier, and Peripatetic opponents of Cartesian ideas were at one in recognizing the danger of this conclusion. The immortality of the brute soul is an opinion "trop choquant & trop ridicule aux yeux de la Raison même" to be acceptable.[67] Moreover, it is proscribed by authority. But either the animal soul is immortal or it is not: if it is not, but is identical with or at least similar in essence to that of man, then human immortality is endangered. If the human soul be not immortal, and yet it is a spiritual substance, then spirituality and immateriality do not necessarily imply immortality. But with this we lose the fundamental metaphysical proof for the immortality of the soul, and one of the most striking claims of the new philosophy to respectability is dissipated.

The recognition of the difficulty was widespread. Guer characterizes the consequences of attributing a spiritual soul to brutes as "effrayantes," and Bayle somewhere describes them as "horrid." It is impossible to doubt that one reason why Peripatetics clung to the sensitive soul, capable of feeling and perception, while denying the applicability of the Cartesian definitions of the spiritual soul, was precisely the belief that only in some such way could the proscribed consequences be avoided. Bougeant says this in so many words.[68] Moreover, the difficulty was apparent to very early followers of Descartes. Pierre Sylvain Régis describes the predicament that the choice between the animal soul and automatism brought about.[69] He insists that Cartesian dualism rendered impossible any escape by searching for a middle

[67] Boullier, Part II, pp. 226 ff.   [68] Bougeant, pp. 13–14.
[69] *Systeme de philosophie, contenant La logique, La metaphysique, La physique, et La morale*, Paris, 1690, Tome II, Livre septième, Part 2, pp. 631–32. In connection with Régis, I must express my indebtedness to the unpublished dissertation on Régis of F. F. Swertfeger.

ground. Nothing is more unreasonable than to attribute to brutes a soul that is a substance really distinct from the body, while at the same time maintaining that it cannot exist independently of the body. For this would be the same thing, says Régis, as the assertion that the brute soul is both a substance and a mode, an independent existence and also an attribute depending upon a subject for its existence. It is equally idle to define it as an incomplete substance. The brute soul would then be either incomplete in itself, or incomplete in relation to the composite of soul and body. If the former, it is not a substance, for it is of the essence of substance to exist by itself. If the latter, it cannot be incorruptible and therefore cannot be spirit. Finally, says Régis, the doctrine that the brute soul is a substance distinct from the body, but of a nature different from the human soul is a perfectly empty hypothesis. It is quite remarkable to note, in Régis and others, how unquestionable is the Cartesian dichotomy of things. One after another agrees with Régis that the mind simply cannot think the thought of a thing which is neither spirit nor matter. As for those who say that the brute soul is veritably a substance that thinks, is distinct from body, and can exist independently of it, we must see that this doctrine cannot be proved. Animals, that is, cannot speak, they cannot give us assurances of an inner spiritual experience. Moreover, if we dally with such an idea, we must accept the consequences, and the consequence of primary importance is the necessity for immortality of the soul of the animal. It is especially this consequence that leads Régis, despite his fidelity to Cartesian doctrine, to the cautious conclusion that whatever "penchant que nous puissions avoir à donner aux bêtes une âme distincte de corps, nous aimons mieux suspendre notre jugement à cet égard." The conception of the animal as an automaton should be taken as a working hypothesis only, and this all the more because of the patent success of the hypothesis. Régis, in short, expresses the discovery that the Cartesian principle of automatism defines a predicament for which no solution comes to mind.

Boullier's efforts to escape from the predicament is a beautiful expression of the artifices adopted for the reconciliation of the

old and the new. In the first place, the *certainty* of immortality
is given only through revelation; to this reason can indeed add
probabilities of a high order, but nothing more. So revelation
and rational probabilities agree in showing that God plans human but not animal immortality. But why does reason indicate
the improbability of animal survival? This survival remains possible, but it is improbable precisely because the immortality of
the brute soul would be derogatory to the work of the Creator.
For the soul of brutes, being purely sensitive, possesses only functions narrowly limited to the body. Its dependence upon the body
is so close that, so Boullier really thinks, its immortality is out
of the question. We could assign no content for an eternal life of
a merely sensitive soul. The matter may be stated in another form:
God has made the brute soul to go with the animal body; they
are so closely proportioned that the soul can have no function
save in strict connection with the animal machine. In addition
we must recognize that the brute soul can neither think the thought
of immortality nor desire it. It would be incredible that God would
give to the soul an end which it was incapable of entertaining
in thought.[70] Anthony Le Grand, the apostle of Cartesianism in
England, states the situation in this way:

. . . supposing the *Souls* of *Beasts* to be *Spiritual* and *Indivisible*, it will
follow that they are also *Immortal*; Neither is there any *Argument* drawn
from the *Light* of *Reason*, whereby we can prove the *Immortality* of
Human Souls, which will not as well prove the same concerning the
Souls of *Beasts*. Besides, if we allow *Knowledge* to *Brutes*, we must also
make them capable of *Religion*; for to imagine a *Knowing* or *Thinking*
Creature, without being under an obligation to obey *God*, and pay *Religious Duties* to him, is repugnant. For if the *Souls* of *Beasts* be *Knowing*,
they will in the first place know themselves; and it is impossible but
that by knowing themselves they should be led to the *Knowledge* of their
Creatour. Which Opinions would pave a ready way to *Atheism*.[71]

Immortality must remain the prerogative of man. The medieval
picture of God, man, and the world provides still the framework
within which Cartesian ideas must be envisaged. The human soul
lies between the angel and the beasts, joining clear ideas and
the confusions of sensation; akin to God in substance, it must work

---

[70] Part II, pp. 233–35.   [71] Le Grand, pp. 255–56.

out its salvation in a momentary alliance with a bodily machine. The world of matter is there according to the divine plan, for the use, for the contemplation, of spiritual souls. Even sensation, in the providence of God, constitutes a part of human happiness: from this, indeed, Boullier thinks, we may perceive that the dogma of the resurrection of the body is comprehensible to reason.[72] But the destiny of the brutes must not be confused with the destiny of man. If, however, we are led to allow the immortality of the brute soul because of its spiritual nature, our conclusion would be virtually a denial of the Creator's whole plan of salvation. Boullier secretly fears, one suspects, that the immortality of the animal soul would imply equally the resurrection of the animal body.

The question of immortality is intimately related to another problem that the possibility of a spiritual animal soul raises. A second set of objections, based upon ethico-theological grounds, must be refuted. These are, in effect, the "effrayantes" consequences to which Guer refers.[73] How can we escape attributing moral responsibility to the brutes? How are the sufferings of brutes to be reconciled with the goodness of the Creator? What meaning can pain have in the case of brutes? Were they machines, they could not suffer. But their endowment of sensitive souls means that pain is a part of their lot. Now the controlling maxim is: "Sous un Dieu juste, on ne peut être miserable sans l'avoir merité." The maxim, Boullier states, is so fundamental that it should be regarded as "une loi éternelle de l'ordre." [74] The meaning of suffering and pain is moral; it is a part of the general pro-

[72] *Ibid.*, ch. xvii.
[73] Guer, pp. 142 ff. Guer tells us that one Le Gendre proposed as alternative hypothesis that the souls of beasts at death go into other animal bodies, or otherwise that we believe the souls of beasts to fall into nothingness, on the grounds that such souls were created by God just to endure through the life of the animal body, but no longer. Guer recounts the arguments drawn from the undeserved sufferings of beasts (pp. 175 ff.).
[74] *Ibid.*, p. 243. Dilly argues to automatism from the same principle. The fact that, were beasts to possess souls, they would suffer without desert, constitutes a proof that they are machines. In the case of man, immortality is the compensation for suffering, and so the goodness of God is saved. But either we must posit the immortality of animal souls as compensation for their sufferings or deny that they have souls and therefore deny that they suffer.

portioning of things by the Creator. To suffer is to indicate demerit. But the brutes suffer, and yet they do not merit punishment,
for they are not moral agents. Boullier's reply to the difficulty
is first of all denial that conceptions of merit and demerit have
any applicability to life below the human level. The maxim applies only to rational souls capable of virtue and of vice. But
there is, of course, the wider difficulty, to the effect that suffering
on the part of the animals is a blemish upon creation. To this
our author replies that the physical suffering of brutes—and of
course there is no other sort—is incidental to the regularity and
systematic character of the world. Suffering is incidental to the
comprehensive plan of God.[75] The preservation of the brute and
its pleasures depend upon conditions which at the same time involve the brute's sufferings. The laws of nature would have to
be suspended from time to time were the brute to obtain pleasure and always avoid pain. In any case, Boullier insists, could
we penetrate the animal soul we should find there a surplusage
of pleasure. The objection takes another form: is it right that
creatures possessing spiritual souls, even if limited to sensitivity,
should be subjected to the use and even to the nourishment of
man? But all bodies exist for the use of the spirit. The question
therefore becomes this: is the human soul sufficiently above that
of the brute so that the instrument of the animal soul, that is, the
animal body, can properly be utilized as an agency for the support of the instrument of the human soul, that is, for the human
body? And finally, is it right that this employment of the animal
should bring to an end the spiritual principle adjoined to the
animal body? Again the reply is a recognition of the divinely
established order of things. In the divine proportioning of the
order of things the lowlier animal, endowed with the lowlier soul,
is a means for the higher animal endowed with the higher soul;
and in turn the whole order of life subserves the life of man in
order that the bodily life of man may support the life of the immortal soul. And if, in the midst of this system of relations, the
spiritual principle of animals is annihilated by the infliction of
death, this is no blemish upon the system.

[75] Part II, pp. 250 ff.

L'anéantissement n'est point un mal pour une creature qui ne reflechit point sur son existence, qui est incapable d'en prévoir la fin, & de comparer, pour ainsi dire, l'être avec le non être. . . . La mort à l'égard d'une âme sensitive n'est que la soustraction d'un bien qui n'étoit pas dû; ce n'est point un mal qui empoisonne les dons du Créateur, & qui rende le créature malheureuse. . . . Enfin, nous n'avons qu'à nous dépouiller une fois pour toutes de ce prejugé, qui, lors qu'on nous parle d'un principe spirituel, nous y fait attacher d'abord cette foule de proprietez excellentes qui se trouvent dans notre âme, & qui la qualifient pour l'immortalité. . . . Nous n'avons qu'à nous bien représenter differens ordres de substances immaterielles qui s'elevent les unes sur les autres presques à l'infini, pour peupler, pour animer, pour orner les differentes parties de ce vaste Univers, alors nous admirerons le plan de la souveraine Sagesse, & nous verrons se changer en des clartez ravissantes ces tenébres même qui nous effrayoient.[76]

The controversy concerning the soul of the animal is an incident in the formation of the modern philosophical tradition. Over a considerable period of time philosophers were busy with the question. One way of defining a philosophical problem is to point to the questions upon which philosophers expend great effort. If this be a test, then the problem of the existence or the nonexistence of the animal soul and of the nature of the soul, if brutes do possess such a thing, was a genuinely philosophical problem. Connected with the problem are ideas that have had a history. The controversy appears to us today somewhat quaint and unreal. In referring to it, the past tense seems appropriate. There is something artificial in asking how an animal can possess a spiritual soul and nevertheless not be destined for eternal life. We may look upon the whole controversy, upon its issues, its arguments, and its oppositions of ideas, with complete detachment. Our interest in its analysis is very much like the interest with which we study a game that has been played, that is over and done with. This incident in the history of ideas we may regard as closed.

[76] Part II, pp. 259–60. It should be added that in chs. xiv–xvi our author considers the problem of the relation of mind and body. He gives an account of what he calls the "Occasionalistic system" (perfectionné by Malebranche, he says), of the system of "pre-established harmony" of Leibnitz (the system of spiritual automata, it is called), and finally the doctrine which assigns to the soul the power to move matter. The last, Boullier thinks, is the most ancient and most reasonable of all; but his doctrine of the animal soul, he believes, is compatible with each of the three systems.

Upon further reflection, however, this conclusion may render us uneasy. If we dismiss the controversy concerning the soul of the brute as unreal we begin to suspect that a similar judgment concerning issues of today would be equally justified. The more we linger over the details of the animal soul debate, the more strongly are we reminded of arguments and issues that have not yet become merely historical. It would be interesting to attempt an experiment. This experiment would consist in translating the debate of Boullier, Dilly, Pardies, and the others into current terminology. Translation, of course, can never be literal; and since ideas have a history, the issue itself would undergo some alteration. But on the whole the general pattern of the conflict of ideas would remain. Peripatetic forms may not appear in the new picture, but entelechies would take their place. After one side of the debate has been pushed to its appropriate extreme, and man, too, has been declared to be a machine, the problem will have lost some of its historical remoteness. Perhaps it is prudent to refrain from pushing the experiment any further. It is enough to indicate that even today there are many who cling tenaciously to the economy of explanation which so appealed to Dilly or hesitate with Guer before consequences that seem "effrayantes" or would like to see, with Boullier, "se changer en des clartez ravissantes ces ténébres même qui nous effrayoient."

Boullier's Account of Sensation

Boullier's treatment of sensation seeks to combine Cartesian principles, Lockean ideas, and a doctrine of "petites perceptions" derived probably from Leibnitz. The question of the nature and epistemological function of sensation is forced upon Boullier by his predicament with respect to the animal soul. Sensation must possess a knowledge function, for it is resident in the soul whose essence is thought; moreover, for everything in the human soul there must be something analogous in the animal soul. Knowledge is in some measure a function of the brute. The highest levels of knowledge must be denied the brute, however, or else all distinctive difference between the two varieties of spiritual souls will be eliminated. The sensitive soul of the brute, moreover, must possess a genuine function or God's creativeness is deceptive.

The escape from the first predicament lands Boullier in a second. The rationalistic view makes a radical distinction between thought (the clear and distinct idea) and sensation. The latter is in terms of logical character and epistemological value confused and to that extent not knowledge at all. But sensations are, nevertheless, thoughts in the soul; and the latter's essence is somehow defined by the capacity for knowledge. On the other hand, in the psychological sense, sensations are clear and distinct; each is qualitatively what it is, just this red, this taste, or this feeling of dizziness. The distinctiveness of sensation provides no guarantee of epistemological value.

This defines a dilemma for Boullier with his doctrine of an animal spiritual soul substance. How are clear and distinct ideas of the understanding related to the confused ideas of sense? If clear and distinct ideas are potentially in sense ideas—if sense ideas can somehow develop into or be developed into clear and distinct ideas—then animals really possess knowledge. But then they possess in potency the highest type of knowledge—thought in the eulogistic sense—and this threatens the distinction between man and the animals. On the other hand, if sense ideas and the ideas of understanding have independent sources, the animals are limited to sense ideas. Strictly speaking, they have no knowledge at all. Then there is a radical difference between the souls of men and those of animals. If sensations have no knowledge function, then *what* function can it have? If it be a mere incident in the chain of stimuli-reactions, we might as well drop it entirely, with the result that automatism seems a satisfactory explanation of animal behavior. With this would fall the scheme of explanation based upon God's providence. Finally, whatever the source of clear ideas, knowledge of the external world depends on sensation. For animals, especially, that certainly have no knowledge of a spiritual world, the object of knowledge is the external world of things. We—and presumably the animals— inevitably attach to things the qualities of sense—that is, the confusions of sensation. The situation is that we must preserve a distinction between the clear and distinct ideas of understanding and the confused ideas of sense, despite a Lockean natural history of ideas; we must preserve a genuine knowledge function for the ideas of sense; we must discover a trustworthy connection between the sense perceptions and the things of the world which they in no way resemble in order that the providential arrangement of animal life may be indubitable. With all this it must be possible still to maintain that the essence of spiritual substance is thought.

Boullier turns to the conception of "petites perceptions." Our ideas are either simple or compound. The simple idea is in one sense a logically simple entity. But sensations are confused. They do not reveal anything of the real nature of the material object which causes or occasions sensations. In God's providence the correlation of sensation and thing (or physiological perceptual process) is fixed and regular. Sensation, as thought, discloses nothing at all concerning this objective correlate. But sensation, precisely because it *is* thought, ought to make such disclosure. Now sensation is an "assemblage" of "petites perceptions" that follow one another so rapidly and in such number that the soul is unable to distinguish them. The ("psychological") distinctiveness of a sensation is due to the different blurrings of two different sets of minute perceptions. In correspondence with the minute perceptions are "petits mouvemens" communicated to the nerves. The soul is present in, or compresent with, the sensorium, where the movements from without terminate.

Two observations must here be made. First, Boullier expresses himself in two quite different ways concerning the minute perceptions. At one time his language suggests that the "petits mouvemens" are physiological, while the blurring of telescoping of these *is* the sensation itself—in which case the blurring occurs in the soul. At another time he suggests that there corresponds to every minute movement a minute perception in the soul; and the blurring of the minute perceptions within the soul is the sensation. In the second place, the distinction between the clear and distinct, as against the confused ideas, is here connected with the notion of a Lockean simple idea. The sensations, being in the soul and being thought, ought to be clear, but are not. But the sensations' confused character may be due to its nature as a blur. If, then, we assume that the minute perceptions are in themselves and in principle clear and distinct, they possess the properties belonging to thought. But since we cannot perceive the minute perceptions, but only a series telescoped into a blur, the confusion of sensation may be maintained with the essential clarity of thought. If the blurring did not occur, if the soul were capable of taking cognizance of each minute perception, then sensations would be identical with minute perceptions, and each would be a clear idea representing a particular minute movement. It would be true that the sensation would represent unambiguously the minute movement which is its correlate.[77] Our ordinary perceptions are combinations of pure ideas and sensations. Thus, if I perceive a red circular area, my cognizance of its circularity is due to the clear idea, and that of the red color is due to the "suite rapide de petites secousses" which is the correlate of and the occasion of the sensation.[78]

Boullier summarizes his "hypothesis" as follows: "Notre âme entant qu'Etre intelligent, peut avoir l'idée des corps, sans être unie au Monde matériel, sans qu'il soit besoin de supposer que ce Monde existe. Mais posé l'existence de ce Monde, l'âme connoît ce Monde existant, & lui est unie par les sensations que Dieu lui donne. Les sensations sont des idées représentatives de ce Monde existant, non précisément tel qu'il est en lui-même, mais dans son raport a une portion de matière organisée sur laquelle les différens objets corporels font diverses impressions. L'âme est rendue présente à ce corps organique, par l'idée confuse que Dieu lui en donne, & par son aplication immédiate continuelle & involontaire à se représenter un certain endroit du cerveau apellé le *Sensorium,* auquel aboutissent tous les nerfs. . . . L'âme réunissant son attention sur cet organe, aperçoit, ou plutôt sent distinctement, toutes les diverses modifications de mouvement qu'il reçoit. L'union de l'âme au corps consiste moins dans l'action par laquelle elle se meut, que dans cette perception involontaire & continuelle qu'elle a de tout le corps par l'entremise du *Sen-*

[77] Cf. Part II, pp. 152–53, 156–58.   [78] Cf. p. 167.

sorium, perception qui se modifie & qui se subdivise en une infinité de sensations differentes." [79]

Boullier points out that with this we have the situation within
which knowledge must be defined. The central difficulty is this: the
clear and distinct ideas of understanding (especially that of extension) provide us with the schematic outline of natural knowledge, or a subject matter "en gros," as Boullier expresses it. Between the definition of the field of knowledge in the understanding
and the realm of nature whose universal structure is known lies
the infinitely variable content of awareness, spiritual states, qualitatively distinct, but with respect to knowledge unclear and confused. As representation and as spiritual state, the sensation is
not potential thought, but *thought.* With respect to knowledge,
however, it is confused, and therefore not knowledge at all. Nevertheless, without sensation we can never fill in the schematic out-
lines of a science of nature; but with it the case seems hopeless.
Finally, we must recognize that a fixed correspondence, if it exist,
between sensation and the minute movements in the brain, is not
guaranteed by the deliverances of sense itself.

Our escape depends on a twofold appeal to God's Providence.
The irresistible impulse that leads us to attribute to the external
world the sense qualities that are within the soul indicates the
legitimacy of this appeal. God has seen fit to supplement the
mechanical by the spiritual in order that the spiritual may make
us aware of the mechanical. To know is part of God's plan for
man. This guarantees that sense is genuinely a vehicle of and
for knowledge. Since the essence of spirit is thought, since sensation is within spirit, and finally since thought means above all
clearness and distinctness, it follows that sensation *must* be somehow clear and distinct in its ultimate character, although not for
our immediate experience. Sensation is a blurring of a sequence
of elementary minute perceptions or ideas, that, as ideas, are
clear and distinct and are in fact Lockean simples. If we could be
aware of the minute ideas, if our intelligence were vast enough
to comprehend each one as a separate state of the soul and as a
logical entity, immediate experience and knowing would be

[79] Pages 169–70.

identical. But if man's intelligence were so vast, man would not be man at all, and the divine purposes in creating humanity and the world would be unintelligible.

Enfin je croi qu'une Intelligence capable de faire l'analogie de la sensation genérale que nous avons de notre corps, & de toutes les sensations qui s'exerce dans l'âme a son occasion; auroit une Science complette, non seulement de la structure du corps humain, jusques aux plus petits details, & jusques aux ressorts & aux mouvemens les plus imperceptibles, mais aussi de tous les raports du corps humain, avec les autres parties de l'Univers.

But such a science is forever impossible for the human mind. We do possess, in terms of clear ideas, knowledge "en gros" of the world. But we are forever committed to the possession of the confusions of sensation corresponding to equally confused physiological events, and by extension our knowledge of things is doomed to confusion.

Cet esprit n'est pas capable de voir avec clarte ce qu'il aperçoit confusément en petit; il seroit accablé par une multitude d'idées disproportionnées à son étendue; cependant il jouit de ces mêmes idées sous la forme de perceptions confuses, de la manière dont cela lui convient & dont il en peut jouir.

This is due to the Province of God.

Elles sont pour lui une source d'utilitez & de plaisirs: Et la sagesse de Dieu en tout si digne d'être admirée ne sauroit mieux mériter notre admiration que par cet endroit (pp. 172–73).

Giacinto Sigismondo Gerdil As Illustration of a Later Stage in the Controversy

Gerdil's dissertation on the distinction between men and animals possesses interest because it illustrates the change of emphasis and background in the later stages of the controversy. For Gerdil the question is not the existence of an animal soul, but the demonstration of the human soul's existence. The problem is not defined primarily by the opposition of automatism and anti-automatism; rather, the controversy is defined now by full-blown materialism. Gerdil's opponent is the materialist. Animal autom-

atism had been absorbed into materialism; mechanical explanation had become the instrument of scientific explanation. At an
earlier period in the controversy no one had seriously pushed the
argument from animal automatism to the conclusion that men
are machines. But in Gerdil's era materialistic metaphysics is a
serious movement. For Gerdil the problem is to show that there
exists a distinctive difference between man and the brute, so that
even if we grant automatism as an incident in the materialist's
doctrine, nevertheless the human soul escapes the materialist's
net. There is something more than matter in man.

The problem therefore is *not* to show that man differs from the
animal *in degree,* but *in kind.* There exists a distinctive difference. The difference upon which Gerdil insists is precisely the
difference which materialism denies or minimizes. The factor in
question is the power of forming abstract ideas and of attaching
them to signs. This power is denied by the materialist—for he
denies the very existence of the abstract and universal idea.
Gerdil is obviously writing against de la Mettrie, whom he quotes.
He says:

Les Matérialistes ont senti combien il étoit difficile, ou, pour mieux dire,
impossible d'accorder leur systême avec les idées abstraites ou universelles, dont l'empreinte ne peut se rapporter à l'impression d'aucun
objet corporel. . . . Ils ont donc pris le parti de trancher le noeud de
la difficulté. . . . Ils ont nié . . . qu'il y ait des idées universelles; ils
ont prétendu y suppléer par les idées des signes, & réduire toutes les
manières de connoître à l'imagination (pp. 152–53).

Gerdil must insist, therefore, that abstract ideas constitute an
order essentially different from ideas of the sensible qualities of
bodies. The animals, indeed, may possess the latter; and in this
sense may be regarded as possessing an intelligence. But the
intelligence that cannot know abstract ideas and that is limited
to distinguishing objects by sense impressions is far lower than
the soul endowed with the faculty of abstract truth (p. 109). The
animal does not form combinations of ideas, such as are the fruits
of reflection. The animal intelligence, accordingly, differs from
the human, not in degree, but in kind. Nature in all creatures has
joined to their faculties an inclination that leads them to use these

faculties for their own conservation, increase, and propagation. Man, of course, falls under the scope of the principle; but in his case this inclination is related to a capacity for rational reflection.

Since the human intelligence differs from the animal in kind, but not in degree, Gerdil directs his attention to the refutation of the argument based on degree. There exist within the realm of animal life insensible gradations of intelligence. But we cannot infer that human intelligence is merely the highest degree in the scale. However high in the scale an animal may be, the brute intelligence is subordinated to an instinct directing it upon sensible objects, so there never result abstract ideas. Moreover, the argument based on degrees of bodily organization is equally invalid. We cannot argue that since human bodily constitution is only better in degree than the animal's, and since the more delicate and intricate the organization of animals, the greater the range of sensible objects and ideas from sense, therefore, the human mind differs from the animal merely in a still greater range of sense activity corresponding to an even greater delicacy of organization. In refutation, Gerdil insists that because men do possess abstract ideas, different in order from ideas derived from sense, the real conclusion to be drawn from the argument is that the degree of bodily organization cannot explain human intelligence. Just because the human body differs only in degree from the animal bodies, therefore the bodily organization cannot explain the difference in kind which actually distinguishes the human from the brute intelligence.[80] Gerdil states the usual dilemma: either we must attribute to animals feeling and perceptions and therefore a soul principle different from matter, however inferior to the human soul, or else we must regard their instincts as wholly dependent upon bodily organization, which would leave the brute neither feeling, perception, nor thought. Gerdil states that he will refrain from estimating the relative merits of these two positions. It is evident, however, that Gerdil regards the distinction between the idea from sense and the abstract idea as critically important. In comparison with abstract ideas, sense knowledge can scarcely be called knowledge at all.

[80] Pages 115–20.

The argument that, as God has given perception and hence some degree of knowledge to animals, therefore to the more perfect organization of man he has given a higher degree of knowledge, is invalid. Processes arising from sense and directed toward sensible objects—and animal "sagacity" is always so directed—can scarcely be called knowledge at all.

There are important subsidiary reasons why Gerdil insisted upon the critical importance of universal ideas as the distinctive difference between man and the animals. He recognizes that the materialist will argue as follows: the differences between man and the animals can be explained by differences of bodily organization plus the education process. That animals can be trained suggests that the differences are merely matters of degree. If this be granted, it follows that ideas of religion and morality are merely the fruits of education and therefore have a purely conventional nature. They are "prejudices." To this Gerdil replies that the very differences in the training of man and that of the animals reveals a fundamental unlikeness in kind in their respective capacities. The man born deaf and dumb, later cured of his ailments, did not possess ideas of God, the soul, and morality. But education, urges Gerdil, does not place in the mind such ideas; rather it *educes* them, and does so only because of the original endowment of a capacity for thought present in man alone.[81]

The materialists "sont forcés de rejetter les idées universelles, pour pouvoir tenir dans leur systême," but experience, "en nous assurant ces idées, nous force de rejetter leur systême." [82]

[81] Page 125.   [82] Page 156.

CLAUBERG AND THE DEVELOP-
MENT OF OCCASIONALISM

IN NO AGE was the effort to acquire knowledge more persever-
ing than in the medieval period. Not often has mind possessed a
livelier curiosity. If the Middle Ages be adjudged sterile with
respect to knowledge, at least with respect to that knowledge now
called science, it was not for lack of zeal. Moreover, the conviction of the utility of knowledge was not lacking. Alchemy and
astrology were nothing if not efforts of mind to assist in the control of human destiny. There is but a half truth, not a whole truth,
in the statement that modernity is marked by the ideal of the
control, through knowledge, of nature in the interests of human
welfare. Nevertheless, such statements as these are seemingly
paradoxical.

What, then, is the reason for the appearance of paradox? What
is the difference between the meaning and the employment of
knowledge, especially knowledge of nature, in the Middle Ages
and in modern times? The difference does not reside in the depreciation of knowledge by the one and its appreciation by the other,
whether we think of knowledge as an end in itself or as an agency
of control. Both ages are in agreement that through knowledge
the control of human destiny is to be assured. The difference turns
upon dissimilarity in the conception of what constitutes the
destiny of man and of what constitutes human welfare. The
medieval mind defined this destiny and this welfare in theological
terms. Human welfare was salvation of the soul. The end of man
was delineated by revelation; the application of knowledge for
the control of human life was directed to the attainment of this
end, and the church was the agency of its accomplishment. The
Christian Epic, to summarize by adopting Santayana's phrase,
defined the boundaries of nature and life and human welfare. The
progress of knowledge must occur within the sphere thus defined
for the imagination. Advance in knowledge meant the increasing
convincingness of the intellectual presentation of the doctrinal

content. It meant augmentation of the power of the Divine Institution, practical efficiency in bringing the human race to salvation. These things implied the growing effectiveness of control over life and a more adequate direction of human energies towards the consummation of its destiny. Nature was not forgotten. Perhaps it is erroneous to think that nature was not construed in what were thought to be its own terms. Given the drama of Salvation as defining the world for imagination, to view comets and plagues as portents and disciplinary functions was for that mentality to conceive nature in its own terms. To exorcise a demon or to suppress heresy was to be intensely practical when nature, conceived as a hierarchy of means and ends, is the scale or ladder of things leading to God. To realize on earth the Kingdom of God required the control and effective alteration of nature, and of the inner and outer man. There remained the qualifying thought that even were this embodiment of righteousness attained upon earth it would be only a prefigurement and a symbol of a transcendent destiny.

That such statements are not a matter of words only is indicated by the character of the early modern reaction. This reaction did not involve a rejection of medievalism as such. It did not cast aside as so much rubbish the medieval scheme of things. The radical step taken with the inception of the modern point of view was a sundering of the medieval whole into two portions. The distinction was made between that which is theological and that which is natural; the subject matter for theological investigation is separated from the subject matter for the investigations constituting the philosophy of nature or science. The medieval integration of theology and science, of God and nature, is abandoned. The statement that the medieval mind conceived man and nature theologically may be misleading; it suggests that the medieval mind brought together two things that could have been and had actually been conceived as separable. But such a statement reflects modernity's view of medievalism, not medievalism's view of itself. The modern mind began with the assumption of the position that the study of nature could be conducted independently of theology and theology could flourish independently of the former type of investigation. The Christian Epic, in the large sense, was not rejected. It was excluded methodologically from the study of the stars, of human anatomy and physiology, and of human nature and society. But many of those who were inaugurators of the new movements proclaimed, and with sincerity, their fidelity to ecclesiastical authority, to revelation, and to the destiny of man as defined in the Drama of Salvation. The epistemological and metaphysical skeptic did this. The founders of mathematico-physical science did it. Despite the differences between Protestantism and Catholicism, this twofold loyalty was common to Protestant and Catholic innovators alike. Perhaps the generalization may be hazarded that ultimacy of explanation was recognized as given by the medieval scheme, while men were skeptical of obtaining knowledge by the application of this scheme to the details of life and nature. Or, rather, knowledge (at least of nature) is taken to mean something for which medieval patterns of thought are useless. Theology becomes the horizon of the field of natural inquiry. It is supposed to encircle and, indeed, to define this field. Inquiry, attaining this limit in its exploration, is supposed to recognize the limitation with due humility. So the theologico-epical scheme becomes a final refuge when independent interpretation of things reaches its ordained boundaries. Thus, Occasionalism appealed to divine operation when the explanation of the relations between things seemed to terminate in insuperable contradictions. While this plan secured a somewhat qualified independence for investigation, at the same time it retained the comforting assurance of the ultimate harmony of the results obtained with the traditional cosmic scheme.

How this breaking apart of the medieval whole came to be effected needs explanation. If for modernity medieval science and its applications did not seem to be science at all, whether pure or applied, it was not because the newer mind took from the very first a radically different view of the essence of human welfare and of the final destiny of man. It appears necessary to think that, having separated nature and life in their details from the traditional view concerning ultimate ends and meanings, the new reaction on its negative side was a matter of detail, not, so to speak, a sweeping wholesale rejection of the medieval standpoint. Perhaps this two-sided reaction was in part born of sheer weariness. On the whole, the geocentric and the anthropocentric theories concerning the structure of the solar system fitted very neatly the medieval epical scheme. Dissatisfaction arose, not because the epical scheme was cast aside altogether, but because the details resulting from improved processes of observation could not be fitted into the geocentric plan without excessively complicating it. There is something genuinely expressive of historical fact in the story of the king who, stupefied by the complexities of that Ptolemaic astronomy, felt he could have given the Creator some good advice had he been present at creation. The separation of the epical scheme and the investigation of nature and life may thus have been suggested by the impossibility of carrying out the arrangement in detail. And the separation, in so far as it was effected, in turn cooperated with other elements to turn attention to more accurate observation and interpretation of the details. All the factors commonly enumerated in explanation of the modern reaction—the widening of the intellectual horizon by exploration and discovery, inventions that increased confidence in human resourcefulness, the growth of industrial interests— cooperated in this process of disentangling the general scheme of medievalism and the detailed tasks of investigation in the field of the natural. Newer purposes conceived as practical aims for mankind suggested new ways of observing and interpreting nature and human nature. And reciprocally, as the latter showed results, new aims for man and society, new goals of effort, emerged. Modernity perceived the futility of medieval science and learning, with its alleged uses, not merely because medieval science and learning were illegitimate in principle, but just as much because they seemed irrelevant (rightly or wrongly) to newer ideas as to what human welfare consists of and as to when it can be found. All ages yearn for salvation; they differ only with respect to what salvation is and how it may be attained. Even a slight change in the notion of what salvation is, will involve changes in the methods of getting it. It is even more obvious that the conviction of success as to method will rapidly change the content of the term. Of course, the claims of the Church were admitted. Men insisted upon the truths of revelation and theology. They acknowledged the theological definition of human welfare and destiny. But these admissions concerned the horizon of thought and feeling and action.

These acknowledgments were sometimes mere prudential gestures. On other occasions they expressed the belief that one could both eat and have his cake; the separation of the natural from the supernal, of the field of independent investigation from the field of investigation under the controlling guidance of revelation and authority, suggested the conviction that men could live naturally and die theologically. Men sought everywhere for a new method of controlling this life—and, thinking they were discovering it, tried to turn the results into a new approach to the salvational horizon. It is not in physics alone that men looked for new ways of getting things done. De la Chambre's *Art of Knowing Men,* with all its absurdities, was intended to be intensely practical. This art and its alleged possible fruits fell within the cosmic circle of the medieval schema, and De la Chambre was not prepared to question its finality. He would substitute physiology and psychology for exhortation and exorcism, and political leadership for clerical guidance in the control of life—of *this* life. The other life was to remain in charge of the clerics. Within the more restricted circles of daily human affairs there was room for a knowledge and an art efficacious for the control of human welfare.

Modernity began its intellectual history, not with a radical redefinition of the task of mind, but with hesitating substitutions and apologetics. It did not separate what had been confused. On the contrary, it sought to break apart a system, singularly unified in spirit and in principle. Rejecting one fragment, it preserved tenderly the other. Faced with the need for verification, the early modern mind could find it only by relating the parts in external ways. As the delineation of spheres of influence in world politics breeds quarrels, so with this device of the modern mind. The medieval tradition at last defines, not the power of mind, but its frailty.

From the generality of the preceding description to the details of Clauberg's philosophy may seem to be a long step. The general setting, however, is part of the explanation of the twist that Clauberg gives to Cartesian doctrine and of his sensitivity to certain of its difficulties. He was reared, we are told by Bouillier,[1] in the reformed faith and in great piety. He became a professor of theology and philosophy and an excellent expositor and defender of the Cartesian doctrine. Faithful to Cartesian teaching in general, and even in many details, he extended and altered it in some respects. It is probable that his Protestantism and its theology influenced him in many of these departures from strict Cartesianism.

The problem of the relation of body and mind engrossed Clauberg's attention. The doctrine of the master, of course, had made connection, interrelation, or commerce of either with the other a perplexity. The body-mind question took a form that made it an instance, although it becomes the most aggravated case, of a very general problem. The task of natural science was, in general, the observation and interpretation of the constant relations found within the system of things. When dealing with things of the same order of existence this task presented difficulties enough, as is indicated by the efforts to comprehend the transmission of motion from one thing to another. The Occasionalists raised the question why and how one object striking against another set the second thing in motion. The thing moving possesses its motion. How can it lose that motion? How is the latter, so to speak, detached from the thing and transferred to a second thing? The facts as directly observed reveal no transmission of motion. What perception indicates is a proportionality in the behavior of things—an interadjustment or correlation. The alleged causal operation of one thing upon another is diluted into the undeniable fact of orderly interrelation. Causes are occasions. What is observed must be interpreted in this way, that God, on the occasion of the contact between two objects, effects the diminution of the motion of the one and the beginning of motion of the other. Thus, the relatedness of things implies God.

[1] *Histoire de la philosophie cartésienne,* 3d ed., I, 294.

But when the things related are found in wholly dissimilar
fields of existence, the problem is aggravated. Body and soul,
extension and spirit, in some sense correspond; they function in
harmony and agreement, or form a cooperative unity. Observation suggests this. Teleological conceptions would reinforce it.
This vague notion was a commonplace. Witness Locke's steady
correspondence (the work of God) between ideas of secondary
qualities and the real properties of things; or the notion of sensation as useful signs, indicated by Descartes. The body could not
be regarded merely as a prison of the soul and an impediment
to the spirit. Modernity had discovered nature as a system whose
order is expressible in mathematical terms, which gave an opportunity for exactitude and generality of knowledge. Moreover, it
was discovered to be a vast machine comprising many machines.
When the human body is taken as a machine, the correlating of
the welfare of the soul with the welfare of the body becomes an
irresistible thought. If the body be an instrument of the soul, then
the efficacy of the instrument means precisely the exquisite perfection of its design as a machine. Again if the machine-body has
a soul attached thereto, it assuredly exists in the interests of the
nobler thing, and the soul must be adjusted to the body in a manner insuring the soul's sensitivity to the condition and operation
of its adjunct. Such a view very naturally falls between medieval
conceptions and the simplification of later materialism or spiritualism. Even though philosophers were placing sensations and
perceptions within the mind, and so leaving the external world as
something with which contact was made by way of a state of the
soul, they were not yet prepared to deny the existence of that
external world as a brute fact demanding recognition. They were
still less prepared to overcome the duality of existence by defining the material world as a phenomenal manifestation of the
spirit. God had created it, of course, but as created it was there
and must be reckoned with. Descartes had defined its essence. And
it had been defined as the antithesis of soul substance. The account
of the body in mechanistic terms was, in effect, a disguised but
more perfect teleology. So the study of bodily structure and function tended to confirm, rather than to lessen, the conviction that

the natural welfare of man could be read from the structure of his body.

The union of soul and body is in one sense natural, for man is a part of creation. And there is a union. With regard to the antithetical character of the component parts, the actuality of this union might seem impossible. Why should not the states of the soul happen in their own order and the occurrences in the body and in nature in an order wholly belonging to nature, without the possibility of relating the one to the other? Why should the conviction of systematic relation or harmony be forced upon us, when, since the substances are wholly disparate, no regularity and no correspondence could be deduced from the bare existence of the antithetical substances? What sense could be given to such a statement as that a percept in the one corresponded to an event in the other? It is apparent that to have doubted this correspondence would have been to imply the deceitfulness of the Creator.[2] One might add that a failure of correspondence would have implied not merely the deceitfulness of the Creator but our inability to relate created mechanisms—the mechanism of perception, for example—with notions of utility, and so would imply a questioning of God's providence. If teleology cannot be translated into mechanism in the case of the human body, then in what instance can we effect the translation? If God's providence is to be retained when things are taken as machines, this retention must be possible in the case of the human body, or it must be rejected everywhere.

After all, Descartes had never denied this systematic coherence of the bodily and the mental—he had only made it a metaphysical problem. The problem was framed in such a way that no solution is possible so long as we confine attention to the two finite substances. The body-soul problem, crucial as it was, had to be placed within a wider setting.

The problem, then, falls within the scope of two conceptions. In the first place, it must be considered naturalistically, so to speak; in accord, that is, with the general spirit of the new standpoint of inquiry. Clauberg does not ask why there is a material

[2] This would follow, of course, from *Meditation VI.*

world at all—it is indubitably there. Not asking this question, he does not raise the metaphysical question: why has the mind a body at all? The relation of soul and body—assuming without question the dualism—is to be viewed naturalistically. Studied as any other relation between created things is to be studied, it must be conceived in terms of vital function, of practical efficiency. The meaning of the union of disparate substances is incidental to man's career in a cosmos of things. In this there is an expression of the characteristic conception of control, of the strain of practical interest running throughout even the most theoretically independent efforts of early modern thought.

In the second place, however, the union of the two disparate substances, unquestionable as fact, is also unquestionable as an illustration of God's providence. But it remains inexplicable in terms of vital function and practical efficiency alone. When we have conceived the orderly relation of these substances in terms of efficiency, there remains the persistent problem how there can be any such efficiency and why there should be any such union at all. The limited investigations of physiology, neurology, and physics may explain in some detail the meaning of this efficiency. But they cannot make intelligible the assumptions that must be made before this efficiency is investigated. This more fundamental question leads us to the horizon of thought—and there the medieval schema provides the solution. In this fashion Clauberg solves the Cartesian problem by turning efficiency into God's providence.

This general statement may serve by way of outline. To it we shall return after a survey of Clauberg's doctrine.

Clauberg's physics follows Descartes' faithfully. Physics is the science of natural things.[3] Metaphysics has the supernatural for

[3] "Physica est scientia rerum naturalium." Hereinafter quotations from the *Opera physica, id est, physica contracta, disputationes physicae, theoria viventium, & conjunctionis animae cum corpore descriptio* (Amsterdam, 1691), will be indicated as follows: "Physica contracta," *PC*; "Disputationes," *DP*; "Theoria viventium," *TV*; and the portion described as "Corporis et animae in homine conjunctio," etc., as *C*. The work entitled *De cognitione Dei et nostri, quatenus naturali rationis lumine, secundum veram philosophiam, potest comparari exercitationes centum, duisburgi ad rhenum,* 1656, will be referred to as *CDN*.

its subject matter. The subject matter of physical science, however, is corporeality. Corporeal things, considered generally, consist of things extended in three dimensions. A thing without
length, breadth, and thickness is nothing—that is, so far as we
refer to corporeal things, to which alone extension belongs.
Qualities, asserts Clauberg, are not things at all.[4] He is sensible
of the economy and simplifying power of the Cartesian definition
of matter. He refers to Occam's razor and asserts that extension
is a sufficient basis for motion, figure, position, and all other
accidents.[5] Cartesian physics needs defense, however, and Clauberg proceeds to support the definition of matter as in essence
extension. To figure, situs, motion, and rest we can refer divisibility, continuity, magnitude, rarity and density, porosity and
solidity, place, distance, and the like. Various sensible qualities,
such as color and sound, are perceived in corporeal things. To
these philosophers add occult qualities and regard the latter as
having the same origin as the sensible or manifest qualities in
the substantial form which determines the nature of each thing.

Now it is most interesting to note that Clauberg's defense of
the Cartesian notion of matter is an attack on substantial forms
and that the attack is based on the assumption of the Cartesian
dualism. If the essence of body consist in substantial form, he
argues, this form is either material or immaterial. If the latter,
it cannot be constitutive of materiality. The point is that this
objection would be irrelevant were the distinction between the
material and the immaterial merely the traditional distinction
between matter and form, rather than the Cartesian distinction
between extension and spirit.[6] He proceeds to urge that if the
form be material, the question remains what the essence of the
material thing is, for form neither as a name nor as a notion satis-

---

[4] *DP*, Disputation III. In *PC*, ch. iii, has an interesting title, as follows: "Corporum
formae intelligibiles & utiles: quantitas, figura, situs, motus, quies: in physicis &
mathematicis, naturalibus & artificialibus spectandae."
[5] *DP*, IV.
[6] Cf. *C.*, ch. xlvii. "Animam corporis formam nec assistentem, nec informantem esse."
We can with equal propriety argue that the soul is the form of the body, or the
body the form of the soul. "Si anima rationalis corporis humani *forma* est, quia
motus varios imperando variis illud modis format ac disponit, intuitu situs & posi-
tionis partium . . . cur non simili jure corpus dicatur forma animae, quoniam
varias in ea perceptiones producendo eam format ac disponit mille modis?" (Sec. 9.)

fies the problem. To distinguish between particular things, we must add the notion of accidental forms to that of form. We can, however, accept only that which we clearly and distinctly perceive, and with occult qualities physical science can never be constituted. The context seems to indicate that, for Clauberg, the sensible and the occult qualities stand or fall together when the problem of a universal physical science is envisaged.[7] With respect to the sensible qualities there exist a general and a special prejudice. The former is the belief that all bodies are sensible and, accordingly, that there can be no body where we have no sensible effects. So for many adults and learned men body cannot be defined in any other way than in terms of sense. The more special prejudice concerns the feeling that there is more corporeality in heavy things, such as stones, than in air; so the notion arises that the degree of corporeality varies with weight and hardness.[8]

Reference to the facts of experience—to the variability of the qualities of things—shows that bodies can retain their true nature, that is, extension, while changing or losing their qualities. The same thing can be now hard, now soft. But the essence of body cannot consist in those properties which are variable. This conclusion is reinforced by the consideration that the unity of the world cannot be defined in terms of qualities. Extension is therefore the essence of matter and the principle of the unity of the world.[9] Clauberg recognizes that the new physical science is a reaction against the misuse of the concept of form even more than a reaction against the notion as such. Moreover, there is the additional difficulty of limiting the term to the observed qualities of things, while escaping the ramifications of the idea into the realm of the fantastic and occult. This is the reason for his insistence that forms are to be admitted only in so far as their existence is certain, denied by no one; only in so far as they are manifest to all men as belonging to extended and divisible matter; and finally they may be admitted only when we have as clear a definition of

---

[7] *DP*, VI, sec. 2.   [8] *DP*, VI.
[9] *DP*, VI, sec. 6 ff.; Disputations, VII, VIII, IX.

form as we have a distinct conception of matter itself.[10] Thus, form, if it is to have an acceptable meaning, must apply equally to celestial and subcelestial things.

This virtual rejection of the medieval notion of form, however, is recognized by Clauberg as bringing in its train the problem of finding a substitute. The newer definition of matter as extension increases the possibility of discovering the universal properties common to all things. For scholastic science the forms provided a basis for the differentiation of one thing from another. A thing, indeed, was a collocation of forms caught into unity by a shared inherence in matter. The diversity and specificity of things can be understood as the result of diversity and specificity in the combinations of the forms. The new physics must furnish a substitute means of expressing the particularity of the thing. The diversity of particular things must be conceived as variations in properties that are universal. But the new physics turns the relation of sensible qualities and matter as extension into a problem. Accordingly, it cannot define matter as extension and resort to sensible qualities as the means of differentiating one thing from another. Clauberg recognized that forms and sensible qualities involve a qualitative point of view, and he perceives that the new science is quantitative rather than qualitative. He urges that, since the greater portion of the material world is insensible and imperceptible, sense qualities cannot be universal. Therefore they cannot provide the basis for the distinction of things from one another.[11]

With these trains of thought another coincides in effect. This is the doctrine of the subjectivity of sense qualities. Through habit we are led to attribute to bodies the qualities of sense. Body, it is true, can exist in the absence of man and his senses.[12] Hardness, for example, is merely the experience of resistance. For Clauberg, the source of all the errors of the scholastic physics may be described as follows: the first step was to regard the sensible qualities as objective, or at least to assume them to be

[10] *DP*, XII, sec. 3.   [11] *DP*, XII, sec. 7.
[12] *DP*, VI.

so without contemplating the other possibility; then, in conception the qualities thus taken as objective are duplicated by just so many intellectual distinctions. Finally, thanks to the notion that logical considerations, which have to do with mind alone, are really principles of the nature of things outside the mind, the qualities are thus surreptitiously reified. Of course, once this procedure is followed, the reification of qualities will not be confined to what may be called the natural qualities of things, but will be carried on to include whatever entities are suggested by the distinctions of intellect. In this way the occult qualities are added to the natural and the sensible.[13]

This general character of the Claubergian-Cartesian physics has been indicated. God is the first cause of motion. The quantity of motion in the universe is a constant. A thing is essentially a certain quantity and tends to persevere in the same state.[14] The variations in things can be reduced to differences in figure and in the combination of motion and rest. On the whole, Clauberg regards the Cartesian method as really a reversing of the scholastic. The latter begins with being in general and then proceeds to body in general; from this point it moves to celestial things, and after this deals with subcelestial things, such as men, animals, and plants. Thus the scholastic method acknowledges the hierarchical arrangement demanded by theology. But Descartes, as Clauberg urges in defense of his method, begins with natural things, not as they are in their perfection, but as they are in their simplest properties. From this he passes to the Supreme Cause. Clauberg, it seems clear, sees the Cartesian doctrine mainly in its outward contrast with scholasticism, while its radical difference in principle and in outcome largely escapes his appreciation. Quite

---

13 *DP*, XII, sec. 18.

14 Clauberg formulates what he describes as the first, second, and third laws of nature in the following way: The first law of nature is: "quod unaquaeque res quantum in se est, semper in eodem statu perseveret; sicque quod semel movetur, semper moveri pergat." The second: "quod omnis motus ex seipse sit rectus, & ideo quae circulariter moventur, tendere semper ut recedant a centro circuli quem describunt." The third: "quod unum corpus alteri fortiori occurrendo nihil amittat de suo motu, occurrendo vero minus forti, tantum amittat, quantum in illud transfert." *DP*, XIX, XXI, XXII.

naturally he thinks of the Cartesian doctrine as lying within the circle of the medieval schema.

Body and Soul

Clauberg, like so many followers of Descartes, is acutely conscious of the problem of the relation of body and mind as this is defined in the Cartesian philosophy. When one recognizes how men of lesser stature were wholly dissatisfied with the situation, especially with the artificiality of the pineal-gland theory, one wonders why Descartes did not express dissatisfaction. Perhaps there lay hidden in his mind the thought that, after all, body and mind are finite substances, and the unity of man is not the unity to be found in the infinite substance, or God. The complexity of the situation made the pineal-gland theory, from the standpoint of physical science, both a necessity and a means of eluding difficulties. In the epistemological sense, man is essentially mind, a knower, the subject; and the subject is a principle of rationality set over against a subject matter, nature, or extension. The human body falls within the limits of that subject matter. But the human being is also a subject matter for natural inquiry. The human being is therefore part of the problem of physics. Feelings, perceptions, thoughts, and volitions, however, fall outside the definition of the field of physics. Facts of this order must be studied in their own terms. But sensations, images, and the like seem to be terminations of a causal process beginning with some outside object. The relation of the final term in the causal chain to the earlier terms must be of interest to physics, yet it lies outside the field of physical inquiry. The metaphysical distinction between the finite substances, however, plays a fundamental role in the determination of the subject matter of physics. A universal physics is possible from the Cartesian standpoint only on condition that within the mental substance shall be placed sense qualities and the passions. In the circumstances, the pineal-gland theory is an intelligible hypothesis for science.

Clauberg is evidently of the opinion that the Cartesian dual-

ism, with its attendant physiology and the theory of the automatism of animals, needs further integration. He begins with an
exposition of the doctrine of the animal spirits. The behavior of
animals, he affirms, can be explained wholly by the movements
of the spirits and by bodily structural harmony and interrelation
(*confirmatio membrorum*). The difference between a living and
a dead body, whether that of a man or of an animal, is said to be
like the difference between a clock properly constructed and having the principle of corporeal motion and the same clock that,
when broken, ceases to move because it has lost its principle of
motion.[15] Animals are machines, and God made them. There is,
accordingly, nothing to wonder about with respect to them. On
the other hand, and by contrast, the union of soul and body in man
is genuine matter for wonder. At this point Clauberg indicates
why the Cartesian theologian finds the doctrine of animals as
machines wholly congenial. Immortality follows necessarily
from the very nature of mind. Were animals anything more than
machines—did they possess soul—the immortality of animals
would follow. This, for Clauberg, is a *reductio ad absurdum* for
the assertion that animals are more than machines.[16]

[15] *TV*, chs., xxi, xxii. To the principle of motion in animal bodies Clauberg at-
taches the traditional term *anima*. It seems clear that for him the animal *anima* is
but a name for the animal spirits. As a matter of convention, he uses the expression
"the animal soul." However, in certain passages he seems to suggest that sense and
appetite may belong to the animal soul; and this would mean, of course, that sense
and appetite belong to corporeality and must therefore be excluded from the rational
soul. This suggestion may express a characteristic difficulty experienced by others
besides Clauberg. It is relatively easy to deny the rational soul, that is, rationality,
to animals, but the similarity between animal and human bodily structures makes it
less easy to deny them sense and appetite, sensations and desire. Whether there is
here an inconsistency in Clauberg, or merely a misleading conventionality of expression, may be left undetermined. His main doctrine is certainly uncompromising
in its dualism. Cf. *TV*, ch. xxii, secs. 519 ff. Moreover, he criticizes the arguments
from the similarity of structure. This, he states, leads men to think that the difference
between men and animals is a matter of degree only. Vulgar opinion argues that
since beasts possess eyes and ears, as do we, they must see and hear in a fashion
comparable to ours. As the Nigger Jim in Huckleberry Finn refutes the proposition
that the French do not speak English, but another language, by urging that since
the French are men they must speak as men speak and therefore speak English;
so Clauberg urges that if similarity of structure means similarity of function, then
animals should speak in our manner, since they possess tongue, teeth, lips, and
other organs adapted for the formation of the elements of speech. It is particularly
important to note that the refutation is made to refer, not to thought, but to sensation
and perception.   [16] *TV*, ch. xxii.

How are we to discover what belongs to mind and what to body? And when the apportionment has been made, just what form does the mind-body problem assume?

In replying to the first question, Clauberg enunciates two principles that should govern our investigations of living beings, especially when there is in view the apportionment of the facts between matter and spirit or body and mind. In the first place, he states, anything that we observe in ourselves of such a nature that it can belong also to inanimate bodies must be attributed to body alone. Secondly, anything that belongs to man, but can in no way be conceived as pertaining to any body whatsoever must be attributed to soul (*anima*). In this context *anima* means, not the principle of motion or the vital "go" of the body, but a spiritual entity, as is shown by Clauberg's illustrations. Motion and heat, he points out, by the first test must be attributed to body, that is, to matter; while cogitation, intellect, and will cannot be attributed to any body whatsoever.[17] He asks what possible affinity there can be between cognition and corporeality. Significantly, he continues in these words: "hoc est, inter longitudinem, latitudinem . . . & cogitationem, perceptionem, judicium." [18] With this goes his emphatic rejection of what he calls the common notion that the soul can be divided into vegetative, sensitive, and rational souls.[19] The Cartesian dualism cuts across this triple hierarchy of functions; the functions must be unambiguously assigned either to body or to soul. From Clauberg's standpoint, the sensitive and vegetative souls, if they are to have any meaning at all, must derive that meaning from the bodily mechanism. They are but names of bodily functions.

What, then, is the nature of the human mind? Our philosopher finds that many definitions are unsatisfactory. He would reject those derived from the negation of materiality, from the notion of form or even from the notion of mind as *spiritus* or *res spiritualis*. Of course he has already excluded vital principles as giving the nature of the soul. What remains as the central fact of mind?

At this point Clauberg's doctrine affords a capital illustration

[17] *TV*, ch. xxii, sec. 497.　　[18] *DP*, XXXV, sec. 15.　　[19] *TV*, ch. xxvi.

of the manner in which the consequences of the Cartesian doctrine operate. Descartes, in the first instance, adopted the body-mind dualism, which lay ready to hand, *in the interests of a logical and epistemological problem.*[20] His first interests are defined by the problem of attaining a principle of certainty. The context of the "cogito" is first of all epistemological. The "cogito" does not imply the fact of self-consciousness as the central element in the definition of mind. It is rather the affirmation of rational certainty. The only test of certainty—the only meaning that can be given it—is rational conviction. The dualism defines the subject as over against its subject matter, or nature. In the prosecution of his work, however, Descartes is forced by the consequences of this position to alter the content of the dualism. The substance, the very nature and essence of which is to think, becomes the depository of what we should call all psychological and "psychical" facts. Everything excluded from matter and therefore from the body by a mechanistic physiology is deposited in mind. Mind becomes *res cogitans,* and thinking comprises anything and everything that, being incompatible with extended substance, is existentially of a different character. Thinking and being conscious, thought and conscious states, become equivalent terms. As Brunschvicq puts it, *ego sum* degenerates into *ego sum Cartesius.* The field of and for psychology is defined, and epistemological problems turn upon this psychology.

Clauberg defines the mind as *res cogitans.* But what is signified by *res cogitans?* The answer is to be found by asking what we are aware of as the activities of mind. The mind is conscious of itself when it thinks, wills, doubts, chooses, affirms, denies, enumerates, ratiocinates, loves, hates, and so forth. All this is implied by the one term *cogitare.*[21] Hence mind—*mens seu animus*—is *res cogitans.* But, in order that the human mind may be distinguished from that which is divine or angelic, it is necessary to add: "finita

20 I have set forth in detail this position concerning Descartes in a contribution to *Studies in the History of Ideas* (Columbia University Press, 1925), pp. 83–158. See also the Introduction, above.

21 *TV*, ch. xxv. "Mens enim si intelligit, cogitat, si vult, cogitat, si non vult, cogitat, si admiratur, cogitat, si ratiocinatur, cogitat . . . judicans cogitat, dubitans cogitat, recte sentiens cogitat, errans cogitat . . . (sec. 610). *CDN*, IV.

corpori organico mutuo quasi foedere conjuncta." [22] If a thing is *res cogitans*, it is not extended, it cannot be divided or dissolved or touched; it is not produced by any corporeal force nor by it conserved or destroyed, affected, moved, or given figure.[23] Therefore the principle of explanation that obtains with material things is foreign to the nature of the rational soul.[24]

Mental processes are divisible into two classes, the actions and the passions.[25] The actions of the soul are volitions, and we experience them as coming directly from the soul.[26] The passions are every kind of perception that comes into the soul.[27] The mind is related to its perceptions as wax to the various figures that it receives.[28] The two faculties, the active and the passive, can be distinguished, but not separated. No perception, indeed, can be in the mind without implying the activity of the will.[29]

This apportionment of the facts between body and mind having been effected, the second question arises: What form does the body-mind problem now assume? What is the union or the character of the relation between the two? Quite obviously, perception and will define the problem. On the one hand, Clauberg never doubts the existence of an independent world of material things. On the other hand, pure thinking as such clearly is an intrinsic operation of the soul. But perception and will represent two sets of facts, or at least of appearances, and the peculiar character of these facts, appearances, or experiences lies precisely in this, that they seem to imply the impossible. In perception bodies apparently operate upon the soul; and in every act of will the soul apparently influences the bodily activities and accordingly seems to act upon matter.

---

[22] *TV*, XXV, secs. 612–13.   [23] *Ibid.*, secs. 615–18.

[24] *Ibid.*, sec. 619: "Adeo ut omnes illas rerum materialium affectiones, quas Physicorum pars communis generaliter explicat, a natura Animae rationalis prorsus alienae sint."

[25] The human mind is "actus impurus seu mixtus" and thus has the faculties of *actio* and *passio*. God, however, is *actus purissimus*. *TV*, ch. xxvii, sec. 650.

[26] *Ibid.*, sec. 651: "Actiones voco omnes nostras voluntates quia expermur eas directe ab animo venire."

[27] Passionem generaliter appello omne genus *perceptionis*, quae in nobis invenitur, quia saepe accidit, ut animus noster eam talem non faciat, qualis est, & semper eam recipimus ex rebus, quae cognoscendo repraesentantur," *ibid.*, sec. 652.

[28] *Ibid.*, sec. 655.   [29] *Ibid.*, secs. 657–58.

With respect to perception, the problem assumes several forms. In the first place, there is the difficulty of understanding how sensible qualities, which seem to be the properties of things, and to be given to the soul (so that the soul seems passive with respect to them), can really be, not properties of things at all, but states within and of the soul itself. But the sense qualities are really states of the soul. How they even come by their appearance of being properties of things requires explanation. We are aware of things; but investigation discloses that what we are really aware of resides within the soul itself, not in things. On the other hand, there is an even more fundamental difficulty. Our perceptions are variable and diverse. But experience forces us to the conclusion that this variability and diversity are not due to the mind itself. Perceptions are not the products of an uncontrolled internal spontaneity of the soul. Their system and coherence seems objectively conditioned. In their variety and in their orderliness perceptions seemingly imply something lying without the mind as their cause. Moreover, the world of common sense consists of an immense diversity of particular things. For Claubergian physics this world is really extension. The diversity of things, that is, of perceptions, in so far as extra-mentally conditioned, must be reducible to variations within the common denominator of extension. Things, as they are in the material world, are definable only as combinations of spatial dimensions and motion. If the qualitative diversity that marks the commonsense world be transported into the soul as its perceptions, nevertheless that diversity must be related to and held in correspondence with the field of extension. The qualitative similarities and differences, which seem to be thrust upon the soul, or to be evoked within it by a power operating from without, imply an objective order.

Thus, for Clauberg the problem of the relation of mind and body, so far as suggested by perception, is essentially one of rendering intelligible the correlation of perceptions and things. The diversity and systematic coherence of the perceptions must be related to a diversity and coherence, not qualitative but quantitative, that is, intrinsic to the nature of the material world. The crucial fact is that we cannot escape the conviction of a perfect correlation between the perceptions of the soul and conditions in matter.

Interaction between mind and matter is impossible according to the position of Clauberg. The correspondence of perception and material thing can therefore not be the result of a causal influence of matter upon mind. By "cause" we can mean only occasion.[30] Things, with respect to states of mind, can be only occasioning causes. Cause in the sense of occasion expresses the fact that there is no interaction between the two substances and also that there is a steady correlation between them. This, so far as the *Theoria viventium* carries the matter, is the union of soul and body. Clauberg's thought may be expressed by stating that science cannot carry the problem further.

In physiologico-psychological terms, of course, the question can be more narrowly defined. The mechanistic account of perception implies that the correlation between perception and thing is really the correlation between the perception and the states of the brain. The diversity of perceptions corresponds to the diversity of motions of the animal spirits. Clauberg furnishes the customary account of the mechanism of perception. The first stage is the excitation of the bodily organ, which movement is transmitted to the brain and terminates there.[31] But it is the *animus* that perceives, not the sense organ. The second step is the perception proper, *perceptio mentis;* the third step is judgment, *iudicium, seu animi assensus vel dissensus.* In this third stage alone can error arise.[32] The bearing of this is obvious: the correlation of perception and physiological process within the brain is constant and perfect. The apparent failures of the perception and extra-organic conditions to agree will result, in the first place, from a mistaken insistence upon the correlation of perception

[30] "*Causam* intellige, quae excitat vel occasionem dat," *ibid.,* sec. 665.
[31] The mind is said to be more closely united with the brain than with the body as a whole, *TV,* ch. xxxii.
[32] Clauberg explains the image in terms of brain-habit; the spirits find it easier to go through pores through which they passed on previous occasions. *TV,* ch. xxxix, secs. 951–52. Clauberg's physiological psychology is completed by the study of the passions, which of course are said to be due to the fact that man is composed of body and soul. The immediate cause, *i.e.,* occasion, of the passions is the *agitatio* of the spirits; while the more remote causes are such factors as attention, the "temperament" of the body, and objects themselves.

and extra-organic conditions, and in the second place, from erroneous judgment.

The dualism of spirit and matter, of *res cogitans* and extension, distinguishes the psychological from the physiological and physical. Since the dualism underlies this very distinction between fields of existence, we cannot draw directly from the material or the psychological facts any solution to the problem presented by the correlation of perception and material conditions. The formulation of the correspondence in terms of occasioning cause defines the problem of the union of soul and body as the problem of finding a metaphysical ground for the occasion. The medieval frame of ideas, with due revision, provides the answer.

It is customary to assert that early modernity tried to frame its questions in naturalistic terms, and to answer them appropriately in the same terms. This, we have insisted, is but a half truth. In ethical and political thought, and even in epistemology, the approach is naturalistic, but this is circumscribed by the framework of tradition. The working out of the Cartesian body-mind dualism is a capital illustration.

The study of man is approached naturalistically. Inquiry is directed towards the discovery of his powers and faculties. The structure of the body is examined in order that its functional organization may be displayed. In ethical and political thought the primary question refers to the source of the motivation of conduct, with the purpose of determining how the natural tendencies of human nature can be most effectively employed. Hobbes may have been led to discover the fundamental egoism of human nature because he had a prior interest in certain conceptions of the proper organization of human society. But, having made this discovery, real or imaginary, he believed that his political doctrine was securely grounded. From the epistemological standpoint the powers of man are considered in terms of their functional capacity. It is assumed that we understand human nature in the measure in which we comprehend its natural efficacy. This is perfectly illustrated in that view of sensation which the Cartesian dualism obscured even for Descartes himself. Sensations and pleasure and pain are organic signs. They afford guidance for the activities of the organism in making its adjustments to things. Pleasure and pain are natural symbols of the beneficent or maleficent character of objects. To generalize this point of view, it is clear that the question of the relation of mind and body would take the form of an inquiry into the functional contribution of mind to the career of an animal body. It would have been said that human bodies have minds dwelling within them for the sake of successful living.

All such naturalistic views, however, are checked by the consequences of the Cartesian dualism. The contribution that mind may make to the career of the organism gives way when we inquire how mind can influence body at all. The value to the body of the possession of mind is quite secondary to the question how body can compel mind to take account of bodily needs. That man consists of mind and body is a matter of fact. But, granted the Cartesian conception, it is equally a matter of fact that mind and body are two disparate substances, estopped from communication with one another by the absence of any common nature. Neither the practical efficiency of mind nor the functional organization of the body can be questioned. Eyes, it is clear, exist for the sake of vision. But how can seeing, as it occurs within the body, make a contribution to mind? After all, the purposes that bodily mechanisms subserve lie within mind, not within the mechanism itself. Sensations, let us grant, are unquestionably useful signs. But this utility has nothing to do with mind as such. It is not mind, but body, that is bruised by things. And above all, it must be recognized that man is not equally body and mind. He is body and mind for the time being, but mind alone with respect to eternity. Assuming that mind is of service to the body, this serviceability is only an indirect way of being serviceable to itself. If mind assists the earthly adventure of the body, this assistance is significant only as a means of furnishing the mind with a more adequate instrument.

In this way is defined the framework within which the unity of mind and body must be found. The solution of the problem is to be made in terms of practical efficiency. But the meaning of practical efficiency must be transmuted. Assuming the dualism of substances, mind in the service of body and body in the service of mind lead us to the very boundaries of naturalistic inquiry. At this limit efficiency can no longer be defined in terms of concrete vital situations—it is not enough to know that pain warns us against danger or that eyes supply us with the contours of objects. The efficiency that makes intelligible the unity of mind and body in man depends upon God's providence.

This describes the problem as it arises for Clauberg. In what manner, he asks, can the body be regarded as the instrument of the soul? The body, he states, is to the soul as the pen or the sword is to the hand, as the horse is to the horseman, or the ship propelled by the wind is to the sailors.[33] These are some of his favorite analogies. They indicate that the relation of body and mind is a coherence of mutual assistance.

It is significant that Clauberg describes the relation of mind and body as sufficiently close. That is, this relation suffices. Between the pictured figures of letters and the objects seen, between the objects heard and the sounds we perceive, there is no similitude; nevertheless, certain figures correspond to certain sounds and pictures, and this is sufficient.[34] The necessities of life demand this measure of efficacy; and in turn this efficacy throws light upon vital necessities. If the body usefully heeds the commands of the soul, and the soul expects and receives the admonitions of the body, what further connection can be demanded? These statements, of course, are but more extended applications of the point of view expressed in Descartes' view of sensation as signs of extraorganic conditions. Throughout, the beneficence of the Creator is revealed.[35]

The Claubergian point of view is illustrated in his declaration that the capacity of soul varies with the capacity of the body. His thought seems to be that there is a harmony between the two. Genius and talent illustrate the intimacy of the union. He cannot, of course, assert that the capacity of the soul in principle is the result of the structure of the body. This would be to proclaim the soul as a function of the body and to run counter to the dualism of

[33] *C*, ch. xviii.   [34] *C*, ch. xv.   [35] *Ibid.*

substances. Mental gifts depend upon the union of soul and body. But, we are told, by *ingenium* we are to understand, not pure human reason abstracted from the body, but this reason as assisted by or impeded by the varying disposition of the body. With Descartes, Clauberg declares that the *dotes ingenii* are faculties such as swiftness of thought and facility in imagining things distinctly. The celerity of thinking (*celeritas cogitandi*) depends upon the agility and promptitude of the spirits. He adds that there is no advantage without its disadvantages, and so with men the mobility of the animal spirits leads to vague and light thoughts. In general, the diversity of talents depends upon the human body, especially upon the disposition of the cerebrum and spirits, this disposition being infinitely varied.[36] Besides this, it is to be noted that the soul is no wandering unattached entity. The soul of each man is determined by and restricted to that body to which God has joined it. In this connection Clauberg tells us that he has refuted the doctrine of the transmigration of souls. And, finally, he feels it necessary to argue that the connection of the soul with its own body is narrower than with other things.[37] The mind thinks of objects, not of its own body. When it feels or perceives, it seems to feel or perceive objects, not its own body and sense organs. From such facts one might conclude that the mind is united with objects more intimately than with its own body. Throughout the discussion there is evident a certain embarrassment. Clauberg is secretly struggling against a dilemma. If the soul's capacity be too dependent upon body, the body will seem too self-sufficient. On the other hand, if the body has little effect with regard to the functioning of the soul, the soul will seem to have little need for the body at all. In the end he must maintain the duality of substances unimpaired, while affirming a natural appropriateness in the union. He does not state that every mind is attached to just that body with whose capacities and operations it will be in complete harmony and that to each human body is attached a suitable

[36] *Ibid.*
[37] *C*, ch. xlvi. "Conjunctionis hujus proprium tertium & vicesimum est, quod *anima cujusque hominis determinata ac restricta est ad corpus illud unum, cui Deus illam adjunxit*" (sec. 1). Also: "Mentem aliter atque arctius cum corpore, in quod agit, a quo patitur, quam cum objectis, de quibus cogitat, sociari" (*C*, ch. xii).

mind. But it seems evident that as a part of God's providence there must be an essential appropriateness in every combination of an individual soul with a particular body.

Throughout, then, we have Clauberg's tendency to view the coherence of the two principles as related to the needs of practical life. Mind is limited by the capacity of body, that is, it can be efficient only in so far as the body represents an instrument for acquiring knowledge and for action. The body is steered through dangerous courses, as a pilot steers a ship. Recognizing the facts more or less awkwardly stated in such expressions, Clauberg's problem is to do justice to them, while maintaining the utter disparateness of body and soul. Where the modern biologist would organize the facts in terms of the utility and survival-value of animals possessing imagination and intelligence, Clauberg turns to Providence. It is not merely that the biological conceptions were unknown in his day. This may be true enough, but it is strictly irrelevant. He must appeal to God's providence, not merely because such biological interpretations lie beyond his intellectual horizon but also because the Deity alone could overcome the metaphysical difficulty, that of uniting in one being, in one efficient and coherent unity, two disparate substances. In agreement with this, the union of body and soul is asserted to be both pleasant and desirable. He does not agree with those who would view the body as the prison of the soul—this is an indirect way of expressing the entire harmony of the naturalistic view of man with the theological solution to the metaphysical difficulty. The same observation may be made with respect to his view of pleasure. God has attached pleasure to acts that make for the conservation of the body or for the propagation of the species. The presence in the human being of capacities of imagination, thought, and will is providential. This applies even to perceptions. In principle the soul loves clarity—so speaks the Cartesian. Its union with body, however, is effected by means of confused perceptions. Nevertheless, the union of soul with the body is pleasant.

Despite these practical interrelations of mind and body, mind is really a thing existing in and through itself. It is not merely an appendage. It does not need a body either for its existence or for its operations. There is no necessary connection between the body and the soul.[38] The relation between the two is not that of substance and accident.[39] Likewise, body in no way depends for its existence or operation upon mind. The case of animals, not to mention that of machines, demonstrates the fact.[40] There is no affinity of nature between body and mind, but they exist as contraries in respect to properties and operations. Despite all this —and "despite" here represents Clauberg's consciousness of the difficulty—man must be conceived as one being.[41] The unity of man is such as to permit of the diversity of its component parts. Nevertheless, body and mind are joined neither as two bodies are joined nor as two minds are joined.[42]

The relation, then, of body and soul is not substantial, but consists of a certain mutuality, so to speak, of passions and actions. To understand the conjunction, Clauberg assures us, we must inquire into the matter by reference to the origin of the conjunction. But origin seems to imply a relation of cause and effect. At this point Clauberg refers to earlier propositions concerning the total independence of body and soul [43] to show that no relation of cause and effect between the two is admissable. He then proceeds to argue that the causal relation is not necessary. It is sufficient if there be a mutual reference with respect to actions and passions.[44] He seeks to reinforce this by asserting that mutual reference does not imply even similarity in the actions and passions. The action of the soul is not similar to the action of the body to which it is referred, in the sense in which similarity obtains between one act of the soul and another. The mutual reference is a commerce (*commercium*). Body has its activities and passivities for itself, and the soul for itself.[45] Notwithstanding this emphatic assertion of utter independence in a causal sense, Clauberg again feels the need of an emphatic assertion that the conjunction is "vital and actual." [46] Part of the same reaction is his refutation of the argu-

---

[38] *C.*, ch. xliv, secs. 2, 4. [39] *Ibid.*, sec. 6. [40] *Ibid.*, sec. 8–9.
[41] *C*, ch. v. [42] *C*, ch. viii, secs. 1–2. [43] *C*, ch. iv.
[44] *C*, ch. ix.
[45] Clauberg here takes the relation of teacher and pupil as an analogy. *C*, ch. ix, secs. 10, 11, 15.
[46] *C*, ch. x.

ment that this doctrine is absurd, since it implies a triplicate life, a life of the mind, a life of the body, and the life of the two taken together.

The acts relating body and mind are transeunt, not immanent. The act of the one elicits the act of the other.[47] The process is, so to speak, one of sympathetic induction. Moreover, it works both ways, for Clauberg insists that those who admit the action of the superior on the inferior, of soul on body, while denying the contrary action, are in error.[48] Body can act on mind "by inducing variety and effecting changes in the activities which belong to the mind and are proper to it." [49] Naturally, the same statement applies to the action of mind on body.

At this point the problem must be translated into theological terms. "Actus mentis & corporis nulla cogitatione naturali, at sola Dei voluntate in Homine connecti." [50] The ordering will of God relates affections in one substance with those in the other. It follows that natural cognition can in no may make intelligible why just such and such an act of soul is related to just this and no other agitation of the animal spirits. For the human inquirer there is but the fact to be recognized. There is utility for the soul and utility for the body in this fixed but inexplicable regularity of correspondence. This is the excellence of the union, an excellence reflecting the wisdom of the Creator.[51]

Of course, everything happens as if body effected in the soul such mutations as the soul is capable of, and mind effected in the body such changes as reflect the capacities of the body. But how can immobile mind even induce sympathetically motions in the body, and body, which is without thought, stimulate the soul to think? The first answer to the difficulty is given by drawing a parallel between God's relation to the macrocosm and the mind's relation to the microcosm. God, although immobile, moves everything. If God can be the universal cause of motion, although immobile, the soul (and here, of course, a certain affinity of God and the soul is assumed) can be in a similar way the "cause" of

[47] *C*, ch. xi.
[49] *Ibid.*, sec. 5.
[51] *Ibid.*, sec. 8; *ibid.*, ch. xv, sec. 9.

[48] *C*, ch. xiii, secs. 1 ff.
[50] *Ibid.*, ch. xiv.

motion of the body.[52] Motion cannot be attributed to the soul, for then the soul's influence on the body would mean a transference of its motion to the material world; and this would conflict with the principle that the amount of motion is a constant.[53] The motions of the body are the "procatarctic" cause of changes in the soul,[54] which means that the bodily event induces the soul, from its own resources, to produce just this idea at just this time rather than a different idea or at another time. In general, the bodily event furnishes the occasion for the mental occurrence, and vice versa. In a sense, the mind may be said to be in a certain place and to cause local motion. That is, the mind is where that body which the mind "rules" and by the motions of which it is affected may be said to be. This presence, however, is not a matter of locality or of essence, but an affair of active and passive "virtue." [55] In this sense the soul can be regarded as present to the whole of the body. To assert that the soul is present to the whole of the body is meaningless if something spatial is intended. On the other hand, if nothing spatial is intended the question of the presence of the soul to the body is merely verbal. Presence to body, Clauberg means, is a matter of functional correspondence. The body is an organized unity. With it the soul is joined. This junction means that the soul can be affected (in the sense defined by occasioning cause) by the whole of the body and can act upon the whole of the body. The unity of the operation of the soul corresponds to the unity of the operations of the body.[56]

Claubert translates all this into physiological and neurological terms. He recognizes that the connection of the soul with the body is really by way of the cerebrum. The connection of the soul with the brain is direct, and with the remainder of the body it is indirect. The appearance of inconsistency here may be dispelled by noting that for Clauberg the body is a unified organization or organism. As a system of spatial parts, its connections must be physical. The systematic unity of functioning is, of course, to be

[52] The connection which binds the Divine or angelic mind to body is, of course, different from that obtaining in the case of man.
[53] *Ibid.*, ch. xvi, secs. 1 to 7.   [54] *Ibid.*, sec. 10.
[55] *Ibid.*, ch. xvii.   [56] *Ibid.*, ch. xlviii.

understood by means of the animal spirits. Thus the soul, as a unity, is immediately related to the body, taken as a whole, because that body is a functional unity. The latter functional unity, as a physical thing, is centralized by the nervous system and the operation of the animal spirits, and moreover is centralized in the cerebrum. In this sense, then, the soul may be regarded as united immediately with the cerebrum and mediately with the remainder of the body. In developing this physiological doctrine, Clauberg revises the Cartesian pineal-gland theory. The pineal gland is not that in which body and soul interact, since there is no interaction, but that part of the brain with which the soul is in the most immediate connection, and at which the soul exercises its functions of sensing, perceiving, willing, that is, all of its functions both active and passive. He quite evidently thinks that the unity of the (bodily) organism must be found primarily in the brain, but especially in a central and single organ, which in its centrality and its singleness will be a suitable physical seat of that unity. Thus he effects the retention of the pineal gland as the highest organ of the body, while casting aside interactionism.[57]

It is to be noted that the mutually sympathetic inductions of motion or of thought, as the case may be, that is, the functioning of thoughts and of bodily motions as occasioning causes, is regular, systematic, coherent, a genuine correspondence of fitness. Just this act is the correspondent of such and such a thought, and for a certain bodily motion a certain thought and no other is the necessary correlate.[58] Moreover, there is no time-interval between the one and the other. They are simultaneous—and Clauberg suggests this as a reason why the acts of body and those of the soul are not distinguished by many men.[59] In all these ways the con-

[57] *Ibid.*, ch. xlix and ch. 1.   [58] *Ibid.*, chs. xxi, xxii, xxiv.

[59] In elucidating this systematic connection, Clauberg analyzes the example of one who translates dictated German into written Latin. There are five stages in the process, each of which is specifically twofold, bodily and mental. First, the volition leading to listening, with the adaptation of the ear; secondly, auditory motion and perception of sound; thirdly, the volition directed towards translation into Latin and the bodily preparation for writing; fourthly, a volitional act having as correlate the direction of the eyes to the task of writing; fifthly, the motions of writing and the visual perception on the part of the soul (*animus*) of the written letters. *Ibid.*, ch. xxviii, sec. 8. The soul (*anima*) is said to perceive simultaneously with the excitation of the optic nerve. *Ibid.*, ch. xxvii.

junction of body and soul is specific, immediate, and not indirect. Accordingly, to look for a *tertium quid* is, he affirms, the fallacy of multiplying entities beyond necessity. No celestial spirit or ether is necessary as an intermediary.[60]

Clauberg's psychological explanation of this systematic correspondence assigns two causes for it. The conjunctions of the body and mental functions may be due either to nature or to habit.[61] He assigns God as the cause of the natural conjunction, while, of course, the conjunctions formed through habit are understood in terms of facility through use. Metaphysically, God is the cause of all conjunction. His providence is displayed first of all in the original "joining" of a soul with a body. All other specific joinings are really brought about by God. In short, for Clauberg there is not substitution of the physiology of habit for the causal activity of God. Strictly speaking, habit is a principle of physiological description, while the mental occurrences corresponding to the effects of habit are simply so many instances of the general relation of occasioning causality.[62] Here, in the case of habit, as everywhere, the metaphysical character of the union of body and soul, in general and in detail, demands teleological explanation. Natural functions, useful as making for the conservation of the individual and the race, become a problem, because every such function involves the dualism of mind and body. The bodily function of eating is natural; it is a part of a whole system of events. But the association of the feeling of pleasure with the process of eating is not natural. It is an additional fact, lying within a different realm. In a similar way, the phenomena of habit in the nervous system are natural, but the recurrence of

[60] This may be taken as an illustration of the economy of the Cartesian dualism. It cuts across the hierarchical ordering of entities. For Clauberg a thing is either body or spirit. This needs qualification only where the theological horizon is reached. Thus, man is assigned a middle place in creation: he is midway between the lowest, or wholly corporeal beings, and the angels. *Ibid.*, ch. xx, sec. 5; ch. xxv, secs. 1, 3–7.

[61] "*Per naturam* eas connecti dicimus, quae ab initio vitae nostrae conjunguntur, a quibus vita humana sua capit primordia, ita ut ante quam concurrere incipiant, Homo compositus & factus censeri nequeat. *Per habitum* eas copulari affirmamus, quae postea quam nati sumus, vel repente uno quodam actu satis intenso, vel pluribus remissioribus paulatim per assuetudinem conjunguntur." *Ibid.*, ch. xxxiv, secs. 3–4.

[62] *Ibid.*, chs. xxxv, xxxvi.

an idea in association with a neural process is not. Thus, in place of the medieval point of view, in which the natural is teleological, and the teleological is natural, there is a separation of one from the other. Enjoyments, meanings, and aims are found exclusively within the sphere of mind, and this is a system of events alongside of and independent of the system of physical events. In strict Claubergian terms a bodily process, just as a bodily process, cannot be a matter either of enjoyment or of aim. The bodily machine, of course, implies a design and a designer. But in itself and as a machine it is indifferent. The field of mechanism and the field of meaning and value are completely separated in themselves. Only through the providence of God is a correlation between them effected.

That there should be a composite of body and soul at all and that the correlation of the bodily and the mental should be specific—these things, we have seen, are due to God. The nature of motion implies God as first cause. But the nature of man implies God even more. For man is the most unique phenomenon in the whole of creation. Clauberg asks: What is it in man that we should wonder at? And his reply, significantly enough, is: "Nexus ille, qui est inter mentem & corpus, res toto genere diversas, sui nihil simile apparet in natura." [63] *De cognitione Dei et Nostri*—where should we arrive at knowledge of God save through a knowledge of ourselves?

"Naturalis Dei cognitio philosophiae principium, medium, finis"—this is the title of the second *Excercitatio*. And immediately thereafter Clauberg asserts that arguments for the existence of God must be drawn from our most certain notions, and there is none more certain than those of our mind and its cogitations. He adds the reservations to the effect that while the soul may not be better known than any other possible subject of inquiry—and this is especially true if we consider the difficulties of the relation of mind and body—nevertheless, to the extent that the soul exists and thinks we have most certain knowledge. And from this, he adds, philosophy may draw arguments for the existence of

[63] *CDN, Exercitatio* lxxix.

God.[64] God's existence is not to be demonstrated *a priori*; this means that there is no higher term from which the deduction can be made, since God is uncaused, and there is no higher principle. Demonstration must be *a posteriori* from effects. But of all the effects of God, none is better known than I am of myself, in the sense explained.[65] What underlies and gives specific meaning to this Claubergian standpoint is conveyed in statements to the effect that from knowledge of our minds we obtain not merely an effect from which we can demonstrate God's existence, but a content for our notion.[66] Clauberg's thought may be interpreted in this way: from any point in the created world we should be able to argue to God's existence; if, however, we argue from motion to a cause of motion we prove the existence of a cause of motion, but scarcely what theological tradition would recognize as God. It is within the human soul, and nowhere else, that we find the material which will give the necessary content to the notion of God.[67] When nature has been stripped of all grace and beneficence, of terror and majesty, remaining a mechanical system of concretions of motion within an unending field of extension, the argument from nature cannot demonstrate the existence of God. The human soul, as spiritual substance, is of all created things uniquely a congener of the angels and God. God is infinite substance. There are two finite substances, matter and mind. Whether Clauberg makes the acknowledgment or not, the relation of the infinite substance to the one finite substance differs from its relation to the other. The finite substance mind or the soul is similar in character to the infinite substance. But the contrast between the two finite substances cannot be greater than the dissimilarity between matter and God. Bluntly stated, the human soul is similar, as substance, to God—but this is not true of matter. It is really this vague assumption that underlies the Claubergian arguments for the existence of God.

Clauberg's argument from the idea of God, which is in us, to the existence of God presents difficulties apparently occasioned by the extent to which his thought ran in older channels. The scho-

---

[64] *Ibid.,* III, 5, 6.   [65] *Ibid.,* III, 8.   [66] *Ibid.,* III, 10.
[67] "Ens summe perfectum, aeternum, omnipotens, omniscium, optimum, origo omnium que sunt preter ipsum. . . ." *Ibid.,* VII, 20.

lastic tradition, taken broadly, involves what may be described
as a triple correlation of ideas in the human mind, of nature, and
of God. That which is *form* in the thing, its nature and structural
pattern, is in God *idea;* in the human mind, in knowing, there
appears from intraorganic potentiality the mind's grasp of this
structural pattern. Things, affecting the senses, effect through the
senses the perception of the form. The created world of things
is made according to the patterns which are ideas in the divine
mind; the human mind, so far as it knows, thanks to its commerce
with things, obtains a sort of replica of this structural pattern.
Neglecting terminological niceties, it may be said that there obtains, subject to the finitude of our knowledge, a correlation of
the mind's idea, the form of the thing, and the aboriginal idea in
the divine mind. Now this scheme is seriously compromised by
the reduction of the world of material things to extension. What
had been the forms of things themselves, the causes, resident in
things, of their natural specific diversities, are now, in terms of
the two-substance dualism, effects in the soul-substance.

The triplicate distinction remains, but its character must be
altered. The ideas in the mind of God which constitute the archetypes of things must be primarily mathematical. Clauberg as a
Cartesian must follow the master's formula to the effect that the
infinitude of figures suffices to express the diversity of things.
Moreover, nature "agit en tout Mathematiquement." [68] The archetypes are then primarily quantitative. Cartesianism had driven a
wedge that broke the commonsense world into two portions. Nature, the collection of things, is essentially extension, figure, and
motion. The qualities of things, the qualitative forms, are within
the mind as states of its substance. Within the mind of God, presumably, Cartesianism must introduce a similar bifurcation. The
archetypal ideas defining the essence of things are quantitative
representations of motion and extension. The archetypal ideas
standing for the qualities and properties which common sense
erroneously attributes to things refer, not to external things, but
to states in human soul-substances. Within the field of the finite

[68] *Œuvres de Descartes*, Adam et Tannery, Paris, 1890, Vol. III (*Correspondance*),
letter clxxxv.

there is no longer a duplication in interorganic potentiality of the forms of things as they are in the external world. The duplication is supplanted by a correlation of spiritual entity and physical entity, of mental state with causal processes in a sea of motions. For the correlation itself God is responsible. The correlation is really effected within the divine mind. God's mind affords the very pattern of the correspondence of just this idea in the soul-substance with just this or that process in the field of extension. Strictly speaking, there is as much of a contrast between things as extension and motion and things as perceived when we refer to the archetypes within the mind of God as there is a parallel contrast within the field of the finite substances. That is, the Cartesian dualism in the Claubergian version means that sense-qualities are in no way reducible to or inferable from the properties of material things. In terms of the scholastic system of forms there is no such problem. A thing, in its extension, motion, color, and other properties, is an intersection of forms. Why this given form should be united with such and such other forms in the concreteness of an apple is in one sense inexplicable. The thing is what it is; and it is what it is because God has created just this thing. The scientific point of view of early modernity, however, contained implicitly the proposal to supply a causal connection between the properties really belonging to the thing and those aroused in the perceiver through the effect of the thing upon the sense-organs. This program, it soon appeared, cannot be carried out if the Cartesian dualism cuts across the causal chain. For the alleged terminus of the chain, the sensation let us say, turns out to be a state of a substance wholly dissimilar in nature from the other and prior links in the chain. The problem therefore is to explain how the terminus, which is really no terminus at all, but a correlate, is held in systematic correlation with the physical events. This correspondence of the spiritual pattern with the physical pattern must be referred to God; it is intelligible only in the sense that God must have so willed it.

The situation has important bearings upon the problem of demonstrating the existence of God. We can pass from the ideas and perceptions in our minds to nature only upon the assumption of God as the guarantor of the fixed correlation. From nature, then, we cannot argue to God. The problem of God depends upon the problem of determining how there can be knowledge at all. "In every idea (notion, conception)," says Clauberg, "there is a twofold being (twofold reality or perfection) to be considered: one of the form (*unum formale seu proprium*), in so far as it is an operation of the mind; the other objective (*alterum objectivum sive vicarium*), in so far as it is the image of the thing cogitated, or in so far as it is on account of that thing." [69] He immediately illustrates the distinction by comparing it to the distinction between a word as a sound, or as something figured and colored, and the word as signifying something, that is, its sign-value. In either aspect, he insists, the idea is something. The idea as a state of the soul, in its "formal" being, is real, for it is an operation of the soul. We need not inquire how ideas come to be, for their causes reside within the soul itself; it is the nature of the soul to produce them. The problem of ideas is the problem of their vicarious, that is, their signifying, function. Are ideas real in this sense? They differ in what they signify, but as signifying, they are real or have perfection. [70] Now every idea, says Clauberg, is an image. [71] And every image requires an original (and this original he identifies with its cause). [72] Without this original the idea could neither be nor be conceived, as a sign can neither be nor be conceived unless there be that which is the signified. That is, since there is mind, there are operations of the mind, and so ideas as existences of the kind defined by the nature of the mind and its operations. But ideas differ from one another, not merely, perhaps, because they are different operations of the soul, but because they differ in signification. They present themselves to our minds as signs, as meanings, and to mean is to point to something beyond the idea as an existence. And Clauberg insists that the significant question is, not how we think in general, but why we

[69] *CDN*, VII, 2.

[70] "Cogitationum nostrarum simplicium sive idearum esse vicarium seu objectivum non est nihil, sed aliquid reale & perfectum in ipsis." *Ibid.*, XV.

[71] Clauberg later explains that the term "image" has a broader and a narrower meaning. According to the former, it is equivalent to idea, as when we state that the idea of God is the image of God. According to the narrower meaning, image has reference only to sense. *Ibid.*, XLVI 2, 5, 6, 13.

[72] *Ibid.*, VII, 9.

have just this idea or meaning or form just this conception. Fruitful inquiry concerning things is not concerned with why things are figured, but why they have just such and such a figure, as why the sun is round or flame pointed.[73] The idea in its "vicarious" being cannot be more perfect than its exemplar or cause, and so it cannot have more of perfection and reality than there is in the thing of which it is the image or expression.[74] Just as in nature *ex nihilo nihil fit*, proceeds Clauberg, so the mind cannot form any real concept unless it imitates some thing; and since the whole being of the idea consists in imitation, it cannot contain more than is in the thing represented.[75] But the soul displays to us its lack of the highest perfections; it does not possess goodness without the possibility of the better; it cannot achieve all that it wills; it knows, but also recognizes its ignorance and its doubts. In sum, then, we have the following: there is the idea of God; as an existence, it is due to an operation of the mind, and presumably our possessing the idea is a matter of the natural history of the soul; but the sign-value of the idea, its meaning, cannot be within the soul itself; that is, the soul is not that to which the idea points. The soul is commensurate with the existence of the idea of God in its "formal" being, but not with its objective or vicarious being. For it an adequate cause must be assigned, and therefore God exists. In the temporal order, says Clauberg, my mind knows itself in a positive way and through its own acts, and so knowledge must begin with cognition of myself, not of God. By noticing the imperfections of my own mind I am led to the knowledge of God. I am led, that is, to the extent that the idea of God is formed.[76] But when we consider the idea in its meaning, this leading appears as the occasion for the idea, not an explanation of its claims. Ideas being signs for which there are originals, God must be the cause of the idea.

At bottom, it is clear, the existence of God and the existence of

---

[73] *Ibid.*, 10–11.   [74] *Ibid.*, 16.

[75] Cf. *Ibid.*, VIII, where an extended analogy is drawn between a thought and a picture "ad melius intelligendum pro Dei existentia allatum argumentum utilis," as the title of the *Exercitatio* has it.

[76] "Ut pictor potest semet ipsum delineare; sic potest mens nostra sui ideam formare; & tunc mens causa est & suae ideae & sui ideae, hoc est, diversa ratione est causa efficiens ideae, tam secundum esse proprium, quam secundum esse vicarium spectatae, simul cogitans, simul exemplar cogitationis, diverso respectu." *Ibid.*, VIII, 7.

the world of things stand or fall together. That ideas should be, is not a problem at all. That is, it is a matter of fact that the nature of the soul is to produce ideas. Having souls we have an operative principle. Ideas are its product. But existences of this order, ideas, point to existences that are not ideas at all, to existences that are not even spiritual. Irresistibly they convince us of their correlation with things; and moreover they convince us that this correlation is specific and constant. Things, however, lie wholly beyond our experience. The correlations and coherences of percepts with one another are wholly an internal matter; they concern ideas in the soul and nothing else. The coherences of percepts and ideas are themselves instances of the problem of the correlation of the mental with the physical. Knowledge must begin with the mind itself, with the spiritual soul. The claim that the idea is knowledge can be validated only through demonstration of the existence of God.

The idea of God is in itself but a special case of the representative function of ideas. The form dwells within the soul. Its intentional being is its claim to represent or to point to a thing. The soul produces the idea from its own resources; it claims to represent a thing. The claim is validated in principle when God's existence has been demonstrated. But only in principle. In carrying out the principle the correlation of the soul and the world of things must be viewed as a providential arrangement. The correspondence between the idea and the motions excited in the body remains after all immersed in the mystery of creation. In three ways Clauberg suggests this final resolution of the question. He tells us that it is God's pleasure that this systematic relation should obtain. He says, in addition, that as God shows some of His perfections in the creation and conservation of things, so here, in the correlation of idea and thing, He gives us an example of His liberty and unconstrained power. Finally, Clauberg suggests that in the relation of body and soul we have an image of the relation of God and the world.[77]

[77] *Ibid.*, XCI, 10, 13.

SOME HISTORICAL STEPS
TOWARDS PARALLELISM[1]

THE FUNCTION of psycho-physical parallelism within psychology is somewhat indeterminate. Now and then it is declared acceptable as a working hypothesis. It permits a systematic correlation of subjective experience with observable conditions. The utility ascribed to the hypothesis depends in part upon the type of psychology to which reference is made. Its employment may be advocated in order that the psychologist may escape from the metaphysical problem of the relation between mind and body. To other psychologists the hypothesis is merely a historical monument referring to the day when psychology had not secured its freedom from metaphysics.

Whatever attitude towards parallelism a psychologist may take, he is tacitly recognizing that the hypothesis is not the creation of psychological inquiry. The doctrine was not formulated to organize results attained by specific psychological investigations. On the contrary, it expresses the general metaphysical position under the auspices of which modern psychological inquiry attained its alleged independence. Parallelism affords a striking instance of the controlling power of metaphysical ideas and their consequences for scientific enterprises.

Parallelism emerged from an intricate context within which occurred an interplay of epistemological, metaphysical, and theological influences. The hypothesis did not arise from psychological inquiry, and it was not formulated for the sake of psychology.

[1] The term "parallelism" is used in the sense assigned by MacDougall. He first states that the term is used to denote all doctrines that deny psychophysical interaction, and then gives a stricter account of its meaning. It implies that "physical and psychical processes are equally real; but there is no causal relation between psychical and physical processes; the two series of events, the psychical processes of any mind and the physical processes of the brain with which they are associated, merely accompany one another in time: their relation is one of simple concomitance only. . . . Within each series the law of causation holds good, the successive steps being related to the preceding and succeeding steps as effects and causes; but no causal links stretch across from one series to the other." *Body and Mind*, 3d ed., London, Methuen and Co., 1915, p. 131.

On the contrary, it came into being because of an effort to provide a metaphysics for physical science, and its function was metaphysical and even theological. Psychology, as that term is understood in the history of modern thought, is really a by-product, a
somewhat unexpected incident in a much larger story. It is a by-
product of metaphysical, theological, and methodological inter-
terests in the science of physical nature.

It must be recognized that parallelism is a specifically modern
doctrine. It is neither medieval nor ancient, just as the physics
with which it must be associated is neither medieval nor ancient.
The doctrine usually taken as the opponent of parallelism, that is,
interactionism, is likewise essentially modern. Neither psycho-
physical parallelism nor the hypothesis of the interaction of soul
and body could come into being until the Cartesian doctrine
concerning body and soul had been formulated. Beneath these
hypotheses lie the fundamental ideas of modern physical science.
Animism has, of course, a long history. Descartes, reckoning with
a new program for a universal science of nature, revised in radical
fashion the animistic tradition. The setting within which psychological inquiry must be established was defined by these conditions. Reflection sought to make adjustments between the revised
tradition, the new scientific conceptions, and ethico-theological
interests. These adjustments determined what a positive study of
mind, of consciousness, or of subjective experience must be. It is
not too much to assert that psychology had to be whatever the new
physics and the related metaphysics permitted it to be. Until recent
times, at least, it preserved in its terminology and methods the
influence of these adjustments. Psycho-physical parallelism appeared when the denial of interaction between soul and body
emerged in the development of the Cartesian tradition. This denial
may be viewed both as a consequence of metaphysics and as a
demand for metaphysics. In either event, psycho-physical parallelism appeared as a device for satisfying the demands of metaphysics and theology in the context of a new physics.

Psycho-physical parallelism, then, assumed a double role: it
purported to be a solution of the body-mind problem, and it served
to define the province and the problem of psychology. Here and
there, of course, psychological investigations reflected positions

opposed to the Cartesian. But even in such cases the general context was maintained. In all quarters the situation was fundamentally the same. The problem was to adjust the new view of nature with the animistic tradition and its associated interests.

The parallelistic hypothesis was not attained in a single step. We may discern within the Cartesian tradition a series of approximations to the hypothesis. It is the purpose of this essay to indicate some of the steps that prepared the way for the statement of the hypothesis.[2] In this way, perhaps, light may be thrown upon the historical function of the hypothesis in the development of psychology. The psychologist who adopts psycho-physical parallelism as a device for escaping metaphysics presents an interesting paradox. By a curious inversion, he seeks to avoid metaphysics by adopting a metaphysics.

The metaphysical problem the psychologist wishes to avoid is that usually described as the body-mind problem. More specifically, it is the perplexities of interactionism from which he seeks relief. The psychologist's effort points to an important historical fact, to the fact that parallelism is itself a reaction against interactionism. When the animistic tradition was revised by Descartes, all questions concerning the relation of mind and body were of necessity reformulated. The reformulation, however, made the interaction of body and soul less, rather than more, intelligible. Psycho-physical parallelism emerged precisely in the measure in which this came to be recognized.

The movement toward parallelism, then, is a consequence of the new ideas of which Cartesianism is the outstanding expression. In Descartes' work traditional terminology received new meanings, More than one of his followers and some of his opponents recognized this. Some of the Cartesians, indeed, felt the need of emphasizing this. The Cartesian definitions of spirit and matter, of soul and body, of what it means to be "objective" and what "subjective" were regarded as new definitions. It is misleading to assume equivalences between Cartesian and medieval uses of the same or similar terms. Descartes' philosophy is, of course, in the

---

[2] This paper is based primarily upon a study of the Cartesian tradition as represented in the work of certain followers and opponents. Details and documentation will be found in papers included in this book.

Augustinian tradition. We must emphasize, however, that his followers, even when recognizing this continuity, were keenly aware that it must not be overemphasized. To think with Descartes, they knew, meant to think in new ways, in terms of new ideas, and in an unfamiliar terminological context. Louis de la Forge, for example, makes this abundantly clear.[3] Hitherto, he maintains, the ideas of Descartes concerning spirit, mind, matter, the soul may have been anticipated—particularly in the tradition coming from Plato through Augustine—but anticipation was not attainment. De la Forge admits that St. Augustine, for example, did not make the mistake of confusing spirit with the animal spirit or of identifying processes in the brain with processes in the mind. He urges, however, with equal emphasis, that Augustine did not arrive at the Cartesian truths concerning the soul and mind. De la Forge's reason for this judgment is of the first importance for understanding the place and influence of the Cartesian philosophy in its contemporary setting. The novelty of the latter philosophy, as De la Forge makes clear, was precisely that *Descartes for the first time in history had achieved an adequate and true definition of matter*. The ideas concerning the soul that prevailed in any period in the past had reflected the conception of matter then commanding acceptance. Not even St. Augustine, spiritual forebear of Descartes that he was, had a sound notion of the soul for the reason that he had not known what matter truly is. All the more would it be the case that outside the Augustinian tradition this failure occurred. The attitude of most Cartesian followers may safely be described in some such way as this: you cannot attribute to a philosophy in the past a Cartesian conception of mind or spirit or soul unless you can equally attribute a Cartesian definition of matter to the same philosophy. The definition of matter is, however, the crucial point of the new philosophy, defining the context within which its terms must be comprehended. Therefore, since no one before Descartes knew what matter is, no one knew what mind, or soul, or spirit, or thought is.

Thus, reflection in Cartesian circles was aware of this dissimi-

[3] The paper on De la Forge may be consulted for a more extended discussion of this point.

larity of contexts within which terms received definition.[4] For the
convinced Cartesian medieval conceptions of matter and form
and of their union in a substance, that is, a thing, were doubly
confused. The medievalist might say: a physical thing is corporeal, constituted by the compresence of form (or forms) and matter. The form, then, as the component of a thing, is physical, but
not material. Indeed, for such a thinker as St. Bonaventura, matter is not necessarily corporeal or "physical." It is corporeal and
a component of a physical thing if it be informed by the form of
corporeality, or a "corporeal" form; united with a different form,
matter may be incorporeal—a soul or an angel. For a Cartesian,
however, all of this would indicate that before Descartes no one
had a clear idea as to the nature of matter and consequently could
not define a soul. We have adequate ideas of both matter and spirit
—and then we have Cartesian ideas—or we have adequate ideas
of neither.

In the new context, mind and matter are each substances, possessing essential attributes. So diverse are these attributes that
mind and matter substance are mutually exclusive and antithetical in properties. In these circumstances, if a thing be said to possess form, then by form we must mean the configuration to be exploited in a mathematical physics. On the other hand, if by form
we are to signify something noncorporeal and nonphysical, then a
form must be either a spiritual substance or an ideal within and
dependent upon that substance. The point, for the Cartesian as
against the opposition is not that body and soul, matter and spirit,
are different, but rather that this difference is one of substance,
and the two substances, antithetical in property, divide finite existence between them. Contemporaries of every school were pre-

[4] The animal-soul controversy makes this abundantly clear. Many Cartesians insist
that if a soul is a spiritual substance the essence of which is thought, we must mean
this whenever we use the term. Hence the dilemma arises with respect to an alleged
animal soul: if the animal soul *is* a soul, then there can be no essential difference
between the soul of the animal and the soul of man; if, on the other hand, the
alleged animal soul differs significantly from the human, the expression is meaningless, and there is no animal soul whatever. Either animals are combinations of
soul and body—and so are identical in principle with man—or else they have no
soul in any sensible employment of the term. If the latter is true, it is reasonable to
view them as machines. Régis makes this point emphatically.

pared to admit a difference between thought, mind, or the soul
and body, or matter. In some quarters it was granted that the essence of mind might be thought, yet thinking might be a function
of matter.[5] The Aristotelians might assert the incorporeality of
the rational soul, while urging that the vegetative and sensitive
souls were functions of corporeality. For the Cartesian this was
inadequate, confused, and even verbal. Again, wherever the Cartesian influence penetrated, there came recognition of the confusions due to the long tradition defining spirit as subtle matter. This
notion, associated with that of the animal spirits, eased body-
mind difficulties for some contemporaries.[6] For a Cartesian, however, attenuation cannot define incorporeality. If potency and act
are to receive Cartesian meanings, then the terms will mean one
thing with respect to matter substance and another with respect to
spirit. Between matter and spirit there can be no *tertium quid*.
Existence is never both matter and spirit, but always either one
or the other. This in itself expresses the radical difference of context between Scholasticism and the Cartesian point of view.

The new context, as Cartesians realized, gave man a place
within creation that it is startling and unique. Nothing can be both
matter and spirit. Nevertheless, man is both. He is therefore a
unity of composition and not a unity of nature. Man alone represents this compresence of substances. Since the animals are machines, they do not possess souls. Or, what amounts to the same
thing, since animals have no souls, they are machines. Only in
man are thought and nature conjoined. From this fact there follow important consequences. A problem which involves questions concerning thought or incorporeal being can be solved only
by a study of man. The human being thus becomes the central
fact for epistemology, metaphysics, and theology. Or, stating the
point more accurately, the soul in conjunction with an animal
body is this central fact. For this reason the Cartesian frequently
defines metaphysics as the study of spiritual beings. Metaphys-

[5] For an illustration, see *Objections*, II.
[6] Bayle warns the learned world not to be misled by the word "spirit." The "spirits"
of the "chymists," and the animal spirits in the nerves, or subtle matter, denote
matter in the same sense in which water or minerals are said to be material. Bayle
must have felt that the caution was needed.

ics in some sense is confined to the human soul, the angels, and God. In this the Cartesians were consistent enough. Metaphysics does not grow out of or form a superstructure for physics. Theology and metaphysics furnish a basis for physics. In a sense, physics deals with whatever is excluded from metaphysics, once the field of physics and the validity of the enterprise have received metaphysical confirmation. Thus, the human body, plants, and animals are merely portions of the subject matter of physics. Their significance for metaphysics is indirect. Their metaphysical interest is absorbed into the general interest of physics for metaphysics and theology.

This, however, is not the whole story. In the end, the study of man must provide the means for an account of the relation of nature and spirit, for in man alone do these two come together. The adjustment of physical science to the claims of morality, religion, and theology depends upon the study of man. Physics by itself is incapable of throwing light upon the problem. It may discover that nature is mechanism—but never that mechanism is evidence of the existence of God. Metaphysics, surveying the soul and its junction with matter, must evaluate physics for theological uses. Metaphysics, then, centering upon the investigation of the soul, becomes the enterprise of adjusting the claims of science and the demands of morality and religion.[7]

The consequences are not yet exhausted. The Cartesian context imposes the problem of discovering a new content for the old terms. Nature, now defined in terms of the new conception of matter, cannot directly contribute to the discovery of spirit. In a hopelessly negative sense, physics may assure us that "mind," "soul,"

---

[7] The controversy concerning the animal soul is peculiarly illuminating with respect to contemporary attitudes. Concerning such questions as to how animals could get along without souls, or the purposive functioning of animal bodies, science could be content with mechanism. There was an aggravating problem with respect to man—that is, what the possession of a soul could contribute to the career of man's body—and the defenders of animal souls were not slow to charge that, if brutes could dispense with souls, then man too does not need an additional substance. The argument was powerful, for it would be impious to set limits to God's competence as a designer of machines. But such arguments were really devices of controversy. For the true Cartesian what animals and the human body are is the question of science. Animals are not thinkers or knowers. If nature as a machine with its own laws can be understood as the product of a designing God, then the life of organized bodies presents no difficulty in principle.

and "spirit" possess meanings antithetical to the meaning of matter. Thus, we know that spirit is unextended; we know that, if corporeality means extension, then spirit is incorporeal. A positive content for the terms, however, can be found only by a scrutiny of immediate experience. The test of what belongs to spiritual substance must be found in immediate experience. Spirit, or mind, is the thing that thinks, and this thing that thinks exhibits its nature not in thinking alone but also in sensing, feeling, and willing. The study of spirit is not the investigation of form and logical structure, but the apprehension of the contents of consciousness. This is certainly not what Descartes had in mind in the First Meditation—but it is what he reached in the Sixth. And with this the point of departure for a Cartesian was fixed.

Thus, we perceive how Descartes, writing a metaphysics to insure a universal science of nature, provoked the psycho-physical problem. The problem of man, of this exceptional unity of composition, is to discover how consciousness and things, how immediate experience and an alien world of objects, how personality and mechanism can be related. The question must be resolved upon the dualistic foundation, not despite it. Moreover, the question is real: for the conviction is somehow rooted in the facts. Indeed, only if man be a unity is it possible to understand how consciousness could discover the outer world and the soul become convinced that it has a body.

Given these conditions, what is the central point upon which a science and a metaphysics of man must be pivoted? It is that the substantial components of man's nature retain the characteristic of independence which is the very mark of substance. A unity of composition—which means an external unity—must take the form of a precise interadjustment of components without prejudice to the essential and mutual exclusiveness of spiritual and material substances. Experience forces upon us the conviction that mind influences body and body influences mind. At least, these words describe even to common sense an almost inevitable belief. Since Descartes has discovered at last what mind is and what body is, it is now possible to discover also the facts represented, with or without distortion, in the belief. Beneath this belief lies a unity of composition, and the belief must reflect an interrelation between component substances. A Cartesian, Louis de la Forge or any other, must view the situation in this light.

The exact point, however, has not yet been precisely stated. We must add that each soul or mind is the soul or mind of somebody; it is a consciousness or self, or the substantial basis of a consciousness or self. Moreover, each soul seems to be in possession, not of *a* body, but of *the,* of *its,* body. A soul's relation to the world of things is exclusively by way of a particular body. In perceiving, in thinking, feeling, and willing and in every spiritual activity, Peter's mind is engaged with contents that somehow reflect the career, the organization, and the environment of Peter's body, not of body in general or of some other soul's body, let us say, Paul's. Bergson has described the fact in defining the body as a privileged image. There may be events in Peter's body that are not reflected in Peter's soul; and possibly there are occurrences within Peter's spiritual substance owning no relation to Peter's body. But these exceptions, if they exist, do not affect the conclusion that the unity of composition must be at least a partial and systematic relation between one sort of event and another. The unity implies a conformity, or, to use a favored expression of the Cartesians, a proportionality between the components of the composition. It is a functional cooperation or correlation. Metaphysical principles lead us to account for the common-sense belief by pointing to the necessity for such a definition of the unity of composition. In return, from the popular belief so grounded we must pass back to a metaphysical and theological completion of the explanation. We may regard the pineal-gland theory as a *deus ex machina.* It was derided by Descartes' Peripatetic opponents—on their principles such a hypothesis was neither necessary nor intelligible. But Cartesians could not deride it: the god from the machine is the evidence of God.

Even for Locke, for whom matter may conceivably be the seat of thought, the adjustment of immediate experience to what he regarded as the disclosures of science defined a similar problem of correlation. His "constant correspondence" represents what happens when the notion of substance is omitted from the context of thought. Between the conditions, we know not what, existing in the minute parts of the primary qualities of things themselves and the secondary qualities within us (whatever this expression may finally mean) there obtains a constant correspondence. This doctrine interprets in its way the irresistible conviction of common sense. Cartesian metaphysics explicitly complicates the question. If we are to have a science of man, we must take account of three things: (1) the interactions of (other material) things and the human body, which is a subdivision of physics; (2) the happenings within the human body, and this again is a portion of a universal science of nature; (3) the events arising within spiritual substance and deriving their specific character from this source. Even with this, however, our science of man is far from complete. For the mind seems to have a body, and the human body, at least, seems to have a mind. It is not, then, sufficient to study the bodily events and the spiritual events each in their own terms. The unity of man is thus resolved into a system of specific interinfluences (by way of the pineal gland, perhaps) or of specific correlations. If there are interactions, and these occur by way of the gland, then extended explanation involves the argument from the machine to God. If there are no interactions, but only correlations, then again complete explanation is teleological in a somewhat more circuitous manner.

Experience suggests the problem; metaphysics is responsible for the form it takes. And metaphysics—or, by extension, theology—must solve it. From the standpoint of this metaphysics, be it noted, there can be no empirical solution of the problem. Experience, from this standpoint, is just what needs explanation. The Cartesians became fully aware of the precise locus of the difficulty. From the accepted fact that man is a unity of composition whose terms are two antithetical substances, nothing whatever can be inferred concerning either spiritual or physical events or their interrelation. Moreover, the event in spiritual substance —the conscious state or immediate experience—tells us nothing whatever concerning things or events in the other substance. Finally, our (physical) knowledge of bodily occurrences tells us neither that there must be some correlative event in the soul substance nor what that event must be. The Cartesian saw this clearly. The problem, they recognized, is defined by specific correlation. The animal spirits, following one channel, coincide with the immediate experience of a toothache; following another nerve pathway, the specific correlate in conscious experience is a blue color sensation. Throughout the range of neurological and conscious events the correlation of the one type of event with the other is specific and theoretically constant. But this cannot be made intelligible from the nature of the animal spirits alone or from the character of conscious experience alone. The animal spirits certainly cannot be responsible for this specificity of correlation, for within the animals the operations of the spirits have no correlated event whatever. Ordinary human experience, however, suggests almost irresistibly the principle of exact proportionality or of constant specific correlation. Granting that there are two components in the nature of man, granting that these components are as the Cartesians defined them, then experience convinces us that the correlation between the two sets of events is not sporadic and unpredictable, but systematic and theoretically predictable. Were this not the case, a Cartesian would have no problem of the external world. The clear and distinct idea of spiritual substance affords no information concerning matter; the idea of matter does not involve the idea of spirit. Were we limited to a conscious state, the Cartesians implied, and to this alone, we should never suspect that the animal spirits course through the nerve tubes. Were we somehow limited to a contemplation of physiological events, we should never suspect that sensations and feelings happen within finite existence. That a man, being hungry, should seek food is a fact that contains no mysteries for common sense. In a deeply serious sense, however, for a Cartesian the fact that a man, needing food, should not merely seek food, but should feel hunger, not envy or anger, is deeply mysterious. It is so mysterious that theology alone can provide a clue. A Cartesian, beating his dog, must admire the skillful contrivance of God in that there should be so curious a similarity of action between the beaten dog and the beaten man, while there exists so profound a difference in the natures of the two creatures. How can a body need a soul, since for lowlier bodies souls are dispensable? And how can a soul need a body, since a soul is a finite substance and by fact is defined as independent of everything save God? The anti-Cartesians exploited this to the utmost, and a Cartesian's charge of verbalism directed against a Scholastic's forms was neatly countered by Peripatetic derision of a wholly superfluous soul.[8]

From these perplexities there was a sole avenue of escape for the Cartesian. The proportionality of body and soul must be ascribed to the competence of God as creator. Moreover, this proportionality must itself be defined as an aim involved in divine purpose. And finally, the unity of composition, having been resolved into and virtually supplanted by the idea of proportionality, must be further transformed into a law of correlation. This having been accomplished, the notion of substance may be permitted to vanish from the context of science.

Leaving Descartes himself, let us turn to the efforts of his followers. Controversy revealed quickly the artificiality of the pineal-gland theory.[9] It was perplexing for a Cartesian to know how to remain a Cartesian and escape artificiality. Let us summarize fully the factors defining his problem:

(1) A correlation, harmony, fitness, or proportionality of body and soul is suggested by experience and demanded by piety.

(2) This correlation or proportionality is not necessarily complete. Obviously it must obtain with respect to sense experience and its derivatives in memory and imagination, and also with respect to certain voluntary activities expressive of sense experience.

---

[8] Cf. the paper on the "Animal Soul," referred to in note 2, above.

[9] The pineal-gland theory did not involve for Descartes an intrusion of mind into physical nature or of the latter into mind, because of his principle that the quantity of motion in the universe is a constant. The soul's influence upon the body being limited to a deflection in the direction of the motions of the animal spirits, the quantity of motion remains unaffected. An irregularity in the physical system may be implied; but appearances are saved for Descartes by two considerations. In the first place, interaction did not imply that an existential fact changed its essential substantial nature. And again, the interaction of body and soul, even if implying irregularity from the standpoint of the physical system, was in itself a regularity in a more inclusive system, embracing human souls and nature within the whole of finite existence.

(3) We have adequate ideas of spiritual and material substance. No relationship of body and soul can be deduced from these ideas alone. The master's interactionism expressed rather than made intelligible common-sense convictions. Moreover, interactionism did not imply in any case causal continuity between body and soul. In these conditions the solution of the problem must lie, not within creation, but within the Creator.

(4) The soul is a substance: a substance is something more than its states, the momentary activities and manifestations which are born of substance and express its nature, but do not exhaust it. Thinking processes of all sorts express the inner traits and native structure of the soul's substantial reality. But there may be portions of the total mental life which spring from the intrinsic energies of the soul substance and for which there are no correlatives or specific proportionalities within the sphere of the body. Soul and body are in harmony: but there may be within the soul powers and the fruits of powers which lie outside the system of correlations. Similarly, there may reside within the mechanism of the body functions not directly expressed in systematic correlations. These elements, residing outside the proportioning of body and soul in a more limited sense, really fall within this harmony in a deeper meaning.

(5) The crux of the body-soul problem is the fact of the *constancy* and *specificity* of the correlation or harmony of events in the soul and events in the body. The world of matter is a realm of causal law; if an event reoccur, then its consequences will reoccur. The system of correlations is equally a realm of law. If an event, say a sensation of red color, occur within the soul, then there occurs, and always occurs when just this sensation is experienced, a certain specific event in nature. The correlation of event in the soul and event in extra-corporeal nature is not regular; but if we bear in mind that the soul is in harmony, not with nature directly, but with the human body, a portion of nature, and only through this with nature as a whole, then we must assert that the correlation of spiritual and physiological events is constant, specific, and systematic. To be quite exact, we must define the relationship as obtaining between the mental occurrence and

the behavior of the pineal-gland. But in any case, this is what common-sense belief turns out to be when given sound metaphysical grounds.[10] Man, in essence, lies beyond nature; but, nevertheless, man's relation to nature can be made intelligible. All that is, is providential—but this is to say that creation is rationally planned.

From this summary we may pass directly to the Cartesians' efforts to meet its difficulties. Out of these efforts psycho-physical parallelism emerged. But the doctrine did not come at once, and we can indicate only a portion of the story.

The situation above described contained two factors warring against one another. Two substances define two types of existence, which we may call for the sake of brevity psychical or spiritual states and physical or material states. In so far as emphasis falls upon the diversity of substantial natures, then the irreducibility and merely external relatedness of the two kinds of existence occupies the foreground. When interest is empirical, relatedness is of primary importance. The science of man emphasizes the affiliation of events rather than their diversity. Moreover, morality demands that the efficacity of the soul be maintained. Knowledge implies that mind can and does deal with things. Most important of all, it is impious to minimize the intimacy of the relation of body and soul; otherwise the Creator would be pictured as a bungler. But even while we emphasize this consideration arising from theology, opposing considerations arise. Immortality is imperiled in the measure in which intimate linkage between the soul and the body is emphasized. Descartes had prudently confined himself to the position that in showing the soul to be of an imperishable substance he had done all that metaphysics could well do for religious belief. But when it becomes necessary to harmonize a vast structure of science with theology, more explicit and complete adjustments are necessary. As nature is resolved into mechanism, perhaps the soul will be resolved into a swarm of mental atoms or its substantial reality be supplanted by a set of psychological laws. The disparateness of Cartesian substances has its obvious advantages for supernatu-

10 These points are illustrated in detail in other papers in this book.

ralistic interests. At the same time, we cannot make experience intelligible and furnish theology with a content to replace revelation, unless a systematic relation obtains between the two substances. Abstractly speaking, the Cartesian substances would be expected to generate, each from within itself and by means of their respective intrinsic resources, phenomena for which all proportionment would be irrelevant. Moreover, if spiritual and material phenomena be not kept rigorously separated, natural sciences would be jeopardized by the undermining of their metaphysical foundations. This situation could be worked out in many details. But enough has been said to indicate the central difficulty: How can the irreducible diversity of substantial natures be retained, with its advantages, while providing the relatedness through which alone man could be included within the sweep of science and the program of social control?

In the main, the efforts of thinkers within the sphere of Cartesian influence were marked by three tendencies. First, the regression of the concept of substance from the foreground of thought and in the end the resolution of the dualism of substances into opponent orders of finite events. Secondly, the correlation of psychical and physical existence is defined in terms of occasional causation. Finally, occasional causation is absorbed into theology.

There were many considerations—more than can be recounted within the limits of this paper—that led to the restrictions placed upon the meaning of substance and to the virtual disuse of the concept. Substance implied intrinsic powers or energies. It possessed functions of origination, or active agency. The picturesquely labeled souls of tradition—the vegetative, sensitive, and rational—were adjusted to the requirements of the Cartesian dualism. If these various souls were represented in the body at all, they must be interpreted as specialized activities of the bodily mechanism. To that extent the term "soul" becomes inappropriate. Cartesians perceived clearly and stated emphatically that the term "soul" can mean but one thing, that is, spiritual substance. For Régis, for example, if animals have souls they are unities of composition and like man; if spiritual substance were lacking, animals are not unities of composition and there is no sense in which they could be said to possess souls. On the other hand, if the functions indicated by labels such as "vegetative," "sensitive," and "rational" souls deserve those names, then these functions are intrinsic powers or faculties of the spiritual substance. Now the rational soul had proved particularly bothersome, for it possessed capacities or produced effects not directly due to sense-experience and possibly not even dependent upon it. At least for the anti-empiricist this is the case. Within the context of the dualism the innate idea expresses the revision of this difficulty. Innate ideas are expressions of the inner potencies of the spiritual substance. The range of these original powers, however, is not easily determined. For example, all abstract ideas may be regarded as innate, in the sense that they reflect primarily the character of spiritual substance itself. Experience, from this point of view, may provide occasions for stimulating the soul to an apprehension of its implicit content, but does not account for the coming of these ideas. On the other hand, an idea, whatever its source, is a spiritual state; for even sense, memory, and imagination are functions of the soul substance. Abstract ideas, even innate ideas, possess in this sense no superiority over the most rudimentary idea from sense. And sense, too, is as much an aboriginal function of soul substance as is the power of forming abstract ideas. The idea from sense in its own way expresses the native energies of the mind as much as does the abstract idea. The Cartesian substantial soul thus engulfs all experience.

It is not easy, however, to define the functions of the soul. An intrinsic power for producing innate ideas is no more explanatory of the facts than an aboriginal faculty of sensation. The soul must possess, as substance, all the powers necessary for producing everything that idea, experience, mind, consciousness, and spirit can signify. With an emphasis such as this, a conflict emerges. The soul, not the correlation of psychical and physical states, furnishes the clues to experience. On the other hand, the emphasis may fall elsewhere. Inquiry may turn, not upon the intrinsic energies of the spiritual substances as its pivot, but upon the correlation of mind and nature. Then the system of correlation between the psychical and physical orders tends to deflate the notion of substance. If nature is to be understood as a series of events, the mind tends to become just another series. The Cartesians' perplexities are obvious. If the soul, through its native powers, can produce *some* ideas without even the need of occasioning excitement through sense—and there were Cartesians who thought this—then its dependence upon association with a body for other states is prejudicial to its substantial status. If the soul be not a substance, it is not a soul at all—at least in a sense that would facilitate the adjustment of theology and philosophy. And if it be a substance, nothing more natural can be assumed than a capacity for producing ideas independently of the system of correlation between the spiritual and the corporeal. Against this was the recognition that exceptions to the system of correlations or occasional causation threatened the intelligibility of the system itself. In short, the idea of universal occasional causation led to neglect of the notion of substance; and in the place of the intrinsic powers belonging to spiritual and extended substance, reflection emphasizes the idea of God's providence. Agency belongs to the Creator.

This situation may be illustrated in some detail. For the early Cartesian physical science and common sense unite in pointing to a specific correlation between psychical states and bodily events, at least with respect to sense experience and its derivatives. On the other hand, innate and abstract ideas, in their universality, seem to express an essential independence of sense experience. We may represent the Cartesians' point of view somewhat as follows. Experience may be necessary as occasion for the soul's exercise of its higher faculties and the apprehension of a content it possesses because it is rational and spiritual. But the occasioning function of experience is general, not specific, with respect to such ideas. Ideas from sense, on the contrary, are specifically occasioned. If in my body the animal spirits have never run a certain course, then in my soul there has never been a sensation of blue. But, so long as my body is affected by things and my soul enjoys sensations and perceptions—it matters little what the things may be and what the sensations are—my soul may respond by discovering within itself the idea of God or the idea of matter.

In a general way sense experience is the occasion for the inner activity which makes explicit the idea of God. But within wide limits one man's sense experience is as good as another's for this result. The idea of God—or a process of abstract thinking— either has no specific correlate in the course of the animal spirits or it has no physiological correlate at all. In either case this activity of soul falls without the system of specific correlation holding in the field of sense, memory, and imagination. The man born color-blind can never perceive color, but he may think of God and comprehend that the essence of matter is extension. The spiritual substance thus explains, not merely that ideas, including universals, are spiritual entities, but also that there are universal ideas. On the other hand, this substantial nature enables us to understand why a toothache is a spiritual entity or event, but in no direct sense why toothaches ever occur. This is a new way of denying that everything in the intellect is first in sense.

In such ways the effort to relate concretely the physical and the psychical through the system of occasional causation restricts the role of substance, and the latter idea in turn limits the extension of the occasionalistic theory. In a similar way this competition appears with respect to volitional processes. Are all volitions occasioned by or in specific correlation with movements of the animal spirits? There were Cartesians who thought that certain volitions related to abstract and universal ideas sprang from the intrinsic powers of the soul substance, independently of specific bodily occasion. Most volitions are related to sense experience; with respect to these, the system of occasional causation holds. But other volitions, such as those due to the resolution of the will in a moral crisis, seem to transcend the impulsions of appetite as the universal idea seems to transcend the materials of sense. The productive agency of the soul substance is thus retained. Louis de la Forge illustrates both points. He implies that there are no bodily processes corresponding to certain (innate and abstract) ideas and that there are volitions having no occasions in bodily processes. These ideas and volitions express the innermost being of the soul substance. This, then, is what remains of the extraordinarily exceptional position that man, as the sole possessor of a soul, enjoyed in the Cartesian universe of creation.

This position, indeed, is the clue to most of the hesitancies and reservations marking the development of occasionalism and explains the postponement of an unambiguous psycho-physical parallelism. If the problems bequeathed by the Cartesian dualism are to be solved by the concept of occasional causation, the momentum of its logic will carry reflection beyond doctrines such as that of Louis de la Forge. To preserve the unique position of man implied, so it appeared to the Cartesian, the limitation of occasional causation to human experience and even to a portion of human experience. The first limitation seems anthropomorphic, and the second arbitrary. If in man alone spiritual states are occasioned by bodily processes, this is understandable only upon the condition that man alone possesses soul substance. That is, the maintenance of the substance concept is necessary in order to preserve man's unique position as the only creature enjoying psychical being. With this, however, the very meaning of "occasioning cause" becomes ambiguous. Does the movement of the pineal gland elicit from the soul substance an activity expressive of the nature of that substance and not in any exact relationship to the movement? Upon a repetition of this movement are we justified in believing that *some* activity of the soul substance will occur, but not necessarily a repetition of the psychical process previously elicited by this movement? If this be the actual relationship signified by occasional causation, then the unity of composition is not a unity at all, and the relation of soul and body is haphazard. What has become of the harmony and proportionality of the components of man which, we have been assured, is expressive of the handiwork of God? The difficulty is sharply defined in the case of volitions. If the soul, by its powers, resolves an issue and decrees a course of action, are we to believe that a certain bodily movement in the pineal gland and no other is occasioned? Or are we to believe only that some movement will occur without certainty as to its appropriateness to this very resolution of the will? In the former case the relation of occasional causation seems indistinguishable from interaction. If an activity of the will, because of its specific character, is responsible for the bodily motion being just what it is, then this seems equivalent to the statement that the soul causes the bodily motion. The more the nature of the soul as substance is emphasized, the more we must emphasize its inner springs and spontaneities; then causal interactionism seems to be demanded. On the other hand, if we take the second supposition, that is, that there is no fixed relation between the particular volition and bodily motion, then occasional causation ceases to be causation in any intelligible sense whatever. No orderly connection of soul and body remains, and we cannot speak of the divine laws for the union of soul and body. The predicament was real. With many Cartesians interactionism was regarded as unintelligible. On the other hand, what could be meant by asserting the laws decreed by God for the union of body and soul unless the correlation of movement and conscious state be specific? If divine law govern the union of soul and body, then assuredly movement A is accompanied by psychical state A′ and no other; and the recurrence of A must mean the recurrence of A′, not B′ or C′.

If occasional causation, as the relationship of the bodily and the mental, be freed from traces of meaning deriving from the notion of interacting substances, then clearly the unity of man receives a new definition. Man is not a unity of composition, the components being substances of antithetical properties. The unity of man is not defined by the notion of substance at all, but by something described as the Creator's laws of the union of soul and body. That is, we must give a merely conventional meaning to "soul" and "body." The real fact is the systematic correlation of a psychical state with a movement. To assert that by divine law a certain thought arises "in the soul" upon the occasion of a certain movement "in the body," deprives substance of spontaneity and agency. In effect, to say "in the soul" is nothing more than saying that psychical states or conscious processes, or, more exactly, psychical events, do occur.

In so far as these considerations are pressed, the anthropological dualism dissolves. If the fundamental fact be that by divine arrangement movement and psychical events are in constant correspondence, there is no reason for confining this to man. The analogies between animal and human bodily activities suggest that a similar law obtains throughout; in the animal world, too, the double series is found, and psychical event accompanies bodily movement. Man is no longer unique amid created things.

There is more to be said concerning this situation. There was a danger lurking in the substance notion itself. If we stress the hidden potencies that substance may possess, the Lockean supposition that matter may be capable of thought will appear to be both rationally tenable and economical. But in this direction lies materialism, and such a solution was repugnant to the interests of theology. Moreover, the critique of substance, associated with the empirical movement, was destroying the idea of substance, especially as defined as an unknown substratum. In the circumstances, it was natural to resolve man's composite nature into the systematic correspondence of two series of events.

We have seen indications of the close relation between developments in Cartesianism and theological requirements. With the resolution of the dualism of substances into the correlation of two series of events, the situation persisted. In the earlier stages of the movement, difficulties had been surmounted by appeal to the creative competence of God. But arguments based upon divine competence have a slippery way of adjusting themselves to the most diverse positions. Controversy after Descartes abundantly illustrated this fact. After physical science had defined nature as a realm of law, and things as machines, theology made of these achievements a capital argument for the existence of God. In the same manner, after a universal system of occasional causation had been defined, it was employed for the same purpose. When occasional causation, as a system, has become a foundation for theology, the situation changed with respect to the limitations of occasional causation. There was no longer any reason to admit exceptions to the specific correspondence between psychical and bodily processes. Physical science had obviated the need of miracles in order to provide evidence for God. In the same way, if the system of occasional causation be grounded upon theology, exceptions to the system would express impiety rather than piety. It is not exceptions, appeal to obscure potencies of the soul, or volitions that have no bodily correlates which express the craftsmanship and providence of God. Piety forces us to acknowledge that God *could* have proportioned the psychical and physical so perfectly that there should be bodily occasions and correlates for every mental event. Mechanism is not in conflict with the notion of final causation; on the contrary, mechanism is the vehicle by means of which divine design is realized. The universality of the correlation of bodily and mental events is then the evidence of a providential perfection of harmony between the spiritual life and mechanism. The unity of creation is found in the universal network of law; the unity of man is found in the special laws governing the relation of psychical state and bodily occurrence. There is, to be sure, a residual difficulty in this, that only *some* bodily movements are accompanied by spiritual events. This conclusion cannot be avoided after mind, spirit, and soul come to mean consciousness and a substantial substratum is removed from beneath consciousness. This difficulty is all the more perplexing because the spiritual has lost efficacy. Nevertheless, the thought must prevail that by this limitation the wise economy of the Creator is expressed. The vegetative soul, in short, is reduced to bodily mechanism without psychical accompaniment and for reasons of economy. The instabilities of this position need not detain us. To preserve the essential disparity of the psychical and the physical, the conception of occasional causation is employed. But the conception itself needs explanation. The irreducibility of the two series does not in itself provide an explanation of their systematic correlation. Neither in the sensation of blue, let us say, nor in the neural processes that form the occasion for the sensation, do we find ground for the fact that this sensation and this process are specifically in fixed correlation. In Cartesian circles the question is generalized. No connection whatever is intelligible in terms of the events said to be connected. We say (to use an illustration favored by Cartesians) that the movement of the billiard ball A causes the ball B to move exactly as it does move. This, however, is mere verbal statement. What is given to observation is A's ceasing-to-move and B's beginning-to-move. This is all that causal connection can mean in terms of A and B and their motions. Thus, the mystery concerning the concurrence of a certain sensation and a certain bodily motion is no greater than the mystery of this other "correlation"—that physical event A is followed by physical event B, not by X or Y or Z. In this manner the perplexity is generalized; all causes are occasions; the hidden potencies of material and spiritual substances are banished and replaced by the problem of God's relation to finite existence, of reality to its twofold appearance.

These are, in part at least, the conditions within which psychophysical parallelism was formulated. This essay began with a statement to the effect that both interaction and parallelism were peculiarly modern doctrines. It would be more accurate to say, after reflecting upon the preceding sketch, that these doctrines are characteristic products of the interplay of ideas in the seventeenth and eighteenth centuries. Psychology, as it has been generally understood, emerged as a by-product of the historical situation partially outlined above. Assuredly neither the hypothesis of interaction nor that of parallelism was generated within the context of psychological inquiry or because of the peculiar needs of such inquiry. Metaphysics arose to justify a growing physical science, to defend the validity of its implicit claims, and to provide a systematic foundation. As an incident in this program, it appeared that what was left out of physics might be the province of psychology. Interaction and parallelism express the difficulty of determining just what physics does omit—and how what it leaves out is related to what it includes. Descartes, we know, was bewildered by his discovery of what the human soul is. Doubtless he was puzzled by the conditions under which a scientific study of it must be undertaken. The Cartesian bewilderment, one suspects, has been strikingly persistent throughout the history of modern psychology. When psycho-physical parallelism is defined as merely a working hypothesis for psychology and all responsibility for the solution of the problem of mind and body is disavowed, resignation seems to replace the Cartesian bewilderment.

CARTESIAN REFUTATIONS
OF SPINOZA

IF THE STUDENT stray from the great highway of philosophy's history, to wander in its collateral byways, he may be sure of adventures. Quite possibly he will attain, here and there, a vantage point from which the highway itself may be viewed in a new perspective. The highway itself and the world through which it leads may be glimpsed from a bypath that in itself leads nowhere.

The relation between the doctrines of Descartes and Spinoza is a matter of frequent reinterpretations. The extremes of opposing interpretations can be easily characterized. On the one hand, Spinozism is defined as a revised and systematized Cartesianism. On the other hand, the relation of the former to the latter may be regarded as extrinsic rather than essential; Spinoza, it may be urged, employed Cartesianism in order to facilitate the expression of a radically different philosophical vision. These opposite views concerning the relation of the two philosophies emerged quite promptly after Spinoza's works became accessible. The settlement of the question was not a matter of merely academic and historical interest. It was rather a matter of living importance. The exciting controversial issues of the day borrowed weapons from one or the other philosophy. The philosophic defense of theology was at issue. Materialism was in process of formulation. Empiricism was coming to the continent from Britain. If the doctrines of Descartes and Spinoza were essentially one in spirit, they could be evaluated in a single process. But, if similarity of expression and to some extent of idea masked a profound difference of meaning, the controversial situation was doubly complicated.

The philosophic defense of theology, it was remarked above, was involved in the Descartes-Spinoza issue. The question of the relation of the later to the earlier philosophy received intense treatment because of controversial associations. In the course of a century an extraordinary transformation occurred. The Cartesian philosophy, in a word, became the foundations for the refutation of Spinozism. To demonstrate the incompatibility of the two philosophies was the first step. The second, and important step, once this incompatibility had been established, was to employ Cartesian doctrine for the refutation of Spinoza. To insist upon the essential harmony of the two philosophies, to emphasize their kinship, was to infect Cartesianism with the horrors of Spinozism. In that measure Cartesianism was unavailable for the purposes of apologetics. To separate the philosophies was, then, the necessary preliminary. The second step, however, the basing of the refutation of Spinozism upon Cartesian doctrine, in itself reflects a transformation effected by the passing of decades.

After all, the earliest reactions to Cartesianism were not wholly unlike the earliest reactions of Spinozism. The Cartesian philosophy appeared as the doctrine of a *novateur*. Here and there it was suspected of a secret harmony with Protestantism. On the whole, however, Protestant and Roman Catholic theologians alike doubted Cartesianism's utility for apologetic purposes. In the case of Spinoza, the question of apologetic employment scarcely arose. Occasionally there appeared a defense of Spinoza against the charge of atheism. In the main, however, the refutation of him became a favorite exercise of piety. The horror aroused by Spinozism is a historical commonplace. All fears born of new ideas, whatever their kind and origin, were concentrated upon it. Those who were alarmed by Deism pointed to Spinoza as its chief proponent. For the self-appointed guardians of society against materialism and atheism, Spinozism was recognized as the chief fortress of the enemy. A striking bit of evidence of the emotional intensity involved—and it is, perhaps, also evidence of the power of Spinozism—is found in the belittling of the enemy's doctrine. Gerdil astonishes us by disparaging the philosophy he is at such pains to refute. The "absurdities" of this *impie novateur* are said to shock common sense, and Gerdil solemnly asserts that there is no philosophy whatever that does not supply a sufficiency of principles with which to combat these absurdities.[1]

[1] Cardinal Gerdil (1718–1802): *Receuil de dissertations sur quelques principes de philosophie et de religion,* par le R. P. Gerdil, Barnabite, Professeur de Théologie en

Gerdil's statement that any philosophy whatever would serve for the refutation of Spinozism renders all the more interesting the selection of Cartesianism for the purpose. It is significant that in the interval between the dissemination of Cartesian doctrine and the appearance of Spinozism, Cartesianism had become the ally of piety and the intellectual arsenal of theology. The defense of Descartes turns out to be equivalent to the refutation of Spinoza. At the same time, the refutation of Spinoza is the overthrow of "atheism" and "materialism." Thus, the earlier *novateur* becomes the bulwark of defense against the later and more dreaded innovator. Cartesian doctrine, once so widely viewed as a threat to religious and theological interests, Protestant and Roman Catholic alike, had become adjusted to the uses of apologetics. Descartes becomes the defender of the faith. In the face of the new adversary, the opposition to Descartes was liquidated. After all, as Gerdil indicates, the defense against innovation must depend either upon the scholastic philosophy or upon Descartes. The enmity between the School and the Cartesians, however, simplified the choice. The net outcome, in brief, was this: the polemic against deism, materialism, atheism, and ethical naturalism must take Cartesianism as its arsenal, or else there would be no modern armament at all for the polemic.

Cousin has called attention to this transformation of the role of Cartesianism. In 1755, he writes, the French Academy discussed *l'esprit philosophique*. The essay that won the prize eulogized Descartes because of this twofold service to philosophy, the freeing of thought from the yoke of Aristotle and his service to the cause of Christianity. It is, perhaps, worth while to quote a few lines from the lengthy selection given by Cousin: [2]

Disciple de la lumière, au lieu d'interroger les morts et les dieux de l'école, il ne consulta que les idées claires et distinctes, la nature et l'évidence. Par des méditations profondes, il tira toutes les sciences du

la Royale Université de Turin, de l'Académie de l'Institut de Bologne, à Paris, chez Hugues-Daniel Chaubert, & Herissant Imprimeur, 1760. The volume contains four dissertations, the fourth of which bears the title: "Sur l'incompatibilité des principes de Descartes & de Spinosa. The reference is to p. 228.

[2] V. Cousin, *Fragments philosophiques pour servir à l'histoire de la philosophie*, 5th ed., 2d part, Paris, Didier et Cie., 1866, pp. 418–21.

chaos, et par un coup de génie plus grand encore il montra le secours
mutuel qu'elles doivent se prêter; il les enchaina toutes ensemble, les
éleva les unes sur les autres; et se plaçant ensuite sur cette hauteur, il
marcha, avec toutes les forces de l'esprit humain ainsi rassemblées, à
la découverte de ces grandes vérités que d'autres plus heureux sont venus
enlever après lui, mais en suivant les sentiers de lumière que Descartes
avoit tracés. Ce fut donc le courage et la fierté d'un seul esprit qui
causèrent dans les sciences cette heureuse et mémorable révolution, dont
nous goûtons aujourdhui les avantages avec une superbe ingratitude. Il
falloit aux sciences un homme qui osât conjurer tout seul avec son génie
contre les anciens tyrans de la raison; qui osât fouler aux pieds ces idoles
que tant de siécles avoient adorées. Descartes se trouvoit enfermé dans
le labyrinthe avec tous les autres philosophes; mais il se fit lui-même
des ailes, et il s'envola, frayant ainsi une route nouvelle à la raison
captive.

Cousin then asks:

Qui prononçait en 1755 ces fortes paroles? Était-ce un professeur de
l'Université de Paris, devançant et surpassant son confrère Thomas dans
son Éloge de Descartes? ou bien encore quelque ardent disciple de
l'Oratoire ou de Port-Royal? Non: c'est un père jésuite, le père Antoine
Guénard.

Descartes' efforts to placate Jesuit opposition were not, after all,
unavailing. To Guénard and to others Descartes had become the
defender of the faith.

It is evident that the resulting situation was intricate. Because
of the association of Cartesianism with the defense of theology, it
was necessary to insist upon the diversity of the two philosophies.
The points of diversity must be specified. On the other hand,
granted the diversity of doctrine, the refutation of Spinozism by
means of Cartesianism must pivot upon these points which were,
at one and the same time, viewed as the points of greatest diversity
and also as fundamental in the Cartesian philosophy. In this way
the essentials of Cartesianism—at any rate the essentials as comprehended by the controversialists—receive definition by the controversial situation itself and the controversy is reciprocally
defined by determining what ideas in the earlier philosophy are
essential. The refutations of Spinozism by means of Cartesianism,
accordingly, reflect the discoveries effected within Cartesianism
by apologetic interests. The pillorying of Spinoza as atheist and

materialist may or may not be informing with respect to the spirit and intention of Spinozism; but it furnishes insight into the speculative interests of the age. The Cartesian refutations of Spinoza are highly revealing. They express one way in which Cartesian doctrine became a historical force. They indicate, not, perhaps, what Descartes intended to emphasize, but what some of his followers discovered to be vital in his doctrine.

The worthy Gerdil [3] may be selected, somewhat at random, to illustrate the first step in the refutation of Spinoza drawn from Cartesian sources—namely, the demonstration of the "incompatibility" of the principles sponsored by the two men. Gerdil is not unaware of the history of the Cartesian movement. The system, he admits, alarmed both the believer and the unbeliever. Of utmost importance is the fact that it had undermined the older support of apologetics. The "School" had effected the reconciliation of philosophy and dogma. But Cartesianism overthrew the very principles upon which this pretended reconciliation had been based. From this an erroneous conclusion had been drawn, to wit, that Descartes himself would have none of these dogmas. This had aroused hostility towards Descartes, and Gerdil states that a whole group of "écrivains licensieux" had proceeded to attack his philosophy. Interestingly enough, Gerdil states that this reaction to Descartes was intensified by the belief that the philosophy of Spinoza was the "funeste conséquence" of the Cartesian teaching. In contrast with this group, Gerdil admits, there is another party; the latter regarded the Cartesian principles as in themselves favorable to the cause of religion. But even this sympathetic group were disturbed by the conviction that Spinozism was somewhat mysteriously generated by the Cartesian system. Gerdil does not make clear to us the source of this conviction. Perhaps the sympathetic felt that Descartes had been reckless in his proclamation of the competence of reason. In the eulogy of the philosophical spirit referred to above, Guénard distinguished two essential aspects of the philosophical spirit, one a complete independence of every authority save that of reason in the order

[3] See note 1, above.

of philosophy, the other a respect for faith in the order of supernatural truths, and Guénard, as Cousin states, cited Cartesianism as the model of the philosophical spirit so conceived.[4] Complete independence in the order of philosophy, however, might well lead the spirit of libertinage to a neglect of the truths of faith. The *Tractatus theologico-politicus* is scarcely to be compared with the Cartesian gestures towards dogma and homage to the Church. The Cartesian independence in the order of philosophy, it must have appeared to some, might well have generated Spinozism, and thus the Cartesian philosophy, despite its author's piety, may have led to atheism. In any case, Gerdil recognizes a widespread fear that Cartesian principles, despite their value for the cause of piety, were also usable in the interests of atheism.[5] In the circumstances, Gerdil must undertake to calm the fears of those who suspect that Cartesian teaching leads to Spinozism and atheism. This is all the more necessary if the employment of Cartesian ideas as apologetics is to be justified. The incompatibility of the two philosophies must be demonstrated.[6]

Atheism, Gerdil informs us, whether ancient or modern, always rests upon three principles. The first is the eternity of movement; the second, the absolute or metaphysical necessity of existence, whether of matter or of motion; and the third, the identity of thinking and material substances.[7] Since he is convinced that Spinozism is atheism, we may depend upon him to discover somehow these three principles in Spinoza's system. To accomplish his purpose he must, in addition, prove that they are not discoverable in the Cartesian system. These two tasks once accomplished, the incompatibility of the systems will have been demonstrated.

Of the three principles that have always defined an atheistic philosophy, there is one, asserts Gerdil, which constitutes the essential "venom" of the Spinozistic system.[8] But Cartesianism is

---

[4] *Receuil de dissertations sur quelques principes de philosophie et de religion*, p. 418.

[5] Pages 157–60, 198. Gerdil's dissertation, it should be noted, is directed against a certain "new examination of Spinozism," the author of which he does not mention by name. The author of this "examen," however, is guilty of this very confounding of the principles of Spinozism with those of Descartes. The writer has not been able to identify with certainty the work taken by Gerdil as the object of his attack.

[6] Preface, pp. vi–vii.   [7] Preface, p. iii.   [8] Page 215.

not atheistic at all. Not merely will the Cartesian system lack the three principles of atheism—it will comprise the very antithesis of the venomous principle as one of its fundamental ideas. This antithetical principle will indeed form a peculiarly beneficent property of the Cartesian system. This special opposition of principle will be central in showing the incompatibility of the two philosophies. What are these opposing principles? The venom in Spinozism is the definition of thought or spirit as a mode of matter—in short, the denial of the Cartesian dualism of finite substances. This is, indeed, somewhat startling; the disentanglement of Spinozism and Cartesianism is based upon the body-soul doctrine. This is a striking illustration of the fact that after Descartes the point of departure for apologetics is the matter-spirit dualism. In forsaking Scholasticism as the reconciliation of philosophy and dogma, Cartesianism, and more specifically the characteristic dualism of Cartesianism, becomes the basis for a new procedure of reconciliation.

Gerdil's assertion that Spinoza regards thought or spirit as merely a mode of matter may astonish the reader. It was evidently the task of Gerdil to manipulate the doctrine of the attributes, thought and extension. The Spinozistic doctrine concerning thought and extension as attributes must be interpreted so as to result in the atheistic principle, the venomous principle that thought is a mode of matter. Gerdil's proposal is as follows: Spinoza's teaching concerning substance cannot be reconciled with his doctrine of extension unless substance and matter be identified. If this identification is necessary for Spinozism, then Spinozism is, of course, a materialism. Moreover, Spinozistic materialism in its specific features will be characterized by its antithesis to the characteristic principles of the Cartesian philosophy. In contrast with the latter, Spinozism, whatever its verbal expression, must reduce thought to a mode of extension or of matter. Spinozistic materialism is, of course, an atheism. But the Cartesian system is neither a materialism nor an atheism. Significantly, it is neither, precisely because the system as such is *au fond* a matter-spirit dualism.

In this manner the incompatibility of the two systems is specifically defined. Gerdil's argument in support of his contention depends upon breaking down the Spinozistic distinction between substance and attribute. Spinoza has ascribed to the so-called attribute of Extension certain essential properties. But these properties are metaphysically ultimate. Gerdil does not call them transcendental, but it seems fair to regard them in this way. Extension, according to Spinoza, is immutable, indivisible; it is one and infinite. But substance alone can possess these characters. They are indeed properties of Absolute Being, or, in theological terms, of God. It follows, accordingly, that extension cannot be consistently defined as an attribute of substance, but is rather substance itself. In Cartesian terms, if we may translate Gerdil's thought, extension is the constitutive attribute of matter; then, accepting Spinoza's characterization of extension at its face value, we must conclude that matter is the supreme reality of the system. Spinozism is materialism. Whatever in that system can be signified by "thought" or "spirit," at least this is true, that the terms signify modes of matter. Thought is a derivative of matter.[9]

It is noteworthy that Gerdil repudiates the notion that Spinozism resulted from the reduction of Cartesian finite substances to the status of attributes of a single substance. Obviously, he must do this or he cannot maintain his contention of the incompatibility of the systems. He urges that, whatever others may think, the Spinozistic system could not have been attained by uniting in a single substance, in the form of attributes, the two perfections that Descartes kept independently real as the finite substances, thought and extension, spirit and matter. Whatever the merits of Gerdil's argument, this much can be read between the lines: the Cartesian ontological dualism is for Gerdil, as for other Cartesians, not a hypothesis, but a truth established with finality.

The argument is reinforced, according to Gerdil, by the fact that Descartes maintained the separation of force and matter. Spinoza did not do this. The consequence is that Descartes can reaffirm the argument from motion to a prime mover, while his

[9] Pages 191 ff. Gerdil explains that Spinoza's atheism is the consequence of his three positions: first, that there cannot be two substances differing in essence; secondly, that one substance cannot be produced by another; and, thirdly, that substance is infinite (pp. 215–16).

successor cannot. This auxiliary point indicates that Gerdil believes Spinoza's view of extension to be central to the system. In
technical expression, Gerdil's argument depends upon the concept of independence. This character of independence, for both
Descartes and Spinoza, is the mark of substance. The problem is
to determine whether the concepts of independence in the two
philosophies are identical. To estimate the validity of the claim
that Spinozism is a necessary consequence of the earlier doctrine,
Gerdil urges that we must examine the idea of independence in
terms of the various meanings that existence may possess. Existence may be *per se,* that is, existence in the proper sense of the
term, implying that all modes are determinations of a single subject. Again, by existence may be intended existence *a se,* implying
existence from itself in the sense of independence of a productive
cause.[10] Independence thus possesses two meanings that must not
be confounded. Descartes' definition of substance preserves the
distinction of meanings. Substance as that which can be conceived
by itself without reference to other things comprises only the idea
of an existence proper to the nature of substance. It excludes the
notion of the inherence of substance in another subject. Independence, as the character of substance for Descartes, does not
confuse independence *a subjecto inhaesionis* with independence
ut a causa efficiente—a confusion of which Leibniz is guilty.[11]
Spinoza's failure to keep apart these two meanings is responsible
for his errors.

Spinoza, en définissant la substance, . . . renferme dans cette notion,
sous les termes équivoques dont les sens se développe dans les conséquences qu'il en tire, l'idée d'une existence non-seulement propre, mais
nécessaire; exclut non-seulement l'inhérence de la substance dans un
autre sujet, mais aussi la dépendance qui convient à un effet par rapport
à sa cause, & en un mot toute idée de relation que la substance peut avoir
à quelque autre chose que ce soit. Spinoza, par un sophisme qui ne
pouvoit être que l'effet d'une passion aveugle, conclut qu'une substance
ne peut être produite par une autre substance . . . Une preuve certaine
que Spinoza, dans sa définition de la substance, cachoit, sous des expressions ambigues, un sens bien différent de celui de Descartes; c'est
qu'après avoir distingué l'attribut de la substance, il entend par attribut
précisément ce que Descartes entendoit par le mot de substance.[12]

---

[10] Page 167.   [11] Page 177.   [12] Pages 185–86.

The finite substances of Descartes are genuinely possessed of the mark of substance, for they do not inhere in a subject. They are not independent in the second sense, implying nondependence on an efficient cause. Gerdil thinks it is absurd to regard things as dependent in the sense that they inhere in God as modifications. It would be equally absurd to suppose that souls and corporeal things are independent *a se*.[13] These absurdities are characteristic of Spinozism and follow from the confusion of the two meanings of independence. From this it appears that Spinoza, unlike Descartes, is in a predicament. If substance implies both the *per se* and the *a se*, then to substance alone can be assigned unity, indivisibility, immutability, and infinity. If, further, extension possess these predicates—and according to Gerdil this is really Spinoza's doctrine, extension itself is a substance. Within the Spinozistic system, however, there can be but a single substance. The logical structure of Spinozism, then, implies the identification of substance and extension. All the "funestes conséquences" follow. Spinozism is materialism. Spinoza, who said "God or Substance or Nature," should have said "God or Substance, or Nature or Matter."

The defense of Descartes against the charge of fathering Spinozism rests in the end upon contrasting conceptions of extension. Descartes, Gerdil urges, did not identify space in the vulgar sense or body with extension. For him extension necessarily implied impenetrability, divisibility, and mobility. Extension was thus clothed with properties vulgarly regarded as belonging to body.[14] Descartes' thought is not that body can be reduced to three dimensions, but rather that these three dimensions cannot obtain without involving impenetrability and divisibility. Hence extension is the essence, the primitive fund, of body. According to the Cartesian view, then, immutability and indivisibility are incompatible with the idea of extension. If Spinoza identifies God and extension, and this he must do if he accords to extension the properties of immutability and indivisibility, it follows that Spinoza is giving extension a meaning radically unlike that of Descartes.[15]

[13] Pages 177 ff. [14] Page 188.
[15] "Il est donc visible que Spinoza ne prend pas l'étenduë dans le même sens que Descartes; qu'il reconnoit au contraire aves les partisans du vuide, qu'il n'y a aucune

For Gerdil, the atheism of Cartesianism pivots upon the concept of matter. There are students of Descartes, Gerdil recognizes, who admit that Descartes was not an atheist, but who fear that his principles lead to atheism. But Cartesianism, Gerdil urges, destroys a fundamental article of atheism, that is, the denial of a distinction between a prime mover and matter. In support of his contention, Gerdil invites his reader to recall the state in which Descartes found "la Physique."

Toutes les puissances que les corps ont d'agir les uns sur les autres, toutes leurs qualités sensibles étoient autant de vertus innées, sympathiques ou antipathiques, expultrices ou retentrices, destinées à produire chaque effet en particulier. Descartes conçut que ce pompeux étalage de qualités occultes ne s'étoit introduit dans la Physique, qu'à la faveur de l'ignorance du méchanisme. Il vit, ce que Boyle confirma depuis par mille expériences, que la nature ne fait jouer en effet que la méchanisme dans la production des effets, où l'on peut entrevoir en quelque sorte son procedé. La simplicité de ses voies le persuada que ce procédé dévoit être uniforme. Il ne balança donc pas à rejetter les formes substantielles & accidentelles de l'Ecole, & à leur substituer les affections méchaniques, la grosseur, la figure, le mouvement des particules d'une matière homogene. Mais après avoir rejetté tout l'appareil des formes & des qualités occultes, il comprit qu'il ne pouvoit plus reconnoître dans la matière aucune vertu active proprement dite. . . . Ainsi les derniers pas de l'analyse physique venoient se réunir aux dernières conclusions de la synthèse métaphysique, pour dépouiller la matière de toutes les propriétés qui ne peuvent se déduire de l'étenduë impénétrable; & faire par conséquent de la matière un être purement passif, incapable de contenir en lui-même le principe du mouvement. D'où l'on voit que la nécessité d'un premier moteur distingué de la matière, est comme le centre où vont se réunir tous les principes physiques & métaphysiques de la Philosophie de Descartes.[16]

The Cartesian principle of the divisibility of matter destroys the atheism of Spinoza, for it disproves the ultimate reality of material substance.

---

répugnance à admettre une étenduë infinie, immobile, indivisible; & qu'après avoir adopté la notion de l'étenduë établie par les partisans de l'espace pur, il y ajoûté une absurdité particulière, qui est de l'appeller une étendue corporelle. Ainsi Spinosa ne peut établir sa conséquence qu'en renversant le principe sur lequel Descartes a rejetté le vuide, & fait consister l'essence du corps dans l'étenduë. Descartes n'a soûtenu l'impossibilité du vuide, qu'en soûtenant que toute étenduë est par la nature impénétrable, divisible, mobile. Spinoza n'établit sa doctrine qu'en supposant que l'étenduë peut être indivisible, immobile. La doctrine de Spinosa est donc directment opposée aux principes de Descartes." Pp. 191–92.
[16] Pages 196–98.

Gerdil attempts to augment his case by discovering inconsistency within Spinoza's materialism. He charges that Spinoza admitted the conception of material particles or corpuscles. But this is hopelessly inconsistent with the indivisibility of extension. In any case, Spinoza is a materialist, for extension is given the attributes of ultimate reality. If, however, we overlook the inconsistency, Spinoza is an atomist and a fatalist. He must be included within the group of the "New Epicureans." "Nothing is then more fitting for the destruction of the Atheism of Spinoza and of Epicurus than the principles of Descartes concerning the essence of matter." The divisibility of matter overthrows the unity of substance that forms the basis of Spinoza's edifice. The establishment of extension as the essence of matter excludes from matter the principles of movement, and this destroys the atheism of Epicurus.[17]

The Cartesian concept of matter enables Descartes to separate the finite and the infinite, or at least the indefinite and the infinite. The distinction between finite and infinite substances, in Gerdil's Cartesianism, is fundamental, precisely as the principle of a single substance is basic for Spinozism. The latter doctrine, were it made consistent and given consistency of expression, would define matter substance as the supreme reality. What Spinozism describes as the "attribute" of thought is, if the term be allowed at all, an attribute of matter. Thought is a manifestation of matter, a mode of extension. Gerdil's interpretation of Spinoza presents the system as an epiphenomenalism. The Cartesian concept of matter, distinguishing the indefinite and the infinite, the moved from the creative principle of motion and continuance in existence, also excluded thought and spirit from matter. The Cartesian principles, then, according to Gerdil, provide a new and ample basis for the defense of religion and theology against the threat of materialism, atheism, and atomism. The destroyer of Scholasticism becomes the defender of the faith.

Gerdil's effort to demonstrate the incompatibility of Cartesian and Spinozistic doctrine is, of course, at the same time an attempted refutation of the latter. It will be conceded that the Car-

[17] Pages 209–10.

tesian refutations of Spinoza cannot be regarded as accurate reflections of his doctrine. They indicate, on the whole, what their authors understood as Spinozism. Perhaps such a statement needs some qualification. We may suspect, here and there, a deliberate misrepresentation of Spinoza's teaching in order to facilitate its refutation. Even admitting this qualification, however, the refutations must express, even in the deliberate distortions of Spinozistic doctrine, the position of that doctrine in the intellectual situation. Thus, the critics of Spinoza, however little they tell us of Spinoza, tell us a great deal concerning themselves—and of the grounds of their allegiance to Descartes. What the critic of Spinoza regarded as a successful refutation of Spinozism by means of Cartesian principles expresses that critic's conception not only of Spinoza's teaching but also of Cartesianism. In the main, the refutations pivot upon the identification of Spinoza's philosophy with atheism, or at any rate they depend upon an interpretation of that philosophy judged to be incompatible with traditional theology. This, in itself, however, is relatively unimportant. The more significant fact is the critics' view that Spinoza's doctrine, if an atheism, is a new atheism. With this goes the conviction that new grounds are necessary for the refutation of an atheism that is new. The effort of Lamy, which is the effort of a Benedictine, deliberately seeks to accomplish its purpose by bending to this purpose philosophical ideas borrowed from recent philosophers.[18]

[18] François Lamy, *Le Nouvel Athéisme renversé, ou Refutation du sistême de Spinosa, tirée pour la plûpart, de la connoissance de la nature de l'homme*, par un Religieux Benedictin de la Congrégation de Saint Maur, a Paris, chez Jean de Nully, 1696. Lamy explains in the *Avertissement* that the refutation according to the geometrical order was written before the publication of his *Traité de la connoissance de soi-même*, and his *Vérité évidente de la réligion Crétienne*. Having been requested to write a refutation according to the "common" (or usual) method, he issues this volume containing both forms of refutation. The volume appeared under impressive auspices: it contains "approbations" by Monseigneur de Fénelon, Archevêque, Duc de Cambray, by Monseigneur de Sillert, Evêque de Soissons; by Hideux, Curé de Saints Innocens; and by M. Coulau, Directeur de la Biblioteque Mazarine. It begins with a statement of the "Idée du sistême de Spinosa & de la réfutation qu'on en fait." There follows the First Treatise, containing a refutation according to "la méthode commune"; the Second Treatise, a refutation concerned with the possibility of the Incarnation; and then the Third Treatise, a "Réfutation suivant la méthode des Geometres." The work concludes with a "Parallel" drawn between the religion and morality of Spinoza with the Christian, "& même avec la lumière naturelle."

There can be, of course, nothing surprising in Lamy's assertion that if Spinoza is not an atheist he at least does not rise above
the level of Deism. But after all, Spinoza is an atheist, for the
Spinozistic God is a universal being indistinguishable from the
totality of nature, a being without liberty, nonprovidential, "sans
but et sans fin, sans choix & sans election." That the consequences
of Spinozism are "funestes"—that the young are being seduced
by the doctrine, its adherents increasing, "les Libertins" finding
support in it—all of this is to be expected. Our interests in Lamy's
efforts must turn upon more specific considerations. The Spinozistic philosophy, for our Benedictine, is characteristic of the
new age; it supplies a capital expression of everything that could
be found wrong with the world. For Lamy thinks that Spinoza is
no isolated phenomenon. This philosophy is a response to the
intellectual needs of minds and temperaments in revolt. Let us,
therefore, first inquire of our author: How and why did the Spinozistic philosophy arise? We may then inquire what Lamy takes
this philosophy to be—the "idée générale du sistême de Spinoza,
& de ses principales consequences," as the title of Section II runs.
From this point we are prepared to appreciate the general plan of
Lamy's refutation.

Spinoza's doctrine effects a "bouleversement" not merely in
religion and morality but even in our conceptions of nature. This
change, however, is the consequence of an effort to give a systematic foundation for the modern ethical revolt. What Lamy finds
in Spinozism may be described in one word: naturalism. The
metaphysics of Spinoza is the ground for ethical naturalism: but
ethical naturalism is precisely what demanded the metaphysics.
The modern age, at heart, demands the overthrow of Christian
morality. The essential trait of Christian morality is its uncompromising opposition to natural impulse. It remains, for Lamy,
an ethics of renunciation. The modern revolt seeks a rational justification for its aversion to Christian morality and for its ethical
and political naturalism. To accomplish this, according to Lamy,
philosophy must furnish a metaphysical ground for anti-Christian
morality and politics. But it must do more—for it must provide an
explanation of the fact that there is a Christian morality. Chris-

tian morality must be explained—by explaining it away. To explain it away, as Lamy regards the effort, there arises a conceptual scheme which the eighteenth century employed again and again in many variants. This is accomplished by the doctrine which attributes the rules and laws of Christian morality to a political and social plot. Those who possessed power exploited the superstitions and fears of the masses, developing the Christian code, in order to insure the subjection of men to priestly and political authority. This is the thesis of the naturalists. Lamy urges that the thesis is unsupportable so long as ordinary ideas concerning God and man and the world are retained. A set of new ideas is required. The naturalistic revolt, having speciously explained away Christian morality and institutions, must seek reinforcement by a metaphysical foundation. To do this, it must, on the negative side, destroy the traditional ideas of the providential governance of the world, which will mean atheism, necessity, and mechanism in nature. On the positive side, it must define a point of view from which the equivalence of right and good, on the one hand, and the natural on the other, necessarily follows.[19] In the eyes of Lamy the Spinozistic philosophy, with its specious appearance of compelling logical rigor, is the outstanding effort to provide radicalism with rational justification.

On the grounds that we must fight fire with fire, the refutation must oppose metaphysics to metaphysics, reason to reason. It is important to note that Lamy recognizes the problem to be metaphysical. The horrible consequences—in morality, in political life, in institutional conflicts—are symptomatic. The time has passed when anything can be accomplished by appeal to dogma and to faith. What needs to be accomplished can and must be accomplished by reason—"même avec la lumière naturelle."

What are the principles of this naturalistic metaphysics that must be overthrown? And where, if we are to depend upon the natural light of reason, are we to find the *point d'appui* of this refutation? The purpose of the refutation is to reinstate what this metaphysics threatens to destroy. The negation of the ethical and religious consequences depends upon the refutation of the meta-

[19] Pages 84 ff.

physics devised to support this transvaluation of values so characteristic of the modern age. Now Lamy recognizes that the
Spinozistic teaching is thoroughly consistent in its rejection of all
anthropomorphical ideas—in its designation of the conceptions
of a rewarding, punishing, and providential deity and the ethical
principles correlated therewith as anthropomorphic. Moreover,
Spinoza's Biblical criticism, which deprives Holy Writ of metaphysical significance, is a necessary consequence of the naturalistic metaphysics. The traditional conceptions of Christian
theology, not to say the formulations of its mysteries, so Lamy
recognizes, must necessarily be for Spinoza a set of symbolic
expressions, possessing only an elliptical value. Social serviceability is the pragmatic test of their worth. Thus, original sin
must be reduced by Spinoza to the level of fiction. Even good and
beauty can have no objective significance.[20] Lamy is convinced
that the use by a Spinozist of a phrase such as "the Love of God"
is preposterous. The traditional language of theology is utterly
unfit for the expression of Spinozistic ideas. When Spinoza declares that to admit miracles is to incur the danger of atheism,
Lamy can record only astonishment. It is the paradox of an atheist
who "gives preservatives against atheism." [21] Lamy's real accu-
sation is that Spinozism, by employing traditional verbiage,
surreptitiously seeks to make his doctrine appear to be in harmony with belief, when in fact it is wholly inconsistent with the
faith. Spinoza would attribute values to his doctrine that it cannot
possess, since these values follow only if traditional expressions
convey the traditional meanings associated with them and do not
follow when the expressions have only the significance of meta-
phor, which they must have in the Spinozistic context.

The point of this situation is that for Lamy, Spinozism is a
doctrine devised to support anti-anthropomorphism; the metaphysical principles provide a foundation of a mechanistic view of
nature; this mechanistic science of nature implies determinism;
and accordingly free will and associated theological and ethical
ideas become mere projections of human impulse into objective
nature. In return, this conclusion reflects back upon the nature of

[20] Cf. pp. 48, 53–54.　　　　　　　[21] Cf. pp. 34–35, 39, 55, 59.

man and results in Spinozistic views concerning man equally at
variance with tradition. Spinoza's attitude towards the passions
as expressed in his political thought would have seemed to Lamy
thoroughly consistent. Neither to praise nor to dispraise the passions, but to understand them—this is to take them naturalistically. But taken in this way, human nature appears as an incident
in the system of nature. It furnishes no clues to a reality lying
beyond. Moreover, whatever laws of morality this view of man
may suggest, these laws can have no value lying beyond their
expediency in a social system. The larger fish devour the smaller
fish by supreme natural right, and so with man conceived as an
incident within the system of nature. With organized society civil
right comes into being. The validity of this right, however, is
circumscribed by the life of society. The function of religion
must then be the inculcation of piety. And the entire system of
religious ideas is essentially a set of symbols for a merely socio-
political content. Within the context of Spinozism, as Lamy
thinks, the "love of God" is either an elaborate symbol for social
control or it is nothing. "Sin" may have meaning within a given
social system, but not beyond it. When Spinoza employs expressions such as the "love of God" in his metaphysical context, the
phrase becomes evasive. Its employment may be due to deliberate
artifice expressing a lack of courage. Either Spinoza seeks to
deceive, or else he is pathetically incapable of recognizing the
consequences of his own doctrine.

Spinozism is a "new" atheism. It is a naturalism—but a naturalism that is in some sense equally new. Spinozism reflects a
modern context. What it denies with significance for Lamy's defense of religion, morality, and theology is something also
modern. In brief, Lamy's zeal is not that of a Scholastic contend-
ing against modernity. On the contrary, he represents dissension
within the context of modern reflection. The refutation of the *new*
atheism must be provided by a metaphysics that is equally a
product of modernity. Lamy's refutation, then, is a Cartesian
refutation.

Within these conditions, *the crucial point in the refutation of
Spinozism lies within the nature of man.* Lamy affirms this again

and again. The very title of his book asserts that the refutation is drawn for the greater part, from knowledge of the nature of man. Knowledge of man is "l'écueil du Spinozisme," the reef upon which the wave of Spinozism is shattered.[22] Spinoza may assert the immortality of man; but Spinozistic immortality, whatever it may be, is at least in no sense an immortality which points backward to the nature of man as a clue to reality or forward to the objective validity and metaphysical implications of morality. Within the naturalistic system, Lamy in effect insists, no one thing possesses primacy over another, neither the living over the nonliving nor man over the remainder of the animate world. Man may be the most highly evolved of things—but the adjectival phrase has no value significance.

Spinoza, if he is to be overthrown, must be refuted by arguments drawn from the nature of man. With this we again come upon the central fact presented by the refutations of Spinozism. The Spinozistic metaphysics defines the nature of the Spinozistic man. From this definition of the Spinozistic man flow all those consequences in the context of practical life that Lamy and other opponents describe as "funestes." Metaphysics, however, can be refuted by metaphysics alone. The Spinozistic metaphysical man, so to speak, can be replaced successfully only by means of an opponent metaphysical man. The opposing conception of man, however, cannot be drawn from Scholasticism—this would not be fighting fire with fire. The opposition of ideas, to be effective continuously, must itself be defined by a common context. The refutation of Spinoza must begin with a modern metaphysics that takes its departure from the nature of man. Lamy must ask: Where is there such a metaphysics? To his mind, there is but one answer. The Cartesian philosophy meets the requirements. The Cartesian philosophy supplies not merely an idea of the nature of man but also a true idea of his nature. In the context of Cartesianism we come to knowledge of man. This philosophy, indeed, is founded upon truths concerning the nature of man. Thus, according to Lamy, the refutation of Spinoza depends upon a Cartesian standpoint. More precisely, it depends upon the Cartesian onto-

---

[22] Cf. pp. 25–32, 83.

logical dualism. Descartes becomes the defender of the faith and can fulfill this destiny because he affirms what Spinozism would deny—the real distinction between soul and body.

As for Gerdil, so for Lamy, the first step is a demonstration of the contrast between the philosophies of Descartes and Spinoza. Lamy centers his effort on disproving the position that Cartesianism generated the later system. The exploitation of Cartesian ideas as the basis for refutation is implicit in the Second Treatise, the "Refutation de l'erreur de Spinosa, sur la possibilité de l'Incarnation." It is also implicit in the document called the *Parallele de la réligion & de la morale de Spinosa, avec la réligion & morale de Jesus-Christ, & même avec la lumière naturelle.* But in a second parallel the comparison of the two philosophies is made explicit. The first stage of the disproof of Cartesian responsibility for Spinoza is formed by a reference to the distinction of substances.

Toute sa philosophie ne roule que sur la distinction réelle qu'il met entre la substance étendue & la substance pensante; & qu'ainsi il admit dans la nature pluralité des substances. [Lamy adds that:] nous venons de voir au contraire que la philosophie de Spinosa ne roule que sur la confusion qu'il fait de ces deux substances, & sur la supposition extravagante d'une seule substance dans la nature; le corps & l'esprit dit-il, ne sont que la même chose.[23]

In this fashion Lamy interprets the Spinozistic dictum concerning one and the same thing, viewed under different attributes. In a summary of Cartesian doctrine, he enumerates six principles peculiar to the former and denied severally and collectively by Spinozism. The central point is the Cartesian principle that the soul is not a mode of being (*une manière d'être*), either of God or of body, or of any other thing whatever. Thus, the Cartesian isolation of the soul from nature and its definition as substance undergo a remarkable increase in importance. The mind-body dualism was advanced by Cartesians as an irresistible truth.[24] Descartes alone has revealed to philosophy both what the soul is and what is the nature of matter. In the earlier stages of debate between Cartesians and anti-Cartesians the alleged irresistible

[23] Page 486.
[24] Cf. "Louis de la Forge and the Critique of Substantial Forms.

truth encountered derision. Confronting a new enemy, however, the Cartesian offensive against atheism must be launched from the body-mind dualism. The Cartesians themselves had acknowledged—with reluctance here and there—the absorption of the animals within the single realm of matter substance and mechanical law. Spinozism, as the opponents of Spinoza viewed his doctrine, would complete the engulfing of life within matter. The refutation of Spinozism, then, must begin with the position that in its conception of man Cartesianism stands in irreconcilable opposition to the doctrine of Spinoza. The very meaning of the term "metaphysics" reflects this adoption of Cartesianism: Lamy declares that metaphysics is above all the science "qui nous fait connoître la diférence qu'il a entre les esprits & les corps, qui nous découvre ce qui se peut connoître de la nature de l'âme, & de son immortalité; de la nature de Dieu, de son Existence, de sa Providence, de sa Puissance." [25] The refutation of Spinoza, as the title of Lamy's first treatise assures us, is accompanied by pure reason, which finds in knowledge of the nature of man "l'écueil" of Spinozism and the source of the duties of Christian morality. The first chapter, moreover, is devoted to the "verities, & duties which spring from the distinction of spirit and body," to "the *justesse* of their union," and "to the capacity by which the spirit knows and loves." In the context of controversy before us, Cartesian metaphysics is definitive in principle.

Lamy stands squarely upon his dualistic basis of Cartesian origin. Effects, actions, express the nature of things. In man we find two wholly opposed series of actions. Therefore there must be two principles as the sources of the dissimilar consequences. If, now, these principles are substances and man is a composite of substances, Spinozism is in principle refuted.[26] There are two substances for the reason that either can be conceived wholly independently of the idea of the other. With this the "whole edifice" of Spinoza is ruined, for Spinozism, if it mean anything, asserts the existence of but one substance, and this implies the reduction of all phenomena to a common denominator.

The dissimilarities revealed in man's composite nature are ir-

[25] Pages 5–6.   [26] Pages 98, 99.

reducible. Lamy even derives from this irreducibility an argument for the existence of God. Only an infinitely wise and powerful being could be the author of man, for such an order of power
and wisdom is necessary to effect the union in one being of substances so opposed.[27] The Cartesian dualism, affording a first argument for the existence of God, provides the foundation upon
which may be reinstated the arguments from design. The latter had
evidently become an object of derision. For Lamy asserts that despite the ridicule of his readers one may establish a supreme wisdom ruling the world from the functions of the human body.[28]
With due attention to his dual nature, then, man need not pass
beyond that nature in order to establish the existence of God, that
is, of God in the sense in which Spinoza would reject the conception as anthropomorphic. *Je pense, donc je suis,* is no more evident
than *Je suis, donc il y a un Dieu infiniment sage.*[29] It is quite unnecessary to burden the reader with the details of Lamy's arguments. It is sufficient to note that man's nature provides the source
of two sets of argument: the one, the arguments from design drawn
from man's body; the other, the arguments from the native ethical endowment of the soul. From the very duality of man's nature an infinitely wise and powerful author is demonstrated. Upon
this foundation the body serves to reinstate the arguments from
design, and the soul to give an objective reality to those ethical
ideas that for Spinozistic naturalism (according to Lamy) cannot
be more than projections of social experience.

Moreover, the superiority of the soul to the body is obvious
from the fact that the soul is capable of thought, while the body is
not. From this it follows that human experience must reveal two
sets of values, the one superior to the other. The soul's immortality, which follows from its indivisibility and immateriality of
substance, extends the values of the soul from the finite to the infinite sphere.[30] With this, the whole of Christian morality, against
which the naturalists and free-thinkers are secretly in revolt, is,
of course, reinstated. The spirit of this morality, as Lamy has
made clear, is renunciatory; thus, the Cartesian dualism has

[27] Pages 103–5.   [28] Pages 93–96.
[29] Page 106.   [30] First Treatise, pp. 171 ff.

served to provide a metaphysical basis for an other-worldly morality. The depreciation of sense as a source of knowledge, according to the Cartesian doctrine, becomes in Lamy's hands an auxiliary of this morality. Reflection upon the nature of man, upon the conditions of the union of soul and body, reinforces the anti-naturalistic point of view. Man is not naturally without duties and without law.[31] The doctrine of innate ideas is thus transformed into a doctrine of an original ethical endowment. Correspondingly, the doctrine that the senses are the source of unclear and indistinct ideas takes an ethical turn. The union of soul and body subjects the former to the impact of ideas from sense aroused within the soul upon the occasion of the perceptual process. The sense-ideas, however, have very bad effects upon the soul, turning it towards earthly things. In this way the corruption of human nature may be explained; the soul is thus "disadvantageously" situated with respect to the performance of its chief duties. Just as the obscurity of the sense idea as a knowledge function cannot be dispelled, but is incurable, in the same manner sense experience cannot be expurgated. As Lamy states the matter, our indispensable duties are to flee from sense objects and sense experience. The soul and the body define two utterly dissimilar sets of values: the first, born of the soul, expresses the immortality of its nature; the second, the interests of the body and this life, for the sake of which Spinoza wrote a metaphysics. Cartesianism, not Scholasticism, it seems, is an other-worldly philosophy.

The refutation of Spinoza, so far, has proceeded according to the "méthode commune"—it is a treatise for the generality. The refutation in the third treatise proceeds according to the geometrical method and is the esoteric doctrine. The third treatise is aimed solely at the first book of the Ethics, for with the overthrow of this the whole structure of Spinozism is destroyed. Lamy proposed to conduct his enterprise by accepting, in the main, Spinoza's axioms and definitions. The definitions of substance, mode, and attribute are adopted, but not that of God. Lamy's own axioms begin with this, that "la réalité, la vérité, la bonté ou la perfection & Unité" are properties inseparable from Being. These are

[31] Page 143 ff.

called transcendent because they are necessarily found in everything that is truly Being. Significantly, Lamy's second axiom asserts that thought is nobler than extension.[32] He seeks to establish that the idea of substance necessarily includes the idea of Being. The very idea of attribute involves the notion of substance, and therefore cannot be conceived by itself. This purpose, of course, is to maintain that, from attributes which can be conceived independently of other attributes we must infer the existence of diverse substances. Thus, against Spinoza his refutation must maintain the existence of several substances, not of one substance; or, what for him amounts to the same thing, he must urge that independence of attribute implies substances as diverse as the attributes. With this he establishes the Cartesian dualism of substances as the central principle upon which the geometrical refutation of Spinozism must be based.[33] At the same time he denies that thought and extension are equally attributes of God. For the essential attribute of God is thought, while extension constitutes a being distinguished from God, and excluded from the essence of God.[34]

So much accomplished, there follow for Lamy the propositions which restore the world of extensions as a creation of God, freedom rather than necessity for God, and the existence of thinking substance, man, really distinguished from God and outside his essence. Cousin, examining two obscure documents concerning the relation of Cartesianism and Spinozism, reaches this conclusion.

Mais on peut dire aujourd'hui toute la vérité: ce n'est pas tel ou tel principe cartésien, c'est l'esprit même du dix-septième siécle, qui, après avoir produit le cartésianisme, c'est-à-dire un spiritualisme aussi judicieux que sublime, l'entraînait en même temps vers la double erreur du spinozisme et du jansénisme. Le dix-septième siécle est en effet comme imbu de l'idée de la toute-puissance divine et du néant des créatures. Il incline à ne reconnaître qu'un seul acteur véritable sur la scène de ce monde, une seule cause, un seul être, Dieu. Là est l'unité de la philosophie de ce grand siécle, comme l'unité de la philosophie du siécle suivant est dans l'affaiblissement de l'idée de Dieu, et dans un sentiment outré des forces de l'homme qui aboutit à une sorte d'apothèose de l'humanité.[35]

---

[32] Pages 260–263.   [33] Pages 299–306.   [34] Pages 319, 329.
[35] *Fragments philosophiques pour servir à l'histoire de la philosophie*, I, 295.

If Cousin's characterization of the inner tendency of the seventeenth century be accepted, the importance of the Cartesian dualism in the refutation of Spinoza may be reaffirmed. Descartes' own distinction between infinite and finite substance was shaky. Deny its validity, and it could be argued that Spinozism is generated—or three Spinozisms, according to the manner in which the results are interpreted. Spinozism as a spiritualism, as a materialism, or as a doctrine in which thought and extension, defined as attributes, would be merely *attributes* of substance. In any case, as Gerdil and Lamy would view such a result, it might imply the nothingness of the creature. A conclusion of this order, for the cardinal and the Benedictine priest, could scarcely be tolerable. The Cartesian dualism of finite substances—that is, a concept of substance permitting a distinction between infinite and finite substance—was of critical significance for the controversial interest of Lamy and Gerdil. If the Spinozistic single-substance doctrine could be construed as a materialism, refutation might be facilitated. In the final analysis, however, it was of greater importance to maintain a real distinction between God and creature. The Cartesian dualism is of inestimable importance. As Gerdil and Lamy implicitly believe, it alone meets the facts and satisfies human interests. It provides for the reality of man and the reality of physical nature. Nevertheless, it prevents the absorption of man in physical nature, while assuring his dignity as a creature. And finally, the Cartesian distinction between finite and infinite substances means that God cannot be identified with nature's substance. If Scholasticism be regarded as overthrown, then on the Cartesian basis, and on it alone, as Lamy seems to believe, can atheism be avoided and the revolt against Christian morality be defeated.

MATTER AND SCIENTIFIC
EFFICIENCY

"CREATIVITY" is another rendering of the Aristotelian "matter" and of the modern "neutral stuff." But it is divested of the notion of passive receptivity, either of "form" or of external relations; it is the pure notion of the activity conditioned by the objective immortality of the actual world—a world which is never the same twice, though always with the stable element of divine ordering. Creativity is without a character of its own in exactly the sense in which the Aristotelian "matter" is without a character of its own. It is that ultimate notion of the highest generality at the base of actuality.

This statement by Whitehead [1] suggests a continuity of ideas through the centuries. Indeed, the persistent use of the very word "matter" suggests a continuity of response to an unremitting demand. The significance of the term, from age to age, from thinker to thinker (whether scientist or philosopher), reflects the tension between speculative ideas and the compulsion exerted by sense experience. For this reason Whitehead can clarify the meaning of "creativity" by reference to Aristotelian matter.

Whitehead's words may, then, serve as a preliminary excuse for what would otherwise seem an act of recklessness. For it is daring to attempt, as this essay proposes, to relate the saintly author of the *Summa* to the no less saintly author of *Process and Reality,* even with the mediating function of the somewhat less saintly Descartes. The later saint, it is true, confronts a situation markedly different from that confronted by the earlier. Between them lies the achievement of an extraordinary body of scientific knowledge, or, more prudently expressed, of scientific findings. The saint of the *Summa* had a preparatory function, of which he was not wholly unaware. The latter-day saint's task is consummatory, since he must reckon with these findings. Despite this notable difference, both metaphysicians address themselves to an identical problem. For Thomas, assuredly, the central problem is to define concrete reality, the finite existent—that which can be said

[1] *Process and Reality,* pp. 46–47.

to be, but must be distinguished from absolute being. For White-head, the task is to recapture the concreteness of existence; that is, to define the finite existence in the light of (and in spite of?) scientific findings. The work of Thomas as metaphysician may be fairly described as preparatory for scientific inquiry. Human cognitive powers are proportioned to things. What, then, is a thing? What is the order of things? The philosophy of organism is a metaphysics sophisticated by centuries of interplay between scientific inquiry and philosophical reflection. The angelic doctor, despite his remarkable prescience, scarcely expected what a bur-den he would bequeath to the future by his stubborn insistence on the competence of reason to attain knowledge of things and his saintly conviction that it is the duty of men, the Creator having made them as they are, to seek to know something about every-thing, even if they are not equipped to achieve complete knowl-edge about anything. Our angelic doctor of the twentieth century must reckon with the results. Philosophy becomes the "critic of abstractions." [2]

The injunctions of Saint Thomas, however, could be obeyed only if an efficient procedural basis for inquiry could be devised. This was done. Whitehead affirms it. Having characterized the "scientific philosophy" which closed the seventeenth century, he writes:

We must note its astounding efficiency as a system of concepts for the organisation of scientific research. In this respect, it is fully worthy of the genius of the century which produced it. It has held its own as the guiding principle of scientific studies ever since. It is still reigning. . . . No alternative system of organising the pursuit of scientific truth has been suggested. It is not only reigning, but it is without a rival.

But notably this doctor continues:

And yet—it is quite unbelievable. This conception of the universe is surely framed in terms of high abstractions, and the paradox only arises because we have mistaken our abstractions for concrete realities.[3]

The situation is profoundly disturbing. We have a system of ideas providing astounding efficiency for inquiry, a body of find-ings resulting therefrom so vast as to be unassimilable by one man,

[2] *Science and the Modern World*, p. 86.   [3] *Ibid.*, pp. 80–81.

even an angelic doctor, a conception of the universe defining the program of efficiency—and it is unbelievable. Indeed, it seems highly probable that thinkers far from saintly must have been at work during the interval between our two angelic doctors.

The interval was marked by a tension between metaphysics and existential inquiry, between ideas and the immediacies of experience. No term more fully represents that tension than "matter." Efficiency in the pursuit of science required a notion of matter suitable to be the basis of high abstraction, for abstraction meant an economy appropriate to the limitations of our cognitive powers, those limitations which the good St. Thomas insisted upon no less than upon the competence of the powers. High abstraction, however, implies remoteness from concrete reality. As children and their very own metaphysician, Aristotle, know full well, scientists come perilously near talking nonsense. It is, then, not remarkable that experience (and experimentation) presented incessant demands for the revision of the concept of matter. The demands were concerned with the need for an inner diversification of matter, to the end that the idea might reflect the abounding concreteness of that world which Thomas insisted we could and should know. As Whitehead perceives the need with the sophistication coming from scientific findings, so Thomas perceived it in his metaphysical efforts to determine what scientific inquiry must seek to know. To Thomas, then, let us turn.

There occurs in a few Thomistic texts an intriguing expression —"the indefinite dimensionality of matter prior to the reception of the substantial form." [4] The significance of such a formula de-

---

[4] Since I am not more than an interested student of Thomas, a word of apology is appropriate. My attention was called some years ago to this formula by Professor Mortimer Adler, who courteously supplied me with references. Their consideration led me to occasional speculations concerning the place of the formula in the Thomistic system. My interest, candor requires me to say, was primarily the by-product of an interest in Descartes. A growing tendency to look backward from the father of modern thought to Thomas, who should be defined as the grandfather, led me to believe that such texts were anticipatory of Descartes and of modernity's prolonged reckoning with "matter." The present essay is the result. An earlier draft was courteously and helpfully, but severely, criticized by competent Thomistic scholars —Professor Walsh, of Manhattanville College and Columbia University, and Professor Elizabeth Salmon, of Fordham University. They found my interpretation inconsistent with Gilson and with Forest's *La Structure métaphysique du concret selon saint Thomas d'Aquin* (*Études de phil. médiévale*, XIV, Paris, Vrin, 1931),

pends upon the context within which it is to be interpreted. Now it appears necessary to distinguish two contexts, defined by and integral to the Thomistic system. To indicate this, let us consider the distinction between the Creator and the creature, between God and things, between Being and participated being. The source of existence is the Creator. To express this, a formula may be offered: Whatever can be said to be in any sense, and yet is not God and must be distinguished from God, is a creature, a something whose measure of being is received from God. (For present purposes, no extended refinements of meaning seem necessary. It is assumed that the formula represents Thomas, even if the nature and being of God and the nature and status in being of all-that-is-not-God be left undetermined.) Whatever the disabilities of the human mind, it must employ such a distinction. Thomas certainly does. Thus, mind must view things in two contexts: on the one hand, in a context or type of context that properly omits reference of things to the Deity; on the other, a context whose ultimate significance is precisely this reference to the nature and being of the Deity. The latter may be called the absolute context, the other being subordinate thereto. The subordinate is appropriate to the pursuit of scientific inquiry. The absolute would imply the necessity for metaphysical foundations *for* science, and a metaphysical reckoning *with* the results of science.[5] It is obvious that a term must be used with some equivocation when we pass from one context to the other. (The reference of the term to the Deity —its meaning in a context whose solar idea is the nature and being of the Deity—is, of course, not the same thing as using the

---

a dissertation written under Gilson. This was disturbing. In that earlier version I had explained my reliance upon Gilson. Prayerfully I reexamined Gilson's texts, and made a rather thorough reading of Forest's magistral work. My debt to both— and to my critics—is great. But I found no collision. It was necessary to rewrite my essay in order to take advantage of what I had learned. But in the end my thesis seemed to be confirmed. The reader will understand that I am probably prejudiced— I seek to find the prologue for the drama of modern science within the ideas of the Angelic Doctor, whether or not he at that time foresaw the drama as did Descartes.

[5] For the sake of brevity "metaphysics" is used as the equivalent of "philosophy" and as comprising natural or rational theology. "Theology" will be confined to doctrine dependent upon faith and revelation. In view of the total structure of Thomism, two "absolute" contexts might be distinguished, the metaphysical and the theological. For present purposes the distinction is neglected.

term "Deity.") Finally, it is contended that there are certain ideas, estimates, and points of view from which Thomas would never wittingly depart and that he would never entertain ideas or expressions recognized to be in irremediable conflict with them.

For Thomas, the term "matter" must be understood within these two contexts and by means of the interplay between them. Now matter is not a substance when form is completely absent. Matter does not exist by itself in nature, since matter as such is not an actual being, but only potentiality. It may be described as rather a thing con-created than as a thing created.[6] It is one, not because it has one form, but by the absence of all distinguishing form. Matter, in so far as it signifies bare privation of being, nothingness, is nothing. Referring all existence to the Creator, it would be inappropriate to speak of matter, in so far as it is equivalent to nothingness, as "created." But matter, in so far as it signifies anything other and more than mere nothingness, must be referred to the Deity. And so it is properly asserted that matter is created by God, albeit not apart from form.

Since, however, we hold matter to be created by God, but not apart from form, matter has its idea in God; but not apart from the idea of it as compounded with form. Matter in itself can neither exist nor be known.[7]

Now God's knowledge reaches to matter, individualizing accidents, and forms. For, since His act of understanding is His essence, it follows that He understands all that is *in any way whatever* in His essence: wherein are virtually, as in their first origin, all that have being *in any way whatever,* forasmuch as He is the first and universal principle of being; and amongst these we must include matter and accident, since matter is being in potentiality, and accident, being in another. . . .[8]

The expression "in any way whatever" has been italicized, for assuredly it is not a thoughtless stipulation on the part of so incomparable a dialectician. Matter, then, in whatever way it *is* in the divine essence, is divinely understood. In whatever way it

[6] *Summa theologica,* Q. VII, r. to o. 3. The following abbreviations will be used: *Summa theologica, ST; Summa contra gentiles, SCG;* references to and quotations from the translations by the Fathers of the English Dominican Province are indicated by *E.* References to the original texts are to the Leonine ed., *L.* The work of Forest, referred to in note 4, is represented by *F.*
[7] *ST,* Q. XV, 3d art., r. to o. 3; *E,* p. 220.
[8] *SCG,* Pt. I, ch. lxv; *E,* p. 136; italics mine.

does have being and is not a nothingness it owes that being to God.

A subordinate context, together with such knowledge as may be had of things understood in accord with the idea defining the context, must be rethought in terms of the absolute context. But a subordinate context does not involve a reference to the idea of the Deity as constitutive. Accordingly, it would appear that things—those things which can be said to be, but which are known in the absolute context to be other than God and are not God [9]—can be understood in limited fashion when they are taken *as if* existing independently of God. As the subordinate context must be assimilated to the absolute context, so the latter must ground the former. "Matter" considered in the absolute context is also considered anticipatorily in preparation for its function in the subordinate context. In this way "matter" receives definition so that science may use the term *as if* it stood for something absolute, for science's restricted purposes. The notion of matter must be prepared so as to implement the procedures of inquiry and to be fitted to receive the burden of meanings generated in inquiry. Within the subordinate context, matter will accumulate meanings reflecting this anticipatory preparation and also the cumulative results of scientific inquiry. But in return matter must be re-referred to the absolute context, to the end that the load of meanings may be re-evaluated.

With this in mind, we may turn to the intriguing Thomistic formulae. It is necessary to quote texts.

. . . in the matter of things generable and corruptible, it behooves one to understand indeterminate dimensions before the taking on of substantial form. And therefore the division which is according to dimensions of this kind properly pertains to matter. But quantity, full and determinate, comes to matter after substantial form. Whence the division which is made according to determinate dimensions has regard to species especially when the determinate arrangement of the parts pertains to the nature [*ratio*] of the species, as is the case in the human body.

. . . that which is understood in matter before form remains in matter after corruption: because the latter being removed there can still remain the former. It behooves one, moreover, . . . to understand in the matter of things generable and corruptible, before their substantial form, di-

[9] Hereafter the formula is dropped, and the expression "finite existent" is used. *F* employs "concrete being."

mensions indeterminate, according to which the division of matter may be effected, so that it can receive diverse forms in diverse parts. And so matter, existing under those dimensions whatsoever form it may take, has greater identity with that which had been generated from it than any other part of other matter existing under whatsoever form.[10]

Here are a number of distinctions. There is matter. There are indefinite dimensionalities which must be presupposed as belonging to matter, independently of form. There is the substantial

[10] *ST*, Pt. III, supp., Q. LXXX, art 5, r. to o. 3; Q. LXXIX, art. 1, r. to o. 3. I am deeply indebted to my colleague Professor Walter Montgomery for his translation of these and other texts. The translations were made intentionally as literal as possible. In the translation of the Fathers of the English Dominican Province, the above texts read as follows: "In the matter of things subject to generation and corruption it is necessary to presuppose indefinite dimensions before the reception of the substantial form. Consequently division which is made according to these dimensions belongs properly to matter. But complete and definite quantity comes to matter after the substantial form; wherefore division that is made in reference to definite quantity regards the species especially when definite position of parts belongs to the essence of the species, as in the human body." "That which is understood as though it were in matter before its form remains in matter after corruption, because when that which comes afterwards is removed that which came before may yet remain. Now . . . in the matter of things subject to generation and corruption, we must presuppose undeterminate dimensions, by reason of which matter is divisible, so as to be able to receive various forms in its various parts. Wherefore after the separation of the substantial form from matter, these dimensions still remain the same: and consequently the matter existing under those dimensions, whatever form it receive, is more identified with that which was generated from it, than any other part of matter existing under any form whatever" (*E*, p. 185; pp. 159–60). In *SCG*, treating of Eucharistic problems, the following texts occur: "Among the accidents, indeed, a certain order is to be noted. For, of all accidents, more nearly does dimensive quantity inhere in substance; afterwards, qualities are received in substance by a mediant quantity (*deinde qualitates in substantia recipiuntur quantitate mediante*), just as color by a mediant surface. Whence also through a division of quantity, they are divided *per accidens*. [*E*: Hence the division of the other accidents is identical to the division of quantity.] . . . So, therefore, it must be posited that the accidents of bread, after the aforesaid change, remain, so that only dimensive quantity subsists without a subject, and in this itself qualities are founded as if on a subject . . ." (*L: SCG*, Pt. IV, ch. lxiii; *E*, p. 231). ". . . dimensive quantity has, in contrast with other accidents, this property that it is individualized *secundum se*. This is so because position, which is the order of the parts in the whole, is included in its very nature [*ratio*]: for it is quantity having position. . . . And because dimensive quantity alone has by nature that from which the multiplication of individuals in the same species can happen, the principal basis [*radix*] of multiplication of this kind seems to be from dimension because in the genus of substance multiplication is made according to the division of matter: which could not be understood except as matter is considered under dimensions: for quantity being removed, all substance is indivisible, as the Philosopher states . . ." (*L: SCG*, Pt. IV, p. 209; *E*, pp. 235–36). *E*: ". . . thus in the genus of substance multiplicity is according to material dimensions; in fact, it is inconceivable in matter apart from dimensions; seeing that without quantity all substance is indivisible . . ."

form. Finally, there is the complete and definite quantity which accrues to matter, or, more accurately, belongs to the finite existent in virtue of matter's reception of the substantial form. So far it would appear that dimensionality, or at least a certain indefinite dimensionality, does not come to matter through form but is inherent in matter independently of form.

Obviously, Thomas is facing the problem of the diversity of things. The question is, then, if the analysis of a finite thing is to be accomplished in terms of the distinction between form and matter, to what extent is the diversity the contribution of matter? The issue is one of metaphysical analysis. There is the concrete, the thing, the finite existent—that which is analytically taken to be a composite of matter and form. What content is to be assigned to form? What to matter? The analysis moves in two directions, one of which terminates in "prime matter." In the texts cited, the terminus seems to be described as matter-in-its-indeterminate-dimensionality. Now, matter can neither exist nor be known. Is this matter that can neither exist nor be known the matter to which must be attributed indefinite dimensionality prior to the reception of the substantial form? Let us assume that beyond indefinitely dimensional matter lies prime matter. Prime matter, presumably, is wholly dimensionless. The term is a sign of something characterless at the base of actuality, to adapt the words of Whitehead. It is a sign that analysis of concrete being has come to an end, in one direction at least; it embodies a gesture whereby bare potentiality is granted. Prime matter, assuredly, can neither exist nor be known. With respect to indeterminately dimensional matter, it may be otherwise. It can be understood, in one sense, as both nonexistent and unknowable. Indefinitely dimensional matter is never "a this," a concrete existent, a thing. But it is not nothingness. If words are to mean anything, it is certainly not even the approximate nothingness of bare potentiality as such. It is, so to speak, a dimensional somethingness, albeit indefinitely dimensional. It is potential for determinate dimensionality, and clearly the determinate dimensions must be, at least in part, determinations of that very dimensionality which is said to be indeterminate before being determined. So far this would appear to be plausible: the indefinite dimensionality has a contribution to make to that which can be said to exist when the indefinite shall have become definite. It would appear, then, that to this meager extent indefinitely dimensional matter is knowable.

The issue may be formulated in another way. Matter cannot be reduced to the point where it is identical with *privation,* sheer nonbeing.[11] We begin with the indescribable diversity of things, the multiplicity of existents, the things whose sensible differences Descartes (rightly or wrongly) thought to be sufficiently representable by the infinite multitude of figures. If, now, analysis pivot upon the distinction between form and matter, the matter component must have *some* contribution to make to the existential diversity. Forest offers the following as a quite provisional formulation of the central idea of the Thomistic system: "L'existence concrète ne désigne pas seulement la position pure d'un être, elle est encore l'être d'une nature, cette nature à son tour comporte des éléments constitutifs." [12] He repeatedly characterizes the relation of matter and form as a reciprocal causality.[13] They are causes, doubtless, of different order, but this is not important for the issue at hand. Nothingness cannot be a cause. The term "matter," employed in the analysis of existence and defined as in a

[11] "Avicenne revient ainsi à ce que saint Thomas nomme une doctrine platonicienne: on ramène finalement la matière à un véritable non-être parce qu'on ne la distingue pas de la privation" (*F,* p. 220). ". . . Saint Thomas dit souvent que la matière est *prope nihil;* encore est-il qu'elle doit bien, pour être comptée au rang de l'être, avoir en elle-même quelque existence; on ne saurait l'identifier au néant. Dans son texte très souvent cité, saint Thomas nous dite qu'elle est *prope rem et aliqualiter substantia rei, quia intrat in constitutionem substantiae; et pour cela il refuse de l'identifier avec la privation*" (italics of this last clause not in original). *F* adds that matter is, since it is an imitation of first being; it is not a complete substance; it has a natural relation to the form which comes to achieve it. It is the union of one with the other which alone renders the composite capable of existing (*F,* pp. 213–14).

[12] Page 39. "Le thomisme est un réalisme mystique. Le concret suppose en outre une composition métaphysique, soumise à cette condition de ne jamais détruire l'unité, qui se convertit avec l'être. Le thomisme est une métaphysique de l'unité" (p. 45).

[13] Page 207. Characterizing his own reading of certain texts, *F* concludes: ". . . la matière et la forme présentent une solidarité telle qu'il faut dire en rigueur que l'une est la cause de l'autre. La matière est cause de la forme en tant qu'elle en est le sujet, la forme est cause de la matière en tant qu'elle lui donne acte. L'expression la plus fidèle da la pensée thomiste nous paraît donc, en définitive, devoir être cherchée dans la doctrine de la causalité réciproque de la matière et de la forme" (p. 215; cf. p. 257).

relation of reciprocal causality with form, must possess an inherent constitutive character. It must be somehow characterizable, to avoid its collapse into the monotonous nothingness of nonbeing. Deprive matter of every possibility of contributing to the *specific* diversities of existence—deprive it of dimensionality lending character to its potentialities, then matter tends towards identification with nothingness.

It is a principle common to Aristotle and St. Thomas that matter is always for the sake of the form [*en vue de la forme*], not the form for the sake of the matter. It is therefore impossible to imagine the diversity of forms as due to the necessity of adapting them to the diversities [*la diversité*] of the matters. The truth is the other way about; diverse matters are required to allow diverse forms to enter into union with them so as to make concrete subjects. Systematically applied, as St. Thomas applies it, this principle becomes an essential part of the metaphysical armature of the universe. . . . St. Thomas links it up with the concept of Creation. Then it results that the Christian God creates forms for themselves, and creates diverse matters [*les matières diverses*] only in the measure demanded by the diversity of the forms. . .[14]

Diversity of, in, pertaining to matter; diverse matters; matters —it appears impossible to dispense with such expressions. Doubtless the diversities reflect some contextual limitations of discourse —of this, more hereafter. But so far it can scarcely be denied that to matter must be ascribed an intrinsic constitutive property, a dimensionality proper to it as matter, a dimensionality either expressing a power of self-diversification or at least a nature anticipatory of the diversification effected by forms. Moreover, and this is crucial, it would appear that matter has some role

[14] Gilson, *The Spirit of Mediaeval Philosophy*, New York, Scribners, 1936, trans. by A. H. C. Downes, p. 465; Fr. ed., Paris, Vrin, 1932, *première série*, p. 294. Gilson cites a text which may be translated as follows: "But the cause of the diversity of things is not from matter except as matter is demanded for the production of things, so that, indeed, according to the diversity of matter diverse forms are induced [*inducere*]. It is therefore not true that the cause of the diversity of things produced by God is matter. . . . In addition to this, according as things have being, so they have plurality and unity, for each and every thing, in so far as it is an entity, is also one; but forms do not have being for the sake of matter [*sed non habent esse formae propter materiam*], but rather matters for the sake of forms [*sed magis materiae propter formas*], for act is better than potentiality; moreover, that on account of which something is, must needs be better. Not, therefore, for this reason are forms diverse, that they may be adequate to diverse matters, but matters are for this reason diverse that they may be adequate for diverse forms" (St. Thomas Aquinas: *Compendium theologiae*, Pars I, Cap. lxxi).

in determining what forms are suitable for being received into itself. Either this, in the context of the analysis of finite existence, or else the distinction between matter and nonbeing, privation, collapses. The question is not whether the diversity of matter is there in view of form: the question is rather that of deciding what is meant by there being diversity in matter. How is this to be understood? And what content, other than uncharacterizable potentiality, can be assigned to the term?

Let us consider Forest's treatment of the problem. It is formulated thus: How can a certain diversity be found in matter anterior to the substantial form? [15] The proper nature of form, in the case of material substances, is that of an indeterminate reality. In order to achieve individuality, a complementary element must intervene, and this is matter. St. Thomas defines the role of matter in the simplest fashion when he says that it pertains to matter to terminate form.[16] In nature we find not only accidental but also substantial mutations. Metaphysical analysis compels us to recognize a certain subject of substantial mutation, and this is prime matter. Matter is the possibility of a form becoming other, the very possibility of change. As potentiality, it is ordered to act. If we consider the bare multiplicity of substances, the form appears, not as an act in the proper sense of the term, but as a particular determination of an element which is indifferent to the reception of diverse forms. This factor is prime matter. But then prime matter is nothing more than pure potentiality.[17] Matter cannot be understood by itself as purely indeterminate.[18] But matter is not to be identified with privation. It is intermediary, indeed, between act and nothingness, not between existence and nothingness, and so it participates in being.[19] If matter is only a negation, or a privation, then it follows that the form is a thing —the error of Avicenna. But it is the nature (*le propre*) of form to be the form of a matter. The union of matter and form defines

[15] Page 191. *F*'s concept of the reciprocal causality of matter and form must be kept in mind. "La matière et la forme, prises chacune à part, ont, en effet, un caractère inachevé, incomplet. S'il en est ainsi, la matière et la forme ne présentent aucune priorité l'une sur l'autre . . ." (p. 207).
[16] Page 209.   [17] Page 211.
[18] Page 212.   [19] Pages 213–14.

the first character of a concrete being. A concrete being is indivisible, it is one in itself. Thomas everywhere opposes doctrines that tend to compromise the unity of being.[20] The veritable difficulty is this: matter, in order to individuate form, should be already such and such, and not such and such another. But in itself matter is entirely indeterminate. "Materia prout nuda consideratur se habet indifferenter ad omnes formas." What, then, is the principle that is susceptible of dividing matter, to cause integral parts to appear within it, parts attributed to such and such a composite and not to another? [21]

Forest now proposes to follow the evolution of Thomas' thought.[22] In the first stage, Thomas propounds that dimensions in matter prior to the substantial form proceed from a first form, corporeity. This explains the essential character of matter, extension in space.[23] Later, abandoning this solution, Thomas adopts from Averroës the notion of indeterminate dimensions.[24] For various reasons, declares Forest, this notion is discarded. But something of Averroistic terminology persists. "Il est, en effet, une expression qui est très souvent jointe à celle des dimensions indéterminés et qui constitue avec elle un même tout: materia individuata per dimensiones interminatas praeintellectas in materia." [25] Thomas, indeed, used the preceding ideas only in order to elaborate his own definitive thought.[26] This thought will be disclosed by finding in what sense, neither Avicennian nor Averroistic, but Thomistic, dimensions can be said to be "praeintellectae in materia." [27] The solution of the problem, Forest proceeds, will

[20] Page 225.
[21] Page 236. The "most delicate problem" is said to be: How can quantity intervene before the substantial form itself, at least by a priority of reason, in order to explain the individuation of substance? In general, says Forest, Thomas admits that the solution of the problem of individuation is to be found in the relations of matter and quantity, which he expresses by the classical expression: *materia quantitate signata*. But how, he continues, can quantity effectively play the role to which its essence, taken abstractly, permits us to consider it disposed and which is to introduce distinction into matter? *F* adds that an explicit exposition of this question is not found in Thomas' work (pp. 237–38).
[22] Pages 238–46.   [23] Page 238.   [24] Page 239.
[25] Page 245.   [26] Page 239.
[27] Page 245. *F*, p. 246, n. 1, cites a text from *De Anima*, which may be translated as follows: "From this fact that matter is constituted in corporeal being through forms, it follows immediately that there are dimensions in it, by which matter divisible

be found in a reflection on the solidarity of the material and formal causes, and more especially in a certain conception of matter which is clearly formulated at all of the principal moments of the system. This matter is pure potentiality, and it involves neither the form of corporeity, nor indeterminate dimensions, nor any seminal reason.[28] Forest then summarizes his own findings: the individual involves two characters. It is undivided in itself and distinct from all others of the same species. Matter plays two seemingly different roles, which in the end become identified.

Elle est d'abord le dernier sujet, qui ne peut plus être reçu en un autre, elle vient ainsi limiter la communauté qui serait toujours celle des formes. La matière intervient donc ici en tant qu'elle donne à la forme l'ensemble des éléments dont celle-ci sera l'acte, et c'est par l'union de l'une et de l'autre que l'être est susceptible de l'existence. Mais il faut encore se demander comment cette matière qui de soi est commune, indivisible, peut être déterminée, devenir par suite telle matière susceptible de telle forme. La réponse de saint Thomas nous est connue: la matière n'est telle que par son rapport à telle quantité. Ainsi comprise, elle est le principe de la distinction, puisque le propre de la quantité c'est d'avoir des parties extérieures les unes aux autres. . . . Il est donc impossible de prendre à part la puissance de la matière et sa relation à la quantité; dire qu'elle est en puissance, c'est dire au contraire qu'elle exige telle quantité.[29]

---

through diversity of parts is understood, so that according to the diverse parts of itself it can be susceptive [*susceptiva*—receptive?] of diverse forms; and further from the fact that matter is understood as constituted in a certain substantiality of being, it can be understood as susceptive of accidents, by which it is disposed toward the perfection of further things, according to which matter becomes fitted for the realization of further perfections. *Moreover, such dispositions are pre-understood* [*praeintelliguntar*—presupposed?] *as forms induced in matter by the agent,* though there are certain accidents not proper to form as such, which act as causes in matter only in virtue of the form itself; whence forms are not pre-understood in matters as if they were dispositions, but rather form is pre-understood in them as cause in relation to effects." This text, *F* declares, represents the extreme point of Thomas' reasoning.

[28] Page 247.

[29] Page 248. This may be supplemented by the following. Numerical diversity proceeds, in a sense, simultaneously from form and matter. Both form and matter must be called "*haec*," but no form is *haec ex seipsa.* So the form of sensible substances is not a reality that matter limits. Without matter it would be entirely unreal. "Supposons, en effet, que la forme soit l'acte de tel élément particulier, elle devient alors déterminée par là même. Mais saint Thomas ajoute ici que cette matière, pour être telle, doit être distinguée, et qu'elle l'est par ses dimensions indéterminées; nous savons ce qu'il faut entendre dans sa pensée définitive: elle est distinguée par cela même qu'elle est puissance; cette réalité n'est, en effet, autre chose que celle d'un rap-

Let it be assumed that Forest presents authentic Thomism.[30] It is clear, from the preceding, that matter is not mere privation of being. It participates in being. What exists is a concrete thing: its nature and status are disclosed by an analysis which affirms the reciprocal causality of matter and form and assigns to the matter component of analysis a contribution of its own. It appears equally clear, then, that restrictions are in order. Matter is indeterminate—but in what measure and in what sense? Matter participates in being—what value is to be ascribed to this participation? Matter is indifferent with respect to the forms to be received within it—is this indifference to be described, by a rhetorical device, as absolute, or is this indifference relative to a set of forms? Matter is pure potentiality—is this potentiality illimitable, uncharacterizable? Prime matter, or matter, if you will, does not exist. What exists are things—roses, stones, dogs, and the like. Prime matter cannot be known, at any rate not in the sense in which a composite of matter-and-form is knowable. But matter must function in metaphysical analysis, and must function without collapsing into irretrievable nothingness. Diverse matters and other plural expressions need not be taken seriously —at least in the present context. Nevertheless, the diversification of existence cannot be due wholly to the diversity of the forms.

The authentic answer to these questions lies in the expression *materia quantitate signata*.

. . . d'une part, il n'y a pour chaque composé qu'une seule forme substantielle, de l'autre la matière est rigoureusement en puissance, elle

port à la quantité et à la forme" (p. 251). This seems rather confusing. We learn further that the final form of the problem of individuation is that of the relations of matter to quantity. But matter is not even extended by itself. "La matière apporte donc non une quantité effective, mais l'exigence de la répétition des partiés, à supposer, bien entendu, qu'il y ait un acte, que la forme a pour mission de donner" (p. 252). Later we read: ". . . il n'y a pour chaque composé qu'une seule forme substantielle . . . la matière est rigoureusement en puissance, elle n'intervient dans l'individuation qu'en tant qu'elle est en rapport à telle quantité et non telle autre, c'est ce que l'on traduit par l'expression *materia quantitate signata*. En un mot, l'idée la plus générale qui se présente à notre attention, c'est, en conclusion, celle de la solidarité et de la relation réciproque de la matière à la forme dans les substances matérielles" (p. 257). All of this, taken together, seems baffling. A given quantity, and not some other quantity—to what extent is this specification of quantity a contribution on the part of matter?

[30] Cf. note 4, above.

n'intervient dans l'individuation qu'en tant qu'elle est en rapport à telle quantité et non telle autre, c'est ce que l'on traduit par l'expression *materia quantitate signata*.[31]

The very nature of quantity is to have parts exterior to one another. Matter is quantitatively signate. Matter participates in or contributes to individuation in so far as, and because, it is in relation to a given quantity and not to another. Now, admitting all qualifications and stipulations, can the conclusion be avoided that matter has an intrinsic constitutive property? As pure potentiality, is it not nevertheless limited in that its potentialities are quantitatively signate? Existents are quantitatively diversified. They have their particular respective quantitative characteristics. Doubtless the form, in the reciprocal causality of matter and form, contributes to the quantitative determination, for the existent is this-form-and-this-matter. But matter, by reason of the same reciprocal causality, also contributes. It contributes what it can appropriately provide. A certain very general signateness, signateness for quantity, appears to characterize matter. To speak figuratively, a form could not be received into a matter for which that form is not adaptable. Matter, in virtue of its intrinsic tendency to precipitate quantitative specification, must exclude a form, if any such form there be, which cannot contribute to the existence of a thing with determinate quantitative aspects. Doubtless a form demands this quantity rather than that: but matter, so to speak, is prepared to meet the demand. The matter, or prime matter, functions both indifferently and selectively. It will receive indifferently any form provided that the form is such that it can evoke a quantitatively signate expression of matter's potentialities. But forms of a different order, if such there be, will be excluded from existence if incompatible with matter's inherent limited potentialities. It is contended, in sum, that the notions of reciprocal causality, of matter as not privation, of matter as potentiality, of matter as an analytical component of the finite existent, of the impossibility of separating the potentiality of matter and its relation to quantity, and related notions cannot be assigned a function in metaphysical analysis unless matter be de-

[31] *F*, p. 257.

scribed as endowed with a nature that inherently restricts the possibilities of existence.

For the sake of further clarification, the question may be considered in terms of the absolute context, in which the Deity is the referent fixing the context. What follows may be regarded as conjecture—a speculative conjecture devised for the purpose of illuminating the problem of matter and Thomas' anticipatory role in the formation of the modern scientific tradition.[32]

The absolute context receives definition, and becomes available for thought, in so far as the existence and nature of the Deity can be known to finite mind. It is beyond the scope of this essay to define the context in terms of Thomas' total system. Nevertheless, certain features must be noted. The divine essence is not directly knowable, although something of it may be known by way of negation.[33] It is incredible that Thomas ever *knowingly* took a position really discrepant with this. Whatever is said by Thomas and whatever is rightly construed in the spirit of Thomas must accord with this position: the divine essence transcends man's powers of knowing save by way of negation.[34] This may be taken as a control over speculation.

Whatever things there are, that can rightly be said to be, are creatures of the Creator.[35] Now there are things possible to God's power, although they are not.

God has knowledge of not-beings. Nevertheless not-beings have not all the same relation to His knowledge. For those things which neither are,

---

[32] I trust it will be understood that the expression "speculative conjecture" is used advisedly. It is my belief that the conjecture is quite in harmony with the spirit of Thomism. I believe it to be in harmony with some fundamental ideas of the system, if not with all of them. If authentic Thomism is an incredibly perfect and utterly coherent system, then, if the conjectures are in harmony with some of its basic ideas, it would be presumably in harmony with, and even demanded by, the system as a whole. I am not competent to decide such matters. It is, of course, possible that there are Thomistic texts utterly opposed to my conjectures. But I do not claim that Thomas either thought or advocated the extension of ideas involved in my speculations—in a sense, this would be irrelevant to my purpose.

[33] *SCG*, Bk. I, ch. xiv; *E*, p. 33.

[34] Here, and elsewhere, I am omitting, for the sake of brevity, the intricate qualifications, based by Thomas on revelation and its function, that would be required to make the exposition adequate to the Thomistic system.

[35] Again for the sake of brevity, reference throughout is to "creatures" with respect to which "matter" is pertinent—i.e., souls and angels are omitted.

nor shall be, nor have been, are known to God as possible to His power. Wherefore He knows them, not as existing in themselves in any way, but as merely existing in the divine power.

God knows not-beings in so far as they have being after a fashion, either in the divine power, or in their causes, or in themselves.[36]

God can do all things.[37] The things contained in creation are there because of God, and the things it does not contain are not there because they were not created to be there. Noncreated things have being after a fashion, but obviously not after the fashion of the things that do exist, that are creatures created. Matter, as we have seen above, is created by God.

Let us consider further the not-beings known to God. Two proposals appear in accord with what has been established and prudently recognize the systematic limitations of our knowledge. First, it is assumed that some (if not all) of the not-beings are such that, *if* they were created (which by hypothesis they are not), *then* they would be creatures whose metaphysical analysis would involve "matter." Accordingly, of these not-beings it could be said: their "matter," if they were created, would be created by God, though not apart from form. Otherwise expressed: Not-beings, so far as is determinable by us, may be of two natures; first, of such a nature that "matter" is requisite for their created existence, were they to be created; secondly, of such a nature that, were they to receive existence, "matter" would not pertain to their existence. In view of our ignorance, it might be said concerning not-beings: (1) *All* not-beings are of such a nature that, were they created, "matter" would pertain to *none* of them; or (2) *all* are of such a nature that, were they created, "matter" would pertain *to each and every one;* or, finally, (3) of such natures that, were

---

[36] *SCG,* Bk. I, ch. lxvi; *E,* pp. 141–42.

[37] *SCG,* Bk. II, ch. xxii. I am not unmindful of ch. xxv, "How the Almighty is said to be unable to do certain things." ". . . God is unable to do whatever is contrary to the *ratio* of being as being, or of *made being* as made." "And as God acts by will, so also does He act by *intellect* and *knowledge.* . . . Hence He can not do what He has foreseen that He will not do, or omit to do what He has foreseen that He will do, for the same reason that He cannot do what He wills not to do, or omit to do what He wills. Also each assertion is conceded and denied in the same sense, namely that He be said to be unable to do these things, not indeed absolutely, but on a certain condition or supposition" (*E,* pp. 44–47).

they created, some would be material things and some nonmaterial. Relative to the human mind, these seem to be legitimate speculative conjectures. But how, under the control of Thomas' position, could we be justified in selecting between these alternatives? Have we the right to declare: The Creator did in fact create *all* of the things to whose nature matter would pertain? *all* of the things falling under the principle that God has knowledge of matter, but not apart from the idea of it as compounded with form? Do we know that the nature of the created universe that has been created represents the limits defining all possible material things? Are we warranted in asserting, quite simply: no material thing is possible unless it fits into this created universe? The very suggestion seems to place an indefensible limitation upon the divine power. It is then assumed that material things—to the analysis of which the distinction of matter and form would be pertinent— *might* exist although in fact they do not, have not, and will not exist, at least in this created universe. They have not appeared, and will not appear, in this creation, because this creation does not contain the conditions for their coming-into-being.

The second conjectural speculation is this. Creation is an order.[38] The order is an expression, assuredly, of Divine Wisdom. It is in accord with a divine plan. Creation has the unity of order. How much man may know of this Wisdom, this plan, this order and by what means are questions irrelevant for the present purpose. It then seems reasonable to say: whatever creation does contain, it is an expression of this Wisdom and is compatible with this order. If, then, there are not-beings which the Creator could have created, but did not, so that they have not been and will not be parts of creation, it appears safe to assert that such not-beings are not because their creation was not envisaged in the divine plan and they would be incompatible with the order of creation. Since the divine essence is known to us only by way of negation, it is scarcely befitting to advance this as more than conjecture. Nevertheless, within the absolute context as defined by Thomism, it is legitimate.

Creation is, then, an order of mutually compossible things. But

[38] Cf. *F*, pp. 276–78, and, in general, ch. viii.

must not speculation be carried further? Assuredly, for Thomas
speculation has the function of enlarging the mind's vision and
also of vitalizing its consciousness of limitation.[39] Must we not,
then, expand conjecture by supposing that God could have created
other creations than this one, which in fact He did create? [40] Since
the divine essence is beyond our direct comprehension, it is impossible for the finite mind to determine possibilities as if it did
comprehend what it cannot comprehend. Now, creation has a unity
of order corresponding to the divine purpose leading to its existence. If, then, the Creator's purpose were other than in fact
it is (whatever be that purpose and whether we are vouchsafed
much or little knowledge of it), the creation effected in accord
with a different purpose would presumably be different from the
creation that was in fact created and created in accord with a plan.
Let it then be assumed that, for all we know, an indefinitude of
creations are possible to the divine mind and power.[41] At any
rate, it is conceded that there are not-beings known to God as in
His power. Let $C_1, C_2, C_3, \ldots$ represent the indefinitude of creations that, so far as we know, are possible. It is understood that
one of these, C_w, in fact does exist. Let us revert to an earlier
conclusion. With respect to not-beings, we *cannot* say that *all* not-
beings are such that, *were* they created, the finite existents so
arising would be one and all "immaterial" beings. Analogously,
it is unwarrantable to declare that all possible creations, other
than C_w, would necessarily be through and through "immaterial";

[39] Thomas' incorrigible rationalism must not be overlooked because of the limitations that are for him inherent in the very nature of our cognitive powers. Reason,
too, is from God, and its exercise to the limit, but with consciousness of limitations,
is divinely warranted.

[40] "The very order of things created by God shows the unity of the world. For this
world is called one by the unity of order, whereby some things are ordered to
others . . ." (*ST*, Pt. I, Q. XLVII, art. 3; *E*, pp. 259–60). This statement, it must
be pointed out, is followed by a denial of the existence of many worlds. Now it must
be noted that the "order of things is the best possible" (*SCG*, Bk. I, ch. xlii; *E*, p.
88). But in view of the texts cited in note 37 above, it is clear that Thomas carefully
safeguards the meanings to be attributed to any proposition implying a restriction
upon God's power. Inability ascribed to the Deity is not to be taken absolutely, but
only on a certain condition or supposition.

[41] "Being itself, considered absolutely, is infinite; for it can be participated in by
an infinite number of things in an infinite number of ways" (*SCG*, Pt. I, ch. xliii;
E, p. 96)

that they would be so many orders of existence with respect to which, for an appropriate metaphysical analysis, the factor "matter" would be in every case irrelevant. Given the conditions under which speculation must proceed, it must rather be said: For all we know, some, or all, or none of these creations, C_1, C_2, C_3 . . . would be wholly "immaterial"; for all we know, some or all or none would be "material"; for all we know, some or all or none would contain beings of an immaterial nature together with some existents of a material nature. (It is important to bear in mind that C_w, the creation that does exist, contains created immaterial creatures as well as creatures composite of matter and form.) It seems then impossible to deny that for all we know other creations involving matter are possible to the divine Will, Intellect, and Power.

Now "matter" signifies potentiality. If, then, there are not-beings and not-creations, known to God as in His power, and if some of these not-beings and not-creations are of such natures that, were they to exist, they would be material beings or created worlds at least in part containing material beings: then matter must signify this total range of possibilities. Let C_{m_1}, C_{m_2}, C_{m_3} . . . represent possible creations containing matter-things, C_{mw} representing that actual created world that does contain material things. Now there must be an all-comprehensive meaning of "matter" comprising this range of possibilities. But there must be assigned a meaning relative to the beings and the creation (C_{mw}) that do exist in distinction from the not-beings and not-creations which, by hypothesis, do not exist. Let us call a totality of forms that if materialized would constitute C_{m_1} or C_{m_2} or C_{m_3} . . . a world-set. Then a "matter" appropriate to each world-set must be posited. Every such matter would be the prime matter of its own world-set. Every not-creation, were it created, would presumably have its own unity of order, "whereby some things are ordered to others," reflecting divine Wisdom. This unity of order would assuredly be found in the corresponding world-set, and since diversity of matter is in view of form, there would be a matter appropriate to this world-set. Now it has been shown that matter in Thomism does not and must not signify irrevocably bare privation. It is known to God, though not apart from form.

It is contended that the speculative pathway being pursued is not in conflict with at least a part of Thomistic doctrine. Indeed, it is demanded by it. We are then led to this speculative outcome: The term "prime matter" must be used in two notably different ways. On the one hand, it signifies prime matter, possibility, in relation to, as pertaining to the existence of, a particular creation, possible or actual, C_{m_1}, C_{m_2} . . . or C_{mw}. In the case of C_{mw}, the world that the Deity did in fact create, the prime matter of this world is in relation to the world-set of forms found materialized in C_{mw}. There are, then, or for all we know may be, many such matters. Let each such matter be called a restricted prime matter. Then by analogy this formula might be set up: the idea of each such restricted prime matter is known to God, but not apart from the world-set of forms in view of which a restricted prime matter can in any sense be said to be. For the sake of being explicit, it might be said that every restricted prime matter has its own indefinite dimensionalities. For C_{mw} the expression *materia quantitate signata* may represent *its* restricted prime matter. But now, in view of our limitations, and since it is admitted that there are not-beings known to God as in His power, we must express the competence and the incompetence of the human mind by representing all that is possible to Omnipotence. We must extend the term "prime matter" to cover not-beings and not-creations in order that it may represent the speculative terminus. It is necessary, then, to postulate an absolute prime matter, an unrestricted prime matter, a prime matter of all prime matters, known to God in the way in which matter is known to God. It is, indeed, pure potentiality. It could properly be called indeterminate. A restricted prime matter could be regarded as signate for a world-set, but absolute prime matter has no such limitation. For a world-set, the prime matter that would make possible the reciprocal causality of matter-and-form is indeterminate with respect to the particular forms of that world-set, but somehow determinate with respect to the world-set as a systematic total. Absolute prime matter lacks such limitations upon its indeterminacy. Its indeterminacy must correspond to the inexpressible range of all that is possible to God. A restricted prime matter is relative to a world-set whose contraction of an appropriate prime matter results in a world, a creation, say C_{mx}, and not in some other. If the finite mind can and must take God as absolute referent; if it must acknowledge the unknowability of the Divine Essence save by way of negation; if some meager distillations of an affirmative value come by that way; then that mind must metaphysically represent the illimitable horizon of possibility within that unfathomable Divine Essence. Adopting Descartes' favorite word, the immensity of the Divine Being must needs be indicated. Absolute prime matter serves not uselessly, in the control of speculation, to express our incompetence to know—save by way of negation—the creative power of the Deity. The distinction between restricted and absolute prime matter, in whatever words it may be clothed, appears to be implicit in Thomism. Correspondingly, the notion is warranted that the "prime matter" of the creation that God did create (C_{mw}) possesses an inherent principle of readiness for diversification. It has a capacity for contributing to the being of things that are contained in this creation, so that it is neither bare privation nor a sign of *all* that is possible to God. (After all, this creation does contain immaterial beings.) The restricted prime matter involved in the metaphysical analysis of the creatures that God did create, of *this* creation, must be understood in relation to the unity of order of *this* creation, not in relation to other creations that for all we know the Creator might have created, but which, again for all we know, He did not create. In a subordinate context analysis may proceed as if restricted prime matter were prime matter, bare possibility. The analysis thus prepares the way for scientific inquiry, seeking to carry on the task blessed by the Angelic Doctor and to find out about minerals and plants and animals and stars and other things found within the world. But in the absolute context, metaphysics must distinguish between a restricted and an absolute prime matter.

The metaphysical analysis of Thomas may or may not be the most coherent achieved by man. That is not here in question. The point is that the Thomistic analysis will collapse—or veer towards "Platonism"—unless (restricted) prime matter is endowed with a power of diversification at once limited and positive and indefinite and exclusive. It is intermediary, as Forest declares, between act and nothingness. It is ordered to act; indeed, it is indifferent to the reception of diverse forms—provided that the forms are such that they *can* be received. The prime matter of the world to be studied in the sciences is indeed potentiality—but not globally, illimitably, incomprehensibly.

In the procession of the centuries, one René Descartes cannot be ranked as the very least of the students of St. Thomas.

The Thomistic metaphysical analysis ends in a conception of matter foreshadowing the adaptation of the term for the uses of scientific inquiry. Prime matter, the restricted prime matter relevant to this world, is responsive in a broadly determinate way to the diversity of forms comprising a world-set. It is indeterminate, and yet determinate within its indeterminacy. Grant that *corporeitas*, grant that indeterminate dimensionality in matter prior to the reception of the substantial form, are midway conceptions in the thought of St. Thomas, while *materia quantitate signata* represents the terminus of his thought: it must be conceded that Thomas assigns to prime matter a contributive character. In the reciprocal causality of matter and form, to adopt Forest's phrase, matter makes a contribution out of its own resources, as it were, to the being of a concrete existent. Reduce the role of prime matter to the minimum, if you will, but it responds to the evocative lure of forms by receiving within itself only those forms that can be accommodated to such a prime matter because only such a prime matter can accommodate itself to such forms. Undeniably, Thomas is forcefully maintaining the concreteness and reality of the things to which children and Aristotle point.[42]

The analysis, provided that preceding contentions are sustainable, represents the first stage in the formation of a program adjusted to the needs of scientific inquiry procedurally independent of metaphysics and theology. More accurately, perhaps, it is the first step towards a new and efficient (or differently efficient?) sci-

[42] The Deity, having created creatures, vouchsafes to them careers of their own and in accord with their respective natures. Cf. *F*, p. 297.

entific program. The objectives and conditions for the pursuit of inquiry are anticipatorily sketched by the metaphysical analysis. There is a realm of things—theology knows these to be creatures —and the realm has a unity of order so that these many things do, indeed, constitute a realm. Sciences propose to know these things and this order. In the metaphysical analysis, the many existents are due to the reciprocal causality of matter-and-form. Since the world—it is creation—has a unity of order, and yet existence is concrete, order pervades existence. The existents and this order cannot be dissevered. In some measure human cognitive powers are fitted to know this world, within which, indeed, these cognitive powers are comprised, both as to its unity of order and as to its discrete existents. Speculations concerning other world-sets of forms reducing appropriate prime matters to actualities are of no concern for science. For science is concerned, not with what is possible for Omnipotence, but with what is and is possible in this world which is understood, upon the assurances of theology, to have been created. Metaphysically, the contents of this world are what they are in virtue of a reciprocal causality between a world-set of forms and a prime matter responsive to them in accord with its own indwelling proclivity. It is, of course, emphatically necessary to understand that "world-set" and "prime matter," "matter" and "form," represent metaphysical distinctions of idea and of discourse, not corresponding entitative actualities. As children fully realize, this world before us is a realm of things, of creatures—of dogs and stones and butterflies and spinach and apples, and great are the differences between them. These things, enjoying a career to which their several natures entitle them under an order which theologians know to be creation, are not matter and form, but rather instances of this-matter-and-this-form. There are a very great many of these combinations of this-matter-and-this-form, and perhaps science cannot find out very much about any of them. Even physicists at times leave their laboratories in order that they may enjoy the flowers in their gardens. Again, this order that theologians would call the order of creation is a matter of considerable complexity. It is, however, the task of scientific inquiry to find out something about it. Neither existents nor order can be neglected without insuring the defeat of science; or, at least, without failing to obtain that science which Descartes desired, not only in order to satisfy his passion for certainty, but also in order to enable the race of men to walk with security in this life.

In these conditions a program of efficiency is desperately needed. But the devising of such a program means a reckoning with matter and form. Under whatever masquerade of words the task of science is portrayed, it cannot escape the import of the distinction between matter and form. It is not the words that count, it is rather the necessities of the case. The proposal of science is to secure knowledge of things and of the cosmic order which insures that the field of inquiry is in some sense and in some degree a whole. Grant that scientific understanding of these things and this whole differs not only from theology's understanding of them but also from that which metaphysics seeks to achieve. Nevertheless, the metaphysical analysis of existence, unless through and through illusory, must have significance for science. The distinction between matter and form may be variously interpreted as to the content to be assigned to "matter" and to "form." The tension between reflection and experience makes the distinction inescapable, for scientific inquiry no less than for metaphysics. The terminology of science conserves traces of the metaphysical distinction despite discontinuities and novelties in the symbols employed. It is historically significant, although perhaps deplorable, that "matter" was carried over into the terminology of science. It is a pity that Descartes did not unambiguously reserve the term for metaphysics, devising new terms for the scientific correlates of "matter," as indeed he sought to do for the scientific correlates of "form." However that may be, the scientific use of "matter" suggests that the word carried a load of metaphysical meaning peculiarly pertinent to the task of inquiry. Perhaps the load served to mark out the limits of this task while signalizing its relative independence of metaphysics and theology. Efficiency in the program for inquiry, one gathers from Whitehead, goes along with abstraction. Science must reckon with all the things there are, and there are a great many. It may recognize that each of these things is a this-matter-and-this-form. It must acknowledge that a science of the singular in its imprescriptible singularity is not a science achievable by man. Efficiency demands abstraction, yet that abstraction must be pertinent to the many things that exist, to something that all possess under the over-arching unity of order. If "matter," in consequence of the definition it receives by metaphysical analysis, serves to point towards efficient abstraction, then so much the better.

It may now be profitable to return to St. Thomas. A realm of things lies before us. Obviously, it does not consist of prime matter, on the one hand, and of forms, on the other. Prime matter, even a restricted prime matter, cannot exist. It cannot even be known, save in a certain sense. Moreover, forms do not exist. Things exist. If knowable, and presumably they are, the distinction between matter and form, in so far as truly characterizing what it means to be, to be a finite existent, to be a thing, is fundamental to the total conditions of their knowability. Each term indicates something for which scientific inquiry, in a manner appropriate to its procedural program, must find a content. The diversity of things is analytically resoluble into a diversity of forms in view of which a diversifiability, a capacity for diversification, pertains to matter. With respect to Thomas, the important consideration for the present undertaking is his recognition of the necessity of the situation: content must be assigned to prime matter. Not everything can be attributed to form. The entire realm of creatures, in so far as they are material, share in this content, whatever it may be, that must be assigned to prime matter. Thomas insists that unity pertains to a finite existent. The reciprocity manifested in the fact that the existent is this-matter-and-this-form would be meaningless were "matter" to signify a potentiality so nakedly uncharacterizable that nothing whatever could be said about it. For this and similar reasons it has been contended that an implicit distinction must obtain between the notion of prime matter in some restricted sense and the notion assignable to the term in the absolute context where the relative incompetence of mind is at a maximum. Restricted prime matter is *functionally* absolute, perhaps, in a subordinate context of inquiry. It may be taken, for the purposes of science, *as if* absolute. But in the absolute context, where the total range of possibility must be at least acknowledged by the speculative intellect, the distinction between prime matter as limitable potentiality and as illimitable potentiality must be drawn.

Materia quantitate signata, if the expression stands for Thomas' final thought concerning the problem, is then the restricted prime matter of the world of things which science proposes to examine. Let us proceed to a further conjecture. Thomas, it seems reasonable to suppose, would assert that in this world some things imaginable are impossible. Doubtless that which genuinely involves a contradiction cannot be, either in this world or in any other. It seems probable that Thomas, so curious a combination of saintly humility and incorrigible rationalism, would admit that for all he knew some other world is possible and that in *that other world* things impossible for *this* world might be possible, while things possible for *this* world might be impossible for *that*. Now if "matter" were identical with nothingness, it is difficult to see how "matter" could have anything to do with determining what could or could not exist in this or in any world. But prime matter is not bare privation or nothingness. Presumably, then, it does have something to do with the possible and the impossible. If prime matter be quantitatively signate, something positive concerning its role seems indicated. (It must be noted that, since there are non-material creatures, matter is not implicated in questions concerning the possibility of such beings.) Now the signateness of matter is maximal, it would seem, in the individual singular thing, in that which is a this-matter-and-this-form. It would appear that it approaches a minimum, but nevertheless persists in the genus. ". . . the essences or quiddities of genera or species are individualized by the signate matter of this or that individual, although indeed the quiddity of a genus or species includes form and matter in general . . ."[43] But then quiddity in some degree of attenuation, including form and matter in general, might well be posited throughout the hierarchy. If the expression be permissible, it could be said that a maximal attenuation of quiddity would involve a minimal signateness of matter; it would involve re-

[43] *SCG,* Bk. I, ch. xxi; *E,* p. 52.

stricted prime matter at its maximal indetermination. Now, it is notable that Thomas asserts that "the infinite of quantity is the infinite of matter." This statement ensues upon the following:

We must consider that a thing is called infinite because it is not finite; whereas matter is in a way made finite by the form, and the form by the matter. Matter is made finite by the form, inasmuch as matter, before it receives its form, is in a state of potentiality as regards many forms; but on receiving a form it is terminated by that one. Again, form is made finite by matter, inasmuch as form, considered in itself, is common to many; but, when received in matter, the form is determined to this one particular thing. Matter is perfected by the form by which it is made finite; therefore the infinite attributed to matter by itself contains the idea of something imperfect; for it is as it were formless matter. Form is not made perfect by matter, but rather is contracted by matter; and hence the infinite, regarded on the part of the form not determined by matter, contains the idea of something perfect. . . .[44]

Now if the infinite of quantity is the infinite of matter, if it is the infinite that, as it were, expresses or constitutes the pervasive nature of matter, then the question might be raised: Is that "matter" whose infinite is the infinite of quantity the only possible "matter"? This question might be dismissed as merely speculative. But at any rate, in so far as matter signifies potentiality,

[44] *ST*, Q. VII, art. 1; *E*, p. 72. This text should be considered together with later passages of the same Q. "Anything out of God can be accidentally infinite [*secundum quid*], but not absolutely infinite [*simpliciter*]. As regards the infinite applied to matter, it is manifest that everything actually existing possesses a form; thus its matter is determined by form. Because matter, considered as existing under some substantial form, remains in potentiality as regards many accidental forms; that is, it is simply finite [*E* here reads "infinite," but in the *L* it runs: *sed quia materia, secundum quod est sub una forma substantiale, remanet in potentia ad multas formas accidentales; quod est finitum simpliciter, potest esse infinitum secundum quid* . . .] yet it can be accidentally infinite; as, for example, wood is finite according to its own form, but still it is accidentally infinite, inasmuch as it is in a state of potentiality to an infinite number of shapes. If we speak of the infinite in reference to form, it is manifest that those things, the forms of which are in matter, are simply finite; and are in no way infinite. If any created forms are not received into matter, but are self-subsisting, as some think is the case with angels, these will be accidentally infinite; inasmuch as such kinds of form are not terminated, nor contracted by matter. Because a created form thus subsisting has being, but is not its own being; it follows that its being is received and contracted to a determinate nature. Hence it cannot be simply infinite" (Art. 2, *E*, pp. 73–74). The infinite in essence is to be distinguished from the infinite in magnitude; no natural body can be actually infinite; the infinite is not against the idea of magnitude in general, but is against the idea of any species of it (Art. 3, *E*, pp. 75–76).

then a matter whose infinite is the infinite of quantity is one that by contracting whatever forms it *can* contract, whatever forms it *can* receive, will invariably yield entities having quantity, dimensive quantity, complete and definite quantity.[45] This material creation, say C_{mw}, is a world of things with respect to which quantity is constitutively basic. Of such a world this could be said: whatever a thing may be in its total nature, as a this-form-and-this-matter—an apple, a star, a stone—it is minimally and basically something quantitative. It is something whose intelligibility involves specifications as to quantities, although this measure of intelligibility is far from exhaustive. Now if we take the position that human speculation can determine that there can be but *one* prime matter and that the infinite of this matter is the infinite of quantity, then the distinction between restricted and absolute prime matter collapses. In effect, in this event, matter-possessing-the-infinite-of-quantity is absolute prime matter. In the language of Thomas, in mid-career, the indefinite dimensionality of matter prior to the reception of form would be the indefinite quantitative dimensionality of absolute prime matter. If, on the other hand, it be argued that speculation cannot determine this, but must admit the possibility of other prime matters, it may nevertheless he said that *for science* matter-possessing-the-infinite-of-quantity defines the limit, in one direction, of scientific inquiry.

It is certain that Thomas envisages not-beings. Two alternatives appear. Thomas conceivably might be interpreted as follows: The not-beings known to God, the not-beings which are not, have not been, and will not be, are nevertheless not-beings that in some sense *could* exist in *that* world which, in fact, God did create (C_{mw}), and which is at hand for scientific inquiry. Of these not-beings, those that, if they did exist, would be unities of matter-and-form would be contractions of a matter whose infinite is the infinite of quantity. In this sense, such not-beings would be compossible with the existences that are, that have been, or will be in this creation, C_{mw}. They would possess complete and definite quantity, were they to exist. If, now, on this supposition, it were

[45] Cf. texts cited above, note 10.

asked: What reason can be assigned for this, that these not-beings are not? the reply, presumably, must rest upon the principle that "the order of things is the best possible: since the potency of the first agent does not fail the potentiality of things for perfection." [46] Thus, it would be the case that the Deity has not given existence to all compossibles (compossibles in the sense defined), for the reason that such existences would mean something less than the best possible ordering of things. Scientific inquiry is here disinterested. Its faith, that there is an order of things, suffices—at least provided Descartes demonstrates that there is no malign genius holding sway over the domain of things to render nugatory the efforts of inquiry. With respect to matter, on this alternative, it is necessary to posit only a prime matter whose infinite is that of quantity.

It is difficult to accept the preceding. Would not Thomas find in it an intolerable limitation ascribed by the finite intellect to the knowledge and will and power of the Deity? The governing rule, the incommensurability of the finite intellect and the Divine Essence, would oppose such a limitation.[47] If this be acceptable, then, as an alternative—so runs the contention of this essay—it must be admitted as a speculative possibility that a distinction between restricted and absolute prime matter is becoming to the finite mind. The latter formula is functional in that it signifies the incomprehensibility of the divine knowledge, power, and will. It signifies the untrammeled divine creativity. On what grounds can we abolish the speculative validity of the conjecture that a creation could exist, such that, were there a universal science concerning its existents, quantitative concepts would *not* be basic for knowledge of them? An infinite "matter," whose infinite by hypothesis is not that of quantity, were it to contract appropriate forms capable of reciprocal causality with this matter, would yield existences, precipitates from an illimitable sea of possibil-

[46] *SCG*, Bk. I, ch. xlii; *E*, p. 88.
[47] Granted that we may know that God cannot do what He has foreseen that He will not do or omit to do what He has foreseen that He will do; that He cannot do what He wills not to do or omit to do what He wills: granted that according to Thomas we know this, it is not *thereby* known *what* He has foreseen that He *will* do, or what He *has* willed to do.

ity, material indeed but not in a sense imaginable by us. This is not to contend that there *are* other restricted prime matters. It is not contended that other created material worlds, C_{m_1}, C_{m_2} . . . are known by us to be possible. Rather, the contention is that we are not advantaged to the extent of being justified in a forthright denial of the possibilities. Moreover, it is contended that such considerations are in accord with the spirit, if not the very words, of the Thomistic system.

The metaphysical analysis of finite existence presented by Thomas represents a critical moment of intellectual history. It represents such a moment in many senses that can not be noted in this essay.[48] It may, or it may not, be true that Thomas foresaw the nature of that extraordinary enterprise, carried out with astounding efficiency, which we call modern science. It may, or it may not, be the case that the century of genius which defined the program of efficiency was aware of this significance of the Thomistic system in relation to that program. This metaphysical analysis, nevertheless, provided an opportunity for discerning the bases of the program.

Scientific inquiry confronts the world of things enjoyed by children and described by Aristotle. These things, according to the analysis of Thomas, are singular finite existents, each a case of this-matter-and-this-form. Such a thing is inexhaustible for human knowing. Science can but effect a series of approximations. Indeed, since a science of the singular in its singularity is for the Deity alone, the closest approximations of science will be remote from the full reality of a natural thing. All the more will this be the case if the scientific enterprise be independent of theology, and if this enterprise should systematically neglect teleological ideas. Again, the multitude of diverse beings of this-matter-and-this-form falls within a unity of order. This order likewise may be approximated, faintly, by scientific inquiry. But no approxi-

---

[48] What follows, I beg the reader to understand, is recognized to be exceedingly partial. It is my conviction that Thomas' system provided the *auspices* for the emergence of modern science and its associated ideas. In another essay I am attempting to work this out with the necessary amplitude. For lack of space, in the ensuing pages I must neglect many factors and be content with bare indications of their place.

mations of the singular existent can be satisfactory without approximations of the order and its unity. They must go together. An efficient program for inquiry must meet the need for economy imposed by the limitations of the human mind. The approximations must depend upon abstractions. But the abstractions must be grounded, somehow, in the nature of finite existence and its order.

The Thomistic analysis supplies a certain assurance. This is a world of things concerning which it can be said that the infinite of quantity is the infinite of its matter. Reciprocal causality of form and matter in the natural thing, that is, the case of this-matter-and-this-form, implies an interadjustment and proportionality of the matter and form components. Through the form definite quantitative dimensionality arises from the quantitative potentialities signified by matter. Assuredly it must follow that the thing, the substance, the finite existent, has a certain internal organization expressed in and by the quantitative specifications pertaining to that thing. Now it is one thing to assert that the global nature of the natural entity is expressed by, is representable by, quantitative specifications; it is quite another to assert that this global nature is nothing but, nothing in addition to, such quantitative specifications. However, in the tight unity of the concrete being, so stoutly maintained by Thomas, a correlation, a harmony, must obtain between quantitative specifications and other aspects of its nature. In sum, then, a quantitative reckoning with all material things is suggested by the nature of these things. Moreover, the many things despite their diversities can be brought together under concepts and devices of pictorial representation reflecting this participation of things in the infinite of quantity. One cannot escape recollecting the famous text of Descartes: the infinitude of figures suffices to express the diversity of things. It is of the utmost importance to observe that the statement reads, *suffices* to *express;* it does not declare that diversity of things is nothing but a difference of figure. Now all things fall within the unity of order. The materiality of these things cannot be unrelated to the order, whatever it is, in its totality. To assert this would mean to veer towards the position that matter is nonbeing, mere privation, a nothingness. It would then appear that inquiry might attain laws, principles, ordering ideas of universal scope reflecting the community of matter and the fact that the infinite of quantity is the infinite of matter.

Let us hasten to add that, in terms of the Thomistic analysis, a science so delineated would combine precision and universality with preposterous inadequacy. It would be inadequate to the inexhaustible reality, the veritable this-ness, of a natural being, a dog, a stone, a star, a daffodil. Something of this reality, however, would be expressed and represented, along a line of radical abstraction. Moreover, such a science, achieving universal principle, would be remote from the splendor of that order which theology understands to be a divine plan, glimpsed, perhaps, by faith alone. But such a science, precise and universally relevant, might well suffice for mundane practical purposes—for the purposes summarily described by Descartes in his ideal, that men should walk with security and dignity in this life.

Expostulation may be anticipated. Thomas did not assert that matter is a substance: but Descartes did. Let us turn to another work that commands respect. Maréchal,[49] granting that his interpretations are not misunderstood, urges that Duns Scotus can be viewed as the midpoint between Thomas and Descartes. In sum, he urges that for Scotus matter without form possesses entitative actuality. It is a positive entity. Scotus argues that between an actual entity and nothing there is no mean. Now for Thomas whatever is, is neither matter nor form but the unity of matter and form. Thus efficient causality refers to this unity alone, and the causality of matter is not efficient causality. The Scotist theory, asserts Maréchal, contains, at least in form, a denial of radical distinction between the reciprocal causality of matter and form, on the one hand, and passive and active causality on the other.[50] Thus, a profound difference obtains between the Thomist and Scotist doctrines.[51] It would thus appear that, if Descartes drew upon

[49] *Le Point de départ de la métaphysique*, Paris, Alcan, pp. 88 ff.
[50] *Op. cit.*, pp. 85–86.
[51] The principle of divergence is said to be this: Scotus attributes an objective entitative correlate to every element of the internal structure of the concept; but for Thomas, as for Aristotle, only the totally determined objective concept represents a variety of beings. Pp. 90–91.

historical resources in arriving at his own concept of matter and the use of the term "substance" in relation to it, these resources are Scotist rather than Thomistic.

This may be true, although it is certain that Descartes was a student of Thomas' writings—indeed, the ablest of all such students. The distance between Thomas and Descartes, however, is not so great as it may appear to be. Insufficient emphasis is customarily placed upon Descartes' own qualifications in the use of the term "substance." Properly speaking, the Deity, the absolute in its *immensité*, God, alone is substance. There is an extraordinary shift in meaning, of which Descartes is fully aware, when the term is applied to anything-other-than-God. A finite substance is substance in that it depends solely upon God—the "concurrence" of God—for its existence. Beneath the use of words, however, lie ideas. Let us revert once more to Thomas. Matter does not exist. It does not have "entitative actuality." Since it does not have this, it cannot have efficient causality. But analytically, all material things share in "matter." A restricted prime matter, *materia quantitate signata,* a matter whose infinite is the infinite of quantity, lies at the basis of actuality. If it receive a form, then with fatal certainty there will be a thing of quantitative dimensionalities. Science may take advantage of this. It would be preposterous to say that science comprehends the thing —but it knows something about it, something pertaining to its being, something permitting this thing to be brought together with that thing. The analytical formal factor constitutive of the being of this-matter-and-this-form can be expressed by, represented by, correlated with, the inescapably quantitative dimensionalities evoked in the material constitutive factor by the formal factor. It is a metaphysical absurdity to identify "green" and an electromagnetic wave of such and such frequency.[52] It is not absurd,

[52] This essay cannot, for lack of space, consider questions concerning the relativity of sensed qualities to the percipient organism, or the subjective "psychical" status ascribed to sensation and perception. Modern dualism may involve a certain apportionment of the total reality assigned by Thomas to a natural entity. The duality of body and soul, defined after the Cartesian fashion, may at once express the consequences of formulating the scientific procedural program and also facilitate its formulation. An elaborate system of correlations between that which is directly experienced and that which is defined as independently existing must be instituted.

on Thomistic grounds, to correlate one with the other. In a word, there is in the Thomistic analysis something truly anticipatory of the real significance of Descartes' matter-as-finite-substance. Science can treat things *as if* everything constitutive of a real entity can be reduced to and *sufficiently* represented by matter-quantities. Since science is limited, in its independent career, to the world of things with respect to which our cognitive powers are proportioned, it can treat this world *as if* it were the final referent of thought. It can treat the world of things, known to theology as creation, *as if* a scheme of matter-entities-in-motion were the only pattern of an existential science of things. Matter has no entitative actuality—let it be so. But restricted prime matter can be taken, for the sake of abstractions providing economy and efficiency in science, *as if* it were something within which quantitative specifications suffice to satisfy the limited aspirations of science and the needs of practical art. Appreciation of the full reality of Jones may be gained by means of social intercourse, and metaphysicians instructed by Thomas may insist upon ascribing it to Jones. But to a physician and a surgeon, as such, Jones must be a case, just one more patient. But is all this so remote from Descartes? There is a realm of indefinite comprising an indefinitude of things. It, indeed, could not be save with the concurrence of substance, of infinite being, of God. Science may construe this realm *as if* it were truly substantial, underived, self-supporting, and each of the indefinitude of "things" may be treated as if it were a mode or a set of modes in a "substance" having an inherent constitutive nature. This nature, indeed, lies at the basis of the several actualities, and conditions both their existence and their intelligibility. It may be the case that many properties attributed by children and Aristotle to "things" do not really belong to things. If such is the case, an elaborate set of correlations must be established in order that science may reflect in its abstract quantitative reckoning with the thing as much as possible of the metaphysical entity, the this-matter-and-this-form. The reciprocal causality of matter-and-form becomes resolved into a system of abstract quantitative correlations, and

---

But these additional questions and factors, though pertinent, do not affect the argument of this essay.

restricted prime matter can be posited as the absolute for science. The career of metaphysical finite existents, which are severally cases of this-matter-and-this-form, may be resolved through efficient abstraction into particles obeying laws of motion. The blessed St. Thomas was well-advised. If the matter-component be a nothingness, there would be no economical way in which our limited cognitive powers could secure even slight mastery over the diversity of things or attain by any approximation whatever notions comparable in scope with the vast indefinitude of a happily restricted prime matter. Prime matter does not exist. Prime matter has no entitative actuality. Let it be granted that these are metaphysical truths. They may be unknown to scientific inquiry. Or, what amounts to the same thing, they may be neglected by science because they can be neglected. Since prime matter is not nothingness, it can be postulated *as if* it were the substance of the indefinitude of existence. There can be assigned to it, since its infinite is the infinite of quantity, whatever may facilitate its quantitative exploitation. Thereby we attain a form of scientific knowledge achieved by an astoundingly efficient program, with results, as Descartes foresaw, momentous for the security and dignity of man in this life. With results, not incredible, but incredible if science and metaphysics be simply identified.

Professor Koyré has neatly said of Descartes that he geometrized *à l'outrance*. Undoubtedly he did. It was scarcely avoidable, in view of the content he assigned to that prime matter which he proposed to employ as if it were genuinely substance. But all modern science has abstracted *à l'outrance*. It was an expedient required by efficiency. Provoked by a tension between metaphysics, which must sustain the inexhaustible singularity and undissipatable reality of concrete beings, and the practical necessities conditioning efficiency in inquiry, the expedient has profound consequences for metaphysics. It is one thing to achieve a metaphysics anticipatory of science. It is another to achieve a metaphysics assimilative of the findings of science during centuries and recapturing the concreteness of existence while appraising the high abstractions of science. Whatever the terminology to be employed, the task is to recapture at a higher level that which St. Thomas insisted upon—that existents are this-matter-and-this-form. Somewhere Professor Gilson utters a remark to the effect that no one can be a Cartesian. This is true precisely in the sense in which it is true that no one can be an Aristotelian, a Platonist, a Thomist, or a Kantian. The saintly author of *Process and Reality* is certainly no Thomist. But he, too, must employ the notion of a prime matter, indeed, a restricted prime matter. Creativity is "the pure notion of the activity conditioned by the objective immortality of the actual world"; it is without a character of its own in exactly the same sense in which the Aristotelian "matter" is without a character of its own. It is significant, however, that the Whiteheadian prime matter is called "creativity." It may be that "ultimate notion of the highest generality at the base of actuality," but what it signifies must be distinguished from bare privation as the Angelic Doctor distinguished the prime matter of his analysis from bare privation. There are organisms not decomposable into subordinate organisms.[53] The temptation is irresistible. Might it be said: Creativity neither exists nor can be understood; what exists is organisms, of each of which it can be stated that it is a this-form-and-this-creativity, and each is a substance? The high abstractions of science must be made to converge upon and be absorbed within the concrete existent organism. Whatever may be the value that history may come to place upon Whitehead's metaphysics, he has assuredly offered the general pattern for metaphysical effort that undertakes the task of reckoning with the results of science. Three centuries have elapsed since Descartes assured the scientist that figures, the supply of which is infinite, would suffice to represent the diversity of things. He who seeks to understand the body of scientific findings—and the doctrine of Whitehead—will agree that Descartes did not exaggerate the number of mathematical essences that are available. Indeed, he will be relieved to know that the supply is infinite, since apparently all will be needed! He should be grateful if, perchance, some continuity of ideas reflecting persistent necessities can be discerned in the centuries since Thomas strove so mightily to prevent the collapse of prime matter into nothingness.

[53] *Science and the Modern World*, p. 191.

MAN, THOMISTIC AND CARTESIAN

Qu'est-ce donc que i'ay creu estre cy-deuant? Sans dif-ficulté, i'ay pensé que i'estois un homme. Mais qu'est-ce qu'vn homme? Descartes, *Méditations*, M. II, Adam et Tannery, IX, 20.

MAN, Thomistic and Cartesian—how do they differ? It may be conceded that the two doctrines concerning the nature of man have traditionally been regarded as, to say the least, different. The difference has often been appraised as radical. In some quarters, it appears, the doctrines are viewed as opposed, the Cartesian doctrine of man being summarily described as dualistic, the Thomistic doctrine as nondualistic. Is this characterization adequate? If so, how explain an opposition of doctrine so radical? If not, just how do the doctrines differ? What, in sum, is the root of the difference? [1]

The reader may forgive a few words of reminiscence by way of an introduction to this essay and as an indication of its intent. The questions posed have interested me ever since those far-off days when I was driven, by a dissertation and the austere counsels of one John Dewey (who expressed the distressing opinion that I should know something about the matter on which I proposed to write a dissertation), to read Thomas' *Treatise on Man*. The results were meager. I was confused and perplexed. The Cartesian and Thomistic doctrines tended to converge, whereas, as I gathered from the books, they really diverged. I abandoned the *Treatise*, assured of nothing save that Plato and the Platonists, as I understood St. Thomas, had fathered a considerable number of disturbingly erroneous ideas concerning the nature of man. But

---

[1] In this essay I am not interested in determining the value of the Thomistic or the Cartesian conceptions of man for the pursuit of psychological science. In view of the history of psychology, however, and of the influence of Cartesian conceptions upon that history, it is my hope that the study will not be regarded as of abstruse philosophical interest only.

some twenty years later I reread the *Treatise* and also again studied the doctrine concerning the angels. I succeeded in rediscovering my perplexities. I wondered why St. Thomas had thought that
Plato and the Platonists had erred. I wondered still more why St.
Thomas had thought—as surely he must have thought—that his
own doctrine avoided these errors. In any case, however, such conjectures were unbecoming. Recognizing defeat, I made no further
efforts.

Later, however, I read Gilson's account of Thomistic man. It is
extraordinarily persuasive. I came to the following conclusion:
either Gilson's Thomistic man is truly St. Thomas' own Thomistic man, or else the former accurately represents what St. Thomas
should have maintained, in view of the total conditions that presumably his doctrine was intended to fulfill. In sum, I was content to assume that what a Gilson declares St. Thomas to have
meant is just what St. Thomas did intend. This was helpful. Thomistic man differs profoundly from Cartesian man. But my uncertainties concerning the basis of the difference increased. Recently I happened upon Brennan's *Thomistic Psychology*.[2] At last,
thought I, with the aid of Gilson and Brennan all obscurity will
be removed—and without the need of rereading St. Thomas. My
objective was to arrive at a neat formula wherein the precise differences between the nature of man according to St. Thomas and
his nature according to Descartes can be definitively summarized.
This expectation seemed all the more reasonable in that both authorities have much to say concerning Descartes' account of man.
This essay is an account of adventures in search for the formula.
The search was not successful.

Gilson makes clear the historical conditions and theoretical is-

[2] *Thomistic Psychology, a Philosophic Analysis of the Nature of Man*, by Robert
Edward Brennan (New York, 1944). References will be indicated as follows: Brennan's book by *B*; Gilson's *Le Thomisme* (Paris, 1922), by *T*, and his *Spirit of Mediaeval Philosophy*, English version (New York, 1936) by *S*, the French (Paris, 1932)
by *E*; St. Thomas, *Summa theologica*, Eng. Dominican trans., by *ST*. Where the *Basic
Writings* of Pégis is referred to, the symbol *P* will be used. In this paper I am relying
upon materials used and conclusions advanced concerning the concept of matter in
St. Thomas in the essay, "Matter and Scientific Efficiency." The symbol *MSE* indicates reference to this essay.

sues defining the problem confronting St. Thomas. These may be summarized as follows: [3]

(1) A satisfactory doctrine concerning man must fall under the general principle of accord between philosophical (and scientific) truth, on the one hand, and theological truth, on the other hand. This does not mean that independent thought can demonstrate all the truths concerning man known to theology. It does mean that lack of accord is symptomatic of error somewhere. The requirement indicated may be called the met-empirical accord. In general, it implies the necessary harmony between philosophical and scientific findings with Christian theology. More specifically, of course, St. Thomas' doctrine concerning the nature of man must accord with Christian theology as interpreted and formulated by St. Thomas. It is understood, of course, that the met-empirical accord might equally govern a theologian whose Christian theology differs from that of St. Thomas. As the theologies might differ, so might differ the doctrines concerning the nature of man required by the theologies if the principle of the accord is to govern all reflection and to be made manifest. But for present purposes, the met-empirical accord concerns only the Thomistic science, metaphysics, and theology.

(2) The doctrine concerning human constitution must accord with empirical data. This we may call the empirical accord. It implies that a sound conception of man's constitution will provide a fund of ideas effective in guiding scientific inquiries concerning men. It will be sufficiently flexible to permit assimilation of detailed discoveries and to be modifiable in view of them. In general, of course, the sciences concerning man must be internally consistent and consistent with other bodies of scientific knowledge. Any discord, met-empirical or empirical, is a sign of error somewhere.

(3) The doctrine must represent the unity of man. This condition may be called the metaphysical requirement. A man is a singular thing, an individual thing, a one thing. He is a unitary being,

---

[3] I am following ch. ix of *T*, but still more ch. ix of *S* and *E*. The summary, however, is my own, not Gilson's.

whatever the complexities of his nature. Distinctions found within the constitution of man, whose recognition is necessary for the intelligibility of man as an object of inquiry, must not be construed so as to negate or imperil this basic unity. If man is composite, he must be conceived as composite in a sense that is reconcilable with his unity. His compositeness must, indeed, be expressive of that unity. Man is no accidental combination of parts, natures, or functions. Factors discriminable in his constitution, determining that constitution, are wrongly conceived when the factors are represented as if extrinsically related. It is to be noted that this metaphysical requirement governs the use of analogies. These may be employed to facilitate our understanding of the nature of man. But some historical analogies may be highly misleading, in relation to the conditions and issues to be met by St. Thomas' doctrine. It may be necessary to distinguish soul from body in one way or another. But to liken the relation of soul to body to the relation between pilot and ship may be deemed unsatisfactory, in view of the accords and the metaphysical requirement. St. Thomas, it seems safe to assert, insists upon the reality of the singular, a reality proportioned to its status in being. His doctrine concerning man must satisfy the requirement without impairing the complexity and unity of the individual man. It must make these intelligible. Satisfaction of the metaphysical requirement, however, must not contravene the met-empirical and empirical accords.

It is not unreasonable to contend that Descartes had in mind these accords and this requirement. He says, in effect, that he has demonstrated the immateriality and indestructibility of the soul, and that this should be all that the theologian should expect from the philosopher. The union of body and soul is very intimate. The analogy of the pilot and the ship is judged to be inadequate. He assuredly anticipates that a philosophical conception of man's constitution must be in accord with empirical findings. Now, of course, a preliminary concession must be made: it may be that Cartesian man fails to meet these three specifications and that Thomistic man does meet them. Then certainly Cartesian man and Thomistic man must differ in some fundamental way. Pro-

vided that I understand Gilson's and Brennan's discussions and
interpretations, it is a fair conclusion that these authorities would
declare: St. Thomas met the conditions and achieved a conception of man, sound in principle, if not exhaustive in detail, mani-
festing the accords and satisfying the metaphysical requirements;
moreover, the Thomistic doctrine is radically unlike the unfor-
tunate doctrine of Descartes. Perhaps Descartes conserves the
errors of the Platonic tradition. However this may be, we may
assume that Gilson's Thomistic man and Brennan's Thomistic man
are, at least, close approximations to St. Thomas' own Thomistic
man. What, then, is Thomistic man?

Let us proceed by an examination of Gilson's Thomistic man.
Then Brennan's Thomistic man will be considered. On the authority of Gilson, Thomistic man is certainly not Platonic man—
nor Cartesian man. Gilson's chapter *"Christian Anthropology"*
sets the stage for the exposition of Thomas' view by a historical
survey.

At first sight no philosophy could seem to hold out better promise for
the future of Christian anthropology than that of Plato and his disciple
Plotinus. . . . In the human composite the soul represents the permanent
element, changeless and divine, while the body is transitory, changeable,
perishable. . . . There is no doctrine in which the independence of the
soul with respect to the body is so strongly marked as it is in Platonism,
and that explains why the Fathers, as soon as they awoke to the importance of the immortality of the soul, so readily turned to Plato as a
natural ally (*S*, p. 173).

But, asks Gilson, what becomes of man? He must be defined as a
soul using its body, a formula which Augustine had to accept. Accepting it, however, he could not meet what we have called the
metaphysical requirement. "In the end, then, the man is only his
soul, or, if you prefer it, it is the soul itself that is the man" (*S*, p.
174). In spite of the advantages of Platonism, Gilson continues,
it carried a latent but insurmountable difficulty into the very heart
of Christian philosophy (*S*, p. 175). But the Christian, he affirms,
must admit that the union of soul and body is natural, is willed
by God, and no natural state can possibly be the result of a fall
(*S*, pp. 174 f.). Christian thought turned to Aristotle.

The soul, according to Aristotle, is the act or form of an organized body having life potentially. Thus the relation of soul to body is a particular case of the general relationship between form and matter. There is a sense in which the form and the matter may be said to be separable, since no particular form is of necessity destined by its nature to inform any particular portion of matter, but in another sense we must consider them as inseparable, at least in concrete substances, because forms of this kind could not exist apart from any matter whatsoever. Since the human soul is precisely a form of this kind, the advantages and disadvantages of the definition become at once apparent (*S*, pp. 175 f.).

Gilson summarizes: if we follow Plato, we put the unity of man in jeopardy; if we follow Aristotle, we risk the substantiality of the soul and its immortality (*S*, p. 176).

It is unnecessary to follow Gilson's account of the problem as treated by Avicenna and others. It is to be noted, however, that Avicenna is said to have anticipated Descartes: "if the soul is a substance essentially separable from the body then, whenever I say 'I think,' it is of my soul alone that I speak; and it is the existence of my soul alone that I affirm when I conclude 'therefore I am' " (*S*, p. 182).[4] Thomistic man must be neither Platonic nor Cartesian man. Thomas had to effect a complete reconciliation of the issues. Proper study of Thomas' texts will reveal that his "reconciliation" is not an eclecticism (*S*, p. 182). With this we arrive at Gilson's critical statement:

the Thomist soul is neither a substance playing the part of a form, nor yet a form which could not possibly be a substance, but *a form which possesses and confers substantiality*. Nothing could be simpler; and yet we should look in vain for any philosopher before St. Thomas who conceived the idea (*S*, pp. 182 f.).[5]

Alas, Gilson adds to this a depressing sentence—"There are few enough even today who are capable of setting out its meaning correctly." If Gilson should be in need of an instance of incapacity it will shortly be supplied.

Thomistic man, then, must be conceived as resulting from a

[4] Candor compels me to take the risk of saying that I cannot accept Gilson's interpretation of many points in Cartesian philosophy, as later stages of this essay may well suggest.

[5] Italics mine: . . . *l'âme thomiste n'est ni une substance qui jouerait le rôle de forme, ni une forme qui ne saurait être une substance, mais une forme qui possède et confère la substantialité* (*E*, p. 188).

form which possesses and confers substantiality. The formality of the soul lies at the basis of its substantiality (*S*, p. 183). For Augustine, the question had been whether we can conceive of a noncorporeal substance. For St. Thomas, if the soul exists, its incorporeal nature admits of no doubt. But what of its substantiality? St. Thomas demonstrates this, and the demonstration is said by Gilson to have been based on an insufficiently noticed principle, that is, that every distinct operation supposes a distinct substance (*S*, p. 184). Substances are known by their operations. If there are acts of thought, then there are thinking substances. In Thomistic terminology, there are then intellects, that is, things that think, *choses qui pensent* (*S*, p. 184; *E*, p. 190). The human intellect is an incorporeal substance, in its being and in its operations (*dans son être que dans ses opérations*).[6] But man and the intellect are not to be identified, for men have other operations besides the intellectual.

Now the unity of man cannot be disassociated into two accidentally united halves (against the metaphysical requirement, as it was called above). The substantial form described, Gilson says, is only a part of man.

Everything therefore goes to show that man is a being composed of a corporeal matter organized by a form, and of an intellectual substance which informs and organizes this matter . . . it is the intellect itself, an incorporeal substance, that is the form of the human body (*S*, pp. 185 f.).[7]

[6] A paragraph from Gilson is indispensable. "The operations of which intellects are the principle are cognitive operations. By the intellect we are capable of knowing the nature of all corporeal things. Now the power of knowing all things demands as a first condition that we ourselves shall be no one of those things in particular, for if the intellect had a determinate corporeal nature, it would be but a body among bodies, limited to its own proper mode of being and incapable of apprehending natures different from its own. In other words, a thinking substance that knows bodies could not itself be a body. From this it results that if there are so many beings incapable of knowledge, it is precisely because they are nothing other than bodies, and that if there are corporeal beings that think, the principle of their cognitive activity is not to be found in their corporeity. That is why the human intellect, on account of the very fact that it is an intellect, must be considered as an incorporeal substance, and this, too, in its being as well as in its operations" (*S*, pp. 184 f.; *E*, p. 190).

[7] This sentence is somewhat puzzling. On the one hand, there is the intellectual substance, the intellect, an incorporeal substance; on the other hand, a corporeal matter and the human body. Now just what is the "corporeal matter" which is organized by a form? Just what is the matter informed and organized by the intellectual substance? Is there first a corporeal matter organized by a form, this form being

Acknowledging that the internal difficulties of Thomism begin to look formidable, it is asked: "Grant that the intellect is an incorporeal substance; how, at the same time, could it form part of another substance, and form with it a whole that would be no mere accidental composite?" (*S*, pp. 185 f.). St. Thomas' position, we are assured, is very different from that of his predecessors, and a great deal more favorable. He means that it is man, not a sensibility, that feels, and man, not a mere intellect, that thinks. "Like all facts, this does not need to be deduced, but simply apprehended (*S*, p. 186)." Substances like the human intellect

would be unable to get into touch with the world of bodies save by the intermediation of a body. In order to apprehend sensible forms and thence elaborate intelligibles, they must themselves become the forms of sensible bodies. . . . They would have to do this—and here is the essential point precisely because they are the kind of substances they are (*S*, pp. 186 f.).

The apparent difficulty here is said by Gilson to be due to an illusion of the imagination.

To say that man is a concrete substance and complete in himself is in no way to contradict the thesis of the substantiality of the soul. The error of interpretation . . . is due to imagining body and soul as two substances and attempting out of these two to construct a third which would be the man.

The man alone fully deserves the name of substance, Gilson continues, but he owes all his substantiality to that of the soul.

---

other than the intellectual substance, so that the latter informs and further organizes a corporeal matter which is itself already organized at a lower level? Or is it rather the case that the intellectual substance informs and organizes *prime* matter? If the corporeal matter results from prime matter organized by a form prior to its further organization by the intellectual substance, we surely have something closely akin to the composite Cartesian man. If the Thomistic doctrine insists upon the unicity of form, I presume the components of Thomistic man are prime matter, and the intellectual substance that informs and organizes, and, consequently, everything in the man that is not assignable to prime matter is to be attributed to the informing and organizing principle. This appears to be the teaching of the quotations immediately following in the text above. Souls obtain the cooperation of sensorial organs by actualizing "a matter" and it is due wholly to them that this matter is a body. But to remove all ambiguity, should we not replace "*a* matter" with "prime matter"?

For the human soul is act, and is therefore a thing for itself and a substance; the body . . . although without it the soul cannot develop the fullness of its actuality, has neither actuality nor substance, save those received from its form, that is to say from the soul. That, moreover, is why the corruption of the body cannot involve that of the soul. . . . Thus the substance "man" is not a combination of two substances but a complex substance which owes its substantiality to one only of its two constitutive principles. Souls are immortal substances, which cannot develop their activity without the co-operation of sensorial organs; in order to obtain this co-operation they actualize a matter; it is due wholly to them that this matter is a body, and yet they are not themselves save in a body; the man, therefore, is neither his body, since the body subsists only by the soul, nor his soul, since this would remain destitute without the body; he is the unity of a soul which substantializes his body and of the body in which this soul subsists [8] (*S*, pp. 187 f.).

This, then, is Thomistic man, according to the magistral authority of Gilson. It is a fair inference to conclude that Thomistic man is thought by Gilson—and doubtless by many others —to be exceedingly different from Cartesian man.

Brennan's [9] Thomistic man is said to be a thing remarkably unlike Cartesian man, as Brennan appears to understand Cartesian man. Indeed, one gathers from Brennan's book that there are but two ways open to psychology. On the one hand it could continue along the path defined by Cartesian man; on the other hand it could be guided by the Thomistic conception of man, which Brennan calls hylomorphism.

[8] See also Gilson's Note 19, *S*. pp. 463–64, which is indispensable.
[9] I have not observed a single reference to Gilson in Brennan's book. His name is not in the index, which seems a bit strange. But Brennan's book appears under impressive auspices. It has its *Nihil obstat* and its *Imprimatur*. Moreover, it contains an introduction by Professor Mortimer J. Adler. After referring to his "first enthusiasm for the knowledge and wisdom about man which Aristotle and St. Thomas have taught me," Professor Adler says that he went to the opposite extreme and rejected all modern developments (p. x). In the course of time, he says, he recognized the importance of the modern contribution. He envisaged "an orderly exposition of all the truths we now know about human nature, both philosophical and scientific. The dream I had has come to life in this book; and though Father Brennan would be the first to insist that his work is only a first approximation to the ideal of which we both have been dreaming, he cannot deny that he has completed the pioneer's work. He has not merely seen the promised land: he has surveyed it, marked its boundaries, laid out its thoroughfares, developed its building-sites . . . the edifice of psychology will not be moved from these foundations" (pp. xi–xii).

In the history of philosophic thought, there have been many attempts to
solve the body-soul problem in a manner quite different from that of
Aristotle and Aquinas; yet, in the last analysis, we find but one alternative to the hylomorphic solution. For, if the body and soul of man are
not substantially conjoined, then the union between them must be a
merely accidental one. Two types of explication have been advanced,
under which all nonhylomorphic accounts may be grouped: first, theories
of interactionism, which began with Plato and were repeated by Descartes and the later Cartesians; second, theories of parallelism, which
were first expounded in scientific language by Fechner and Wundt and
afterwards developed with incidental variations by succeeding psychologists. To see that all these accounts are ultimately the same, one need but
reflect that, historically, parallelism stems from the teaching of Descartes, through Leibniz's theory of pre-established harmony and Geu-
lincx's occasionalism; while, philosophically, parallelism is simply an
attempt to show how body and soul can operate side by side without
being causally related. It makes little difference that the Platonists were
less concerned about the body and more about the soul and its spiritual
integrity; and that the parallelists are less concerned about the soul and
more about the body and the law of physical conservation. Fundamentally, the two positions come to the same thing: that body and soul have
only incidental relationships with each other (*B*, pp. 75 f.).

Brennan says later that, for Descartes and his disciples,

man is not one substance, but two different and widely opposed substances: mind, something that thinks, whose very essence, in fact, is
thought; and matter, something that mechanizes, whose very essence is
extension. In the Cartesian picture of man, therefore, the dichotomy of
soul and body, or of mind and matter, is complete and absolute, since
Descartes' unextended mind cannot communicate with his extended body
—except, of course, in a purely mechanical or accidental way (*B*,
pp. 76 f.).[10]

In sum, then, Thomistic man as described by Brennan is not
what Brennan understands Platonic and Cartesian man to be. Let
us assume the validity of the metaphysical requirement: no account of man that jeopardizes his essential unity can be accepted.
It is fair to say, one hopes, that Brennan judges that Cartesian
man does not and Thomistic man does meet the requirement. The
Thomistic account makes intelligible the unity of man in virtue

[10] Cf. p. 178: "Descartes . . . revived the exaggerated Platonic dualism of mind
and matter. . . . After the entrenchment of Descartes' philosophy, mind and
matter were no longer regarded as conjoined in a substantial union."

of the substantial conjunction of body and soul. Let us assume that the metaphysical requirement would be regarded as valid in the sciences of man. Let us further assume that any distinctions, such as that between "body" and "soul," the "psychical" and the "physical," and the like, found necessary for the understanding of the facts, must be so interpreted as not to conflict with the metaphysical requirement. Finally, let it be granted that man as defined by Descartes is such that "body and soul have only incidental relationships with one another," that the "dichotomy of soul and body, or of mind and matter, is complete and absolute," with the understanding that Cartesian man accordingly does not satisfy the metaphysical requirement. Given these conditions, it is evident that Cartesian man, if dominating psychology, will produce a pseudo-science. Again, given these conditions, we should conclude: the Thomistic doctrine satisfies the metaphysical requirement; it renders intelligible the unity of man, providing a foundation for the interpretation of distinctions, while avoiding the difficulties arising from the notion of "two different and widely opposed substances." Thomistic man, then, is *man*. Anticipatorily, the Thomistic doctrine serves to guide the processes of psychological inquiry. Consummatorily, it provides the pattern within which its findings must fall and by means of which they can be organized coherently. In the conditions cited, Cartesian man is not man at all, but rather a monster. Because of the similarities between Platonic and Cartesian man, St. Thomas was well advised to view Platonism with a critical eye. With this, it could be urged, the difference between Thomistic man and Cartesian man has been made sufficiently clear.

Prudence—and Gilson's remark to the effect that even now few are capable of setting forth correctly the meaning of St. Thomas' principle—would suggest an immediate end to this adventure. To continue would be folly. But then there would be no essay.

Thomistic man is man: Cartesian man is a monster. It would be comforting to dismiss all perplexities with this conclusion. We could exclaim, with Professor Adler, What man has made of man! [11] The psychologists could be left to stew in their own—and Cartesian—juice. But, somehow, it seems improbable (that is, to me) that Plato and Descartes described a monster and then thought they had described man. At any rate, Descartes knew quite a bit about St. Thomas, and presumably about Thomistic man, and should have been able to recognize a (or his) monster for what it is. The truly perplexing thing, however, is a matter of words. Thomistic man and Cartesian monster are described, partly by means of the same words and partly by means of similar terms. Perhaps this may be dismissed—but perhaps not. It awakens curiosity. Descartes declares that man is a unity, not indeed of nature, but of composition. The union is said to be very intimate. The pilot-and-the-ship analogy is expressly repudiated. On the other hand, Brennan refers to "the view of Aristotle and Thomas Aquinas that man is a composite substance, made up of matter and mind, the one without physical dimensions, the other possessing all the characters of extended matter" (*B*, p. 56).[12] Strangely, this seems to put Descartes in a company from which one had thought him to be excluded. Verbal identities and similarities, of course, demonstrate nothing. Occurring in different philosophical and scientific contexts, presumably the same and similar words are intended to convey meanings reflecting differences of context. Make what allowances you will—the question is re-evoked: What *is* the difference that makes the difference?

Recklessly, let us resume the adventure, veering first towards Descartes' monster and then towards St. Thomas' man.

The monster is a unity of composition, not of nature. What is meant by the denial? By the unity? By composition? [13] Is man

[11] *What Man Has Made of Man: a Study of the Consequences of Platonism and Positivism in Psychology* (New York, 1937).

[12] The text continues: "if, further, we hold that no single intellectual operation is to be found without its material correlate, no thought without an image, no volition without feeling of some sort—at once the concrete phenomena of man's mental life are seen in their true context, which is both psychological and physiological." To which I can but add: perhaps—but just how different from the Cartesian monster?

[13] In what follows I must make many unsupported statements. I do not accept many traditional interpretations of Descartes, and hope to defend my own, extensively,

composed of two substances? How could Descartes possibly have said this without reservations of the utmost gravity? In the first place, Descartes is emphatic in asserting that the term "substance," in the strict and proper sense, can be applied to God alone. The term cannot be used univocally of God and other beings. For the sake of brevity, let us use the term "Nature" as signifying *all* existents other than God or Substance. In this sense, man is a natural thing, and in so far as "substance" can be used, equivocally, in relation to natural things, man's relation to nature's substantiality or substantialities can be indicated. Is man, then, composed of *two* substances? Certainly not. Granting that Cartesian man has a substantial soul, that his soul is a substance, it certainly is not the case that his body is a substance. His body may be described as of a substance, as a part or portion of a substance, but not as a substance. It is an organized set or system of modes of a substance whose essential attribute is extension. It is, then, highly misleading to describe Cartesian man (or monster) as composed of two substances.

But why use "substance" of Nature at all? What could be meant by saying that Nature is substantial, is composed of substances? Distinguishing between God and the world, reality and appearance, Nature is quasi-substantial. Nature's substantiality as a whole can be described by saying that it depends upon the concurrence of God, and upon that alone, for its existence and for its being what it is. With reference to Nature alone, a natural substance has independence in existence in the sense that it is of the very nature of substances reciprocally to exclude one another. It is possible to take the position, without undue violence to Descartes' thought, that Nature in relation to the divine concurrence has a single conditional substantiality. In this sense, Nature can be described as an internally diversified substantiality.

But disregarding theological references, Nature can be viewed as that which the sciences in their similarities and differences seek to render intelligible. With this, in Cartesian doctrine, Na-

---

on another occasion. Perhaps the reader will graciously accept my statement as hypothetical, in the sense of saying to himself—*if* Descartes did mean this, then this comparative study of Descartes and St. Thomas on man has plausibility.

ture's internally diversified substantiality appears as a plurality of (finite) "substances." This plurality is functional in the pursuit of the sciences. There are several existential sciences. Each science, let us say, views existential matter-of-fact in a perspective determined by a fund of assumptions and basic ideas, the fund, of course, being cumulative and revisional. Reflecting similarities in matters-of-fact, several perspectives may be in part defined by one and the same idea. All sciences have Nature's substantiality as the final referent for *sciences*. The problem is whether this side of the final referent there is a more limited referent, or referents, functionally necessary for the sciences. Descartes, seemingly, was led to a plurality of referents. It was necessary to define a plurality of natural substances. To one he applied the term "matter." Since "substance" cannot either exist or be understood without an internal essential and constitutive character or attribute, the attributes of the substances into which Nature's substantiality proliferates must be defined. Thus, we have as referents for the sciences matter, with its essential attribute of extension, and soul substances, with the essential attribute of thought. For the purposes of scientific inquiry, then, that derivative, dependent substantiality or quasi-substantiality which is called Nature can be regarded *as if* it were unconditionally substantial or as composed of spiritual substances and a matter substance.

It was disclosed to Descartes that man must be viewed in two perspectives, with the consequence that there must be two sciences, or sets of sciences, about man. One science (or set of sciences) refers its findings to Nature's substantiality by way of matter; the other by way of "soul." Let us say that the word "man" signifies an existent thing consisting of a set of matters-of-fact. In the total set of matters-of-fact signified by the word, many, many items are basically extensities, *whatever they may be in addition*. But many items are not basically extensities at all. This may be expressed crudely as follows: in this world, if you look for a tree, a flower, a butterfly, a stone, you must look for something that in every case, however different these things may be, is an extensity. They are things that can neither be without extension nor be understood without reference to "matter" and its essential attribute. Now, in the case of the total matter-of-fact signified by "man," this is not wholly the case. In this world, such items as arms, legs, intestines, cortical neurones, can neither be nor be understood without using the same referent as in the case of the former things. In this world "rose," "stone," "arms," and "intestines" refer to existential sets that are extended, whatever they may be in addition. But there are other items in "man" —so finds Descartes—conditioned neither as to their existence nor as to their intelligibility solely by participation in and reference to matter and its essential attribute. For sciences dealing with man (at least), Nature's diversified substantiality must be interpreted by defining two referents, which may be called, in view of their role in inquiries, "substances," the nature of which is to be reciprocally exclusive and relatively independent.

If we think, not in terms of common sense and common-sense absorptions of (alleged) knowledge and scientific findings, but in terms of the sciences themselves, the real bearing of Descartes' view of man can be restated. It is not the case that man "has" or "is" a body, and *therefore* must be viewed in a perspective defined by "matter." Rather, because some of the matter-of-fact signified by the term "man" cannot be rendered intelligible save by reference to matter, it must be concluded that "man" is to that extent a corporeal thing. His corporeality, then, is a name for an intricate set of scientific findings, many of which seem to be warranted. Because of certain similarities of scientific findings in the case of "dogs," "stones," and "stars," it must be concluded that man is like these things in some measure. But it is equally true that other bits of this matter-of-fact identified by the word "man"—so thinks Descartes—cannot be rendered intelligible by reference exclusively to matter (or, if you will, by reference to "matter" as defined by him). So to speak: look at man in the perspective of what we call "physics" or "chemistry" or "anatomy" or "neurology," and according to Descartes, you will not even see anything identifiable as "envy," "longing for immortality," or "thought." This being the case, if these items are to be seen, you must look at "man" in a different perspective. Whereupon you will see that "man" is or has a soul.

Scientific probing comes to an end by referring these facts to a diversification of Nature's substantiality; of this diversification it cannot be said that extension is universally constitutive. The knowability of man, then, depends upon two different referents. Describe this, if you will, by saying that man is a dual being. Of course, he is a single thing; he is what Aristotle would call a unity of matter-and-form. Possibly he could be seen in some perspective (a metaphysical one?) in which his unity would be manifest and a duality of referents be unapparent. The union of body and mind is said to be very intimate. But if reflection is to begin *after* the perspectival findings of the several sciences are at hand to be reckoned with, then perforce the unity must appear as one of composition. Then "composition," if it is to be made specifically intelligible and in view of different findings because of duality of referents, must take the form of a correlation of items, or else must be interpreted in terms of a systematic interaction between substantial factors. If the behavior of the pineal gland will not suffice, then some other way must be sought. Perchance—one might imagine Descartes saying—the day may arrive when Nature's concurrent substantiality may be reflected in a dominant idea providing a similar perspective for all the sciences. Then, perchance, man's unity of "composition" will be resolved into a unity of "nature." If Descartes ever had such conjectures, he probably thought of their realization as distant.[14]

[14] It will be understood, I trust, that this essay is not concerned with a critical evaluation of Descartes' conceptions. It might be urged that if Descartes' conception of matter were radically revised and the new conception were sufficiently absorptive of today's findings in the many sciences there would be no need for two referents ("substances") for knowledge of the nature of man. Perhaps this is possible. But the new conception must be proportioned to the concrete diversification of nature. It must function so as to embrace all the facts and facilitate arriving at the intelligibility of the total set of matters of fact. Whether the word "matter" would be appropriate for this new conception would be a question of taste and expediency. Or it might be urged that the term "substance" should be abandoned—or that it has been abandoned, on the ground that it is of no use or cannot be made useful. I do not care to urge the retention of a term, or of any historical idea signified by the word, provided the concrete and incredibly rich diversification of Nature be not "impov-

Whether or not this discussion leaves Cartesian man a monster may be disregarded. The question is how divergent are Thomistic and Cartesian views concerning this thing, whether man or monster. Let us further examine Thomistic man under the tutorship of Gilson and Brennan. Identities and differences of terminology have been noted. Why should Thomistic man and Cartesian monster be described in words so strangely alike? Let us take samples from Brennan.

Applied to man, the hylomorphic doctrine states that between the first matter and the first form of every human being there is a bond of perfect substantial union. This means, more concretely, that the body of man, as first matter, is an incomplete substance; that the soul of man, as first form, is likewise an incomplete substance; that body and soul together, in a bond of mutual complementation, make one complete substance which is man (*B*, p. 68).[15]

Brennan supplies a "clarification" for this chapter.

I should like to make it clear from the outset that when the term "body" is used in conjunction with the term "soul" as in the phrases "the body-soul relationship," "man is a creature composed of body and soul," "the soul requires a body for its perfection," and so on, "body" always refers to first matter. Actually, the human soul confers on first matter all the perfections that we witness in the human body. In other words, the soul is united directly and immediately to first matter, as to its co-principle in the constitution of man. Strictly speaking, a body or corporeal substance is something that has already been perfected by union with a substantial form. To be precise, therefore, one should always say that the constitutive principles of man's essence are first matter and rational soul. This is the way in which the "body-soul" phraseology is to be understood in the text (*B*, p. 81).

But later Brennan states:

Now, it is quite manifest that a power which is capable of grasping the universal nature of its objects and of reflecting upon itself must be rooted

---

erished." I adopt the phrase from the paper by Iredell Jenkins, "The Postulate of an Impoverished Reality" (*Journal of Philosophy*, Vol. XXXIX, No. 20). Finally, the "subjectification" of sense-experience does not resolve the issue, since there must be a diversification of nature-other-than-man in correlation with nature-as-manifest-in-man.

[15] How can the *body* of man be *first* matter? Is the body an incomplete substance? Or is first matter? But see the next quotation.

in a substance that is completely devoid of matter; and further, that its proper stimulus, to be able to set it in motion, must be immaterial also (*B*, p. 171).[16]

The incomplete substance, the soul, seemingly is completely immaterial. Let us admit, indeed, urge, that we have no right, at least so far, to identify the meaning of Brennan's terms with Cartesian meanings. Presumably the meanings are Thomistic, or revisionally Thomistic. This is indicated by other statements. Distinguishing natural from intentional modes of being, Brennan says (referring to the "ability to give intentional existence to objects" as "precisely the thing that distinguishes cognitive being from nutritive being"):

This is the gap that separates the sensitive from the vegetative acts of man. This, in a measure, is the dividing line between material and immaterial functions, because even sensitive knowledge, though common to body and soul, is yet immaterial in its way. In the hierarchy of man's acts, therefore, the operations of his senses are placed midway between the operations of his vegetative powers, which are purely material, though immanent and vital; and the operations of his rational powers, which are purely immaterial (*B*, p. 114).

Now it seems obvious that the notion of something midway between the material and the immaterial could not be reconciled with the Cartesian meanings. It would be absurd to refer to the Cartesian soul substance, or "faculties" residing within it, as only somewhat, or slightly, or negligibly material. In Cartesian doctrine, if immateriality be defined by reference to the essential attribute of matter, the notion of "degree of immateriality" seems impossible. Assuredly the immateriality of the soul, of thought,

---

[16] Cf. "It is proper to say, then, that the human mind exhibits an objective dependency on sense, since the data of sense furnish it with the objects of intellection. But in the subjective order, that is, in the act of abstracting and understanding, the intellect of man is completely devoid of matter and the appendages of matter. But if it is immaterial in its intellectual operations, it must be immaterial in its intellectual nature" (p. 309). Again: "An intelligible form . . . is a universalized form, that is, a form which has been denuded of all its concrete characters and thereby removed from the dimensions of space and time. A sensible form, then, is something material. An intelligible form is something immaterial. But, knowledge by sensible species is proper to the animal, just as knowledge by intelligible species is proper to man. Unless, therefore, material and immaterial mean one and the same thing, it is impossible to identify the cognitions proper to man with those proper to the animal" (p. 196).

cannot mean occupancy of relatively little space. Evidently
Brennan finds no difficulty in the notion of something midway,
and presumably finds it integral to the Thomistic conception of
man.[17]

The effect produced in the sense when an object impinges on it is neither
wholly material nor wholly immaterial. It is not wholly material because . . . it is a removal or disengagement of form from matter; yet
it is not wholly immaterial because the modification is wrought in a
material organ (*B*, p. 120).

The epistemological abstractive doctrine is at least intimately associated with the notion of degree of immateriality, although it is
somewhat uncertain as to whether the epistemological doctrine
determines the notion or the notion facilitates the former. In any
case, it is evident that the unassimilability of the notion in the
Cartesian doctrine, and its (apparent) assimilability (if not its
necessity) in the Thomistic conception of man as reported by
Brennan, is due at least in large measure to a difference in the notion of "matter." This suggests the question: Is the difference between the Cartesian and Thomistic conceptions of matter so great
as to render intelligible the difference represented by the impossibility of the notion, "degree of immateriality," in the former and
its congeniality or necessity for the latter?

Postponing this question for the moment, it should be remarked
that the notion seemingly collides with the dual notion expressed
by Brennan.

The vegetative and sensitive functions of man are bounded by the limitations of time and space, though we discern varying degrees of immanence
and remotion from matter in the activities of our psychosomatic powers.
But now, with the advent of thinking processes, a completely new world
is opened up to us: a universe of ideas and volitions, a region liberated
from the palpabilities of sense. The human mind uses no organ in its
actual elaboration of thought, however much it may be extrinsically
limited by cortical substance, nerve centers . . . and all the material
paraphernalia that form the necessary preliminary to its intellectual
achievements (*B*, p. 169).

[17] See text cited in note 16, above. Cf. *B*, pp. 115 f., where the expressions, "the
higher the degree of immateriality" and "a certain degree of immateriality" are
found (although it should be noted that the expressions occur here in connection
with discussion of the nature of knowing).

Distinguishing between the proper objects of sense and of the intellect, Brennan continues:

The restriction of the sensitive power to the apprehension of singulars is due, of course, to its psychosomatic nature. It is inherently dependent on matter for all its operations. By contrast, the extension of the intellectual power to the apprehension of universals is due to its purely psychic nature. It is inherently independent of matter in all its operations. This does not signify that intellect is free of the administrations of sense. Quite the opposite! (*B*, pp. 191 f.).[18]

Brennan divides human powers into two classes: those that belong to the soul and body together, and those belonging to the soul alone. The first are psychosomatic; the second "purely psychic." Continuing, he says:

Moreover, psychic powers are identical with mind; and mind, by extension, is identical with soul. To ask, then: is the mind of man a substance? is really to ask: is the soul of man a substance?

Brennan's summarizing reply is this:

man is a hylomorphic creature. He is made up of two basic principles: matter and form. Each is a necessary part of his essence. As parts, each is incomplete without the other. Each belongs to the category of substance, though neither, alone, is a complete substance, because neither, alone, is a complete species. The point is that, entitatively speaking, the soul of man, like all souls, is a substantial form of matter. This means that it demands a material substrate as a coefficient of its very being, in conjunction with which it establishes the complete corporeal substance that we call man (*B*, pp. 303 f.).

These passages, together with others previously cited, verbally if not really, suggest an unresolved collision of ideas.

What tentative conclusions can now be projected? What is suggested by the expositions of Gilson and Brennan concerning Thomistic man? It seems clear that the Thomistic and Cartesian doctrines were formulated under an approximately identical tension between two sets of considerations. The nucleus of one set is assuredly represented by the metaphysical requirement: man is a

---

[18] Again, on p. 192, it is stated: "To understand the true nature of the dependency on sense . . . it is necessary to distinguish intellect's proper operations, which are immaterial, from the conditions of its exercise, which are material."

unitary being; if in any sense he is compounded, the composition is an organizational conjoining that interprets his composite nature without destroying his unity. The nucleus of the other set is found in this, that inquiry seeking to render intelligible the constellation of apparent facts identified as a man appears to be driven towards the definition of a bi-polarity within the constellation itself. It is contended that the identity of the tension explains the similarity in verbal descriptions together with the Cartesian adaptations of terms found in the Thomistic tradition.[19] Substance, composition, matter—these seem to be the terms reflecting the tension in the highest degree.

Cartesian man and the Thomistic man of Gilson and Brennan seem to be identical—verbally at least—to the extent that the soul is incorporeal. Gilson, in the sources cited, appears to use the term "immaterial" more sparingly than does Brennan. It seems that the soul is distinct from the body: thus the incorporeal is distinguished from and presumably is radically different from the corporeal. Indubitably, analysis of "corporeality" will disclose a factor, "matter," without which corporeality cannot be understood. Presumably, in one direction at least, the soul can be understood without reference to the factor, matter. But the error of interpretation must be avoided—we must not imagine that body and soul are two substances and attempt out of these to construct a third which would be the man. Man is not to be identified with his soul. "En disant que l'homme est une substance concrète et complète en soi, on ne contredit aucunement la thèse qui affirme la substantialité de l'âme" (*E*, pp. 192 f.). Accepting this brave assurance, let us assume that Gilson's formula authentically expresses the central point of Thomistic doctrine concerning man—the Thomistic soul (*âme*) is not a substance playing the

[19] It seems unnecessary to provide a list of identical and similar terms and phrases, in view of the abundance of materials quoted in the text and footnotes. It will be understood that I do not assert that Brennan's interpretations of Thomistic man are identical with Gilson's, nor, for that matter, that either or both give impeccable accounts of Thomistic doctrine. For the purposes of this essay, it appears sufficient to regard Brennan and Gilson as genuinely representative of the Thomistic tradition. In what follows, to avoid over-burdening the essay with footnotes, I omit referring terms and phrases to the quotations from Brennan and Gilson from which they are drawn.

role of a form, nor yet a form which could not be a substance, but a form which possesses and confers substantiality.

Let us postpone the question of matter, to consider "substance," "intellect," and "soul." The intellect is said to be an incorporeal substance. Intellects are things that think. The Thomistic *intellectus* is a thinking thing.[20] But the intellect cannot be identified with the man. The body is some part of man, and this is also the case with the intellect by which he understands.[21] But the intellectual principle is the form of the man.[22] An incorporeal substance, it appears, is the form of the body. There are before us a number of terms whose relations must be determined: soul, intellect, intellectual soul, incorporeal substance, the man (the concrete and complete substance), the form that possesses and confers substantiality, the form of the body, the body. It is not astonishing that the Thomistic doctrine is intricate—or that few are competent to understand its fundamental principle. However, one can but try.

As a first step, it appears safe to make several statements. According to Thomistic doctrine, the man cannot be identified with the intellect. Again, in some sense the soul cannot be identified with the intellect. It is evident that were there a soul lacking the intellectual principle and not describable as an intellectual soul, then that soul could not be called human. That soul could not confer substantiality with the result that there is a man, the concrete and complete substance. The man, then, is not a composite whose components are (1) an intellect, this intellect being exactly equivalent to the soul, being the whole of the soul, and the whole of the incorporeal substance, and (2) everything else belonging to the man. The soul, then, is something more than the intellect. It comprises the intellectual principle. The soul comprising the intellectual principle is an incorporeal substance. Gilson states:

For St. Thomas, if the soul exists its incorporeal nature admits of no doubt, but it is not altogether the same as regards its substantiality, and it is on this precise point that he brings all his forces to bear. [The principle underlying the demonstration is said to be this]: that every distinct

[20] Cf. *E*, p. 199; *S*, p. 184.
[21] *ST*, Q. LXXVI, art. 1, *I answer that* . . . (*P*, I, 697).
[22] *Ibid*. (P, I, 698).

operation supposes a distinct substance. It is only in fact by their operations that substances are known, and conversely, operations are not to
be explained except by substances (*S*, p. 184; *E*, p. 189).

The soul or form that confers substantiality cannot be identified
with the intellect precisely because, as Gilson says, men have other
operations in addition to the intellectual (*S*, p. 185; *E*, p. 191).
The man Socrates exists, and being is the act of existence.[23] The
man Socrates has operations other than the intellectual. What are
the operations of Socrates? What are the relations of the operations other than the intellectual to the concrete and complete substance, the man, and to the form that possesses and confers substantiality? Now, in Thomistic man there is at least a distinct
substance rightly described as an intellectual substance. "The
operations of which intellects are the principle are cognitive operations" (*S*, p. 184; *E*, p. 190). Gilson immediately adds:

Even if we wanted to identify the man with his soul we should be faced
with a difficulty of the same kind. Such an identification would be possible in the doctrine of Plato or in that of St. Augustine, because, for these
philosophers, sensation is an operation proper to the soul and one in
which the body plays no part (*S*, p. 185; *E*, p. 191).[24]

Clearly, there is man; there is the intellect, either an incorporeal
substance or sharing in the incorporeality of the substance; and
there is the soul. It is declared, however, that "the human soul
is act, and is therefore a thing for itself and a substance" (*S*, p.
187; *E*, p. 198). If distinct operations imply distinct substances,
if "intellect" must be distinguished from "soul," if the intellectual
soul is a substance, then just how many substances are there?
From cognitive operations we are led to posit an intellectual substance. The man Socrates is not an intellect or an intellectual substance, but he has one. It is somewhat bewildering, because the
man Socrates is said to be a concrete and complete substance, is
said to be, not a combination of two substances, but a complex
substance which owes its substantiality to one only of its two constitutive principles.

Let us indulge for a moment in free conjecture. Let us say that

[23] See Gilson's indispensable footnote 19, *S*, pp. 463–64, referred to hereafter as
Note 19.
[24] Is it really the case that for these philosophers in sensation body plays no part?

in one sense the soul is a substance, as the principle of all human operations. That is, some operations of the human being, the man, are vegetative-*like*, others animal-*like*, but even these operations are not just vegetative and animal, but *human*, since all human operations are operations of the being called man. In this sense it is difficult to see how the identification of the man (in so far as incorporeal) with the soul can be evaded. We are told that St. Thomas "never loses sight of the fact that just as it is the man, and no mere sensibility, that feels, so it is the man, and no mere intellect, that thinks" (*S*, p. 186; *E*, pp. 191 f.). That Thomas never loses sight of the fact must be conceded. It is his way of effecting the empirical accord. As for the met-empirical accord, that, as we may perhaps find out, is another matter.

It is monstrous to regard man as made up of a soul capable of intellectual operations alone, and of a body which performs all other operations ascribable to man. Gilson's Thomistic man and St. Thomas' Thomistic man are, apparently, not that. Yet there must be something more to be said for Platonic man than has been conceded so far. In some manner all the operations must be referable to the man, for they are operations of the man. In some manner some of the nonintellectual operations, if not all, must be referred to the informing soul or incorporeal substance. Moreover, the man is not made by a combination of two substances, and the incorporeal substance is somehow a unity, not a random collection of souls accidentally conjoined. The soul possesses the intellectual principle, but the soul is not equivalent to the intellect. Yet a man would not be a man without this principle and a soul possessing the principle.

Let us consider the soul and its operations. We may first establish that "the principle of intellectual operation which we call the soul, is a principle both incorporeal and subsistent." [25] "the intellectual principle, which we call the mind or the intellect, has essentially an operation in which the body does not share . . . (*P*, I, 685). Revert now to the principle stated by Gilson: "toute opération distincte suppose une substance distincte" (*E*, p. 189;

---

[25] *ST*, Q. LXXV, art. 2, *I answer that* . . . *P* reads: ". . . the principle of intellectual operation, which we call the soul of man . . ." (I, 685).

S, p. 184). It is evident that the principle cannot be applied loosely. There are operations other than the intellectual. Assume that some of these operations are such that the body has no share in them. A literal application of the principle suggests that there are as many souls, provided these operations are distinct. But the soul of Socrates is no collection of substances. Nor is the man Socrates a collection. The principle must be interpreted in a more recondite way. Adopting Dionysius' position that there are three things to be found in spiritual substances—essence, power, and operation, St. Thomas treats the problem of man accordingly.[26] Now, the power of the soul is not its essence.[27] Yet several powers must be placed in the soul.[28] There are operations of the soul performed without a corporeal organ, such as understanding and will. The powers of these operations are in the soul as in their subject. Some operations of the soul are performed by means of corporeal organs.[29] But all powers of the soul, whether their subject be the soul alone or the composite, flow from the essence of the soul as from their principle.[30] Plurality of powers and operations does not, then, imply a plurality of souls. Now, St. Thomas rules out several possible identifications. First, to equate "man" with "soul," but a particular man, Socrates, with the composite of soul and body. Second, to equate this man and this soul. It is in this context that St. Thomas declares that Plato, supposing that feeling was proper to the soul, maintained that man was a soul making use of a body. But feeling is not an operation of the soul alone.[31] Third, the man cannot be equated with the intellect, for if man is the intellect itself, and Socrates and Plato have one intellect, then Socrates and Plato are one man.[32] In man, the sensitive, the intellectual, and nutritive souls are numerically one.[33] "Of one thing there is but one substantial being. But the substantial form gives substantial being. Therefore of one thing there is

---

26 *ST*, Q. LXXV, introd.; *P*, I, 682.
27 *ST*, Q. LXXVII, art. 1, *I answer that* . . . *P*, I, 720.
28 *Ibid.*, art. 2, *I answer that* . . . *P*, I, 722.
29 *Ibid.*, art. 5, *I answer that* . . . *P*, I, 727.
30 *Ibid.*, art. 6, *I answer that* . . . *P*, I, 729.
31 *ST*, Q. LXXV, art. 4, *I answer that* . . . *P*, I, 688. Would not Descartes grant this?
32 *ST*, Q. LXXVI, art. 2, *I answer that* . . . *P*, I, 701.
33 *Ibid.*, art. 3, *I answer that* . . . *P*, pp. 705 f.

but one substantial form. But the soul is the substantial form of man. Therefore it is impossible that there be in man another substantial form besides the intellectual soul." [34] The intellectual soul contains virtually the sensitive and nutritive souls.[35]

We may now return to the powers of the soul. It seems clear that this conclusion must be maintained: once the essence of the soul shall have been established, then the powers must be such that they are in accord with that essence. They are all resident within one soul. If, for example, it is of the essence of the soul, if it is integral to the nature of the substantial form of man, to be incorporeal and immaterial, then assuredly all the powers, even if their exercise involves a corporeal organ, are rightly described as incorporeal and immaterial. Despite the desperate ingenuity of St. Thomas, does not Platonic man arise before us? Man is a soul using a body. Perhaps the expression is figurative—even for Plato. But in the end, does it not express something indispensable for the Thomistic doctrine concerning man? To this we shall revert later.

If Thomistic man—either that of Thomas, of Gilson, or of Brennan—is to fit the requirements of both the empirical and the met-empirical accords, there are some interpretations of terms, of isolated texts, which must be utterly unacceptable. But it may be clarifying to entertain one of these interpretations. The proposed interpretation, it should be emphasized, would be utterly condemned (I believe) by St. Thomas, Gilson, and Brennan. It is suggested by certain texts, terminological usages, and doctrinal needs—but only by some. It may not be intended even by these. For the sake of brevity, the basis of the interpretation may be defined as the notion of degrees of immateriality, and the doctrine to which it leads may be called the organismic (or naturalistic?) view of man. The latter is not what Brennan intends as the hylomorphic doctrine. It is contended, however, that Brennan's hylomorphism reduces to the organismic view *unless* distinctions of

[34] *Ibid.*, art. 4, *On the contrary* . . . *P*, I, 708. Here, as in many other places, Pégis is far more guarded in his use of the terms "'being" and "existence" than the original *ST* translation, with resulting great improvement.
[35] *Ibid.*, *I answer that* . . . *P*, p. 708.

a Cartesian type are introduced. The same will be true of St. Thomas' and Gilson's Thomistic man, in so far as Brennan's Thomistic man is in accord with the former. Once more, the interpretation is offered purely for the sake of clarification.

Let it be assumed that the soul is the substantial form of man; that the man (says Socrates) is the concrete and complete substance; that the man is not constructed out of two substances; that with St. Thomas we shall never lose sight of the fact that it is the man, not a mere sensibility or intellect, that feels and thinks. It is further assumed that this being, the man, for example, Socrates, is to be understood, and that the distinction between matter and form is indispensable for the purpose.[36] In the conditions hypothetically established, a man is composite in the sense that the analysis of his being—logically conditioning any further investigation of his nature and being—moves in two directions, signified by "form" and "matter." The distinction is one of discourse, but it is relevant to and is referable to the thing, the man. The form of this thing can be identified as an intellectual soul in this sense, that the phrase and others like it describe the nature of the form constituting the intelligibility of this thing when the bi-polarity of analysis is expressed in terms of the distinction between matter and form. Were the thing a stone, an oak tree, a dog, no such description would be appropriate, for no one of these things is a man, albeit the distinction of matter and form conditions the intelligibility of each of them. The form conferring substantiality may be called the soul.

Now this form, or the soul, is evidently to be regarded as immaterial. It is immaterial in the sense that, form being distinguished from matter, form is not matter. Some substantial forms "are subsisting principles of operations proper to themselves as forms, and these are *rational souls;* others are bound up with matter both as to their being and as to their operation, and these are *material forms.*" [37] But the expression, material form, as-

[36] "Being is the act of existence. Posited by this act, the being is posited in and for itself. Since it is, it is by definition itself and no other . . . the being conceived in its undivided unity is called precisely *substance*, and its property of existing as substance, that is to say, for itself and without substantial dependence on any other, is called *subsistence*. Thus the act of being causes the substance and its subsistence." Gilson, Note 19.   [37] *Ibid.*

suredly cannot *negate* the distinction between matter and form; rather it describes something about the nature of the form. Perhaps this may be conveyed by saying that immaterial stones are not: posited by an act of existence, the stone is matter-and-form. This states something pertinent to the essential nature of a stone. The soul, then, is immaterial, in the sense that every form is immaterial. If the soul now be described as incorporeal, the question arises: is this term to be regarded as equivalent to immaterial? If the corporeal signifies a being that is a unity of matter-and-form, the equivalence cannot obtain.

"Soul," "intellectual soul," and similar expressions, furnish content with respect to the form of this thing; the "body," or the "human body," effects something corresponding, in view of the fact that the thing is matter and form. In the case of a stone or a dog, appropriate values must be supplied, for these, too, are unities of matter and form. It may possibly be reasonable to use "body" and "soul" with respect to a dog, but quite inappropriate in the case of a stone. The formula, possessing and conferring substantiality, on this interpretation, could be stripped of all suggestions that man is arrived at by taking two substances and adding them together. It could be made to mean something like this: here is a thing said to be a man; if inquiry does not disclose, as pertaining to its nature, a certain degree and type of organization, then this thing is not correctly called a man. It is the organization that, so to speak, makes the thing a man. In a similar sense, it could be asserted that it is the organization that makes a dog a dog, a reptile a reptile, and so forth.

Containing this plan of interpretation, the notion of degrees of immateriality seems requisite. The matter and form analysis points in one direction towards a terminus which is designated prime matter. Prime matter does not exist. Forms do not exist. Prime matter is what is never "a this." Matter acquires actual being as it acquires form.[38] The potentiality of matter is nothing else but its essence.[39] Now the degree of remotion from bare prime matter, the degree of actualization of its possibilities, could rea-

[38] *ST*, Q. LXXV, *I answer that* . . . *P*, I, 692.
[39] *ST*, Q. LXXVII, *Reply obj. 2, P*, I, 721.

sonably be described as a degree of immateriality. The more matter acquires form, or the higher the form acquired, the more actual being it comes to have. *De*-materialization, or *im*-materialization, is *organization*. In this sense, the higher the actual being, the more immaterial or organized it is. The higher the being subject to investigation under the analytical bi-polarity of matter and form, the more there would intervene for inquiry between this being, let us say a man, and the raw nudity of prime matter. Let us call a thing, composite of matter and form, a body, and reserve the term "matter" for prime matter. Agreeing upon this terminology, immaterialization or immateriality could not be identified with incorporeality. On the contrary, corporeality must signify some degree of removal from matter. The notion of a maximal degree of immateriality does not seem to be impossible. It could be urged that the set of finite existents called the world is somehow limited, in that nothing can have a degree of immateriality beyond a certain degree, whatever that is. In these conditions, maximal immateriality is maximal remotion from bare (prime) matter. But equally, maximal immateriality is maximal *corporeality*. Maximal actualization of the potentialities of matter is maximal corporealization. If prime matter is somehow restricted as to the nature and range of its potentialities, then actualization, organization, corporeality, immateriality are relative to that restriction.

If the preceding seems to be a strange use of words, the underlying ideas are familiar enough. It is equivalent to saying: all existing things are organized; organization may differ in degree. Do not biologists sometimes express their findings in such a manner? It might be contended that the most highly organized things are men. Their organization is such that the thing must be described as capable of rational operations and, therefore, as rationally be-souled. The maximally immaterial function, power, or aspect of organization is the intellect. This being is also the maximally *corporeal* thing, that is, the maximal realization of matter's potentialities. A man is a concrete and complete substance. Let us assume that he is the highest being of that set of beings for the study of which the distinction between matter and form is necessary. This distinction controls investigation. As organization comes to be understood in the various sciences, the "form" of the thing itself comes to be understood. It is understood as an actualization of the potentialities of matter. Inquiry will vibrate between "form" and "matter." But the thing is there, with its unity unimpaired, for distinctions are being made as demanded by its organization. Given this pattern "pre-investigatively," to adapt Brennan's felicitous expression (*B*, p. 336), then science may proceed to supply details, adjusting "post-investigatively" their findings to this pattern. This, then, is the organismic pattern.

It would be preposterous to attribute this interpretation to Gilson or to Brennan. Frankly, I am not wholly convinced that it would be preposterous to attribute it to St. Thomas. The questions, however, are: Why is it preposterous? Under what conditions can Thomistic man escape identification with organismic or naturalistic man? How can we follow the good counsel never to lose sight of the fact that it is the man who feels and thinks and, nevertheless, avoid the conclusion that all the historic distinctions summed up in the distinction between body and soul are nothing more than a distinction between organization and that which, in relation to the purposes of an inquiry, may be regarded as the raw materials of the organization? In great perplexity, I can but suggest this answer: Thomistic man is not organismic man, because the former is astonishingly like Cartesian man. On the one hand, it must be said of Thomistic man that the concrete and complete substance, the man, feels and thinks. This seemingly expresses the empirical accord. But, with Gilson, we must be able to say:

Man . . . is a concrete substance, that is to say a substance in which there are parts which may legitimately be considered separately; but his being is one, first because the substantial elements of his being, that is to say body and soul, cannot subsist apart, and secondly because it is due to the subsistence of one only of these, that is to say the soul, that the substance, man, subsists. The different *rôle* played by the two parts is quite clear, inasmuch as *the soul, once it has obtained the necessary aid from the body, can subsist without the body,* as in fact it does after the death of the man, while on the other hand the body can in no case subsist without the soul, to which latter it owes all its actuality; as the very dissolution of the corpse is enough to prove.[40]

The met-empirical accord is hereby satisfied. We must avoid the identification of the man with the intellect or even with the soul; yet the man must in some sense be identified with the soul; we must maintain the unity of man; we must understand "souls" as "immortal substances which cannot develop their activity without the cooperation of sensorial organs" and yet persist after having obtained the aid needed. Thomistic man must have a Platonic soul. The soul is substantial. It obtains necessary aid from the body. I am willing to concede that this represents faithfully the thought of St. Thomas. What aid does the soul receive because it confers substantiality and the man subsists? How does it use corporeal organs? Are its powers evoked, its operations made specific, by an extrinsic excitation on the part of the body? How are the parts of man to be considered separately? Granting that there are "parts" which can be considered separately, then, when they are so considered, how are their several functions to be conceived, and how the relation between them? Now it must be true, if the met-empirical accord obtains, that the immortal part of the man is genuinely the man.

To make this clear, let us consider that Socrates might have died in early youth. This Socrates would never have become the tutor of Plato. But this youth Socrates, since his soul is an immortal substance, would have immortality and the immortal soul would be that of the youth Socrates. But Socrates is reported to have died full of years. His soul obtained aid from the body for decades more than would have been the case had he died in youth. Surely this lengthened career implies that much accrued to the soul of Socrates which would not have so accrued had he died in youth. It was the man Socrates who thought and felt, who suffered and loved and sought the truth. But are the fruits of all this somehow gathered up into the soul substance which alone is immortal? And if so gathered up, must these fruits not be in and of the soul, participating in its nature, and escaping the dissolution of the body? The difficulty is obvious: the parts of man must be distin-

[40] Note 19; italics mine.

guished; they must be systematically interrelated in such a manner that the unity of the man can be maintained and the metaphysical requirement be met; but the immortal part must be separable, and in some way must be identifiable with the man—Socrates' soul with Socrates, Aristotle's with Aristotle—for otherwise there could be little meaning to the notion of necessary aid from their several bodies. But how can all the conditions be fulfilled unless St. Thomas admits, as an abiding truth, *that man is a soul using a body?* I must confess my inability to see how Thomistic man can meet all the conditions for which it was devised, escape reduction to the organismic or naturalistic pattern, and provide a program for scientific inquiries, unless that program be based upon a radically "dualistic" conception of man's constitution.

Let us return to Brennan's Thomistic man. Does he evade Plato, or Plato and Descartes? We may be assured that his hylomorphism is not intended to be the organismic conception. The vegetative and sensitive functions, he says, are bounded by the limitations of time and space. They are inherently dependent on matter for their operations. Strictly, one assumes, they are dependent on corporeal organs, but corporeality comports prime matter. This does not necessarily imply, of course, a simple identification of the functions with activities of corporeal organs. It implies some form of dependence. This might be construed to mean that the activity of the corporeal organ occasions or somehow elicits a corresponding vegetative or sensitive functioning. Whether Brennan means this, or whether he must accept it, remains to be seen. In any case, he continues: "By contrast, the extension of the intellectual power to the apprehension of universals is due to its *purely psychic nature.* It is *inherently independent of matter* in all its operations. This does not signify that intellect is free of the administrations of sense. Quite the opposite!" (*B*, pp. 191 f.) [41] Again, we read: "To understand the true nature of its dependency on sense, therefore, it is necessary to distinguish intellect's proper operations, which are immaterial, from the conditions of its exer-

[41] Italics mine.

cise, which are material" (*B*, p. 192). Passions are said to be complexes of psychic and somatic elements (*B*, p. 155). According to Aquinas, Brennan says, "both the somatic and psychic features of a passion constitute one affective phenomenon. . . . Body and soul, in such a case, are acting as a single principle of operation" (*B*, p. 160). The operations of sense, he declares, are *"midway* between the operations of his vegetative powers, which are *purely material*, though immanent and vital; and the operations of his rational powers, which are *purely immaterial"* (*B*, p. 114).[42] Immateriality can be understood as signifying form, in the sense that "to understand is to free form completely from matter" (*B*, p. 190). "A sensible form, then, is something material. An intelligible form is something immaterial" (*B*, p. 196). Matter and form are parts of man's essence. Each is incomplete without the other. Each belongs to the category of substance. The soul is a substantial form of matter.

Brennan's terminology, so far as I can see, is incontestably twofold. In part, it is the matter-form terminology. In part, it is what may be called psychophysical. Is the form-matter distinction intended to be identical with the distinction between the psychical and the physical? If form as form is immaterial, in view of texts previously instanced, it is difficult to believe that this equivalence is intended. If form is not matter, no form, whether sensible or intelligible, can be something material. If to understand is to free form completely from matter, then, presumably, if a sensible thing composite of matter and form came to be understood, its form would be divested of matter. It might be the form *of* a thing which could not exist save by being a unity of matter and form, and in this sense be material as the form of a material thing.

Are we to understand that if a stone comes to be understood, its form being freed of matter (which presumably would involve the operations of purely immaterial powers), then that form becomes purely psychic? To man, said to be a complete substance, the distinction between matter and form is pertinent. We have been told that each of the parts of man's essence, matter and form, belong to the category of substance. The statements seem obscure. Ac-

[42] Italics mine.

cepting them, could the following be urged? If form be distinct from matter, or can be distinguished from it and from the thing as a unity of matter and form, and can be regarded by itself in its distinction from matter, then form is certainly immaterial. If, then, it belong under the category of substance, form emerges as an immaterial substance or as something in and of an immaterial substance. Accordingly, the substance, the man, in so far as form alone is regarded, becomes a non matter or other-than-matter substance. But so it would be in the case of a stone, if a stone be a thing of matter and form, and if each factor in the case of the stone belong to the category of substance. Doubtless this is absurd. But to add that the substantial form in the case of man is psychical, while in the case of the stone the term "psychical" has no relevance, involves importing additional considerations. If it be urged that the form of a stone is the form of a material thing, while the form of man is an immaterial psychical something, then two radically different distinctions are employed and the systematic relations between them remain in obscurity.

Consider this text of Brennan:

. . . the soul of man is the immediate subject of his rational powers. As a subject, it does not require to be possessed by anything else. It exists, in short, by its own rightful title, which means that it is a substance. For, obviously, acts suspended in a vacuum are inadmissible. Thinking demands, not only a power that thinks, but also a substance in which the power to think is rooted. Similarly, willing demands, not only a power that wills, but also a substance in which the power to will is embedded. Now, thinking and willing are acts proper to the soul alone, since the soul alone is the ultimate principle of such operations. As a basis of rational processes, then, the soul of man must be a substance (*B*, p. 304).[43]

If such a statement (and others cited in the footnote) cannot fairly be described as closely approximating the traditional description of Cartesian man (or monster), then I must admit utter incom-

[43] "And just as we cannot deny the substantiality of man's body, so we cannot deny the substantiality of his soul" (pp. 305 f.). "What kind of substance is this mind or soul of man? . . . Aquinas replies that the human soul is essentially immaterial. To say that it is immaterial is to say that it is *incorporeal*; that it is not a body. Further, to say that it is immaterial is to say that it is *subsistent*; that it is not intrinsically dependent on a body" (p. 306). On page 311, Brennan assures us that the soul is not made up of quantitative parts. It is a form of matter, which, on conjunction with matter, makes "the composite substance of man."

petence. If Brennan's doctrine does not comprise factors that cannot be derived from matter-form analysis, how does it escape reduction to the organismic position?

It may be instructive to imagine a scientist adopting the matter-form distinction. This living thing (he says) is an organized functioning thing, a unity of matter and form. I must find meanings for matter and form relevant to my particular type of inquiry. I shall distinguish as "form" the organization of the living thing, while what does not concern me in my inquiries I shall designate "matter." By "matter," then, I shall mean that which, in view of the objectives of my inquiry, may be regarded as given, as the "stuff" receiving organization. It designates a terminus of my inquiries. But that which is the matter-terminus for *my* inquiries, may well be *the* or *a* concrete thing (a unity of matter and form) for *other* inquiries. I may be assured by my colleague the chemist that he discerns a high degree of molecular organization below the level, as it were, of the terminus of my inquiries. At some point, needless to say, this reductive process must terminate. In some science, whatever it may be, there will occur a final gesture of acceptance of the bare fact of existence, a recognition that existence involves prime matter. Whatever may be added to this must be the responsibility of metaphysics, not of scientists and their sciences.

Now this imaginary discourse could be given specific illustration by taking man as an instance of existence. It could represent what is meant by saying that man is a composite, a complex, substance. It could interpret what is meant by saying that the intellectual soul is the form of man. It would be a translation of the form-matter distinction into a doctrine concerning the hierarchical organization of the stuff of existence, with the soul at one extreme and prime matter at the other. On this interpretation, it is difficult to see just why it would not be acceptable to a naturalistic philosophy. Now it may be absurd to think that this represents the doctrine intended by St. Thomas. I cannot believe that it would be acceptable to Gilson or Brennan or that either would accept it as an interpretation of St. Thomas' doctrine. But *why* would it be absurd to attribute the interpretation to St. Thomas?

What factors are involved in the real doctrine of St. Thomas which make the interpretation unrepresentative? I can see but one general answer—there remain, in Thomistic doctrine, elements of the Platonic tradition which in the final analysis make that doctrine as "dualistic" as is the doctrine of Descartes. Making due allowance for terminological differences, making due allowance for differences of historical epoch, I cannot avoid the conviction that a dilemma obtains: either Thomistic man is the naturalistic philosopher's man, is organismic man, or else the notion of the soul is so weighted that Cartesian man is basically a revised version of Thomistic man.

The contention may be tested in several ways. It was said that matter and form are parts of man's essence. Let us assume that something parallel could be said of a stone. In some sense, the corporeality of the stone is comprised within its essence, and presumably, in reference to prime matter, so comprised in virtue of its form. That is, incorporeal stones do not exist. There may exist incorporeal things, but they are not stone and do not possess at least some of the characteristics pertaining to stones. If the expression be allowed, we could say that stones have natures and possibly may share something of their natures with other things. But some part of their natures could not be shared with incorporeal things.[44] If the essence of man be such that a man is, in part, incorporeal, he differs from a stone in two ways. First, the stone is not incorporeal, not even in part. The form of the stone, qua form, is, of course, immaterial, although the form is the form of a corporeal thing. Again, man, even if corporeal in part, differs in his corporeality from the stone's corporeality. That is, man's body is not a stone. If it be of the essence of man to be form and matter, but if man is, in part, incorporeal (comprising an intellectual, a "psychic," substance, a soul devoid of matter, an immaterial incorporeal form *possessing* substantiality, and so forth), yet man is in part corporeal, and we "cannot deny the substantiality of man's body," must we not, in reckoning with all this, use the notion of form and matter twice over? Or, if not this, must we

[44] Cf. *MSE.*

not provide an additional distinction, other than the form-matter, but corresponding to it? If the soul only *conferred* substantiality, if it were only a form conferring but *not possessing* substantiality, the situation might be otherwise.

Let us accept the statement—the soul is not intrinsically dependent on a body. Just how this is to be reconciled with the contention that body and soul are substantially conjoined and with other related expressions are aspects of the total problem. In so far as the body is a substance, however incomplete, in so far as it is a something, an existent, and something other than the soul, and in so far as it is not *prime* matter (and certainly it is not that, although it could not exist without it), then the body is a unity of matter and form. The form, we know, is from the soul, the form that possesses and confers substantiality; indeed, it *is* the soul. The soul, too, is an incomplete substance, at least in some respect, or as understood in some perspective. It needs a body, an organized body, not prime matter, although it could not have what it needs if there were not prime matter. The soul achieves the organization of a body and is the form of the body (an incomplete substance in some respect and in some perspective). Yet it is an immortal substance (incomplete or complete?). The soul cannot be conceived, in the conditions stated, as becoming the form of the body in *this* sense that it abandons its (semi-) independent status, its prerogative of *possessing* substantiality, so that it suffers that fate of the corruptible body. Yet the soul *is* the form of the body. The distinction between possessing and conferring substantiality cannot be overlooked.

Let us indulge in conjectures, but refrain from asserting that any of them represent Thomistic man. Suppose the form (the soul) is, as it were, internally fissioned, so that one "portion" informs matter, with the consequence that there arises a body, while the other "portion" does not inform matter, but remains aloof. Or, alternatively, suppose that the form (the soul) is not one, but two, one form informing matter, being of such a nature that to inform matter and give rise to the human body is just what it is fitted to do, the other form being responsible for the possession of substantiality by the soul. In some sense, of course, the form of *man* can be regarded as not one, but two, because he is body (a formed thing) and soul (possessing substantiality, a form-possessing-substantiality). But let us indulge in another conjecture. The incorporeal, immaterial form, identified as substantial, as a thing in itself, which both possesses and confers substantiality, let us suppose, stands aloof from prime matter, not immersing itself within it at all, but *elicits* by a sort of catalytic action the emergence of the organized body from the potentialities of prime matter. The supposition implies that the soul, with respect to prime matter, might be described as an *occasioning* cause, or a *releasing* cause, provoking prime matter to actualize some of its pent-up possibilities. Of course, somewhat mysteriously it must elicit an organized body appropriate to itself. In a sense, on this supposition the soul is the form of the body. In another sense it is not, for it incites the actualization of the body from the resources of prime matter and in some measure both the matter and the form of the body are evoked from prime matter. On the supposition, we could add, that the body so evoked is organized in accord with the needs of this intrinsically independent substantial soul, and in view of this proportionality, the composite thing, the man, could be *figuratively* described as a one thing, a substance. Accordingly, in one sense this being is to be identified with the soul and its catalytic power; in another sense, with the body; and in still another sense, with the thing as a composite being.

These are all conjectures, illuminating one or another aspect of Thomistic man. I do *not* maintain that any of these suppositions represent Thomistic man satisfactorily. One or another supposition interprets or is suggested by sentences or clauses in passages cited from Gilson or Brennan. It is *not* claimed that any one of the conjectures rightly interprets Gilson or Brennan or Thomistic man. The conjectures show how the problem is haunted by Platonic-Cartesian man.[45]

[45] It is to be noted that according to St. Thomas, intellectual substances also are composites—composites, not of matter and form, but of actuality and potentiality, of form and participated existence. Thus, the soul is composite; the man is composite; and presumably, the body, in so far as considered independently, is composite (*ST*, Q. LXXV, art. 5, *Reply obj.* 4). Now the intellectual soul is endowed not only with the power of understanding but also with the power of feeling (*ibid.*, art. 5, *I answer that* . . .). When all of this is put together, the intricacy of St. Thomas'

In *some* sense the relation of Socrates' soul to Socrates' body *is* accidental and, I contend, no less accidental on the Thomistic formula than in Cartesian doctrine. The relation is intimate. It is, however, temporary. Let us keep in mind that we are concerned, not with embryological questions, but with metaphysical analysis. Say what you will, intimate union, the unity of the man Socrates, the composite nature of Socrates, must mean for St. Thomas something approximating that which Descartes called a unity of composition. Doubtless, to assert that the soul is the form of the body is a way of insisting upon the intimacy of the union. The pilot-and-the-ship analogy is unacceptable—but unacceptable also for Descartes. But the soul, functioning as substantial form of the body, must not vanish in corporeality. The Gilsonian doctrine, as represented in the formula, indicates that a man as a composite substance involves a certain proportionment, adjustment, functional reciprocity between that which is a substance and confers substantiality and that to which substantiality accrues in that it has had substantiality conferred upon it. Even this phrase is misleading, in that it suggests that there is a *something,* a substance, upon which further substantiality is conferred. But assuredly neither St. Thomas nor Descartes intended obvious absurdities. The independence of the soul substance, for Descartes, surely did not mean that it was merely a matter of sheer accident that Socrates' soul somehow got attached to the historical corruptible body that Plato would have identified as that of Socrates and that—for all we know—it might as well have become attached to the bodies of Smith, Jones, or Brown, or to each one in succession.

If one abandon form-matter terminology or revise its meanings, due allowance ought to be made in the comparison of doctrines. But surely St. Thomas and Descartes are in agreement that Socrates the man is one thing, but that he is also an incorruptible soul and a corruptible body, an immortal soul substance and a corporeal thing that is not immortal. Would not Descartes—who was not unaccquainted with the Angelic Doctor's thought—speak

doctrine, its ingenuity, and its failure to escape the "Platonic" view of man becomes apparent.

somewhat as follows? Whatever be the unresolved mysteries concerning the nature and coming-into-being of a man, Socrates the soul is largely responsible for this, that Socrates the man has, not *a* body, but *Socrates'* body. Since we must make a distinction between a man's body and his soul, as St. Thomas insists, then we must interpret the empirical facts while maintaining the distinction. Would St. Thomas, Descartes might ask, deny the multitude of facts summed up in saying: the soul uses the body; it suffers and is sometimes constrained by the body; there is sometimes hostility between soul and body, and sometimes cooperative peace; that profiting by the body means on occasion and in some measure adjusting the soul to the body, and so forth? When human beings become objects of scientific investigation, provided that "soul" is to mean something more than the way in which matter-modes are organized, then some hypothesis conceived in terms of the distinction between soul and body must be provided for achieving the empirical accord.

This seems to be a reasonable representation of Descartes' thinking. The pineal-gland hypothesis works in two ways: it represents a measure of dependence of Socrates' soul upon Socrates' very own body and indicates the possibilities of his soul's profiting by intimacy of union; it also represents a measure of independence, for the will can cause the gland to deflect the animal spirits, to the profit, perhaps, both of Socrates' soul and Socrates' body, and in sum to the profit of Socrates. Moreover, this hypothesis is intended to interpret empirically the truth that it requires just that form possessing and conferring substantiality which is Socrates' soul to "inform" prime matter to the end that Socrates the man shall have a body. The form possessing and conferring substantiality identified as Plato, Aristotle, Smith, Jones, could not achieve Socrates' body.

Now, the pineal-gland story may not today be regarded as a very likely one. There may be philosophers and scientists today who would insist that Socrates is simply an organized body, just as a stone is an organized body, and that to understand the differences of organization is to appreciate the complexities of matter's manifestations. This is as it may be. But such thinkers are discarding, not the thought and language of Descartes alone but the thought and language of St. Thomas as well. If the demand for a met-empirical accord be valid, and if this requires that the soul be an immortal substance; if the empirical accord must be realized, then, say what you will, qualify the figurative language as may be necessary, but the Thomistic and Cartesian men are Platonic souls using the body. If, then, the metaphysical requirement also is to be sustained, scientific myths must interpret the intimacy of union between the form possessing and conferring substantiality and the body, which would not be what it is and have the temporary career that it does have, without its union with that form. The career of the man Socrates is cumulative. Socrates, the man who drank the hemlock, was something other than and more than the Socrates of the days of his youth. But the cumulative Socrates is not just the cumulative bodily Socrates; he is also the cumulative immortal substance called Socrates.

Now, in so far as the body is body, or can be scientifically investigated independently of the soul, there may be a perspective in which the soul can be neglected as if it were not. Since according to Thomistic doctrine the soul is the *form of the body*, and the body in its organization is the soul-as-informing-prime-matter, presumably such a perspective is in principle definable. Since the soul is a form *possessing substantiality*, there may be definable a perspective in which it can be investigated independently. Nevertheless, for both St. Thomas and Descartes, there must be a perspective in which science may see that the soul uses the body and the body uses the soul, with the result that the immortal soul of Socrates may become enriched with the fruits of the career of Socrates the man. The sciences must strive to accomplish all this, if they begin with the Thomistic-Cartesian notion of man. Or the sciences may abandon that notion, adopting the organismic notion. Perhaps, thereby, the empirical accord and the metaphysical requirement may be realized. Perhaps not. But the met-empirical accord, as vital to Descartes as to St. Thomas, would then presumably be denied.

Having said "it is the intellect itself, an incorporeal substance, that is the form of the human body," Gilson continues: "It is just here perhaps that the internal difficulties of Thomism begin to look most formidable" (*S*, p. 186). I submit that they do not merely look most formidable; they *are* most formidable. They are more. They are insuperable, *if* the doctrine is to be internally consistent and *if* at the same time a fundamental and fundamentally meaningful difference between Thomistic man and Cartesian man is to be sustained. If Thomistic doctrine concerning the nature of man, not in its details, but in its essentials, is simply false, one might as well, without more ado, pass a similar judgment upon Cartesian doctrine concerning man.

But a final test may be necessary. It may be urged that Thomistic doctrine has in view *prime* matter, but that Cartesian matter is something else. Let us agree to abandon particular Cartesian scientific hypotheses, such as animal spirits, pineal gland, and other more or less likely stories. Perhaps, then, the irreconcilable difference between Thomistic and Cartesian man, for which we seek, can be found in the direction to which the word "matter" points.

Surely, by no form entering prime matter could something be actualized which surpasses the potentialities of prime matter. Prime matter could not receive any form, if such there be, that is not proportioned to prime matter and its potentialities. But for St. Thomas prime matter is not nothing. It is not bare *privation* of being, sheer emptiness, unrelieved lack of internal resources.[46] It has an internal, intrinsic, constitutive nature that defines its not-illimitable range of potentialities. Prime matter *is* this restricted range of potentialities. It contributes something of itself, however indefinite in character, its contribution to the diversification of existence, to the multiplicity of finite existents, in so far as the existence of these existents is referable to prime matter and they are corporeal.

Following excellent authority, we may define St. Thomas'

[46] Here, as elsewhere, the argument is based upon conclusions concerning the Thomistic doctrine of matter that were established (I hope) in *MSE* (see note 2 above).

prime matter as *materia quantitate signata (Mqs).*[47] If it be the very nature of quantity to have parts exterior to one another, which St. Thomas seems to maintain, and if prime matter is *Mqs*, then *Mqs*, by its very own intrinsic character, must set restrictions upon the reception of forms. A form hostile, so to speak, to quantity could not directly enter into *Mqs*. Suppose there are such forms, and that such forms, moreover, *possess* substantiality. Suppose these forms, possessing substantiality, are such that they cannot tolerate having parts exterior to one another. It is difficult to understand how such forms could inform prime matter, if prime matter is *Mqs*, in the sense that these forms are in consequence the forms of corporeal things. On the other hand, if such forms were endowed with an eliciting catalytic power, so that, while remaining aloof from prime matter, *Mqs*, they could evoke from *Mqs* the actualization of a thing having parts exterior to one another, the thing so emerging would have a form. It would be a corporeal thing. The form of this thing, however, could be not identified with, but only *correlated* with the form which had the inciting power. Thus, the soul substance—to return to a previous conjecture—might in this manner possess and also confer substantiality. Provided it had the catalytic power, it could occasion the emergence of a body fitted to its needs, from the resources of *Mqs*. If it did elicit anything from *Mqs*, it would have to be content with eliciting a body having parts exterior to one another, a material corporeal thing, because it could get nothing else out of prime matter.

It is as if Descartes were to say: if a soul substance can participate catalytically in getting something out of the resources of matter substance, then the thing so arising, as sure as fate, will be an extended thing, a body to be understood as basically a set of modes of the attribute of extension. No soul can evoke from matter a satellite for itself that is not extended, because the resources of matter are restricted in the sense that, whatever a material thing or body may be in addition to being extended, it is basically extended. In relation to St. Thomas' *Mqs* or Descartes'

[47] Cf. *MSE*, pp. 654 ff. The authority referred to is Forest. I use the symbol, *Mqs.*, not only for the sake of brevity, but because the formula appears open to many interpretations, a consideration of which does not seem necessary for present purposes.

matter-substance, the catalytic action of a form possessing substantiality must be proportioned to the intrinsic endowment of the one or the other. If the form evoked a body from *Mqs* in the fashion indicated, it could remain serene in the possession of its own substantiality. It could be called the form of the body in an indirect sense, in that it is assumed that the catalytic power of each form is its own, and the body arising is adjusted to its individual power. Socrates' body, then, would be such that Socrates' soul could use it.

Man, viewed in terms of this effort to understand Thomistic man, is, indeed, a soul-possessing and conferring substantiality, plus an organized body. In one sense the latter would owe its organization to the soul; in another sense, to matter. The soul would possess serenely its incorruptible substantiality. The met-empirical accord would be satisfied in principle. Presumably, in view of the history of modern psychology, the demand for the empirical accord could be satisfied. Further and prolonged examination would, perhaps, be necessary to determine whether the metaphysical requirement had been measurably satisfied.

Alas! the search has failed. I have not discovered a difference, *the* difference, a really fundamental difference, that opposes Thomistic man and Cartesian man. I believe that I have discerned a vast alternative—that between Platonic-Thomistic-Cartesian man, on the one hand, and hylomorphic organismic man, on the other. Either there is dualistic man in one or another variant of historical doctrine or in still other doctrines yet to be formulated, or else there is man as perhaps matter's highest manifestation of its own inherent unassisted resources. If Thomistic man is to satisfy the conditions enumerated at the beginning of this essay, that man is formed upon a plan as essentially dualistic as the plan of Cartesian man, however the plans may differ as to detail. Not even St. Thomas, I submit, can eat his cake and have it too—but no, I retract that statement. Perhaps St. Thomas can. But I must confess that I do not see how he achieves this, and I submit, with deferential apologies and with gratitude, that neither Gilson nor Brennan has shown us either that or how St. Thomas can accomplish the feat.

A new perplexity besets me. How does it come about that those having mastery of Thomistic doctrine nevertheless believe that Thomistic man is so very different from Cartesian man? John Dewey's opinion was evidently sound. I should not have embarked upon an adventure whose record must end with a confession of failure.

INDEX

Âme, use of the term, 55 f.

Âme naturelle, De la Chambre's theories of, 58

Animals: De la Chambre's attribution of reason to, 49 ff.; Gerdil's distinction between them and men, 154 ff.

Animal soul: Descartes' doctrine of, 106 ff.; *see also* Animal spirits; Automatism

Animal spirits: Cordemoy's conception of, 5, 12 f., 22; De la Chambre's rejection of Descartes' theory of, 43 f.; ambiguity of the term, 53 f.; Clauberg's exposition of Descartes' doctrine of, 172; *see also* Animal soul

Aristotle, Cartesian agreement with, 31

Atheism: Gerdil's discussion of, 223; Gerdil's contention that it is destroyed by Cartesianism, 228 f.; charged against Spinozism by Lamy, 230 ff.

Augustine, Saint, De la Forge's adherence to, 82

Automatism, attitude of various philosophers toward Descartes' doctrine of, 106 ff.

Bayle, Pierre, 128 f., 132 f.

Bodies, Cordemoy's conception of, 8, 17 f.

Body, *see* Dualism

Body and soul, *see* Mind-body relationship

Bouillier, Francisque: attitude toward Cartesian automatism, 111 ff.; account of sensation, 149 ff.; quoted, 152 f.

Brennan, Robert Edward, *Thomistic Psychology,* 280, 287 ff., 295 ff., 310 ff.

Cartesianism: possibility of its conflict with religion, 32 f.; opposition to, 42 ff.; controversies concerning, 42; defended by De la Forge, 83 ff.; ambiguities in, 84 ff.; arguments in favor of its superiority to Spinozism, 218 ff.

Chambre, Louis de la, *see* De la Chambre, Louis

Clauberg, Johann, attitude toward Occasionalism, 163 ff.

Clerselier, Claude: understanding of Cartesianism, 30; Rohault's lectures evaluated by, 31; belief in Descartes' faithfulness to religion, 33; quoted, 34; evaluation of Descartes' theory of dualism, 36 ff.

Cogito argument, 67 f.

Common sense, Cordemoy's belief in its universality, 14

Condorcet, Marie Jean Antoine Nicolas Caritat, Marquess de, quoted, 28, 45

Consciousness, Cartesian doctrine of, 29

Cordemoy, Geraud de: interpretation of Cartesianism, 3 ff.; *Le Discernement et de l'âme,* 3; objections to Descartes' theory of matter, 8

Corporeal species, the theory examined by De la Forge, 88 ff.

Cousin, Victor: eulogy of Descartes, 220 f.; quoted, 240

Daniel, G., 121, 130

Deffand, Marie de Vichy-Chamrond, Marquise de, Cordemoy's faith in, 6 f.

Deity, *see* God

De la Chambre, Louis, 42 ff.; opposition to Cartesianism, 42 ff.; opposition to Descartes' materialism, 43 f.; piety of, 45; symptomatic value of his work, 46; *L'Art de connoistre les hommes,* 46 f., 53; *Connaissance de bêtes,* 49; *Traité des animaux,* 49 ff.; conflicting views of body and soul, 55 f.; diagnostic value of his ideas, 63; *Art of Knowing Men,* 162

De la Forge, Louis, 80 ff.; belief in Cartesianism, 81

Descartes, René: faithfullness to religion upheld by Clerselier, 33; Clerselier's understanding of, 34 f.; indivisibility of his philosophy, 67 f.; novelty of his ideas, 198 ff.

Desgabets, Robert, 80, 93, 94

Design: relation to Cordemoy's theories, 16 ff.; De la Chambre's concept of, 59 f.

Dilly, 118 ff., 129 ff., 140